INFLATION: THEORY AND POLICY

Also by A. J. Hagger (with Ajit K. Dasgupta)

The Objectives of Macro-Economic Policy

Inflation:
Theory and Policy

A. J. Hagger

Reader in Economics
University of Tasmania

First published 1977 by
THE MACMILLAN PRESS LTD
London and Basingstoke
Associated companies in New York Dublin
Melbourne Johannesburg and Madras

ISBN 978-0-333-21246-2   ISBN 978-1-349-15735-8 (eBook)
DOI 10.1007/978-1-349-15735-8

Typeset in IBM Press Roman by
PREFACE LTD
Salisbury, Wiltshire

To my
daughter,
Stephanie, and
my son, Michael

CONTENTS

PREFACE

My aim in writing this book has been to produce an undergraduate text that would be suitable both for specialist courses in the economics of inflation and for general courses in macroeconomics which emphasise inflation, as many now do. In keeping with this aim, I have tried to make the discussion as comprehensive as possible and to strike a reasonable balance between theory and policy, between developed and underdeveloped economies and between normal and abnormal inflation. I have also tried to avoid heavy concentration on technicalities and fine points, hopefully without loss of rigour, and to cater for a wide range of experience, technical equipment, ability and interest.

Like most other areas of economics, the study of inflation has been deeply penetrated by econometrics in the last decade or so, and no textbook on inflation of the mid-1970s which avoided the econometrics of the subject could reasonably be said to be up to date. Certainly, in this book I have given the econometric literature considerable, though not, I believe, undue weight. At the same time I have recognised that many potential readers of the book, particularly students in their first or second undergraduate years, will have virtually no knowledge of econometric method. I have tried to safeguard the interests of this group by making the empirical, econometric discussion as non-technical as possible and by including a brief account of basic econometric method in Section 4.1 for the benefit of the entirely uninitiated. It would not be unfair to say, therefore, that the book assumes no knowledge of econometrics. This is not to say, of course, that the book assumes no mathematical knowledge. On this point a fair statement, I think, would be that the book calls for no mathematical equipment beyond the school mathematics which is nowadays assumed by virtually all basic texts in economics.

The potential reader should be warned that the book adopts a definite and somewhat uncompromising methodological stance. This is spelt out in detail at various points in the book, notably in Section 2.1, and there is no need to dwell on it here. Suffice it to say that the essence of the methodological viewpoint from which the book has been written is that the usefulness of economic models, models of the inflationary process included, is to be judged in terms of predictive success, not in terms of 'realism' of assumptions. This viewpoint appears now to be very widely accepted among professional economists, though by no means universally, and certainly is basic to the whole of the econometric work which has been undertaken in the field of inflation in recent years.

Finally, I should like to record my debt to the many people who have assisted in the writing of the book. In particular my thanks are due to several colleagues who read and commented on the book as it developed, especially Mr D. W. Challen of the University of Tasmania, to Mrs Yvonne Melotte for her careful and painstaking work in preparing the index and to Mrs Patricia Combes for her excellent typing of an untidy and complicated manuscript.

A. J. Hagger

University of Tasmania
May 1976

1

DEFINITION AND MEASUREMENT

1.1 What is Inflation?

The aim of this book is to give a comprehensive treatment of the problem of inflation. Thus the questions to be examined are: What are the causes of inflation? Why does it matter? How can it be stopped, or at least restrained? What other problems arise when action is taken to restrain inflation? Are these other problems so serious that it would be better, on balance, to allow a certain degree of inflation coupled with a comparatively small dose of these other problems than to have no inflation at all coupled with a somewhat larger dose of these other problems? If so, how large is the 'certain degree' of inflation that will have to be tolerated if the undesirable consequences of restraining inflation are to be kept within desirable limits?

It need hardly be said that before we can come to grips with questions such as these we must know what inflation is and how it can be measured. The main purpose of this opening chapter will be to consider these matters. In the present section we shall be concerned with the problem of defining inflation, and in subsequent sections with the problem of its measurement.

Like many economic concepts, inflation has been defined in different ways by different writers, and there is still no single definition that is generally accepted by inflation specialists. Accordingly, before presenting and discussing the definition of inflation to be used in this book we shall first mention some alternative definitions which are prominent in the literature, and which, in some cases, are still quite widely used in popular discussions of the subject.

A definition which found considerable favour in the early post-war years is that inflation is a state of affairs in which there is excess demand for commodities in the economy as a whole.[1] By this we mean that the level of spending being directed towards home-produced commodities exceeds the maximum output of home-produced commodities which is attainable in the long run, given existing productive resources. The qualifying pharase 'in the long run' is important. It signifies that, for the purposes of the excess-demand definition, 'maximum attainable output' is reckoned on the basis that there is no excessive overtime, that machinery is shut down at the presribed times for maintenance, that normal stocks of raw materials are maintained, that only fit workers are employed, and so on. In the short run none of these restrictions need apply. In the long run, however, they must all apply. Hence the maximum output which is attainable in the long run is a good deal less then the maximum which is attainable in the short run; and it is the former (*potential* real G.N.P.) rather than the latter (*capacity* real G.N.P.) which is relevant in connection with the definition of excess demand.

A much-used paraphrase of the excess-demand definition of inflation is that inflation is a condition in which 'too much money is chasing too few goods'. This paraphrase can be criticised on two grounds: in the first place, it is the *flow*, spending, which 'chases goods' not the *stock*, money; second, there is a redundancy – excess demand means *either* that desired spending is 'too much' in relation to the available goods, *or* (equivalently) that the available goods are 'too few' in relation to the desired spending. To introduce both 'too much' and 'too few' is to say the same thing twice. Thus a more acceptable paraphrase of the exess-demand definition would be that inflation is a condition in which 'too much *spending* is chasing the *available* goods'.

A second definition of inflation which is worth mentioning is that employed by Paish. A natural way to approach the problem of defining inflation is to ask: 'What exacly is being inflated when inflation is in progress?' In effect, the answer which Paish gives to this question is: 'in inflation money incomes are being inflated relative to real potential G.N.P.' He puts the point in the following way:

> A better definition of inflation [than one based on prices] is that it is a condition in which money incomes are rising faster than the flow of goods and services on which to spend them – that is to say, faster than real national income. But this definition is also not adequate, for an accelerated rise of money incomes may be accompanied for a time by an equally rapid rise of output and real income, achieved by a higher level of employment. But while the rise of incomes can continue indefinitely, and indeed is likely to accelerate as unemployment falls, the rapid rise of output can be maintained only until full employment is reached, and must then slow down to equality with the long-term trend of growth. The inflation, already implicit in the rapid rise of incomes, now comes into the open. The definition of inflation must therefore be a condition in which incomes are rising faster, not than the current rise in real national income, but than the *maintainable* rise. Apart from the effects of changes in the terms of trade and in net income from foreign investments, this is the same thing as the maintainable rise of output, or, as it is sometimes called, the rise of productive potential.[2]

The definition given by Paish in the above passage differs from the excess-demand definition in two main ways. In the first place, it runs in terms of a comparison between aggregate money income and real potential G.N.P. rather than a comparison between aggregate spending and real potential G.N.P. Second, it runs in terms of the rates of increase of variables rather than in terms of the levels of the variables.

A third well-known definition of inflation is that proposed by Turvey.[3] According to Turvey, inflation is a 'process of general price and/or wage increases *starting under conditions where the general level of output cannot be increased in the short run*[4] and resulting from 'competition in attempting to maintain total real income, total real expenditure and/or total output at a level which has become physically impossible or in attempting to increase any of them to a level which is physically impossible'.[5]

This definition has some interesting features. To begin with, it allows either the general price level or the general level of wages to be the variable which is 'inflated' in an inflationary situation. In this respect it is a wider definition than that proposed by Paish. Second, it restricts inflation to situations in which the general level of output is incapable of being increased, even in the short run, that is (using the terms introduced earlier) to situations in which *actual* real G.N.P. has risen so far above *potential* real G.N.P., for example as a result of excessive overtime or the temporary recruitment of physically unfit workers, that the upper limit set by real *capacity* G.N.P. has been reached. This is a narrower class of situations than that envisaged by the first definition. All situations such that the desired level of real G.N.P. (= level of spending directed towards home-produced commodities) exceeds real potential G.N.P. constitute inflation on the first definition. However, not all such situations constitute inflation on Turvey's definition. For on his definition desired real G.N.P. must not only exceed real potential G.N.P.; it must do so by a sufficient margin to ensure that actual real G.N.P. reaches the upper limit set by capacity real G.N.P. In other words, the excess of desired over potential must be at least as great as the excess of capacity over potential before inflation can exist on the definition which Turvey proposes.

While all three of the definitions just examined have much to commend them, they suffer from the disadvantage that they are rather too much economists' definitions; they provide a good basis for economic analysis, but the inflation they describe is not the inflation which worries the ordinary man and hence not the inflation which is of interest to the policy-maker.

In popular discussion inflation is invariably taken to mean rising prices in some ill-defined sense. Largely because of their deep involvement in this popular discussion economists themselves have increasingly adopted a definition of this type in the last ten or fifteen years.

We shall follow this trend here. The definition of inflation which will be used in this book – one which would be acceptable, we believe, to most economists as well as being familiar to the layman – is as follows: by inflation we shall mean a situation in which there is a persistent upward movement in the general price level, or in which there *would be* such a persistent upward movement but for the presence of direct controls over prices.

Three points should be made here by way of elaboration. In the first place, the definition covers not only a situation of *actual* increase in the price level (open inflation) but a situation of *potential* increase (*repressed* inflation) as well. It is not uncommon for governments, faced by especially rapid price increases, to pass legislation making further price increases illegal, either for a specified time or indefinitely, except in limited, well-defined circumstances. Most governments passed such legislation during the Second World War and the governments of the

United Kingdom and the United States are two which have imposed 'price freezes' since 1945. Suppose that such legislation is passed and that prices cease to rise. Even so there would still be inflation on our definition because prices, though stable, *would be* rising but for the price-freeze legislation. This must be so, because, if it were not, there would be no need for the legislation; and since this type of legislation is highly unpopular, one can reasonably assume that it would have been repealed if the need for it had passed.

Second, for inflation to exist on our definition, the upward movement (actual or potential) in the general price level must be *persistent* in character. Thus if the price level is rising merely because of influences which can reasonably be expected to operate in reverse at some time in the future (which are causing prices to rise now but will cause then to fall at a later stage), then the current upward movement of prices could not be said to be persistent and hence would not constitute inflation on our definition. For example, if the general price level is rising because of a seasonal increase in the prices of key raw foodstuffs or because drought conditions have led to an increase in the prices of certain important agricultural raw materials (for example wool and wheat) or because the prices of certain basic commodities (for example petrol and tobacco) have risen through government fiscal action (for example the removal of a subsidy, the imposition of a heavier sales tax or excise duty), in all these cases we would say that the observed rise in the general price level is not part of a continuing upward movement (not persistent) and hence that it does not constitute inflation. In the first case, the argument would be that the seasonal increases in foodstuffs' prices will be reversed in due course as the seasons change; in the second case, that bad seasons will be followed, in the future, by good seasons at which point the prices of agricultural raw materials will tend to fall; and, in the third case, that with a change in general economic conditions the government will consider it appropriate to take fiscal action of the opposite kind to that now being taken (that is to reduce sales taxes or excise duties or to increase subsidies) and so induce a fall in the general price level.

Third, when we say that inflation is a situation characterised by a persistent upward movement of the general price level, we do not necessarily mean that it is a situation in which the movement in the price level is *always* upward. A succession of years in which the price level has risen, quarter by quarter, without ever once falling, would undoubtedly be a period of inflation on our definition; but so would a succession of years in which the price level has risen in some quarters and fallen in others so long as the rises have outweighed the falls, that is so long as the general direction of the movements has been unmistakably upward.

As indicated already, a desirable feature of the definition just presented is that it fits in with the ordinary man's notion of inflation and so helps to keep professional discussion of the inflation problem in touch with popular discussion. There is, however, one *un*desirable feature which must be set against this, namely that inflation, as we have defined it, and *dis*inflation, as usually defined, are not opposites as their names would suggest. By disinflation the economist means a reduction in excess demand through a restriction of the level of spending on home-produced commodities; he does *not* mean a persistent *downward* movement in the general price level, that is he does not mean the reverse of inflation, as this term has been defined. This lack of symmetry in the terms is a likely source of confusion. For example, one could easily imagine a fruitless argument between *A* and *B*, *A* claiming that there is no inflation because there is no sign that excess demand is getting larger and *B* claiming that there *is* inflation because prices are rising. Confusion has arisen because *A*, while remembering the definition of disinflation, has made the mistake of treating inflation as its opposite. Again, one could imagine a confused discussion arising between *C* and *D*, *C* asserting that a particular policy action has not been disinflationary because the price level has continued to rise, and *D* asserting the reverse because excess demand has been reduced; *C* has remembered that inflation means rising prices but has created havoc by forgetting that disinflation is not just the opposite situation.

The definition of inflation which we propose to use has disadvantages, therefore, as well as advantages. However, we feel that the advantages far outweigh the disadvantages and that we are conforming closely, both to current professional usage and to popular usage, in employing it.

1.2   Measurement of Inflation: Choice of Price Index

The measurement of inflation, as defined in the previous section (a persistent upward movement in the general price level), involves three main problems:

(i) The problem of choosing the price index which is to represent 'the general price level';

(ii) The problem of measuring the *extent* of the upward movement in the chosen index over any specified period of time; and

(iii) The problem of measuring *variations in the speed* of the upward movement in the chosen index over the specified time period.

In this and the two following sections we shall consider each of these three problems in turn. The discussion will be developed in the Australian context, but it will be applicable, with small modifications, to most advanced industrial economies.

In most countries the choice of a price index to represent the general price level in the measurement of inflation is quite wide. In the case of Australia the main possibilities are as follows:

(*a*) the consumer price index (C.P.I.);

(*b*) some component of C.P.I.;

(*c*) either of the wholesale price indexes (W.P.I.) or   some component of either;

(*d*) the implicit deflator of G.N.P.;

(*e*) the implicit deflator of some category of gross national expenditure (G.N.E.);

(*f*) the implicit deflator of non-farm G.N.P. at factor cost.

The problem to be considered in this section is the problem of deciding which of these six indexes is the most appropriate. We shall approach this problem by first listing the characteristics of a price ind which would be ideal for the purpose in hand (the measurement of inflation) and then examining each index to determine the extent to which it possesses these characteristics.

The first characteristic of an ideal index is that it would relate only to commodities produced within the economy or group of economies whose inflation is being measured. For example, if we are attempting to measure the extent of inflation in Australia or in Western Europe, we should like the price index which we use for the purpose to relate only to commodities produced within Australia or within Western Europe, as the case may be. Thus an index which covers imported, as well as domestically produced commodities, is less than ideal for the purpose of measuring inflation.†

Second, an ideal index would be comprehensive in the sense that it would relate to all goods and services produced within the economy, or economies, being studied. For example, an index which relates only to retail goods would fall short of the ideal in the present context, as would one relating, say, to goods consumed by wage-earners.

Third, an ideal index would take proper account of improvements in the quality of the various commodities covered by the index, whether they be goods or services. In other words, it would be recognised, in constructing the index, that over a ten- or fifteen-year period, say, the *nominal* rise in the price of a commodity may considerably overstate the true rise in price. For example, suppose that in constructing an index it is assumed that the rise in the *price* of medical services between any two points in time is equal to the rise in the *cost* of medical services between the same two points in time. Such an index would be less than ideal because, in constructing the index, no allowance is made for improvements in the *quality* of medical services. Because of quality improvements the true rise in the price of medical services will be less than the nominal price rise, that is less than the rise in cost. By equating the two the index would overstate the rise in the price of medical services over any period, which means that it would overstate the rise in the general price level over that period and in turn the extent of inflation as we have defined it in the previous section.

---

†Of course when we refer to an index which 'covers imported commodities' as being less than ideal we mean one which covers them *specifically*, not one which covers them only in the looser sense that it relates to commodities produced at home with imported materials or with materials which themselves incorporate imported materials.

The final characteristic of an ideal index is that it would not be affected by price increases which are temporary, in the sense that they are likely to be reversed at some time in the future, for example price rises which can be attributed to unfavourable weather conditions or to government fiscal action. This requirement is necessary because of the way in which inflation has been defined. According to our definition reversible price increases are not part of the upward movement in the price level which constitutes inflation (see p. 4 above), and for this reason we would like them to have no affect on the index which is to be used to represent the general price level in the measurement of inflation.

We shall now consider each of the indexes in the list presented earlier, in the light of these four requirements, with a view to deciding which of them is the most appropriate for the purpose of measuring inflation.

(a) *The C.P.I.*

While the C.P.I. stands up reasonably well in relation to the third requirement, it appears to fall well short of the ideal when considered in relation to the first two and the last. Many imported goods are included in the C.P.I. regimen. Also, since the index is intended to measure only variations in the retail prices of those goods and services which attract a substantial proportion of the aggregate expenditure of wage-earners, it is far from comprehensive. Finally, the index covers all important raw foods and all commodities whose prices are subject to significant variation through fiscal action, as is only to be expected given the purpose for which it is designed. As a result the index is by no means unaffected by the type of temporary price increase that we exclude in our definition of inflation.

(b) *Some Component of the C.P.I.*

Instead of using the C.P.I. itself, one could use one of the five component indexes from which it is built up, namely the indexes for food, clothing and drapery, housing, household supplies and equipment, and miscellaneous. However, all of these fall down on the score of comprehensiveness, being worse in this respect, of course, than C.P.I. itself. Also, all are deficient in relation to at least one of the other three requirements. For example, the housing index is deficient in relation to the first requirement – the problem of allowing for improvements in quality is especially acute in relation to a housing price index and is only partially solved in the case of the housing component of C.P.I. Again, the household-supplies index covers most of the commodities which are subject to sales tax, and for this reason does not stand up well in relation to the fourth requirement. The food index is deficient in this respect also, since it covers all of the important raw foods.

(c) *The W.P.I.s or Some Component*

The C.P.I. and its component indexes are *retail* price indexes. As alternatives for the purpose of measuring inflation, one could consider one of the two *wholesale* price indexes (the index of materials used in house-building, or the index of materials used in building other than house-building), or possibly one of the component indexes from which the W.P.I.s are constructed. However, all of these indexes fall far below the ideal in relation to the second requirement since even the most comprehensive of them is restricted to some class of building materials. In addition, since they all cover imported, as well as locally produced building materials, they are less than ideal from the standpoint of the first requirement.

(d) *The Implicit Deflator of G.N.P.*

The implicit deflator of G.N.P. is not a price index in the ordinary sense, and, before attempting to assess its suitability for the purpose of measuring inflation, it may be desirable to explain the way in which it is calculated. The implicit deflator of G.N.P., say for any quarter, is obtained by dividing the G.N.P. for the quarter in terms of *current* prices by the G.N.P. for the quarter in terms of *constant* prices. For example, Australia's G.N.P. for the September quarter 1968 was $6446 million in current prices and $6133 million at average 1966–7 prices. Hence the implicit deflator of G.N.P. for this quarter was 1.051 (= 6446/6133) on the base 1966–7 = 1.

It will be clear from this explanation that, while the implicit deflator of G.N.P. is not a genuine price index, it can be interpreted in the same way as a price index. Specifically, it can be thought of as a price index relating to all goods and services comprising G.N.P., that is to all goods and services produced within Australia. For example, Australia's implicit deflator for the September quarter 1968 (1.051) can be interpreted as indicating that the prices of all goods and services produced within Australia was a little over 5 per cent higher, in this quarter, than the average level for 1966–7.

Since the implicit deflator is, in effect, a price index relating to the goods and services comprising G.N.P., it clearly stands up well on the first two of our four requirements; it relates *only* to goods and services produced within Australia and it relates to *all* such goods and services. On the other hand, it is rather unsatisfactory from the point of view of the third and fourth requirements. Let us take them in turn.

From the explanation, given earlier, of the way in which the implicit deflator is calculated for any period, it is apparent that a critical element in the calculation is the estimate of G.N.P. at constant prices for the period. In the Australian case this estimate is obtained by making estimates of G.N.E. at constant prices, exports at constant prices and imports at constant prices and then using the identity: G.N.P. at constant prices = G.N.E. at constant prices *plus* exports at constant prices *less* imports at constant prices. Thus whether or not the deflator makes proper allowance for quality improvements (third requirement) depends, in the end, on whether or not there is due allowance for quality improvement in the constant-price estimate of G.N.E., exports and imports. In particular it depends on whether there is proper allowance for quality improvement in the constant-price estimate of G.N.E., since G.N.E. is the dominant element in the right-hand side of the G.N.P. identity. If inadequate allowance is made for quality improvement in the constant-price estimate of G.N.E., the figure for G.N.P. at constant prices will tend to be too low and the figure for the implicit deflator too high. For example, in revaluing the x motor-cars purchased in year t in terms of the prices ruling in some base year (this would be part of the job of making the constant-price estimate of G.N.E. for one year t) one would have to recognise that the number of 'base-year' motor-cars purchased in year t was really more than x because the year t motor-car was of better quality than the base-year motor-car. If one failed to take the quality improvement into account, one's estimate of expenditure on motor-cars in year t in terms of base-year prices would be too low, and, to this extent, one's figure for the implicit G.N.P. deflator for year t would be too high.

To determine whether in fact due allowance is made for quality improvement in the Australian constant-price estimates of G.N.E. one must examine the procedures which the statistician uses to make these estimates.[6] If this is done one is forced to the conclusion that, through no fault of his own, the statistician makes a quite inadequate allowance for quality improvement in his constant-price estimate of G.N.E., and hence that this estimate understates the true constant-price figure, and in turn that the implicit deflator of G.N.P. overstates the extent of the rise in the general price level over any specified time period.

The implicit deflator of G.N.P. falls down, then, in relation to the third of our four requirements. Nor is it satisfactory in terms of the fourth requirement. The main reason is that since G.N.P. includes the value of production of the Australian farm sector as well as the value of production of the non-farm sector, the figure for G.N.P. in current prices for any quarter, say, will reflect price increases caused by production difficulties of a temporary kind in the farm sector. And since the G.N.P. deflator for any quarter is obtained simply by dividing the figure for G.N.P. in current prices by the figure for G.N.P. in constant prices, the deflator must also reflect the temporary price increases, contrary to the fourth of our requirements for an ideal index. A second reason why the implicit G.N.P. deflator is unsatisfactory in terms of the fourth requirement is that, since G.N.P. measures the value of production in the Australian economy as a whole *in terms of market prices*, the figure for G.N.P. in current prices will reflect price increases caused by the imposition or stiffening of indirect taxes or the removal of subsidies. Hence the implicit deflator of G.N.P. will reflect these price increases also, contrary to the fourth requirement for an ideal index once again.

(e) *The Implicit Deflator of Some Category of G.N.E.*

Instead of choosing the implicit deflator of G.N.P. to represent the movement of the general price level in the measurement of inflation, one could use the implicit deflator of some component of G.N.E. ('a G.N.E. deflator', for short). For example, one could use the implicit deflator of personal consumption expenditure

(P.C.E.), this being the 'index' arrived at by dividing P.C.E. in current prices by P.C.E. in constant prices.

A G.N.E. deflator lacks the advantages of the G.N.P. deflator in that it fails to measure up against the first two requirements. This is so because a G.N.E. deflator does not cover all the goods and services produced in the Australian economy and covers some goods and services which are produced outside the Australian economy. For example, the implicit deflator of P.C.E. fails against the first requirement because P.C.E. covers only goods and services purchased by persons for purposes of consumption, that is it excludes purchases by persons for purposes other than consumption (for example purchases by persons of new houses) and all purchases by entities other than persons (for example purchases of roads and bridges by governments and purchases of plant and equipment by companies). On the other hand, the P.C.E. deflator covers *all* consumer goods purchased by Australian persons whether they be home produced or imported and so fails against the second requirement.

Not only does a G.N.E. deflator lack the advantages of the G.N.P. deflator; it also shares its disadvantages. Take the P.C.E. deflator as an example once again. This deflator fails to make adequate allowance for quality improvement because, as will be clear from earlier discussion, the constant-price estimate of P.C.E. fails to do so. Thus this particular G.N.E. deflator fails in relation to the third requirement. It also fails in relation to the fourth requirement. P.C.E. in current prices reflects 'temporary' price increases, both because the P.C.E. aggregate measures consumer purchases at market prices, that is inclusive of indirect tax, and also because it covers all the consumer goods produced by the Australian farm sector, fresh fruit and vegetables for example, and since the P.C.E. deflator emerges by dividing P.C.E. in current prices by P.C.E. in constant prices, it must be the case that the P.C.E. deflator will be affected by temporary price increases and hence that the P.C.E. deflator is less than ideal on the basis of our fourth requirement.

f.   The Implicit Deflator of Non-Farm G.N.P. at Factor Cost

This 'price index' is derived, for any given quarter, by dividing the figure for non-farm G.N.P. at factor cost in terms of current prices by the figure for non-farm G.N.P. at factor cost in terms of constant prices. Like the implicit deflator of G.N.P. it stands up well in relation to the first two of our four requirements; only goods and services produced within the Australian economy are embraced by the index, and all such are covered except for the goods which are produced on farms. The index is highly satisfactory from the point of view of the fourth requirement also. Unlike G.N.P. in current prices, the current price figure for *non-farm* G.N.P. at *factor cost* is unaffected by price increases arising from temporary production difficulties in the farm sector or from an increase in the severity of indirect taxation. Hence the implicit deflator of non-farm G.N.P. at factor cost is not affected by such 'temporary' price increases either. The non-farm deflator is not satisfactory, however, as regards the third requirement. In fact, our assessment of the implicit deflator of G.N.P. from the point of view of this requirement applies without essential modification to the implicit non-farm deflator as well. That this is so becomes clear once it is realised that the constant-price estimate of non-farm G.N.P. at factor cost is made by using substantially the same identity as is used to make the constant-price estimate of G.N.P., namely non-farm G.N.P. at factor cost and at constant prices = G.N.P. at constant prices *less* indirect taxation at constant prices *less* farm product at factor cost and at constant prices = G.N.E. at constant prices *plus* exports at constant prices *less* imports at constant prices *less* indirect taxation at constant prices *less* farm product at factor cost and at constant prices.

It will be recalled that the purpose of this section was to consider the problem of choosing between the six price indexes which we might use to represent the general price level in the measurement of inflation. It will be remembered, too, that we decided to approach the problem by first listing the characteristics of an index which would be 'ideal' for this purpose and then examining each index in the light of these characteristics. We have now completed this task. It is clear from our assessment that none of the six indexes is entirely satisfactory in the light of the criteria we have proposed. However, some are more satisfactory than others, and the one which comes closest to the ideal, in our view, is the implicit deflator of non-farm G.N.P. at factor cost. This index falls down in relation to the third requirement of an ideal index but has strong claims for selection in terms of the other three.

Clearly, however, there is an element of judgement in the selection procedure which we have adopted. In the first place the set of criteria against which we have assessed the six indexes is not the only reasonable set which could be proposed. Second, there is room for judgement in the application of our criteria; all six indexes are good in some repects and bad in others, and which is best, on balance, is a matter of opinion. In view of this element of judgement it must be recognised that our conclusion in favour of the implicit deflator of non-farm G.N.P. at factor cost, while entirely reasonable, is by no means the only conclusion which is logically possible.

The preceding discussion suggests that one should approach the seemingly straightforward question – 'How much inflation has there been?' – with a certain amount of caution. For in any actual situation there will usually be several price indexes which can be legitimately used to measure inflation, and it may well be that the answer that one gives to the above question will depend significantly on which of them is chosen.

1.3 Measurement of Inflation: Extent of Upward Movement

The first problem to be faced when one sets out to measure inflation (defined as a persistent upward movement in the general price level) is the problem of deciding which price index to use to represent 'the general price level'. This problem was discussed in the preceding section. Suppose now that it has been dealt with. The next problem is that of determining the extent of the rise which has occurred in the chosen index.

To be specific, suppose that we are interested in measuring inflation in Australia over, say, the years 1952–3 to 1957–8 and that we have dealt with the first problem involved in this exercise by selecting the implicit deflator of non-farm G.N.P. to represent the general price level. The next problem would be to determine the extent of the rise in this price index over the period in question.

The simplest way of handling this problem would be to calculate the percentage increase in the non-farm deflator between 1952–3 and 1957–8. Thus if the deflator stood at, say, 102.6 in 1952–3 and at 124.2 in 1957–8, we would answer the question 'How severe was inflation in the period 1952–3 to 1957–8?' by saying that the implicit deflator of non-farm G.N.P. rose by 21.1 per cent $[100(124.2/102.6 - 1)]$ over this period.

This approach would be satisfactory enough if there were no call for a comparison between the inflationary experience of the years 1952–3 to 1957–8 and that of some other period – 1960–1 to 1970–1, say. Suppose, however, that having answered the question 'How severe was inflation between 1952–3 and 1957–8?' by saying that the implicit non-farm G.N.P. deflator rose by 21 per cent over this period we were then asked: Was inflation more severe in the period 1952–3 to 1957–8 than in the period 1960–1 to 1970–1? Suppose, too, that we proceeded to answer this new question by calculating the percentage increase in the non-farm G.N.P. deflator over the second period and comparing this figure with the corresponding figure for the earlier period. To be specific suppose that we observed that the deflator stood at 140.7 in 1960–1 and at 195.2 in 1970–1 and proceeded to calculate the percentage increase implied by these two figures, that is $100(195.2/140.7 - 1) = 38.7$ per cent. Would we now be in a position to answer the supplementary question? At first sight it might seem so. Could we not say that, since the non-farm G.N.P. deflator rose by 38 per cent between 1960–1 and 1970–1 and by only 21 per cent between 1952–3 and 1957–8, inflation was more severe in the second period than in the first? Unfortunately this simple answer would be misleading because it would ignore the crucial fact that the 21 per cent increase in the deflator took place over a period of *six* years whereas the 38 per cent increase took place over a much longer period of *eleven* years.

Because of this difficulty the problem of determining the extent of the rise in the chosen price index is usually approached by determining the average annual percentage increase in the chosen index over the period of interest, rather than the total percentage increase. The figure obtained in this way provides an effective summary of the inflationary experience of a particular period and has the added advantage that it is directly comparable with the corresponding figure for another period even though the two periods may be of widely differing lengths. The percentage increase in the chosen index between successive years or quarters is frequently termed the *rate of inflation* or the *inflation rate*, and the average annual or quarterly percentage increase, the *average rate of inflation*. We shall employ these terms throughout the book.

The usual method of calculating the average rate of inflation for any period is the *compound-interest* (C.I.) method. Under this method one assumes that the chosen index grew in compound-interest fashion over the period and then uses the compound-interest formula to calculate the rate of compound interest implied by the first and last values of the index. Thus on this method we obtain the average rate of inflation from the following formula:

$$r = 100 \left[\left(\frac{P_n}{P_0} \right)^{1/n} - 1 \right],$$

where r is the average rate of inflation and P_0 and P_n the first and last values of the index respectively.†

The C.I. method of calculating the average rate of inflation suffers from the disadvantage that it is based *only* on P_0 and P_n, the first and last values of the index; no intermediate values affect the calculation in any way. As a result the figure obtained by this method is highly sensitive to small changes in the period on which the calculation is based. For example, the calculated average rate of inflation for the period 1952–3 to 1967–8 may well be very different from that for the period 1952–3 to 1966–7 and very different again from that for the period 1951–2 to 1967–8, despite the fact that, for all practical purposes, the same time period is involved in the three calculations.

An alternative method of calculating the average rate of inflation which avoids this difficulty, at the cost of being a little more complicated, is the *least-squares* (L.S.) method. Under the L.S. method an equation of the form:

$$P_t = ab^t$$

is fitted to the observations on the chosen index, for the period of interest, by the method of least squares.‡ The least-squares estimate of b (call it $\hat{b}$) is then taken

---

†If the index is on a quarterly basis the above formula will give the average *quarterly* percentage rate of increase of the index. This can be converted to an annual basis by application of the following formula:

$$r' = 100[(1 + r/100)^4 - 1],$$

where r' is the average *annual* percentage rate of increase.

‡The mechanics of this operation are as follows. First, the equation is reduced to linear form by taking logarithms. Thus we have:

$$\log P_t = \log a + (\log b)t.$$

The $n + 1$ observations on P_t for the period of interest $(P_0, \ldots, P_n)$ are then converted to logarithms, to get $n + 1$ observations on $\log P_t$. Next, a time origin is selected and the $n + 1$ time periods are numbered on the basis of this time origin to get a set of $n + 1$ observations on t. The $n + 1$ observations on $\log P_t$ and t are then used to form the following sums: $\Sigma \log P_t$; Σt; $\Sigma t \log P_t$; Σt^2. Next the to be the average *ratio* of increase in the chosen index over the period, so that the average rate of inflation is given by: †

$$r = 100(\hat{b} - 1).$$

Unlike the C.I. method the L.S. method is based on *all* of the observations on the chosen index. This is because all of the observations on the index are involved in the calculation of $\hat{b}$. That this is the case can be seen from the formula for $\hat{b}$. Assuming that the time origin is taken to be the mid-point of the period of interest, $\hat{b}$ is given by (cf. second footnote on p. 13):

$$\hat{b} = \text{antilog}\left(\frac{\Sigma t \log P_t}{\Sigma t^2}\right).$$

Since all of the observations on the chosen index are used in calculating $\Sigma t \log P_t$, they are all used in the calculation of $\hat{b}$ and hence in the determination of the average rate of inflation by the least-squares method.

1.4. Measurement of Inflation: Timing of Upward Movement

Having chosen our price index and determined the extent of its upward movement, we shall have gone a long way towards measuring the inflationary experience of the period in which we happen to be interested. However, one task will still remain. As well as a measure of the *extent* of the rise in the chosen index, we shall need to provide a measure of the *way in which this rise was distributed* over the period in question before we can claim to have given a reasonably complete picture of the inflationary experience of the period. For example, suppose that we wished to measure the inflationary experience of the ten-year period 1955–6 to 1964–5 and that, to do so, we merely determined the average rate of inflation for the period. The information that the average rate of inflation was, say, 3 per cent per annum over the period would be a vital piece of information; but would it tell us all we wished to know? Clearly not. The

---

'normal equations':

$$\Sigma \log P_t = (n + 1) \log a + \log b \; \Sigma t$$

and

$$\Sigma t \log P_t = \log a \; \Sigma t + \log b \; \Sigma t^2$$

are solved for log a and log b to get the least-squares estimates of log a and log b. Taking antilogs we then get the least-square estimates of a and b.

†Once again, if the index is on a quarterly basis, the above formula will give the average quarterly percentage rate of increase and the further calculation indicated in the previous footnote would have to be undertaken to obtain the average rate of inflation on an annual basis.

statement that the average rate of inflation was 3 per cent per annum means that the index rose by something over 30 per cent over the ten-year period in question. This 30 per cent rise in the index could have been fairly well spread out over the period or it could have been largely concentrated in one or two years – the inflation of the period could have been of the 'creeping' variety or it could have taken the form of a single sharp inflationary burst. To take the extreme cases, the entire 30 per cent increase in the index could have occurred in a single year or the index could have risen by exactly 3 per cent in each year; in both cases the average rate of inflation would have been 3 per cent per annum. Now 'creeping' inflation and 'sharp-burst' inflation are very different things; and we could not reasonably say that we had effectively measured the inflationary experience of the ten-year period in question without having measured the degree to which one possibility, rather than the other, had been realised.

One simple way of measuring the distribution of the observed rise in the chosen index is to identify the sub-period in which the most rapid increase in the chosen index occurred, and then to calculate the 'coefficient of concentration of price increases' from the following formula:[7] coefficient of concentration = proportion of observed increase in index occurring in sub-period x proportion of period outside sub-period. Should the observed increase in the index be perfectly evenly spread over the period (that is should the percentage increase in the index be equal to the average rate of inflation in every single quarter or year), the coefficient will be zero because, in this case, the sub-period of most rapid price increase will coincide with the full period so that the second term in the product will be zero. This is one extreme. The other extreme occurs when the entire increase in the index occurs in a single year or quarter as the case may be. In this event the first term in the product will be unity, and the second term will be very close to unity, giving a value of the coefficient not appreciably different from unity. The coefficient, therefore, is easily interpreted: the nearer the coefficient is to unity the more heavily concentrated is the observed increase in the index (the closer the experience approximates to 'sharp-burst' inflation); the nearer the coefficient is to zero the more evenly spread is the observed increase (the closer the experience approximates to 'creeping' inflation).

1.5 Why Bother About Inflation?

In the chapters which follow, our main task will be to examine the cause of inflation and the ways in which it can be prevented. Before embarking on this task, however, it is natural to ask why inflation is undesirable and why most modern governments consider that it *should* be prevented. The purpose of the present section will be to deal with this question.

Perhaps the main reason for trying to prevent the persistent upward movement in the general price level, which constitutes inflation according to our definition, is that it leads to a redistribution of real income which is arbitrary and which, therefore, may well be socially unjust. People whose money income rises less rapidly than the general price level will lose relatively in times of inflation, while those whose money income rises more rapidly than the price level will gain. The losers will probably include pensioners, people whose main source of income is interest or rent, professional people such as lawyers, doctors and academics and the producers of some primary products sold on world markets. The gainers will include other primary producers, strongly organised wage-earners and business-men. While some of this redistribution may be socially desirable, it is clear that much of it will not be.

The redistributive effects of inflation are not confined to real income; they extend also to real wealth. People or institutions whose wealth is comprised mainly of assets with a fixed, or virtually fixed, money value, such as bank deposits, government bonds and private debt of various kinds, will lose relatively in terms of wealth under inflationary conditions. Persons whose assets consist mainly of real property or whose liabilities remain fixed in money terms will gain relatively. Once again, while some of this redistribution may be in a socially desirable direction, much of it will not be.

A second reason for regarding inflation as undesirable is that it faces a person who wishes to save in order to provide an income for his old age, or to educate his children, or to build a house, with a very serious dilemma. If he invests his savings in a life-assurance policy or in government bonds, or if he places them with a bank on fixed deposit, he can be sure that on certain dates in the future certain fixed sums of money will be forthcoming. But he takes the risk that inflation will reduce the real value of these sums to such an extent that he will find it impossible to meet the needs for which the savings have been made. On the other hand, if he invests his savings in some form of real property he avoids the inflation risk because it is reasonably certain that property values will rise at least as rapidly as the general price level. But he lacks the assurance that certain fixed sums of money will become available to him at certain specified dates in the future because, while the value of property *in general* is likely to rise with the general price level, the value of *his* property may well fall, for example because of the establishment of some source of noise, or other pollution in the vicinity, or because a bridge connecting the suburb in which his property is located with the rest of the city collapses. This is the dilemma referred to earlier; and the fact that inflation faces the ordinary, prudent individual with a choice between such unpleasant alternatives is a strong argument for trying to prevent it.

A third reason why most governments are anxious nowadays to avoid inflation is that it may lead to balance-of-payments difficulties. This, of course, is an especially important consideration for countries like the United Kingdom, where foreign trade plays a major role in the economy. Inflation can weaken the balance of payments both by stimulating imports and by restricting exports. Imports will be stimulated because when the price of the domestic product rises, the foreign product becomes more attractive to the domestic purchaser, other things remaining the same, than was previously the case. On the other hand, the growth of exports will be checked by rising domestic costs and prices because, *ceteris paribus*, rising costs weaken the competitive position of domestic producers in foreign markets.

Of course, if the costs and prices of foreign producers are also rising, along with those of domestic producers, the consequences of inflation for the balance of payments will be less serious than if the costs of foreign producers are stable or falling. For, in the former case, the competitive position of foreign producers in the home market will be strengthened less, and the competitive position of domestic producers in foreign markets weakened less, by inflation than in the latter case. Thus from the point of view of the balance of payments it is not inflation as such which is undesirable but rather more rapid inflation than in the rest of the world.

We turn now to a fourth reason for thinking that inflation should be prevented. When the general price level rises the real value of a given sum of money declines. For example, if the price level rises by 10 per cent between the beginning and the end of a particular year, a sum of $100 expressed in beginning-of-year prices will be $100/1.1 at the end of the year as compared with $100 at the beginning of the year. That is, the real value of $100 will decline by a little over 9 per cent in the course of the year. Because of this fact, wealth-holders have a strong incentive, under inflationary conditions, to keep as little of their wealth as possible in the form of money and as much as possible in the form of assets whose price rises at least as rapidly as the general price level, and which, therefore, do not decline in real terms. This means, in turn, that both individuals and firms face certain real costs (loss of welfare) under inflation that they would not have to face if prices were stable. First, there is the time and effort (physical and mental) which they put into the task of economising on money balances; then there is the inconvenience associated with illiquidity which they suffer if they are successful in this task. If the rate of inflation is moderate – say less than 5 per cent per annum – these real costs will probably not matter very much. However, once the inflation rate climbs to something like 15–20 per cent per annum they can no longer be ignored. And in extreme inflations, when the loss of real wealth consequent on holding money becomes a major consideration and people seek to pass on money as quickly as possible after receiving it, the real costs in question are undoubtedly very large indeed.

A fifth reason for rejecting inflation, which is closely related to the one just discussed, has been well expressed by Hicks in the following way:

If one examines the balance-sheet of a business 'at a moment of time' it will usually be found to have among its assets not only some money which is not earning interest, but also some debts owing to it on which it is not charging interest. If one asks why it should hold assets in this latter form, the answer is surely that it is a matter of convenience, just like the reason for holding money. A debt that is due from a regular customer is not regarded in isolation; it is part of the regular relation between customer and supplier, which it is to the interest of both to maintain in a way that is convenient to both. On this, as on the money holding, inflation exercises a pressure. When money rates of interest are high ... the loss of interest that is involved in unpaid debts becomes more serious. It thus becomes profitable to take more trouble in collecting debts promptly, exerting pressure on debtors which would otherwise not need to be exerted. There is a real loss, measurable in labour-time, in exerting such pressure. And since the debtor himself has a similar incentive to delay payments, it is easily intelligible that the loss can be considerable.[8]

A final reason for rejecting inflation is that it distorts the institutions which lie at the heart of modern capitalist society. Once again it is hard to improve on Hicks's treatment. He says:

The habits — business habits as well as personal habits — which are based on the assumption of stable prices are too strong to be easily broken. Nor is it just habits ... it is also institutions. The accounting system, the tax system, even the general legal system, all are based on the assumption of a stable value of money; if the value of money is seriously changeable, they are twisted out of shape. The accountant's 'profits' cease to be true profits; the taxes that are imposed are different to what was intended; the fines and penalties imposed by the courts, as well as the compensations which they award, lose their proper effect. Now it is of course true that these things can be put right (for a time) by legislation; but only by re-opening issues that had been taken to be closed. There is waste of time in re-discussing them — surely a much more serious waste of time and energy than is involved in holding 'too small' money balances.[9]

We can sum up by saying that inflation needs to be prevented because it redistributes income and wealth in an arbitrary and potentially unjust way; because it complicates the task of the individual who wishes to smooth out his lifetime patterns of consumption and income; because it is a potential source of difficulty in the balance of payments; because it imposes a variety of real costs both on individuals and on firms; and because it distorts the basic institutions of modern capitalist society.

Some economists argue that these troubles would not be serious if inflation were steady and if exchange rates were flexible. For if the inflation rate were to settle at, say, a steady 5 per cent per annum, year-in-year-out, an annual 5 per cent inflation rate would come to be generally expected, 'interest rates would ultimately reflect the pace of inflation; salaries and other sticky incomes and the entire institutional framework would be increasingly adjusted',[10] that is the bad redistributive effects of inflation would disappear. And if exchange rates were flexible, the ill effects on the balance of payments of more rapid inflation than in the rest of the world could always be nullified by an appropriate adjustment of the exchange rate.

Clearly, however, this line of argument lacks force unless there is some prospect of steady inflation and flexible exchange rates. While the latter is arguable, there is little room for argument about the former. As we shall see in Chapter 7, steady inflation presupposes that the authorities are able to control the growth of aggregate demand so that a steady unemployment rate is maintained; and further that certain other variables over which the authorities have virtually no control happen to behave in a steady fashion. In view of this it must be said that there is little prospect of steady inflation. In any case the line of argument in question disposes only of the bad redistributional and balance-of-payments effects of inflation; the bad welfare and institutional effects would still be present even if, by some chance, a perfectly steady inflation were to be achieved.

2

MODELS OF THE INFLATIONARY PROCESS IN DEVELOPED ECONOMIES

2.1 Introduction

As pointed out in the opening section of Chapter 1, one of the important problems to be discussed in this book is the problem of stopping inflation, or at least of keeping it within prescribed bounds. Clearly, however, we cannot hope to say anything useful about possible ways of curbing inflation until we know why it occurs. We must begin, therefore, by considering the question of the causes of inflation. This is our task in the present chapter.

We shall begin by digressing briefly to discuss the general procedure which the economist adopts when called on to explain why some particular economic phenomenon is observed, for example why inflation happens, why there is sometimes substantial unemployment, why consumers purchase what they do, why firms produce what they do in the way they do, and so on. Having cleared our minds on this fundamental matter we shall be in a position to indicate the approach to be adopted in this chapter to the task that has been set — the task of answering the question: How is inflation caused?

When required to explain why some economic phenomenon occurs, the economist begins by building an appropriate model. By this we mean that he formulates a set of relationships which, between them, suffice to determine the economic variables which relate to the phenomenon to be explained (these are called the 'unknowns') once the values of certain other variables (called the 'data') have been specified.† For example, the model set up for dealing with the question 'Why does inflation occur?' would be a set of relationships which determine (among other variables) the chosen price index or its rate of increase, given specified values for certain data, such as the rate of increase of labour productivity.‡ Having formulated his model the economist then explains the

†The set of relationships can be formulated in literary terms, in terms of diagrams or as a set of mathematical equations — which form is chosen is entirely a matter of convenience.

‡The data vary considerably from one model to another. However, as we shall see, they commonly include some type of labour productivity variable.

phenomenon in question by showing that, if the data behave in a particular way, the relationships of the model will generate a pattern of behaviour in the unknowns which corresponds to the phenomenon to be explained. Continuing our inflation example, having formulated his model of inflation, the economist would explain the inflation phenomenon by showing that the relationships of the model will generate a continuous upward movement in the chosen price index given that the data behave in a particular way, for example provided there is an initial downward movement in labour productivity.

Suppose that the economist has succeeded in explaining the phenomenon concerned in this fashion — by setting up a group of relationships between unknowns and data and showing that these relationships will generate the required pattern of behaviour in the unknowns when a certain pattern of behaviour for the data is fed in. How can one tell whether his explanation is satisfactory or otherwise? Only by examining the underlying model and determining whether that is satisfactory or otherwise. How is this to be done? This is a difficult and important question and we must investigate it closely.

The first point to note is that, in building his model, the economist will have made no attempt to be 'realistic' in the sense of specifying a set of relationships which conforms in all respects to what is known about the real world. On the contrary, he will have deliberately departed from reality; his aim will have been to capture in his relationships what, in his judgement, is the *essence* of the real situation and to exclude the rest. In support of this procedure he would argue that a completely realistic model would be useless as a basis for explaining the phenomenon concerned because it would be so complicated as to be unintelligible. Hence his is the only really sensible way in which to proceed. If it is argued against this view that the model need not be completely realistic but only 'sufficiently' realistic, the economist would reply by asking: 'How does one tell when a model is "sufficiently" realistic? On what basis can one say that one type of departure from reality is acceptable and another unacceptable?'

It follows from this discussion that criticism of a model based on its unreality is completely misconceived. Such criticism misses the essential point that a model is a conscious abstraction from reality, and that it would be useless if it were otherwise. But if we cannot assess a model by asking whether it is 'realistic' or 'sufficiently realistic', how can we assess it? The answer to this question is that the test of a model lies in whether or not it predicts better than competing models. The usual situation is that the given economic phenomenon can be explained in terms of several very different models, each of which stresses a different aspect of reality or is 'unrealistic' in a different way. Each of these competing models will generate its own set of predictions which can be tested against actual economic data. If model A predicts better than models $B, C, \ldots$, then model A is to be preferred to models $B, C, \ldots$. The testable predictions generated by a model can take various forms. The values of the unknowns which are generated by the model over any specified period, on the basis of the values observed for the data over that time period, constitute one obvious form of testable prediction. Suppose, for example, that the model in question is one designed to explain the observed movement of the rate of inflation and the percentage rate of increase of money wages per man-hour (these are the unknowns) and that it is set up with real G.N.P. per man-hour and the unemployment percentage as data. By obtaining observations on the two data variables for each quarter from first quarter 1956–7 to fourth quarter 1965–6, say, and substituting these into the model, values of the rate of inflation and the rate of increase of money wages per man-hour could be generated for each of the forty quarters in question. These 'predicted' values could then be compared with the corresponding actual values, that is the predictions made by the model could be tested against the appropriate facts.

Sometimes the model can be made to generate testable predictions of a less obvious kind. Consider, for example, the textbook model of consumer choice. This explains the household's purchases of individual commodities by saying, in effect, that the household behaves as if it possessed a given utility function and maximised this function subject to a budget constraint in which household income and commodity prices appear as data. Now, by appropriate manipulation of this model, it can be shown that it implies household demand functions of a particular form and, in turn, market demand functions of a particular form. This is a prediction generated by the model. It can be tested against the appropriate facts by estimating market demand functions from data on aggregate commodity purchases, on commodity prices and on aggregate household income, and seeing whether these estimated market demand functions possess the properties which they should possess according to the traditional consumer-choice model.

It may be that there is nothing to choose between a group of competing models on the basis of predictive success. In this case other selection criteria will be called for. Those commonly employed are 'simplicity' and 'fruitfulness'. Given two models which stand up equally well under test, the simpler of the two, in terms of number of relationships and complexity of relationships (call it model A), will normally be preferred to the less simple (model B), though we may be prepared to suffer the added complexity of model B if it is more 'fruitful', in the sense that it generates a more varied set of predictions than model A and hence achieves its equally good test record under more stringent conditions than does model A.

Let us now return from this digression on methodology and, using the ideas developed there, proceed to set out the plan to be followed in the present chapter.

We have seen that to explain inflation, as it has been defined in the opening chapter, the economist first formulates a model of the inflationary process. As will be clear from our preliminary discussion, this is a set of relationships which includes among the unknowns either the level of the chosen price index or its percentage rate of increase between successive years or quarters, and which determines the price variable and the other unknowns for each time period (year or quarter) once values have been allotted to the data. Since the value of the prices variable is determined for each period by the values allotted to the data for the period, it is clear that the *time path* of the price variable is determined once the time paths of the data have been specified. Having formulated his model the economist then shows that, if certain time paths are imposed on the data, the model will generate a time path for the price variable, which constitutes inflation as we have defined it. If the price variable is the *level* of the chosen price index, this time path will take the form of an *increase in the value* of the price variable in every period; if the price variable is the *percentage increase* of the chosen price index over the preceding period, the time path generated by the model will take the form of a *positive value* for the price variable in every period. In both cases the time path generated for the price variable is an inflationary time path because it implies a continuous upward movement in the chosen price index. Thus inflation is explained by saying that the relationships which link the price variable with the data are such that, when the data follow certain time paths, an inflationary time path for the price variable must result.

A great many models of the inflationary process, in the sense of the preceding paragraph, have been proposed in the last thirty years or so, and it would not be possible to discuss them all in the present chapter. In any case it would not be desirable to do so since many of the models exhibit close similarities, and the discussion, therefore, would be rather repetitive. On examination, the models appear to fall into five broad groups which, for ease of reference, we shall designate as follows: (1) Keynesian; (2) Mark-Up; (3) Expectational; (4) Monetarist; and (5) Wage Leadership. In the following five sections of this chapter we shall present a prototype model, as it were, for each of these five groups, that is a model which possesses the essential characteristics of all models falling in the group in question though not necessarily coinciding with any actual model in that group. By this means we hope to give a birds-eye view of the model-building work of the last two or three decades. As far as possible our approach in this chapter will be non-mathematical even though this may result in a certain lack of precision from time to time.

Before beginning our theoretical survey there is one further point which must be stressed, namely that the models to be discussed in this chapter are intended to explain *normal* inflation in *developed market economies*. They are *not* intended to explain abnormal inflation (or 'hyperinflation' as it is sometimes called) nor are they intended to explain the inflationary process either in centrally planned economies or in developing economies. In recent years many models have been designed specifically for these latter purposes, and, as one would expect, these models are quite different in character from the models to be discussed here. We shall turn our attention to models of inflation in developing economies in Chapter 10 and to models of hyperinflation in Chapter 11.

2.2   Survey of Inflation Models: Keynesian Models

As already indicated, the object of this and the following four sections is to present a prototype model for each of the five main classes of model that have been proposed in recent years to explain normal inflation in developed market economies. We begin with Keynesian models.

As our prototype Keynesian model we shall take the model sketched by Keynes in his famous pamphlet, *How to Pay for the War*.[1] Several of the models proposed in the late 1940s and early 1950s were inspired by this model and share its essential features. It is this group of early post-war models to which we are attaching the label 'Keynesian'.

We shall begin by quoting the relevant portions of Keynes's discussion, which is remarkable both for its clarity and its persuasiveness:

> Let us suppose that the value of the output of the country is £5,500 million at pre-war prices, that individual incomes (including transfer payments) come to £6,000 million, that the yield of taxation is £1,400 million . . . and that the expenditure of the Government, also reckoned at pre-war prices is £2,750 million, i.e. £2,250 million excluding transfer payments. After deducting £1,400 million which they pay in taxation, individuals are left with £4,600 million which they are free to spend if they choose. But since the Government has already purchased £2,250 million of the output, there is only £3,250 (£5,500 − £2,250) million of goods (valued at pre-war prices) left for the public to buy with their remaining incomes of £4,600 million.

> Let us suppose . . . that the voluntary savings of the public are, in the first instance, only £700 million, and that they try to spend the rest of their incomes, namely £3,900 million, on goods worth only £3,250 million at pre-war prices. Obviously prices will have to rise 20 per cent which will equate supply and demand; for the goods will then be worth £3,900 (£3,250 + £650) million, which is just equal to the desired expenditure. Moreover, those who have sold for £3,900 million goods which only cost them £3,250 million will have the balance of £650 million left over as extra unspent income.

> A certain time will elapse before this sum reaches those who will be entitled to spend it. But in the next innings, so to speak, it will be added to the total of potentially spendable incomes, so that we shall have incomes of £5,250 million (£4,600 + £650) facing goods which, after allowing for the continuance of the 20 per cent price rise, are only worth £3,900 million. Moreover, it will be impossible for the Government to keep down the prices of its own purchases if open market prices have risen 20 per cent. Thus we shall soon find ourselves in much the same position as before with a substantial discrepancy between the amount of money which the public are preparing to spend and the value (at the new price level, 20 per cent higher than before) of the goods available for them to buy. A further rise in prices will be required to provide a temporary respite; and so on. Fortunately this is not a complete picture of the second chapter of the story . . . . More than half . . . of the £650 million will become payable as taxes. Moreover it is likely that a considerable proportion of the balance will be voluntarily saved . . . . Thus, in fact, only a small part of the £650 million (or

of this figure augmented by such higher prices as the Government may pay for its own purposes) will come on the consumption market in the second innings. Instead of another 20 per cent rise of prices being required to preserve equilibrium, it may be that a rise of 2 or 3 per cent would be sufficient.

Unfortunately this is not yet the complete story; for we have now gone to the other extreme, having slipped in an assumption much less troublesome than the facts. We have assumed that, in spite of the rise of 20 per cent in prices, workers are content with the same money-wages as before .... But in fact the workers will press for higher wages – with at least partial success. For employers will put up much less resistance than usual to a rise in wages. The scarcity of labour will force them to agree if they are to retain their men; and, since the Government is taking away in taxation 75 per cent of their excess profits, it will not cost them much to share their profiteering with their employees and their salaried staff. If, indeed, wages and other money costs were to go up fully in proportion to the cost of living, we should be faced, as before, with an unlimited inflation, proceeding by 20 per cent at each step – the process generally known as the vicious spiral.

In this passage Keynes has formulated a model of the inflationary process, and has shown that it will generate a continuous upward movement in the price index provided the data are allotted appropriate time paths, that is he has explained inflation. His argument may be briefly summarised as follows.

Inflation occurs, according to Keynes, when the *volume* of output, (Keynes's 'output at pre-war prices') is virtually fixed in the short run.† Suppose that, in such a situation, the government increases its own spending without taking any steps to reduce private spending by an equivalent amount. Then aggregate spending will increase. But if aggregate spending increases, the *value* of output must increase by the same amount because aggregate spending and the value of output are identically equal. Now with volume of output fixed, the only way in which the value of output can increase, so as to keep in line with the higher level of aggregate spending, is by means of an increase in the price index. This is because $V = PV^c$ where V denotes value of output, V^c volume of output and P the price index. In fact with V^c fixed an increase in aggregate spending must *cause the same proportional increase* in P; if aggregate spending increases by, say 5 per cent, prices must rise by 5 per cent also. According to Keynes, this is how inflation begins. An increase in aggregate spending, with V^c at its upper limit, results in an equal proportional increase in the price index. By this means the value of output

†For all practical purposes situations in which physical output has reached an upper limit are confined to periods of total war and its aftermath; in more normal times it is usually possible to increase the volume of output significantly in the short run, even in the absence of idle productive resources, by resort to additional overtime working, by using workers who are normally outside the labour force, and so on.

is restored to equality with aggregate spending. However, the increase in the value of output will be matched by an increase in aggregate income because the value of output is identically equal to aggregate income. This increase in aggregate income will consist partly of an increase in wage income and partly of an increase in profit income. Wage income will increase because, after a time, wage-earners will press for, and gain, increases in wage rates (wage-earnings per man) to compensate for the rise in the cost of living induced by the earlier rise in prices. With employment fixed this rise in wage rates will produce an equal proportional increase in wage income. Part of the increase in aggregate income, then, will take the form of an increase in wage income. The rest will take the form of an increase in profit income since, by definition, profit income is merely aggregate income *less* wage income.

Regardless of its disposition between wage income and profit income, the increase in aggregate income will lead to an increase in private spending. Also, assuming that the government is determined to maintain its *real* expenditure at the higher level achieved at the outset of the process, government spending in actual money terms must increase in proportion to the increase in the price index. Thus, both directly through government spending and indirectly through private spending, the initial increase in the price index will cause a further increase in aggregate spending and so lead to a re-opening of the gap between aggregate spending and the value of output. In other words, the initial price increase will both close the spending–output gap and, at the same time, make inevitable its re-emergence at a later point of time, through its effects on profit income and wage income and on the real value of government spending.

We are now back to our starting-point. Once again, we have aggregate spending increasing in relation to the value of output. And, once again, this results in an equal proportional increase in the price index, which both closes the spending–output gap and leads, in due course, to its re-appearance and hence to a further price increase. Thus the whole process is repeated indefinitely; the initial increase in the price index is followed by a further increase which is followed, in turn, by a further increase, and so on. In other words, we have a process of inflation as we have defined it in the opening chapter.

By means of this argument, then, Keynes shows that the model presented above will generate a continuous upward movement in the price index provided the data have appropriate time paths – specifically provided volume of output and employment remain fixed at their initial levels and provided real government spending first increases above its initial level and then remains fixed at the higher level thereafter.

2.3   Survey of Inflation Models: Mark-Up Models

Having set out a prototype Keynesian model we turn now to the second of our four groups of inflation models. To these we have given the label 'mark-up models', and it may be helpful to begin by explaining the significance of this label.

In the developed-market economies to which the theoretical material presented in this chapter relates (see p. 23), prices of individual commodities can be divided into two broad groups: (i) prices which are fixed impersonally on an auction-market basis; (ii) prices which are fixed as a result of some administrative decision. The prices which fall into the first group are those which emerge, typically, through a process of offer and counter-offer. An example is the price of a particular lot of wool. This would be fixed after an auctioneer had taken bids and counter-bids from prospective buyers. Another example is the price of a particular pen of sheep at an abattoir. Here again the price would emerge from a process of bid and counter-bid on the part of prospective buyers. By contrast, the prices in the second group are simply announced. Sometimes the price (to the seller) is announced by a public official or a Cabinet Minister, for example when some agricultural commodity is marketed through a public marketing authority. More commonly, however, the announcement is made by one of the parties to the transaction. In some such cases it is the *buyer* who announces the price and the seller who accepts it, for example when a cannery advertises its willingness to purchase the whole of a particular fruit crop at a specified price. But in most cases where the price is announced by one of the parties the roles are reversed; in particular in the case of nearly all manufacturing, wholesale and retail prices, it is the seller who fixes the price and the buyer who accepts it. Such prices are frequently described as 'mark-up' prices because the process by which the seller fixes the price of a unit of output is to 'mark-up' the cost of a unit of output (unit cost), that is the process is to add on to unit cost some fraction of the figure, the sum added being known as the *profit margin*.

Now the distinguishing feature of the 'mark-up' class of models, and the reason for attaching this particular label to them, is that they conceive of inflation as the continuous upward movement in some index of mark-up prices, and accordingly have such an index or its percentage rate of increase as their unknown price variable. Of the indexes discussed in Chapter 1, the one which would appear to be most suitable for use in a mark-up model is the implicit deflator of non-farm G.N.P. Another index which would be appropriate, and which has sometimes been used in mark-up models, is an index of manufacturing prices.

All mark-up models take the mark-up process as their starting-point. Thus the framer of a mark-up model sees price as being determined in the following way:

$$\text{price} = \text{unit cost} + (x \times \text{unit cost}) = (1 + x) \times \text{unit cost},$$

where x is some fraction such as $1/10$ or $1/4$ or $3/10$. The term ($x \times$ unit cost) is the profit margin; clearly it is equal to price *minus* unit cost. The fraction x is referred to as the *relative* profit margin because it represents the profit margin (price *minus* unit cost) expressed as a proportion of unit cost.† Alternatively, $100x$ is

†From the above expression we have:

price − unit cost = x × unit cost

Therefore, $x = \dfrac{\text{price} - \text{unit cost}}{\text{unit cost}}$.

called the *percentage* profit margin since it is the profit margin expressed as a *percentage* of unit cost. For example, if x is 1/10 the price-maker in question would be said to be operating with a profit margin of 10 per cent ($100x = 100 \times 1/10 = 10$).

Starting from this relationship between price and unit cost, the framer of a mark-up model proceeds, step by step, towards a 'price equation' for the 'mark-up sector' of the economy as a whole, this being the sector in which mark-up pricing, as defined above, applies. This price equation constitutes the basic relationship of his model of the inflationary process.

The price equation for our prototype mark-up model is:

$$p = \beta_1 w - \beta_1 o + \beta_2 s + m,$$

where p denotes the percentage increase in an index of prices, w the percentage increase in an index of wage-earnings per man, o the percentage increase in an index of output per man, s the percentage increase in an index of unit non-labour cost and m the percentage increase in an index of mark-up factors, all indexes relating to the mark-up sector of the economy. We shall now outline the argument by means of which this equation can be derived from the basic micro expression presented above, namely:

$$\text{price} = (1 + x) \times (\text{unit cost}),$$

where x is the relative profit margin.

We first note that if the price of the current period (say the current quarter) is given by:

$$\text{price} = (1 + x) \times (\text{unit cost}),$$

then the *percentage increase* in price between the current quarter and the preceding quarter is given by:

$$\hat{p} = \hat{m} + \hat{c}, \qquad (2.1)$$

where $\hat{p}$ denotes the percentage increase in price between the current quarter and the previous quarter, $\hat{m}$ the percentage increase in the 'mark-up' factor $(1 + x)$ and $\hat{c}$ the percentage increase in unit cost. This expression is an approximation which gives good results so long as both $\hat{m}$ and $\hat{c}$ are small.

To illustrate this formula[2] take the following hypothetical figures:

	Unit cost ($)	Percentage profit margin	Price ($)
Quarter 1	100	20	120
Quarter 2	105	21	127.05

According to our formula the percentage increase in price is approximately equal to the percentage increase in unit cost *plus* the percentage increase in the mark-up factor $(1 + x)$. The percentage increase in unit cost is 5 while the percentage increase in the mark-up factor is $|(1.21 - 1.20)/1.20| \, 100 = 0.83$. Hence according to our formula the percentage increase in price is 5.83. This is very close to the true percentage increase which is $7.05 \times 100/120 = 5.88$.

Relationship (2.1) relates, of course, to a single price-maker, for example a single manufacturing firm or a single retailer. The analogous expression for the mark-up sector of the economy as a whole is as follows:

$$p = m + c, \tag{2.2}$$

where p denotes the percentage increase, between the current quarter and the previous quarter, in some *index* of mark-up prices, m the percentage increase in some index of mark-up factors and c the percentage increase in some index of unit cost in the mark-up sector.

We next note that the variable c can be decomposed in various ways. In particular, it can be written as:

$$c = \beta_1 n + \beta_2 s, \tag{2.3}$$

where n denotes the percentage increase in some index of unit *labour* cost in the mark-up sector, s the percentage increase in some index of unit *non*-labour cost in the mark-up sector and β_1 and β_2 two constants which sum to unity.†

---

†Denote the unit cost of a price-maker by C, the unit labour cost by N and the unit non-labour cost by S. Then:

$$C_0 = N_0 + S_0$$

and

$$C_1 = N_1 + S_1,$$

where the subscripts denote successive periods. Hence:

$$\frac{C_1 - C_0}{C_0} = \frac{(N_1 + S_1) - (N_0 + S_0)}{(N_0 + S_0)}$$

$$= \frac{(N_1 - N_0) + (S_1 - S_0)}{N_0 + S_0}$$

$$= \left(\frac{N_1 - N_0}{N_0}\right)\left(\frac{N_0}{N_0 + S_0}\right) + \left(\frac{S_1 - S_0}{S_0}\right)\left(\frac{S_0}{N_0 + S_0}\right).$$

Hence:

$$\hat{c} = \beta_1^* \hat{n} + \beta_2^* \hat{s},$$

where the denotes 'percentage increase' and

$$\beta_1^* = \frac{N_0}{N_0 + S_0}$$

and

$$\beta_2^* = \frac{S_0}{N_0 + S_0}$$

The decomposition of c can be taken one stage further. It can be shown that:

$$n = w - o, \qquad (2.4)$$

where w denotes the percentage increase in some index of wage-earnings per man (or per man-hour) in the mark-up sector and o the percentage increase in some index of output per man in the mark-up sector. Like (2.1), (2.4) is an approximation which gives good results so long as o is small.[3]

If we substitute (2.4) into (2.3) and then substitute the resulting expression into (2.2), we obtain:

$$p = \beta_1 w - \beta_1 o + \beta_2 s + m. \qquad (2.5)$$

According to this expression the current percentage increase in the index of mark-up prices (the percentage increase between the current quarter and the preceeding quarter) can be found (approximately) by taking a weighted sum of: (i) the current percentage increase in the index of wage-earnings per man in the mark-up sector (weight = β_1); (ii) the current percentage increase in the index of output per man in the mark-up sector (weight = $-\beta_1$); (iii) the current percentage increase in the index of unit non-labour cost in the mark-up sector (weight = β_2); and (iv) the current percentage increase in the index of mark-up factors in the mark-up sector (weight = 1).

Relationship (2.5) constitutes the central relationship of our prototype mark-up model.† To complete the model we shall introduce a second relationship which explains w, the current percentage increase in the index of wage-earnings per man in the mark-up sector. This relationship is as follows:

$$w = \phi(u, p^*), \qquad (2.6)$$

where u denotes current unemployment, expressed as a percentage of the labour force (the current 'unemployment percentage' or 'unemployment rate'), p^*

---

are two constants which sum to unity. The analogous expression for the mark-up sector as a whole is:

$$c = \beta_1 n + \beta_2 s,$$

where c is the percentage increase in the *index* of unit cost, n the percentage increase in the index of unit labour cost, s the percentage increase in the index of unit non-labour cost and β_1 and β_2 two constants which sum to unity.

†The procedure used to obtain (2.2), the relationship which forms the basis of (2.5), is an example of 'aggregation by analogy'. This is a crude form of aggregation whereby a macro relation (for example (2.2)) is obtained from the corresponding micro relation (for example (2.1)) by retaining the form of the micro relation and replacing the micro magnitudes by the corresponding macro magnitudes. Aggregation by analogy is also used in the derivation of (2.3) (see previous footnote).

denotes the percentage increase in the index of mark-up prices at some time in the past† and ϕ denotes 'is a function of' or 'is determined by'.

Relationship (2.6) states that the current rate of increase in the index of wage-earnings per man in the mark-up sector is determined by: (i) the current unemployment percentage; and (ii) the rate of increase in the index of mark-up prices at some time in the past.

In setting out (2.6) we have made no stipulation as to the precise *nature* of the dependence of w on u and p^*, but it is usually assumed that given the level of p^* w increases as u decreases, and that given the level of u, w increases as p^* increases. In other words, the usual assumption is that the index of wage-earnings per man in the mark-up sector will rise at a faster rate than before if the unemployment percentage falls and/or if the index of prices in the mark-up sector rises at a faster rate than previously.

Indeed it is usual to go even further in specifying the precise form of the function ϕ. We have said in the preceding paragraph that one usually assumes that w increases as u decreases, given p^*. In graphical terms, one assumes that with w on the vertical axis and u on the horizontal axis, the curve of w against u, for a fixed level of p^*, is a curve which falls continuously from left to right. Usually, however, one goes further and postulates that the curve of w against u, for given p^*, is a curve which falls continuously from left to right *in the special way indicated in Figure 2.1*. The features of this curve are: (i) that it cuts the horizontal axis at some level of u, denoted by $\bar{u}$; and (ii) that it becomes more and more steep as one moves from right to left. Thus it is usually assumed: (*a*) that

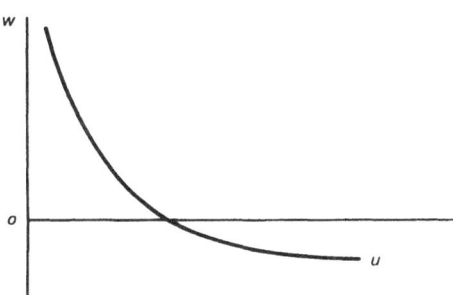

Fig. 2.1

---

†The vagueness involved in the use of the word 'past' is deliberate. In some contexts such vagueness cannot be tolerated. For example, if one wishes to examine the stability properties of a particular model of the inflationary process, precise dating of the variables is absolutely essential. Again, as we shall see in Chapters 4 and 5, precise specification of the lags at work in relationships like (2.4) is of critical importance when one is undertaking empirical work. In the present context, however, we gain nothing by attempting to be more specific and lose by adding considerably to the complexity of the discussion which follows.

there is some level of u beyond which w is negative, that is to say that if the unemployment percentage rises far enough, the wage-earnings index will actually fall; and (*b*) that a fall of one percentage point in the unemployment percentage will have a much more powerful effect on w when u is already low than when u is high, for example a fall in u from, say, 1.5 per cent to 0.5 per cent will cause a more rapid rise in the rate of increase of the wage-earnings index than a fall from, say 5 per cent to 4 per cent.

The curve shown in Figure 2.1 is now known as the *Phillips curve*, after the economist who first proposed it,[4] and we shall describe it in this way from now on.

Our prototype mark-up model of the inflationary process consists, then, of the two relationships (2.5) and (2.6). Of the six variables which appear in these two relationships, namely p (currrent and past), w, o, s, m and u, the first two are regarded as unknowns while the remaining four are regarded as data. Thus (2.5) and (2.6) can be thought of as a system of relationships which together determine p (the percentage increase – current and past – in the index of prices in the mark-up sector) and w (the current percentage increase in the index of wage-earnings per man in the mark-up sector) once values are allotted to the four data, namely o, s, m and u.

It remains to show that our model is, indeed, a genuine model of the inflationary process, that is to say, that it will generate a continuous upward movement in the index of mark-up prices if an appropriate set of time paths is specified for the four data. Now the *index* of mark-up prices will exhibit a *continuous upward movement* so long as *the percentage rate of increase* of the index is *continuously positive*. Hence to show that our mark-up model will generate a continuous upward movement in the index of mark-up prices, if appropriate time paths are specified for the data, we have merely to show that it will generate continuously positive values for the unknown p, if the data of the model are given appropriate time paths. This we shall now do.

Let us postulate an initial situation in which both s and m remain fixed at zero, that is a situation in which both the index of unit non-labour cost and the index of mark-ups remain constant in the mark-up sector. Let us suppose, too, that o, the percentage increase in the index of output per man in the mark-up sector, remains fixed in the initial situation, though not necessarily at zero. Finally, we postulate that in the initial situation the unemployment percentage is such that the ordinate of the relevant Phillips curve is equal to o, i.e. such that $w = o$. We denote this particular unemployment percentage by $\bar{u}$. Then, in the initial situation, it will be the case that p is zero, that is to say, that the index of prices in the mark-up sector is constant. (This follows from relationship (2.5) which implies that p is zero when $w = o$ and when s and m are both zero.)†

Suppose, further, that this initial state of rest is disturbed by a 'step' increase in

†This means of course that the 'relevant' Phillips curve referred to at an earlier point in this paragraph will be the curve corresponding to $p^* = 0$.

the index of unit non-labour cost in the mark-up sector. By this we mean that the index of unit non-labour cost increases in some quarter and then stays put at the new, higher level thereafter. For example, if the index was initially constant at 100, if it rose to, say, 105 in some particular quarter and if it then remained constant at 105 forever after, the increase from 100 to 105 would constitute a 'step' increase of 5 points in the index. Quite obviously, the postulated step increase in the index of unit non-labour cost can be expressed in terms of *s* (the current *percentage increase* in the index); what we are supposing is that *s* (one of our data) is constant at zero in the initial situation, that it rises to some positive value (say 5 per cent) for one period (one quarter, say) and that it assumes its original value of zero forever after.†

Suppose, finally, that the index of mark-up factors and the index of labour productivity both remain fixed at the constant levels followed in the initial situation, that is to say, that both *o* and *m* stay at their initial zero levels, and that *u* remains fixed at $\bar{u}$.

In the last two paragraphs we have, in effect, postulated a set of time paths for the data of our model. This set of postulated time paths can be summarised as shown in Table 2.1.

Table 2.1

Datum	Postulated time path
s	Zero in initial situation; positive for one quarter; zero thereafter
o, m	Zero for all time
u	$\bar{u}$ for all time

As we have seen, with this set of time paths for the data, our model implies that $p = o$ in the initial situation or that the index of mark-up prices is constant in the initial situation. However, the model also implies that *p* will become postive in the quarter in which the intial situation is disturbed by the rise in unit non-labour cost and remains positive thereafter, or, equivalently, that the index of mark-up prices will move continuously upward from the point in time at which the disturbance occurs. In other words, with this set of time paths for the data, our model generates inflation.

†The postulated increase in the index of unit non-labour cost could be the result of an increase in the domestic prices of imported raw materials – caused either by an increase in their foreign-currency prices with fixed exchange rates or by an exchange devaluation with fixed foreign-currency prices. Alternatively it could result from an increase in the prices of raw materials produced in the market-price sector and used in the administered-price sector, for example wool used in clothing manufacture.

To see that this is so let us return to the two relationships which form our model, namely (2.5) and (2.6). From (2.5) we see that, with s positive and w, o and m zero, p will be positive. Thus, in the quarter in which the step increase in the index of unit non-labour cost occurs, the index of mark-up prices will rise. Relationship (2.6) implies that, after a delay, this increase in p will shift the Phillips curve to the right (recall that, given u, w increases as p^* increases). Consequently with u still held at $\bar{u}$, w will become positive. With o and m continuing at zero, with s now back at zero and with w positive, (2.5) implies that p will continue to be positive. With p positive the Phillips curve will remain in some position to the right of its position in the initial situation. Hence with u still at $\bar{u}$, w will continue to be positive. However (2.5) implies that, with o, m and s continuing at zero and with w still positive, p will continue to be positive. And so on. Thus we see that, given the time paths imposed on the data in Table 2.1, the relationships of our model ((2.5) and (2.6)) will generate continuously positive values for the unknown p, that is will generate a continuous upward movement in the index of the mark-up prices.

Table 2.2†

Datum	Set 1	Set 2	Set 3
o	B	A	A
m	A	C	A
u	D	D	E

†A denotes 'zero for all time'; B denotes 'zero in initial situation, negative for one quarter, zero thereafter'; C denotes 'zero in initial situation, positive for one quarter, zero thereafter'; D denotes '$\bar{u}$ for all time'; E denotes '$\bar{u}$ in initial situation, $\hat{u}$ for one quarter ($\hat{u} < \bar{u}$), $\bar{u}$ thereafter'.

The set of time paths imposed on the data in Table 2.1 is not the only set for which (2.5) and (2.6) will generate an inflationary process. Three others, designated as 'set 1', 'set 2' and 'set 3', are shown in Table 2.2. In the case of set 1, the 'shock' which initiates the inflationary process is a step *decrease* in the index of output per man in the mark-up sector. (In this terminology the shock in Table 2.1 is a step increase in the index of unit non-labour cost.) In the case of set 2, the shock is a step increase in the index of mark-up factors. Finally in the case of set 3, the shock is a one-period decrease in the unemployment percentage. (The difference between a one-period decrease and a step decrease is that, in the case of the former, the lower value is maintained for one period only, whereas in the case of the latter the lower level is maintained indefinitely.) It will be left to the reader to adapt the argument of the preceding paragraph to show that relationships (2.5) and (2.6) will indeed generate an inflationary process if any one of these three sets of time paths is imposed on the data.†

2.4   Survey of Inflation Models: Expectational Models

Our prototype expectational model is a fairly straightforward extension of the mark-up model discussed in the preceding section. It consists of the following two relationships:

$$p = \psi(u) + p^e \qquad (2.7)$$

and

$$\Delta p^e = \theta(p - p^e). \qquad (2.8)$$

In these expressions, p and u have the same meanings as before, while ψ is the symbol, once again, for 'function of'. The new symbols are p^e, Δp^e and θ. The first denotes the percentage increase in the index of prices in the mark-up sector which is *expected* in the current quarter (as distinct from p, the percentage increase which *actually occurs* in the current quarter), the second denotes the *change* in the expected percentage increase between the current quarter and the previous quarter, while θ is a constant lying between zero and unity.

The unknowns of the model are p and p^e while u is the sole datum. Thus (2.7) and (2.8) are to be thought of as a system of relationships which, between them, determine p and p^e (both current level and current change in level) once u is specified.

Relationship (2.7) is a combination of (2.5) and (2.6) – or, more precisely, of modified versions of these two relationships. To obtain (2.7) we start with (2.5) and simplify it by assuming: (i) that $\beta_2 = 0$, that is to say that *labour* cost is the only cost element in price; (ii) that the index of output per man grows at a constant rate (constant rate of increase of productivity) so that o is some constant, say r; (iii) that profit margins remain fixed over time so that m remains constant at zero. On these assumptions the price equation takes the simpler form: ‡

$$p = w - r. \qquad (2.9)$$

---

†The four sets of data time paths specified in Tables 2.1 and 2.2 are characterised by *constant* values for each of the data subsequent to the period in which the shock occurs. More complicated sets could be specified in which one or more of the data follow non-constant paths subsequent to the shock. An example is the following: o, m zero for all time; u at $\bar{u}$ for all time; s zero in initial situation; *positive* thereafter. In the case of this set the 'cause' of the inflation is a *continuous* increase in the index of unit non-labour cost, as distinct from the step increase of Table 2.1.

‡Recall that $\beta_1 + \beta_2 = 1$ (see above, p. 29). Thus $\beta_2 = 0$ implies $\beta_1 = 1$.

We next modify (2.6). Instead of:

$$w = \phi(u, p^*),$$

we postulate:

$$w = g(u) + p^e, \qquad\qquad (2.10)$$

where g denotes 'function of'. It will be recalled that, in the case of (2.6), the curve of w against u, for a fixed level of p^*, is assumed to be of the form shown in Figure 2.1 (see p. 31 above). The corresponding assumption is made in relation to (2.10). That is, we assume, when writing (2.10), that for a fixed level of p^e, the curve of w against u is of the form shown in Figure 2.1. Thus (2.6) and (2.10) are alike inasmuch as they both embody the concept of the Phillips curve. In other important respects, however, they are very different. In the case of (2.6) it is assumed that, given u, w will be higher *the higher is* p*. In other words, it is assumed that an increase in the percentage rate of increase of prices in the mark-up sector will shift the Phillips curve upwards, albeit after some delay. Moreover, nothing is postulated about the *extent* of the shift which results from, say, a one-point increase in the rate of increase of prices. By contrast, in the case of (2.10), it is assumed that, given u, w will be higher *the higher is* p^e. Thus, here, wage-earners are assumed to be guided by *likely future* price developments, when formulating wage claims, not by *historical* price development; it is, an increase in the *expected* rate of price increase which shifts the Phillips curve upwards, and not an increase in the *actual* rate of price increase. Furthermore, unlike (2.6), (2.10) is quite specific about the extent of the shift in the Phillips curve which results from a one-point increase in p^e. From the fact that p^e appears additively on the right-hand side of (2.10) it is clear that a one-point increase in p^e (say from 4 per cent per period to 5 per cent per period) will produce a one-point increase in w at a given level at u (and hence of $g(u)$). In other words, it is clear from the form of (2.10) that a one-point increase in p^e will displace the Phillips curve upwards *by one percentage point at all points*.

Together (2.9) and (2.10) imply that:

$$p = [g(u) - r] + p^e .$$

Therefore

$$p = \psi(u) + p^e,$$

where the function $\psi(u) = g(u) - r$.

The expression just derived is, of course, (2.7), the first relationship of our expectational model. We turn now to (2.8), the second relationship of our prototype expectational model.

Recalling that θ is a constant lying between zero and unity, we see that, according to (2.8), Δp^e is zero if p and p^e are equal, is positive if p exceeds p^e and is negative if p falls short of p^e. Thus it is implied by (2.8) that if expectations as to the rate of price increase are fulfilled ($p = p^e$) there will be no revision of expectations – previously held expectations will continue to be held ($\Delta p^e = 0$). On the other hand, any non-fulfilment of expectations will cause expectations to be revised in one direction or another. If the actual rate of price increase exceeds the rate that was expected ($p > p^e$), the expected rate will be revised upwards ($\Delta p^e > 0$) by some fraction of the excess. Conversely, if the actual rate falls short of the expected rate ($p < p^e$), the expected rate will be revised downwards ($\Delta p^e < 0$) by some fraction of the deficiency.

Relationship (2.8) is an instance of the so-called 'adaptive expectations hypothesis' which has found wide application in dynamic economics since it was first introduced by Cagan some fifteen years ago.[5]

As with the prototype Keynesian and mark-up models discussed in earlier sections we have now to show that the above expectational model is indeed a model of the inflationary process, in the sense that it will generate a continuous upward movement in the index of mark-up prices if an appropriate set of time paths is specified for the data.

Let us postulate an initial situation in which the index of prices in the mark-up sector is expected to remain constant at all points of time. This amounts to saying that, in the initial situation, p^e is zero at all points of time and hence that Δp^e is zero at all points of time. Now from (2.8), $p^e = 0$ and $\Delta p^e = 0$ together imply that $p = 0$. Thus the index of mark-up prices is not only *expected* to remain constant at all points of time in the initial situation but actually does so, that is in the initial situation price expectations are continuously realized. Moreover, from (2.9), if $p = 0$ then $w = r$, that is the rate of increase of wage-earnings per man is equal to the (constant) rate of increase of output per man (see also p. 35). Hence from (2.10) we have for the initial situation:

$$r = g(u).$$

In other words, the unemployment rate must be at a level (call it $\bar{u}$) such that the ordinate of the relevant Phillips curve (the curve corresponding to $p^e = 0$) is r, as illustrated in Figure 2.2.

So much for the state of rest in the initial situation. We now postulate that this state of rest is disturbed by a permanent decrease in the unemployment rate; the unemployment rate falls from $\bar{u}$ to $\bar{\bar{u}}$, say, and stays at this lower level thereafter. Given this decrease in the unemployment rate, the expectational model (2.7) and (2.8) will generate a continuous upward movement in the price index, that is continuously positive values for the unknown, p. That this is so can be seen by referring to relationships (2.7), (2.8), (2.9) and (2.10) and to Figure 2.2.

Recall that in the initial situation, where $u = \bar{u}$, we have $w = r$, and hence, from (2.9), $p = 0$. When u falls from $\bar{u}$ to $\bar{\bar{u}}$ the following sequence occurs:

(i) w rises above r (see Figure 2.2) and hence, from (2.9), p becomes positive.
(ii) With p positive and p^e still at the zero level characterising the initial situation, $p - p^e$ becomes positive and hence, from (2.8), there is a positive

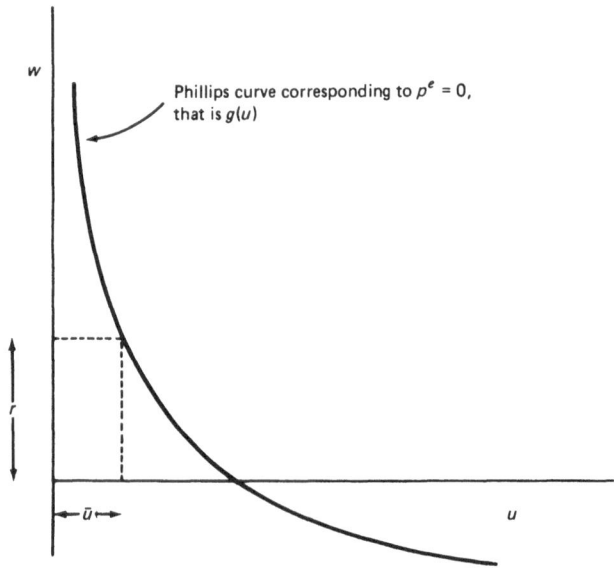

Fig. 2.2

change (an increase) in p^e. Since p^e was previously zero this amounts to saying that p^e now becomes positive. But from (2.10) we see that, with p^e positive, the Phillips curve will move to the right of its position in the initial situation where $p^e = 0$. Hence, after the increase in p^e, w must still be in excess of r (see Figure 2.2), and hence from (2.9) p must remain positive. Moreover, p must be *more* positive (the rate of increase of the price index must be higher) after the increase in p^e than before because of the rightward shift of the Phillips curve produced by the increase in p^e.

(iii) Even after the increase referred to in (ii), p^e is still below the level of p which prevails prior to the increase since $0 < \theta < 1$. Consequently it must certainly be below the level of p which prevails after the increase since the level of p after the increase in p^e exceeds the level of p prior to the increase (see (ii)). Hence, after the increase in p^e, $(p - p^e)$ must still be positive, and hence, in turn, there must be a further increase in p^e (from (2.8)). From (2.10) it follows that the Phillips curve must shift still further to the right, and hence that the sequence outlined above must be repeated.

We have shown, therefore, that the model of (2.7) and (2.8) will generate continuously positive values for p if the single datum of the model, namely u, follows an appropriate time path — specifically if u falls from the level $\bar{u}$ characterising the initial state of constant prices to a level $\bar{\bar{u}}$ and stays thereafter at this lower level. We have also shown that, in the case of this model, p is not only continuously positive but is also continuously increasing, that is to say, that the rate of price increase is *continuously increasing*. Thus we have shown that our prototype expectational model is, indeed, a genuine model of the inflationary process.

2.5 Survey of Inflation Models: Monetarist Models

In the present section we shall introduce a prototype 'monetarist' model of the inflationary process. The hall-mark of a 'monetarist' inflation model is that it incorporates some form of the so-called 'new quantity theory of money', and it will be helpful to begin with a brief discussion of this particular theoretical development.

'New quantity theory' is the name given to a demand-for-money function which Milton Friedman and his associates developed during the 1950s.[6] There are several versions of this function (we shall refer to it as the N.Q.T. function), but the basic version is one in which the dependent or explained variable is the total demand for nominal money balances. This function is developed in three stages. First, the determinants of the demand for nominal money balances by an *individual household* are formulated. Second, the determinants of the demand for nominal money balances by an *individual firm* are formulated. Finally, the micro demand-for-money functions which emerge from the first two stages are aggregated to give the function governing the demand for nominal money balances in the economy as a whole. We will not attempt to consider each of these three stages in detail but will merely indicate the general drift of the underlying argument.

The first stage, in which the determinants of the *household's* demand for nominal money balances are derived, starts from the conventional model of consumer choice. One of the implications of this model is that the household's demand for a particular consumer good will be determined by its nominal income, by the price of the good in question, and by the prices of all other consumer goods. Proceeding by analogy we can say that the variables determining the household's demand for a particular *asset* – in particular the asset money – will be: (i) its total nominal wealth; (ii) the proportion of human wealth to total wealth; (iii) the real-rate-of-return stream expected from one unit of money; and (iv) the real-rate-of-return streams expected from one unit of each of the other assets over which the household's available non-human wealth can be spread. The first two variables in this list are treated as data by the new quantity theorists. But it is considered undesirable to treat the rate-of-return variables in this fashion, and accordingly an attempt is made to find the variables which determine them. Once found, these determining variables are used to replace the rate-of-return variables in the function governing the household's demand for nominal money balances. Proceeding in this way, the new quantity theorists arrive at the following as the determinants of the household's demand for nominal money balances at a particular point in time t: (i) its total nominal wealth at time t; (ii) the proportion of human wealth to total wealth; (iii) the price index at time t; (iv) the expected rate of change of the price index at time t; (v) the constant income streams attaching in perpetuity to a consol at time t, divided by the price of a consol; (vi) the constant income stream attaching to an equity at time t (viewed as a consol with a purchasing-power escalation clause) divided by the price of an equity.

The second stage, in which determinants of the demand for nominal money balances by the individual *firm* are explored, takes traditional firm theory as its starting-point. It is argued that, from the firm's standpoint, a money balance is nothing more than a source of productive services, like a machine or a building. The conclusions of firm theory as to the determinants of the firm's demand for productive services in general are therefore applicable to money balances. Proceeding in this way the authors of the N.Q.T. function are led to the view that the list of determinants already developed for the household suffice to explain the demand for money balances by the individual firm also.

The third stage in the development of the basic version of the N.Q.T. function is concerned with the problem of aggregating the micro functions which emerge from the first two stages. An aggregation problem arises because (i), (ii) and (iv) in the above list of determining variables assume a different value for each decision-making unit, so that the macro function is not merely the aggregative counterpart of the micro functions. The authors of the N.Q.T. function are unable to resolve this problem and settle for an approximation to the true macro function in which the determining variables are (iii), (v) and (vi) in the above list, together with the economy-wide total of (i) and the economy-wide averages of (ii) and (iv).

The basic version of the N.Q.T. function thus takes the form:

$$M^d = f(P, r_b, r_e, p^e, w, W), \qquad (2.11)$$

where M^d denotes the total demand for nominal balances, P denotes some price index, p^e its average expected rate of increase, $r_b(r_e)$ the fixed nominal income attached to a bond (equity) divided by the price of the bond (equity), W aggregate nominal wealth and w the average ratio of human wealth to total wealth and where f is to be read as 'function of'.

A second version of the function runs in terms of the flow, income, rather than the stock, wealth. Aggregate nominal income, Y, and aggregate nominal wealth, W, are so defined that Y/W is equal to the rate of interest. Hence W can be replaced in (2.11) by Y times the rate of interest. However, the rate of interest can be omitted because it can be taken to be a weighted average of r_b and r_e and hence to be fully represented by those variables. The second version, then, is:

$$M^d = f(P, r_b, r_e, p^e, w, Y). \qquad (2.12)$$

The other versions are derived directly from (2.12) by the new quantity theorists with the help of the assumption that the function f is homogeneous of the first degree in P and Y. They are:

$$\frac{M^d}{P} = f(r_b, r_e, p^e, w, \bar{Y}) \tag{2.13}$$

and

$$\frac{Y}{M^d} = v(r_b, r_e, p^e, w, \bar{Y}) \tag{2.14}$$

where Y denotes *real* National Income (i.e. Y/P) and where v denotes 'function of'. In the first of these functions, the dependent variable is the demand for *real* money balances while in the second it is the desired income velocity of money. According to the N.Q.T. approach, therefore, the demand for real money balances and the desired income velocity are determined by the same variables but through different functions – in general, the functions f and v will not be the same.

We now introduce a simple model of the inflationary process which incorporates one of the above versions of the N.Q.T. function and which can be regarded, therefore, as a prototype for the class of models which carry the 'monetarist' label.

Our prototype monetarist model is as follows:

$$\frac{M^d}{P} = \alpha \bar{Y}^\beta \tag{2.15}$$

$$M^d = M \tag{2.16}$$

$$p = \phi[(\bar{Y}/\bar{Y}^f)^*] + p^e \tag{2.17}$$

$$\Delta p^e = \theta(p - p^e) \tag{2.18}$$

Here M^d and M denote, respectively, the desired and the actual nominal stock of money balances, P denotes the price index chosen to measure inflation, p and p^e denote, respectively, the actual and expected percentage rate of increase in P, $\bar{Y}$ denotes real National Income and $\bar{Y}^f$ full-employment real National Income. Finally, α, β and θ are positive constants, θ lying between zero and unity. As before, * denotes 'past' while ϕ stands for 'function of'.

The function ϕ is such that ϕ' and ϕ'' (the first and second derivatives) are both positive for all values of $(\bar{Y}/\bar{Y}^f)^*$ and such that $\phi = 0$ at some positive level of $(\bar{Y}/\bar{Y}^f)^*$.

The data of the model are M and $\bar{Y}^f$. Thus the above four relationships can be regarded as a system which determines p^e, $\bar{Y}$ and M^d, together with the price index (both current level and current rate of change), once M and $\bar{Y}^f$ have been specified.

The first, second and fourth relationships of the above prototype monetarist model require no more than a brief comment. Relationship (2.15) is the 'real-balances' version of the N.Q.T. function with all determining variables apart from real National Income suppressed (the idea is that under normal inflationary conditions, $\bar{Y}$ will be the dominant influence on M/P) and with the function f given a specific form. Relationship (2.16) postulates that the *desired* level of nominal money balances adjusts instantaneously to exogenous changes in the *actual* level. Relationship (2.18) has been discussed already in Section 2.4.

Relationship (2.17) requires somewhat fuller treatment. This relationship is closely connected with (2.7). For any fixed value of p^e (2.7) gives a curve of p against u of the type shown in the left-hand diagram of Figure 2.3, while for the same fixed value of p^e (2.17) gives a curve of p against $(\bar{Y}/\bar{Y}^f)*$ of the type shown in the right-hand diagram. (Recall the restrictions placed on the function ϕ.) The left-hand curve shows p increasing with *decreasing* u, given p^e, while the right-hand curve shows p increasing with *increasing* $\bar{Y}/\bar{Y}^f$, given p^e. But *increasing* $\bar{Y}/\bar{Y}^f$ implies *decreasing* u. Hence, the two curves are effectively showing the one relationship. Also, just as (2.7) implies that a one-point increase in p^e will displace the *left*-hand curve upwards by one percentage point at all points, so (2.17) implies that a one-point increase in p^e will displace the *right*-hand curve upwards by one percentage point at all points.

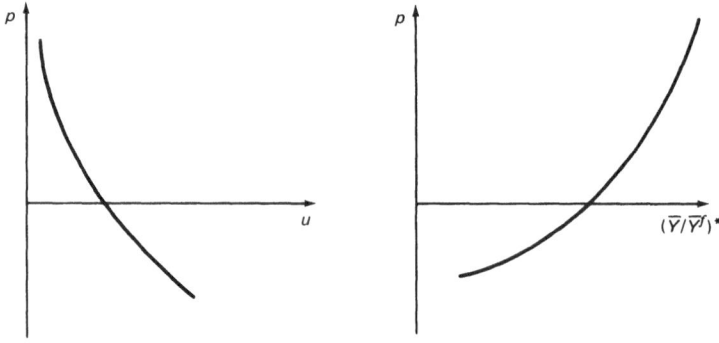

Fig. 2.3

It remains to show that the above monetarist model will indeed generate an inflationary process when appropriate time paths are imposed on the data, M and $\bar{Y}^f$.

To this end we first put the model in a more convenient form. For notational convenience we replace $\bar{Y}/\bar{Y}^f$ by Z throughout. We also use (2.16) to replace M^d by M in (2.15) which then reads:

$$\frac{M}{P} = \alpha(Z\bar{Y}^f)^\beta. \tag{2.19}$$

Next we write (2.19) in terms of percentage rates of increase rather than absolute levels. Since α is a constant the percentage rate of increase of M/P equals the percentage rate of increase of $(Z\bar{Y}^f)^\beta$. Hence:

$$m - p = \beta z + \beta \bar{y}^f, \tag{2.20}$$

where each lower-case letter denotes the percentage rate of increase in the variable denoted by the corresponding upper-case letter, for example m is the percentage rate of increase in the nominal stock of money balances.† Finally, we rewrite (2.20) with z on the left-hand side and m on the right-hand side. This serves to emphasise the fact that the causal sequence runs from m to z rather than in the reverse direction, M being a datum and Z (through Y) an unknown.

After these manipulations our prototype monetarist model reads:

$$z = \frac{1}{\beta}(m - p) - \bar{y}^f \tag{2.21}$$

$$p = \phi(Z^*) + p^e \tag{2.22}$$

$$\Delta p^e = \theta(p - p^e) \tag{2.23}$$

We now postulate an initial situation in which p is constant at zero, that is in which there is no inflation, and in which p^e, m and $\bar{y}^f$ are also constant at zero. With p, $\bar{y}^f$ and m constant at zero, z and Δp^e will aslo be constant at zero (from (2.21) and (2.23)) while Z will be constant at the value, say $\tilde{Z}$, given by the point at which the curve of p against Z^*, for $p^e = 0$, intersects the horizontal axis (see Figure 2.3). Let this initial state of rest without inflation be disturbed by an increase in m from zero to some positive figure — say 2 per cent per annum. Assuming that $\bar{y}^f$ the rate of increase of full-employment real National Income, remains fixed at zero, the immediate effect of this increase in m will be to turn z, hitherto zero, into some positive figure (see (2.21)). In other words, the immediate effect will be to cause an increase in Z. Since $Z = \bar{Y}/\bar{Y}^f$ we can also say that the immediate effect of the expansion of the stock of money balances will be to increase $\bar{Y}$ relative to $\bar{Y}^f$ or to increase excess demand (make it more positive if $\bar{Y}$ was initially above $\bar{Y}^f$ or less negative in the reverse case).

The postulated increase in m will have no immediate effect on p, the inflation rate. However the increase in Z which results from the increase in m will eventually turn p from zero into some positive figure, that is the price index will

---

† In the derivation of (2.20) we have made use of the following: (i) the percentage rate of increase of a ratio is approximately equal to the percentage rate of increase of the numerator *minus* the percentage rate of increase of the denominator; (ii) the percentage rate of increase of a variable raised to some power is approximately equal to the power *multiplied by* the percentage rate of increase in the variable; (iii) the percentage rate of increase of a product is approximately equal to the sum of the percentage rates of increase of the two variables concerned. The first and third of these approximations have been used already (see above p. 28 and p. 30).

begin to rise (see (2.22)). Once p becomes positive, p will exceed p^e (recall that p^e is initially zero). Consequently p^e will also rise (see (2.23)); and this rise in p^e will reinforce the effect on p of the increase in Z (see (2.22)).

We now postulate that m rises yet again by whatever amount is necessary to keep $m - p$ positive despite the increase in p, that is to keep z positive. With z positive, Z will continue to rise, and hence, after a delay, p will continue to rise, that is the upward movement in the price index will continue at an accelerating rate (see (2.22)). The effect on p through Z will be reinforced by a further rise in the expected inflation rate *via* (2.23).

Clearly, so long as m continues to increase by whatever amount is necessary to keep $m - p$ positive, the upward movement in the price index caused by the initial expansion of the money stock will continue — and continue, moreover, at an accelerating rate. Putting the point in another way, we can say that according to our monetarist model accelerating inflation will result provided the monetary authorities expand the stock of nominal money balances sufficiently rapidly to ensure some expansion in the stock of *real* money balances.

2.6   Survey of Inflation Models: Wage-Leadership Models

One well-known classification of models of the inflationary process is the following: (*a*) demand-inflation (or demand-pull) models; (*b*) cost-inflation (or cost-push) models; and (*c*) mixed models. *Demand-inflation* models are models whose data consist exclusively of 'demand' variables, that is variables such as aggregate demand for commodities, some component of this aggregate, excess demand for commodities, the demand for labour, some proxy for the demand for labour (for example the level of employment), excess demand for labour, some proxy for the excess demand for labour (for example the unemployment rate). *Cost-inflation* models are models whose data include *no* demand variables. Finally, *mixed* models are models whose data include both demand variables and non-demand variables.† Thus a demand-inflation model implies that inflation *always* arises from the demand side, a cost-inflation model that it *never* arises

---

†Closely connected with the above threefold categorisation of *models of inflation* is the popular categorisation of *inflationary episodes* into: (*a*) demand inflation; and (*b*) cost inflation. That is, one frequently finds the inflation of a particular period described as 'demand inflation' and that of some other period as 'cost inflation'. What the users of these labels usually have in mind is that in the former period the changes which were the ultimate cause of the inflation were changes in demand variables, whereas in the latter period the inflation could be traced ultimately to changes in non-demand variables. Clearly 'demand inflation' in this sense could be accounted for in terms of any model which includes demand variables among its data, that is either in terms of a model from category (*a*) or one from category (*c*). Similarly 'cost inflation' could be explained in terms of a model either from category (*b*) or from category (*c*).

from the side of demand, and a mixed model that it *can* arise from the demand side but need not do so.

All four prototype models discussed so far in this chapter prove, on examination, to fall in category (*c*), as do the great bulk of the models which they typify. By contrast, the class of models to be considered now (wage-leadership models) fall, by and large, in category (*b*).

As our prototype wage-leadership model we shall take a model in which there are two mark-up industrial sectors, the first consisting of 'leading' industries and the second of 'following' industries. The distinction between the two sectors is based on the pace of productivity growth. Leading industries are those characterised by rapid growth of productivity (output per man) while following industries are those in which the rate of productivity increase is below that of the economy as a whole.

Leading industries have a choice between (i) holding price constant (or increasing price) and at the same time allowing money wage-earnings per man to rise at the same rate as output per man, and (ii) reducing price while limiting the rate of money wage-earnings per man to a figure below the rate of increase of output per man. In the first case unit labour cost remains constant while profit margins remain fixed or rise according to whether price is held constant or raised. In the second case unit labour cost falls while profit margins remain fixed or increase according to whether the proportionate price reduction is equal to or less than the proportionate reduction in unit labour cost. In our prototype wage-leadership model it is assumed that leading industries take the first course, this being the less troublesome of the two from their point of view. Thus we have:

$$w^1 = o^1, \tag{2.24}$$

where w^1 denotes the percentage increase in the index of money wage-earnings per man in the leading industries and o^1 the percentage increase in the index of output per man in those industries.

The second assumption of the model is that the main determinant of the rate of increase of money wage-earnings per man in the *following* industries is the degree of pressure for wage increases exerted by the unions in these industries, and that this, in turn, is determined mainly by the pace of wage increase in the leading industries. More specifically, it is assumed that the percentage increase in the index of money wage-earnings per man in the following industries in any period will be the same as that in the leading industries is some past period — that the unions in the following industries take the pace of wage advance achieved in the leading industries as their target and, in time, always reach this target. Thus we have as the second relationship:

$$w^2 = (w^1)^*, \tag{2.25}$$

where w^2 denotes the percentage increase in the index of wage-earnings per man in the following industries and, as before, * denotes 'past'.

Finally, it is assumed that in each sector the percentage rate of increase in the index of prices is equal to the excess of the percentage increase in the index of wage-earnings per man over the percentage increase in the index of output per man, or:

$$p^1 = w^1 - o^1 \tag{2.26}$$

and

$$p^2 = w^2 - o^2, \tag{2.27}$$

where p^1 and p^2 are the percentage rates of increase in the price indexes of the leading and following sectors, respectively, and where o^2 is the percentage increase in the index of output per man in the following industries. These relationships can be regarded as simplified versions of relationship (2.5), the price relationship of our prototype mark-up model.

By substituting (2.24) and (2.25) into (2.26) and (2.27), respectively, the above four relationships can be reduced to two, namely:

$$p^1 = 0 \tag{2.28}$$

and

$$p^2 = (o^1)^* - o^2. \tag{2.29}$$

To round off the model, we add the following:

$$p = p^2, \tag{2.30}$$

where p is the percentage increase in the index of prices in the mark-up sector as a whole. Relationship (2.30) can be justified by treating the price index in the mark-up sector as a whole as a weighted arithmetic average of the indexes in the leading and following sectors.†

---

† Denote levels of price indexes by P and use a '-1' subscript to denote 'previous period'. Then, using the fact that P^1 remains constant at its base-period value of unity (see (2.28)) we have:

$$P = w_1 P^1 + w_2 P^2 = w_1 + w_2 P^2$$

and

$$P_{-1} = w_1 P^1_{-1} + w_2 P^2_{-1} = w_1 + w_2 P^2_{-1},$$

where w_1 and w_2 are constants which sum to unity. Hence:

$$p = \frac{P}{P_{-1}} - 1 = \frac{w_1 + w_2 P^2 - w_1 - w_2 P^2_{-1}}{w_1 + w_2 P^2_{-1}}$$

$$= \left(\frac{P^2 - P^2_{-1}}{P^2_{-1}} \right) \times \frac{w_2 P^2_{-1}}{w_1 + w_2 P^2_{-1}}$$

$$= \alpha p^2,$$

Of the five variables which appear in (2.28)–(2.30), the three price variables, p, p^1 and p^2, are regarded as unknowns and the two productivity variables, $(o^1)^*$ and o^2, as data. (Since no demand variables are included among the data, the model is a clear case of a cost-inflation model, as defined above.) Thus we can think of (2.28)–(2.30) as determining p, p^1 and p^2, given values for $(o^1)^*$ and o^2.

That this model is capable of explaining inflation can be shown as follows. Imagine an initial situation in which the rate of growth of labour productivity is identical in both sectors $((o^1)^* = o^2)$ so that p^2, p^1 and p are all zero. Suppose, too, that this initial situation is disturbed by an increase in the rate of growth of output per man in the leading sector, and that the higher rate of growth is maintained thereafter, while the rate of growth of output per man in the following sector remains fixed at its original level. Then eventually p^2 will become positive and will remain positive thereafter (see (2.29)). From (2.30) it follows that the same will be true of p. Thus there will be a continuous upward movement in the price index for the mark-up sector as a whole as a result of the permanent increase in the rate of growth of output per man in the leading sector.

Clearly, we reach the same conclusion if we postulate that the rate of growth of output per man in the *following* sector *decreases* as compared with the initial situation, while the rate of growth in the leading sector remains fixed at the original level. In fact any set of time paths for the two data which implies that $o^1 - o^2$ becomes positive at a given point of time, and remains positive thereafter, will suffice to generate an inflation within the framework of our wage-leadership model.

2.7 Recent Inflationary Experience

Towards the end of the 1960s the developed market economies entered a strikingly new inflationary phase. Until then the broad facts of their post-war inflationary experience were fairly steady inflation at rates of the order of 2 per cent to 5 per cent per annum, coupled with consistently low unemployment rates. Round about 1968 all this changed dramatically. As will be clear from Table 2.3, the inflation rate rose sharply throughout the developed world in, or just after, 1968, and continued to climb throughout the first half of the 1970s. Moreover, this 'price explosion', which all developed countries experienced in greater or less degree, was not accompanied by abnormally low unemployment rates, as might perhaps have been expected. On the contrary, in some of the developed countries

---

where

$$\alpha = \frac{1}{1 + \dfrac{w_1}{w_2} P^2_{-1}} \simeq 1.$$

Table 2.3

Country	Average annual percentage rate of increase of index of consumer prices, 1955–67*	Percentage rate of increase from previous year of index of consumer prices ‡							
		1968	1969	1970	1971	1972	1973	1974	1975
Canada	2.1	4.1	4.6	3.3	2.9	4.9	7.4	10.9	10.8
United States	1.9	4.1	5.5	5.8	4.3	3.8	5.5	12.2	9.1
Japan	3.9	5.4	5.2	7.8	6.1	4.7	11.7	24.4	11.8
Australia	2.6	2.7	2.8	3.9	6.0	5.9	9.8	15.1	15.1
Austria	3.0	2.6	3.4	4.1	4.7	5.7	8.1	9.5	8.5
Belgium	2.3	2.7	3.8	3.9	4.4	5.8	7.3	12.9	12.7
Denmark	4.2	8.7	4.4	5.6	6.0	8.8	8.8	15.4	9.9
Finland	5.7	8.7	2.9	2.8	6.2	7.5	11.4	18.1	17.6
France	4.4	4.6	6.7	5.5	5.6	5.9	7.1	13.9	11.7
Germany	2.3	1.8	2.7	3.8	5.1	5.7	8.1	9.0	6.0
Greece	2.3	0.0	2.7	3.5	2.5	4.9	14.8	29.0	13.7
Iceland	7.5	15.8	21.9	13.1	6.9	9.3	20.5	43.3	49.0
Ireland	3.4	4.7	7.4	8.3	8.9	8.3	11.9	19.0	20.9
Italy	3.3	1.4	2.6	4.9	4.9	5.7	10.8	19.1	17.0
Luxembourg	1.9	2.6	2.3	4.6	4.7	4.8	8.4	9.6	10.7
Netherlands	3.4	3.7	7.5	4.4	7.6	7.4	7.8	9.6	10.2
Norway	3.5	3.4	3.3	10.2	6.4	7.5	7.0	9.8	11.9
Portugal	2.8	5.9	8.7	6.6	11.6	10.7	12.9	25.1	15.3
Spain	6.0†	2.1	5.4	8.4	8.0	8.3	12.0	16.9	16.9
Sweden	4.0	1.9	2.7	7.1	7.3	8.5	8.1	10.7	9.7
Switzerland	2.6	2.4	2.6	3.5	6.6	8.5	8.8	9.8	6.7
Turkey	9.3	5.3	4.3	8.3	18.6	15.1	14.6	n.a.	n.a.
United Kingdom	3.1	4.8	5.4	6.4	9.5	7.3	9.4	15.9	24.3

*Calculated by C.I. method from figures given in *Main Economic Indicators: Historical Statistics 1955–1971* (Paris: O.E.C.D.).
† Based on years 1958–67.
‡Calculated from figures given in *Main Economic Indicators: Historical Statistics 1955–1971* (Paris: O.E.C.D.) and *OECD Main Economic Indicators* (April 1974, April 1975 and April 1976).

(for example the United Kingdom and the Netherlands) the highest unemployment rate since 1955 occurred in the years of accelerating inflation, while in
others (for example Japan, the United States, Canada and Sweden) unemployment rates only slightly below the highest post-1955 figure were recorded in those
years.[7] In short, 'stagflation' — accelerating inflation accompanied by high
unemployment rates and hence by low and even negative rates of growth of real
G.D.P. — was a common phenomenon in the developed world in the first half of
the 1970s.

It is natural to ask whether the models of the inflationary process which have
been surveyed in the preceding sections can explain these dramatic events, or
whether, as some have suggested, an entirely new theoretical approach, perhaps
sociological rather than economic in character, is called for. The view taken in this
book is that existing models are quite capable, not only of explaining inflation in
general — this has been demonstrated already — but also of explaining the special
brand of inflation experienced by all of the developed countries in the last five
years; and that if new theoretical work is required it is because existing models
lack *predictive* power (see Section 2.1 above) not because they lack *explanatory*
power.

To support this view we shall now set up an expectational model which is just a
little more elaborate than the prototype presented in Section 2.4, and proceed to
show that this model can easily explain the fact that all developed countries have
experienced stagflation in greater or less degree since the end of the 1960s. In
concentrating on this one model we do not wish to suggest that it is the only
expectational model which can explain the events in question in a satisfactory
way nor that models of different types altogether, for example monetarist models,
provide a less convincing explanation in some sense than the model we have
chosen. It is just that the chosen model is both straightforward and comparatively
easy to handle and so provides a convenient vehicle for demonstrating the
explanatory capabilities of the entire range of models surveyed in this chapter.

The expectational model referred to in the previous paragraph is as follows:

$$p = \beta_1 w - \beta_1 o + \beta_2 s + m \tag{2.31}$$

$$w = g(u) + p^e + \Psi(A, P) \qquad \left(\frac{\partial \Psi}{\partial A} > 0; \frac{\partial \Psi}{\partial P} > 0 \right) \tag{2.32}$$

$$\Delta p^e = \theta(p - p^e) \tag{2.33}$$

This model differs from the prototype expectational model in two ways. First, the
price equation is the full equation of the mark-up model rather than the truncated
version of this equation which appears in the prototype expectational model.
Second, an additional term, $\Psi(A,P)$, has been included in the wage equation. This
term is some function of the variables A and P such that the function increases
with A for given P, and with P for given A. The variable A, which is treated as a
datum, is some numerical indicator of variations in the aggressiveness, militancy or
pushfulness of wage-earners in relation to money wage demands while the variable

P, which is also treated as a datum, is some indicator of variations in the vigour with which the policy-making authorities preach the need for wage restraint. The implication of the revised wage equation is that *w*, the percentage rate of increase of money wage-earnings per man, will increase, at a given unemployment rate and a given expected inflation rate, if wage-earners press their money wage demands more aggressively than before or if the authorities oppose excessive wage increases less vigorously than before.

Our task, then, is to demonstrate that the above model can explain the fact that all developed countries have experienced stagflation, in greater or less degree, since the last years of the 1960s. Before attempting this task we shall spend a little time on the mechanics of our model.

Let us contemplate an initial situation in which all the data of our model (that is *o*, *s*, *m*, *A*, *P* and *u*) are constant, and in which, therefore, the three unknowns, *p*, p^e and *w*, are also constant. Since p^e is supposed to be constant, Δp^e must be zero, which means, from (2.33), that the constant level of *p* and the constant level of p^e must be equal. What happens if, for some reason, wage-earners begin to press their wage demands more aggressively than before? In other words, what will be the result of an increase in *A*? If all other data remain unchanged, and if p^e remains unchanged, the immediate effect will be an increase in *w*, that is money wage-earnings per man, which hitherto have been rising at a constant rate of, say, 5 per cent per annum, will begin to rise more rapidly — say at 7 per cent per annum (this is evident from (2.32)). But with *o*, *s* and *m* fixed, an increase in *w* must lead to an increase in *p*, as is clear from (2.31). That is, the inflation rate which hitherto has been constant at, say, 3 per cent per annum will rise to, say, 4.5 per cent per annum. If p^e were to stay fixed at the initial level, this would be the end of the story. It is clear, however, that p^e will not remain fixed. With *p* at 4.5 per cent per annum and p^e still at 3 per cent per annum, $p - p^e$ will become positive instead of zero, which means, from (2.33), that Δp^e, which has hitherto been constant at 3 per cent per annum, will rise to, say, 4.2 per cent per annum. As is clear from (2.32), this rise in p^e will mean an equivalent rise, in terms of percentage points, in *w*, so that *w* will move from 7 per cent per annum to 8.2 per cent per annum. In turn, this rise in *w* will mean a further increase in *p* to, say, 5.3 per cent per annum. Thus the excess of *p* over p^e will persist and lead to a further upward revision of p^e, and through this to a further increase in *w*, and through this to a further increase in the inflation rate; and so on. Evidently, then, once the model is 'started up' by an increase in wage-earner aggressiveness it will generate a continuous upward movement of the inflation rate ('accelerating' inflation).

It is also clear that the model will generate accelerating inflation in response to an increase in *P*, that is, if for some reason the authorities adopt a more lenient attitude towards excessive wage increases than hitherto, and also in response to an increase in *s*, that is if, for some reason, there is an increase in the rate of increase of unit non-labour cost.

We turn now to the task of showing that an expectational model, comprised of (2.31), (2.32) and (2.33), can explain, in a quite straightforward way, why the developed countries generally should have experienced stagflation since the end of the 1960s. We divide this task into two: (*a*) the task of showing that the model can explain why inflation has accelerated throughout the developed world since the end of the 1960s; and (*b*) the task of showing that the model can explain why this accelerating inflation was accompanied, at least in some developed countries, by unusually high unemployment rates.

The acceleration of inflation in all developed countries since about 1968 can be explained in terms of our expectational model in the following way. Towards the end of the 1960s all of the developed countries experienced a sharp break in worker attitudes, the character and origins of which will be explained shortly. One of the manifestations of this break in attitudes was a much more aggressive approach to securing wage increases. As a result of this increased aggressiveness, the rate of increase of money wage-earnings per man rose throughout the developed world. In turn, this generated a continuous upward movement of the inflation rate (and of the rate of wage increase) in all of the developed countries, through the process of interaction between the actual inflation rate and the expected inflation rate, described earlier (see p. 50). The sharp break in worker attitudes which the developed countries as a whole experienced in the late 1960s was accompanied in most of them by a more relaxed attitude towards excessive wage increases. The origins of this particular development will also be explained shortly. Its immediate effect was to add a further autonomous stimulus to the rate of increase of average money wage-earnings in the developed countries. This gave a fresh start to the process of interaction between the actual and expected inflation rates, and thus strengthened the cumulative upward movement of the inflation rate resulting from the break in worker attitudes. This is not the end of the story. Early in 1973 the rate of increase of unit non-labour cost rose sharply in the developed countries and stayed at the new higher level throughout 1973 and into 1974. This movement, which will also be examined more closely in a moment, provided a further autonomous stimulus to the inflation rate within developed countries. This, in turn, reactivated the process of interplay between the actual and expected inflation rates and thus kept alive the continuous upward movement in the inflation rate which the inflationary shocks of the late 1960s had set in motion.

In short, the continuous upward movement in the inflation rate which occurred in the developed countries as a whole in the late 1960s and early 1970s can be explained by our expectational model in terms of three inflationary shocks which all of the developed countries experienced in varying degrees – the increase in the aggressiveness of wage-earners which emerged in the developed countries round about 1968, the increase in the permissiveness of the authorities towards excessive wage increases which appeared in these countries at about the same time, and the sharp increase in the rate of increase of unit non-labour cost which hit the developed countries as a whole in 1973. Each of these shocks triggered off the actual inflation rate–expected inflation rate interaction, and by this means set the actual inflation rate in each country on some continuously rising time path.

The three, conceptually separate time paths which were generated in this way then fused to produce the upward-sloping time path actually observed for a particular country in the years after 1968.

In the course of the preceding discussion we undertook to look a little more closely at each of the three inflationary shocks which have impinged on the developed countries as a whole in recent years and which play a critical role in the above explanation of the recent inflationary experience of these countries. We now fulfill this undertaking.

As regards the break in worker attitudes, the main point to be grasped is that in all of the developed countries the outlook of wage-earners who entered the labour force after the Second World War was bound to be very different from that of the older men who began work before the war. There are several reasons for this but one stands out as far more important than the rest. In the words of Phelps Brown, it

> is the unprecedented maintenance of a high level of employment. By giving the individual employee less reason to fear that if he withdraws from his job he will not get it back, it will have increased his readiness to strike, and to join with or support others who are striking. By giving him more independence of the employer it will have changed the texture of relations, making subordination less acceptable and deference less natural, so removing an invisible but powerful sanction against pressing claims against one's immediate superiors.[8]

Now, in the immediate post-war years those with exclusively post-war work experience constituted a small minority of the labour force, and hence the new outlook made very little impact; the dominant attitudes were still those that had been formed by the hard pre-war years. But, of course, this could not last. As Phelps Brown puts it:

> year by year, as the 1950s and 1960s went on, the older men who had grown up in a world where job security took precedence over pay claims were leaving the labour force, and their place was taken by entrants whose experience was to be of a demand for labour so sustained as to give the individual worker a substantial independence of the employer. ... In country after country the time must have come when the number with solely postwar experience attained a critical mass, sufficient to outweigh the force of tradition and the respect accorded to older men.[9]

Thus the break in worker attitudes at the end of the 1960s, and the increased worker militancy which accompanied it in the developed countries as a whole, was just the attainment of a 'critical mass' by the new outlook – the tipping of the scales in its favour which was bound to occur sooner or later in every country, and bound to occur, moreover, at about the same time.

We turn now to the second of the three shocks – the more permissive attitude of the authorities towards excessive wage increases. The essential point here is that the developed countries fall into two distinct groups as regards anti-inflation policy. On the one hand, there is the United States, where the authorities can frame anti-inflation policy without much regard to the effects of their actions on the external position of the country. On the other hand, there is the rest of the developed nations which have balance-of-payments equilibrium as a prime economic objective and where the authorities are subject to a definite external constraint in the field of anti-inflation policy. When the external position of these countries deteriorates, the authorities are bound to intensify their anti-inflation policies, this being the only effective way of halting the deterioration given a regime of fixed, or virtually fixed, exchange rates such as has existed since the end of the Second World War. Conversely, when the external position improves, the authorities can take a more permissive attitude towards inflation and some relaxation of anti-inflation policy normally follows. Having made this point, we can now explain why a more permissive attitude towards excessive wage increases should have appeared in the developed countries – more precisely in the second group of developed countries – round about 1968. The reason is that, at about this time, the authorities in these countries became less concerned about inflation than they had previously been, and hence less concerned about the inflationary consequences of excessive wage increases, because of marked improvement in their external position. A major reason for this improvement was the intensification of the Vietnam War after about 1966, which led to a big increase in foreign spending by the U.S. government, and, by stimulating inflation in the United States, to a worsening of the competitive position of U.S. producers.

We come now to the third inflationary shock – the increase in the rate of increase of unit non-labour cost which occurred early in 1973 and which resulted from a sharp jump in the rate of increase of the prices of imported raw materials. The main features of this development have been well sketched by Manser as follows:

> The prices of world commodities – of food, metals, minerals, textiles and other natural substances – had not moved by more than 3 per cent (either way) in any one year for the previous twenty-five years. In 1973, they began to soar. By the end of the first quarter, they stood some 15 per cent above the average for 1972 .... By the mid-year, commodity prices were 23 per cent, and by the end of the year no less than 50 per cent, above the average level for 1972 .... In October, 1973 came the Arab–Israel War and, out of it, first a short lived embargo, then a devastating multiplication of the price of oil. In the United Kingdom, for example, oil had been landed in 1973 at somewhat below £8 per ton. By June, 1974 it was coming in at £32 per ton.[10]

Having now shown that our expectational model can explain why the inflation rate has been on a rising path in the developed countries since the end of the 1960s, we turn to the second part of our task, which is to show that the model can also explain why, in some countries, accelerating inflation has been accompanied, during this period, by unusually high unemployment rates.

Let us begin by contemplating, once again, an initial situation in which all of the data of our expectational model (o, s, m, A, P and u) are constant, and in which, therefore, the actual and expected inflation rates are both constant. Further, let the constant levels of the data be such that the actual and expected inflation rates are not only constant but equal. Now suppose that the authorities raise the unemployment rate and keep it fixed at the new, higher level. Then, according to our model, the following sequence will ensue. Since, for fixed levels of A, P and p^e, the curve of w against u given by (2.32) is of the form shown in Figure 2.1 (see p. 31 above), the increase in u will cause a reduction in w, which, in turn, will cause a reduction in p (by (2.31)), which, in turn, will cause a reduction in p^e (by (2.33)), which, in turn, will cause a further reduction in w (by (2.32)), which, in turn, will cause a further reduction in p (by (2.31)), and so on. In other words, the model implies that an increase in u will initiate a continuous *decline* in the inflation rate, other data being held *fixed*, that is it suggests that raising the unemployment rate will be one way of countering an undesired upward movement of the inflation rate.

It appears, then, that the higher than usual unemployment rates can be explained, in terms of our model, as a direct policy response to the accelerating inflation. In all countries, it can be argued, the authorities were set on checking the upward movement of the inflation rate, and, in some, they were prepared, by appropriate management of aggregate demand, to raise their unemployment rate to an exceptionally high level in an effort to do so. That the inflation rate continued to rise in these countries nevertheless (that stagflation emerged) was due to the fact that the downward pressure generated by the increase in the unemployment rate was less than the upward pressure generated by the three inflationary shocks discussed earlier. To stop the upward movement of the inflation rate altogether, it would have been necessary for the authorities to raise the unemployment rate to a higher level still, that is to accept an even more severe check to growth than in fact occurred.

3

TESTS OF INFLATION MODELS

3.1 Testable Predictions

In Chapter 2 we presented a series of five competing models of normal inflation in developed market economies. Each of these models represents an attempt to capture the essence of the inflationary situation in such economies. The Keynesian model is based on the view that the essence of the inflationary situation in economies such as the U.S., the U.K. and the Australian economies is the rigidity of output in the face of rising demand. To the author of the mark-up model, the essential feature of normal inflation in developed market economies is the two-way link between price and money wages, while to the author of the expectational model it is the two-way link between the actual and the expected rate of inflation which appears to be of central importance. In the case of the monetarist model, emphasis is placed on the response of real output and prices to changes in the quantity of money, while in the case of the wage-leadership model it is the drive towards rising money wages provided by the unions in the fast-growing industries which is highlighted.

As pointed out in Section 2.1 one cannot assess the worth of an economist's model, such as these five, by asking 'is it realistic?' because economists' models are not intended to be realistic. On the contrary, they purport to be drastic simplifications of reality — to be 'realistic' only in the very limited sense that they capture the *essence* of the reality to which they relate. The only basis for assessing the worth of any such model is predictive success. More precisely, to determine whether a model is useful we must take the model and use it to generate statements of the form: 'If the model gives an essentially correct picture of reality such and such will be the case.' These statements we call 'testable predictions'; and we deem the model to be useful if its testable predictions stand up well when confronted with the relevant facts.

In the last few years a considerable volume of empirical work has been undertaken in the field of inflation from this methodological standpoint and in this chapter we shall give an account of this work. As we shall see, most of it centres around the expectational model discussed in Section 2.4. To assist the reader we shall employ a uniform notation, in line with that used in Chapter 2, throughout the chapter. As a consequence the notation used in presenting a particular piece of empirical work will not necessarily be identical with the original notation and the reader who turns to the original studies after working through this chapter should keep this in mind.

3.2   The Expectational Model: Turnovsky and Toyoda

We begin with a test of the expectational model undertaken recently by
Turnovsky.[1] To understand the character of Turnovsky's test it is best to begin by
recalling a point which was made clear in Section 2.4, namely that the
expectational model comprises three distinct relationships:

$$p = w - r \qquad (3.1)$$

$$w = g(u) + p^e \qquad (3.2)$$

$$\Delta p^e = \theta(p - p^e) \qquad (3.3)$$

where w denotes the percentage increase from the previous period in money
wage-earnings per man and r some assumed constant percentage increase in output
per man.

Now consider the expression:

$$\alpha_0 + \alpha_1 u_t^{-1}, \qquad (3.4)$$

where α_0 is a negative constant and α_1 is a positive constant, and the subscript t is
a 'time subscript'.† If we plot this expression against u_t we obtain a curve of the
type shown in Figure 3.1.‡ Thus the curve of $\alpha_0 + \alpha_1 u_t^{-1}$ against u_t has precisely
the form of the curve of the function $g(u)$ (see above, p. 38) — the first term of
relationship (3.2). In fact the expression $\alpha_0 + \alpha_1 u_t^{-1}$ is nothing more than a
specific form of the general function $g(u)$ in (3.2). It follows from this that the
wage equation:

$$w_t = \alpha_0 + \alpha_1 u_t^{-1} + p_t^e, \qquad (3.5)$$

where α_0 and α_1 are negative and positive constants, respectively, is just a specific
form of (3.2), the wage equation of the expectational model.

Turn now to the wage equation:

$$w_t = \alpha_0 + \alpha_1 u_t^{-1} + \alpha_2 p_t^e, \qquad (3.6)$$

where α_0, α_1 and α_2 are constants. Comparing (3.5) and (3.6) we immediately see

---

†A time subscript is a subscript attached to a variable to designate the
particular time period (month, quarter, year, and so on) to which the variable
belongs, t designating 'current period', $(t - 1)$ 'last period', and so on.
  ‡This can be seen as follows: as u_t tends to infinity $\alpha_1 u_t^{-1}$ tends to zero.
Hence as u_t tends to infinity $\alpha_0 + \alpha_1 u_t^{-1}$ tends to the negative constant α_0. On
the other hand, as u_t tends to zero, $\alpha_1 u_t^{-1}$ tends to infinity. Hence $\alpha_0 + \alpha_1 u_t^{-1}$
also tends to infinity as u_t tends to zero. Further $d(\alpha_0 + \alpha_1 u_t^{-1})/du_t = -\alpha_1 u_t^{-2}$,
which is negative for all values of u_t since both α_1 and u_t^{-2} are positive. Thus the
curve of $\alpha_0 + \alpha_1 u_t^{-1}$ against u_t has a negative slope at all points. To sum up, the
curve of $\alpha_0 + \alpha_1 u_t^{-1}$ against u_t is one which gets closer and closer to the vertical
axis as u_t approaches zero, and closer and closer to the negative constant α_0 as u_t
approaches infinity and which has a negative slope at all points. In short the curve
has the properties shown in the diagram.

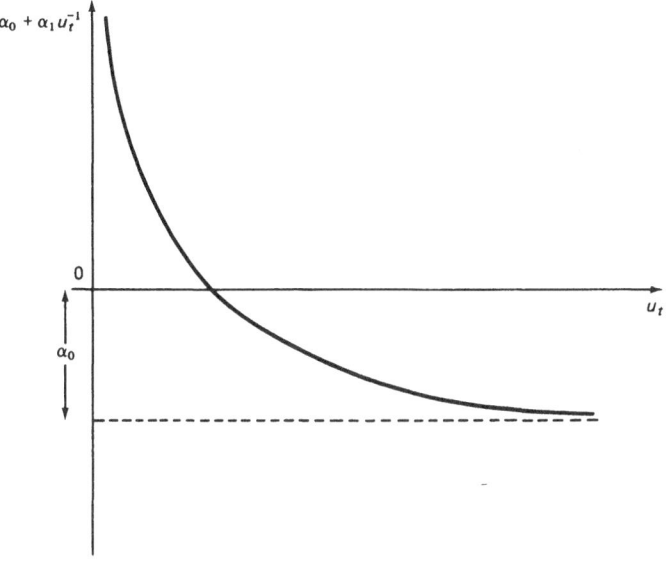

Fig. 3.1

that the expectational model (or rather the wage equation of that model) generates the testable predictions that the constant α_0 in (3.6) is negative, that the constant α_1 is positive and that the constant α_2 is unity. Thus one test of the expectational model would be to estimate (3.6) and see whether, in the numerical equation, the intercept is negative, the coefficient of u_t^{-1} positive and the coefficient of p_t^e approximately unity. If so, the model would be vindicated; if not it would be refuted. This is the test which Turnovsky has applied.

Using six-monthly Canadian data he has, in fact, derived *two* numerical versions of (3.6) — one using a p^e series based on expectations for six months ahead and the other using a p^e series based on expectations for twelve months ahead. These are as follows:[2]

$$w_t = -1.137 + 22.396u_t^{-1} + 0.768p_t^e$$

and

$$w_t = -1.597 + 24.373u_t^{-1} + 0.876p_t^e.$$

It will be seen that the predictions of the expectational model are well supported by these numerical relationships. In both cases the intercept is negative and the coefficient of u_t^{-1} is positive, as predicted; and in the latter case, at least, the coefficient of p^e is close to the predicted value of unity.† Thus the expectational

---

†The t test indicates that, at the conventional levels of significance, the true coefficient is not significantly different from unity.

model is strongly supported by the Canadian data on the basis of Turnovsky's test.

A test which is identical with the Turnovsky test in all essential respects but which differs in detail has been applied to quarterly Japanese data by Toyoda. There are two main differences of detail. In the first place, instead of estimating (3.6) Toyoda estimates an equation in which y, the percentage rate of increase of real G.N.P., appears as an explanatory variable in addition to u^{-1} and p^e:

$$w_t = \alpha_0 + \alpha_1 u_t^{-1} + \alpha_2 p_t^e + \alpha_3 y_t. \tag{3.7}$$

Second, whereas the p^e series which Turnovsky uses in the estimation of (3.6) are genuine price-expectation series, in the sense that they were constructed from answers provided by a group of business economists to direct enquiries about expected price developments,[3]† the series used by Toyoda (ten different series are used) are artificial series constructed from a series of p with the help of the expectations-formation equation (3.3). Let us consider this point in more detail.

Relationship (3.3) can be written in the 'time-subscript' form as:

$$p_t^e - p_{t-1}^e = \theta(p_{t-1} - p_{t-1}^e),$$

or as:

$$p_t^e = \theta p_{t-1} + (1 - \theta)p_{t-1}^e. \tag{3.8}$$

Suppose now that we have a time series for p and that the first five items in the series are those set out in column (1) of Table 3.1. Suppose further that we allot a value of 0.5 to θ (recall that θ lies between zero and unity) and a value of 2 to p_1^e (the expected rate of price increase for the first period). Then using (3.8) we can generate a value for p_2^e in the following way. From (3.8) we have:

$$p_2^e = \theta p_1 + (1 - \theta)p_1^e.$$

Table 3.1
$\theta = 0.5, p_1^e = 2$

Period	(1) p_t (per cent per period)	(2) θp_{t-1}	(3) p_t^e (per cent per period)	(4) $(1 - \theta)p_{t-1}^e$	(5) (2) + (4)
1	2	–	2	–	–
2	4	1	2	1	2
3	6	2	3	1	3
4	2	3	4.5	1.5	4.5
5	3	1.5	3.75	2.25	3.75

†It will be noted that the Turnovsky p^e series relate to the United States rather than Canada. Thus their use in the estimation of (3.6) for Canada presupposes that U.S. price expectations represent a satisfactory 'proxy' for Canadian price expectations.

Table 3.2
$$\theta = 0.1, p_1^e = 2$$

Period	(1) p_t (per cent per period)	(2) θp_{t-1}	(3) p_t^e	(4) $(1 - \theta)p_{t-1}^e$	(5) (2) + (4)
1	2	–	2	–	–
2	4	0.2	2.0	1.8	2.0
3	6	0.4	2.2	1.8	2.2
4	2	0.6	3.58	1.98	3.58
5	3	0.2	3.42	3.22	3.42

Inserting the values allotted to θ and p_1^e and the observed values for p_1 we obtain:

$$p_2^e = (0.5 \times 2) + (0.5 \times 2) = 2.$$

Using (3.8) once again we can now generate a value for p_3^e. We have:

$$p_3^e = (0.5 \times 4) + (0.5 \times 2) = 3.$$

Obviously we can continue in this way indefinitely and generate a whole series for p^e. The first five items in this series are shown in column (3) of Table 3.1. All we need, then, to generate a p^e series is a series for p, a 'starting value' for p^e (that is a value for p_1^e) and a value for θ. Relationship (3.8) will do the rest.

Of course, if we were to allot a different value to θ, we would finish up with a different series for p^e. The p^e series generated by the same p series and the same values for p_1^e as before but with $\theta = 0.1$ instead of 0.5 is shown in column (3) of Table 3.2. It is equally clear that we would finish up with a different p^e series if we were to allot a different value to p_1^e. The p^e series generated by the same p series and the same value for θ as in Table 3.1 but with a starting value for p^e of 3 instead of 2 is shown in column (3) of Table 3.3.

Table 3.3
$$\theta = 0.1, p_1^e = 3$$

Period	(1) p_t (per cent per period)	(2) θp_{t-1}	(3) p_t^e	(4) $(1 - \theta)p_{t-1}^e$	(5) (2) + (4)
1	2	–	3	–	–
2	4	1	2.5	1.5	2.5
3	6	2	3.25	1.25	3.25
4	2	3	4.63	1.63	4.63
5	3	1.5	3.82	2.32	3.82

Returning now to Toyoda's study, we have seen that the basis of his test is a numerical version of (3.7). Actually ten different numerical equations are derived from quarterly Japanese data, corresponding to ten different artificially generated p^e series. These correspond, in turn, to ten different values for θ — the same starting value for p^e is used throughout. The 'most satisfactory' of these equations (using goodness-of-fit as measured by $\bar{R}^2$ as the criterion) is as follows:[4]

$$w_t = -2.892 + 15.467u_t^{-1} + 0.476p_t^e + 0.233y_t. \tag{3.9}$$

We see from this expression that the intercept is negative and the coefficient of u_t^{-1} positive, as predicted by the expectational model. The coefficient of p_t^e however, is well below unity contrary to prediction. Thus, on the basis of the Turnovsky–Toyoda test, the expectational model is supported in part only by the Japanese data.

3.3   The Expectational Model: Donner and Lazar

We have seen in the previous section that (3.5) is a specific form of the *wage equation* of the expectational model. It follows that a specific form of the model *as a whole* (written in 'time-subscript' notation) is:

$$p_t = w_t - r_t \tag{3.10}$$

$$w_t = \alpha_0 + \alpha_1 u_t^{-1} + p_t^e \qquad (\alpha_0 < 0; \alpha_1 > 0) \tag{3.11}$$

$$p_t^e - p_{t-1}^e = \theta(p_{t-1} - p_{t-1}^e) \qquad (0 < \theta < 1) \tag{3.12}$$

The test to which we now turn — a recent test undertaken by Donner and Lazar[5] — is based on the second and third of the above three relationships. Several testable predictions are derived from these two relationships and are then confronted with the facts as a means of assessing this part of the expectational model.†

To derive their testable predictions Donner and Lazar (henceforth to be abbreviated to DL) set up the following equations:

$$w_t = \alpha_0 + \alpha_1 u_t^{-1} + \alpha_2 p_t^e \tag{3.13}$$

and

$$p_t^e - p_{t-1}^e = \theta(p_{t-1} - p_{t-1}^e), \tag{3.14}$$

†The Donner–Lazar test is thus a test of *two* of the three relationships which constitute the expectational model, in contrast to the Turnovsky –Toyoda test which relates to *one* of the relationships. It should also be pointed out that the empirical work referred to here as 'the DL test' is not described as a 'test' by the authors themselves, though it might well have been.

where α_0, α_1, α_2 and θ are constants. They next substitute (3.14) into (3.13) to obtain: †

$$w_t = \theta\alpha_0 + \alpha_1 u_t^{-1} - \alpha_1(1 - \theta)u_{t-1}^{-1} + (1 - \theta)w_{t-1} + \alpha_2\theta p_{t-1}. \qquad (3.15)$$

Now the expectational model predicts that the constant α_2 in the wage equation (3.13) is unity, as is seen by comparing (3.11) with (3.13). Hence it predicts that, when the expectations-formation equation (3.14) is combined with the wage equation (3.13), the coefficient of p_{t-1} in the resulting equation will be equal to θ, that is to say, that the coefficients of p_{t-1} and w_{t-1} will sum to unity. Hence a test of (3.11) and (3.12) combined would be to estimate (3.15) and see whether, in the numerical equation, the coefficients of p_{t-1} and w_{t-1} do indeed sum to approximately unity. Further, the expectational model (more precisely the specific form of the model represented by (3.10)–(3.12)) predicts that $\alpha_0\theta$, the intercept of (3.15), will be negative (since it specifies $\alpha_0 < 0$ and $0 < \theta < 1$), that the coefficient of u_t^{-1} will be positive (since it specifies $\alpha_1 > 0$), that the coefficient of u_{t-1}^{-1} will be negative (since it specifies $\alpha_1 > 0$ and $0 < \theta < 1$), and that the coefficients of w_{t-1} and p_{t-1} will both be positive. These further predictions can also be confronted with the facts by examining the estimates of the intercept and the coefficients in a numerical version of (3.15).

To perform their test, then, DL derive a numerical version of (3.15) by applying standard econometric methods to quarterly *Canadian* data. Their numerical

---

†(3.14) can be written as:

$$p_t^e = p_{t-1}^e - \theta p_{t-1}^e + \theta p_{t-1}.$$

Therefore
$$p_t^e = (1 - \theta)p_{t-1}^e + \theta p_{t-1}.$$

Therefore
$$\alpha_2 p_t^e = \alpha_2(1 - \theta)p_{t-1}^e + \alpha_2\theta p_{t-1}.$$

Substituting in (3.13) we obtain:

$$w_t = \alpha_0 + \alpha_1 u_t^{-1} + \alpha_2(1 - \theta)p_{t-1}^e + \alpha_2\theta p_{t-1}.$$

From (3.13) we have:

$$p_t^e = \frac{1}{\alpha_2}w_t - \frac{\alpha_0}{\alpha_2} - \frac{\alpha_1}{\alpha_2}u_t^{-1}.$$

Therefore
$$p_{t-1}^e = \frac{1}{\alpha_2}w_{t-1} - \frac{\alpha_0}{\alpha_2} - \frac{\alpha_1}{\alpha_2}u_{t-1}^{-1}.$$

Substituting this expression for p_{t-1}^e in the above wage equation we obtain:

$$w_t = \alpha_0 + \alpha_1 u_t^{-1} + \alpha_2(1 - \theta)\left[\frac{1}{\alpha_2}w_{t-1} - \frac{\alpha_0}{\alpha_2} - \frac{\alpha_1}{\alpha_2}u_{t-1}^{-1}\right] + \alpha_2\theta p_{t-1}.$$

Therefore
$$w_t = \theta\alpha_0 + \alpha_1 u_t^{-1} - \alpha_1(1 - \theta)u_{t-1}^{-1} + (1 - \theta)w_{t-1} + \alpha_2\theta p_{t-1}.$$

equation is:[6]†

$$w_t = -0.360 + 23.55u_t^{-1} - 18.713u_{t-1}^{-1} + 0.756w_{t-1} + 0.265p_{t-1}.$$

Examination of this numerical equation in the light of the above discussion shows that, for the Canadian economy, the expectational model stands up extremely well under the DL test. The numerical intercept and all of the numerical coefficients have the predicted signs and the numerical coefficients of w_{t-1} and p_{t-1} sum to just a little over unity – again in line with the expectational prediction.

A test which is basically the same as the DL test but which differs in detail has been applied to quarterly U.K. data by Parkin.[7] There are two main differences between the Parkin and DL tests.

In the first place, the money-wage and expectation-formation equations which form the basis of the Parkin test differ slightly from those which form the basis of the DL test, that is (3.13) and (3.14). The Parkin equations are:

$$w_t = \alpha_0 + \alpha_1 u_t + \alpha_2 p_t^e \qquad (3.16)$$

and

$$p_t^e - p_{t-1}^e = \theta(p_t - p_{t-1}^e). \qquad (3.17)$$

Comparing (3.16) with (3.13), we see that, in the case of (3.16), w_t depends linearly on u_t, whereas in the case of (3.13) it depends *non*-linearly on u_t (linearly on the *reciprocal* of u_t). Thus (3.16) can be regarded as a linear approximation to (3.13). Comparing (3.17) with (3.14), we see that the two are identical except that p_t appears on the right-hand side of (3.17) whereas p_{t-1} appears on the right-hand side of (3.14).

Since Parkin's basic wage and expectation-formation equations differ in these ways from the corresponding DL equations, the equation which he obtains on substituting his expectations-formation equation (3.17) into his wage-equation (3.16) also differs from the corresponding DL equation, namely (3.15). The Parkin equation corresponding to (3.15) is: ‡

$$w_t = \theta\alpha_0 + \alpha_1 u_t + (1 - \theta)w_{t-1} - \alpha_1(1 - \theta)u_{t-1} + \alpha_2\theta p_t. \qquad (3.18)$$

---

†Note that their $\Delta w/w$ is our w, their $\Delta p/p$ our p, their α_9 our α_1, their α_8 our α_2, their α_{10} our α_0, and their δ_3 our θ.

‡We have from (3.17):

$$\alpha_2 p_t^e = \alpha_2(1 - \theta)p_{t-1}^e + \alpha_2\theta p_t.$$

Substituting in (3.16) we obtain:

$$w_t = \alpha_0 + \alpha_1 u_t + \alpha_2(1 - \theta)p_{t-1}^e + \alpha_2\theta p_t.$$

From (3.16) we have:

$$p_t^e = \frac{1}{\alpha_2} w_t - \frac{\alpha_0}{\alpha_2} - \frac{\alpha_1}{\alpha_2} u_t.$$

So much for the first of the two differences of detail between Parkin's test and the DL test. Turning now to the second difference, it will be recalled that DL's test procedure is to formulate the testable predictions of the expectational model in terms of the intercept and the coefficients of their 'combined equation' (that is (3.15)) and then to confront those predictions with a numerical version of the combined equation. Parkin's procedure, on the other hand, is to formulate the testable predictions of the expectational model in terms of one of the two elements of his combined equation, namely (3.16), and then to confront those predictions with a numerical version of this equation which he derives from a numerical version of the combined equation.

What are the predictions of the expectational model in terms of (3.16)? One of them, as we have seen, is that the coefficient α_2 will be unity. What of the intercept α_0 and the coefficient α_1? The predictions here are: $\alpha_0 > 0$ and $\alpha_1 < 0$. To see that this must be so, recall that the expectational model specifies that the plot against u_t of the non-linear expression $\alpha_0 + \alpha_1 u_t^{-1}$ takes the form of the unbroken curve in Figure 3.2. This being so, it must also specify that the plot

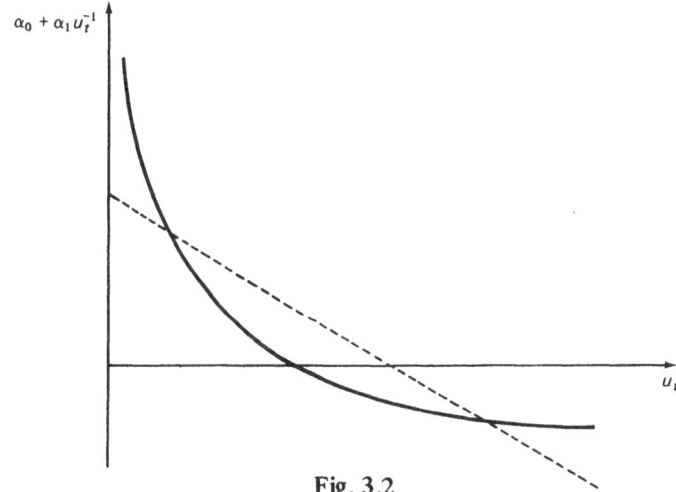

Fig. 3.2

Therefore

$$p_{t-1}^e = \frac{1}{\alpha_2} w_{t-1} - \frac{\alpha_0}{\alpha_2} - \frac{\alpha_1}{\alpha_2} u_{t-1}.$$

Substituting this expression for p_{t-1}^e in the above wage equation we obtain:

$$w_t = \alpha_0 + \alpha_1 u_t + \alpha_2 (1 - \theta) \left[\frac{1}{\alpha_2} w_{t-1} - \frac{\alpha_0}{\alpha_2} - \frac{\alpha_1}{\alpha_2} u_{t-1} \right] + \alpha_2 \theta p_t.$$

Therefore

$$w_t = \theta \alpha_0 + \alpha_1 u_t + (1 - \theta) w_{t-1} - \alpha_1 (1 - \theta) u_{t-1} + \alpha_2 \theta p_t.$$

against u_t of a linear approximation to this non-linear expression $(\alpha_0 + \alpha_1 u_t)$ has the form of the broken line in this diagram; and this, of course, is a line with a positive intercept and a negative slope.

These are the predictions, then, which, in the Parkin test, are confronted with the facts *via* a numerical version of (3.16).† Actually, Parkin derives six different numerical versions of (3.16). Three of these are presented below: ‡

$$w_t = -0.098 + 1.701u_t + 0.347p_t^e$$

$$w_t = 6.967 - 2.542u_t + 0.472p_t^e$$

$$w_t = 2.097 + 0.069u_t + 0.650p_t^e$$

As explained earlier, these numerical equations have been derived from the corresponding numerical versions of the combined equation (3.18). The method of conversion can be seen from a comparison of (3.16) and (3.18). First, the estimate of the coefficient of w_{t-1} in (3.18) was subtracted from unity to get an estimate of θ. Then the estimate of the intercept of (3.18) was divided by this estimate of θ to get an estimate of α_0, the intercept of (3.16). Obviously, the estimate of the coefficient of u_t in (3.16) was obtained directly from the estimate of the coefficient of u_t in (3.18). Finally the estimate of the coefficient of p_t^e in (3.16) was obtained by dividing the estimate of the coefficient of p_t in (3.18) by the estimate of θ.

Examination of the above three numerical equations shows that the predictions of the expectational model are largely refuted by the U.K. data on the basis of Parkin's test. The estimate of the coefficient of p_t^e is less than one-half in two of the three equations and still well below unity in the third. The coefficient of u_t has the right sign in only one of the three equations while the intercept has the right sign in only two of the three.

---

†It will be seen that Parkin has fewer testable predictions to confront with the facts than if he had followed DL in formulating his predictions in terms of the intercept and coefficient of the combined equation (cf. p. 61 above). Otherwise there is nothing to choose between his test procedure and the DL procedure.

‡The last of the three numerical equations presented above was estimated from quarterly data relating to the entire period from the 3rd quarter of 1948 to the 1st quarter of 1969; it is the equation labelled 'entire' in Parkin's table 1. The first and second equations were estimated, respectively, from data relating to those quarters in the above period in which an incomes policy was in force and those quarters in which no incomes policy was in force; they are the equations labelled 'policy on' and 'policy off'. It will be noticed that Parkin presents alternative 'entire', 'policy on' and 'policy off' equations in his table 2. These differ from the three which we have presented in the text in that they embody a more general assumption about 'the error term' in the combined equation. We have chosen to ignore this econometric refinement, especially as the second three equations tell much the same story as the first three.

3.4 The Expectational Model: A Second Turnovsky Test

While the model of Section 2.4 (reproduced in (3.1), (3.2) and (3.3)) is the most frequently discussed expectational model, it is by no means the only one to be found in the inflation literature. (It will be recalled (see p. 23 above) that this particular expectational model was put forward in Section 2.4 merely as a prototype – as typical of the class of expectational models.) Indeed the next test to be dealt with in this chapter relates to a group of three expectational models, each of which differs somewhat from (3.1)–(3.3). All three incorporate relationships (3.1) and (3.2), but either modify (3.3) or replace it with an expectations-formation equation of a completely different kind. As we have seen (p. 58 above) (3.3) can be written in the form:

$$p_t^e = p_{t-1}^e + \theta(p_{t-1} - p_{t-1}^e) \qquad (0 < \theta < 1).$$

In the first of the three expectational models referred to, this is modified to read:

$$p_t^e = p_{t-1}^e + \theta(p_t - p_{t-1}^e). \tag{3.19}$$

In the second of the three models (3.3) is replaced by:

$$p_t^e = p_t + \gamma(p_t - p_{t-1}), \tag{3.20}$$

while in the third it is replaced by:

$$p_t^e = \lambda_0 p_t + \lambda_1 p_{t-1} + \ldots + \lambda_n p_{t-n}, \tag{3.21}$$

where it is assumed that $\lambda_0, \lambda_1, \ldots, \lambda_n$ sum to unity.

According to (3.19) ('adaptive expectations') the rate of inflation expected for the current period is determined by taking the rate expected for the previous period and correcting it by some fraction of the 'expectation error' of the previous period. According to (3.20) ('extrapolative expectations') the expected rate of inflation for the current period is determined by taking the *actual* rate of inflation and correcting it by some fraction of the most recent change in the actual rate. Finally (3.21) ('distributed lag expectations') implies that the expected rate of inflation for the current period is determined by taking a weighted arithmetic average of the actual rate of inflation of the current period and the actual rates of some finite number of previous periods.

Each of the above three expectational models has been tested by Turnovsky.[8] Turnovsky's test procedure is essentially the same as the DL procedure discussed in the previous section. That is, he begins by deriving for each model the combined wage and expectations-formation equation which is to constitute, so to speak, the vehicle of the test for that model. The test equations for the three models, which are derived by a series of manipulations corresponding exactly to those used by DL (see above p. 61), are respectively:

$$w_t = \theta\alpha_0 + \alpha_1 u_t^{-1} - \alpha_1(1 - \theta)u_{t-1}^{-1} + (1 - \theta)w_{t-1} + \alpha_2\theta p_t \tag{3.22}$$

$$w_t = \alpha_0 + \alpha_1 u_t^{-1} + \alpha_2 p_t + \alpha_2\gamma(p_t - p_{t-1}) \tag{3.23}$$

$$w_t = \alpha_0 + \alpha_1 u_t^{-1} + \alpha_2\gamma_0 p_t + \alpha_2\gamma_1 p_{t-1} + \ldots + \alpha_2\gamma_n p_{t-n} \tag{3.24}$$

Turnovsky then formulates the testable predictions of the first model in terms of the coefficients of (3.22), those of the second model in terms of the coefficients of (3.23) and those of the third model in terms of the coefficients of (3.24). As we have seen already, the first model yields the testable prediction that in (3.22) the coefficients of p_t and w_{t-1} will sum to unity. It also predicts that both of these coefficients will be positive, that the coefficients of u_t^{-1} and u_{t-1}^{-1} will be positive and negative, respectively, and that the intercept will be negative (see above p. 61). The second of the three models predicts that in (3.23) the coefficient of p_t will be unity,† that the coefficient of u_t^{-1} will be positive (p. 57 above) and that the intercept will be negative (p. 57 above). Finally the third expectational model yields the testable prediction that the coefficient of u_t^{-1} will be positive and that the coefficients of $p_t, p_{t-1}, \ldots, p_{t-n}$ will sum to unity.‡

Turnovsky's final step is to derive numerical versions of (3.22), (3.23) and (3.24) by the use of standard econometric methods and to see whether these predictions are borne out, or refuted by, the data.

The above test procedure has been applied by Turnovsky both to Canadian data and to U.S. data. The results for Canada are highly favourable to the expectational models and hence support the results of the DL test of (3.1)–(3.3). On the other hand, the models are clearly refuted by the U.S. data.

The numerical versions of (3.22), (3.23) and (3.24) which Turnovsky derives for Canada are:[9] ¶

$$w_t = 12.968u_t^{-1} - 5.834u_{t-1}^{-1} + 0.448w_{t-1} + 0.507p_t \qquad (3.25)$$

$$w_t = 13.874u_t^{-1} + 0.773p_t - 0.393(p_t - p_{t-1}) \qquad (3.26)$$

$$\text{(a) } w_t = 11.942u_t^{-1} + 0.478p_t + 0.316p_{t-1} + 0.065p_{t-2} + 0.120p_{t-3} \Big\}$$

$$\text{(b) } w_t = 12.451u_t^{-1} + 0.458p_t + 0.278p_{t-1} + 0.142p_{t-2} + 0.049p_{t-3} \Big\}$$

$$(3.27)$$

It will be seen from these equations that the testable predictions of the three expectational models in question are strongly supported by the Canadian data. Taking (3.25) first, we note that the coefficients of u_t^{-1} and u_{t-1}^{-1} have the signs predicted by the first of the three expectational models and that the sum of the coefficients of p_t and w_{t-1} is very close to unity — again as predicted. Thus, apart

---

† All three models predict that α_2 will be unity. See p. 57 above.

‡ Recall that it is assumed in (3.21) that $\gamma_0 + \gamma_1 + \ldots + \gamma_n = 1$.

¶ Turnovsky does not report the intercepts of these numerical equations since they proved to be insignificantly different from zero. The two versions of (3.24) correspond to two different econometric methods for estimating the coefficients from a given set of data. Note that n, which is, of course, arbitrary, has been put equal to 3.

from the non-appearance of a negative intercept (cf. footnote on p. 66) (3.25) bears out the predictions of the first model remarkably well. The second model is also well supported by (3.26) in that the coefficient of p_t is close to unity (though perhaps not close enough for unequivocal support) and the coefficient of u_t^{-1} is positive. Once again the non-appearance of a negative intercept is the main blot on the predictive record. Turning finally to (3.27) we see that, in both equations, the coefficient of u_t^{-1} is positive and that the sum of the remaining coefficients is very close to unity. Thus both relationships are well in line with the predictions of the third model — apart, of course, from the intercept.

On the basis of Turnovsky's test, then, the class of expectational models is strongly supported by the Canadian data.

The numerical equations corresponding to (3.22), (3.23) and (3.24) which Turnovsky derives for the United States are:[10]†

$$w_t = 1.610 + 21.914u_t^{-1} - 10.209u_t^{-1} + 0.493p_t - 0.021w_{t-1} - 2.346d_t$$

$$\text{(3.28)}$$

$$w_t = 1.432 + 13.320u_t^{-1} + 0.427p_t + 0.153(p_t - p_{t-1}) - 2.509d_t \qquad \text{(3.29)}$$

$$w_t = 1.199 + 14.556u_t^{-1} + 0.466p_t + 0.143p_{t-1} - 0.354p_{t-2} + 0.129p_{t-3}$$
$$- 2.417d_t \qquad \text{(3.30)}$$

Starting with (3.28) we see that the testable predictions of the first model are borne out in part only by that equation. The coefficients of u_t^{-1} and u_{t-1}^{-1} have the predicted signs but the sum of the coefficients of p_t and w_{t-1} is far short of unity, the sign of the coefficient of w_{t-1} is the reverse of the predicted sign and so is the sign of the intercept. Similarly, the predictions of the second model are not well supported by (3.29). The coefficient of u_t^{-1} has the predicted sign but the sign of the intercept is wrong and the coefficient of p_t is well below the predicted value of unity. Finally (3.30) gives only weak support to the third of the expectational models under test. The coefficient of u_t^{-1} has the predicted sign but not the intercept, while the sum of the coefficients of p_t, p_{t-1}, p_{t-2} and p_{t-3} falls far short of the predicted value of unity. All in all, it must be concluded that the expectational class of models are clearly refuted by the U.S. data on the basis of the Turnovsky test.

---

†The d variable which appears in each of these equations is a 'seasonal dummy'. As the name suggests, it is not a genuine explanatory variable but merely an econometric device for taking care of the purely seasonal influences in the (six-monthly) time series from which the three equations have been estimated. Thus its appearance in (3.28)–(3.30) does not mean that there is a discrepancy between these equations and (3.22)–(3.24) — the former can be described quite legitimately as numerical versions of the latter. It should be pointed out that there was no need for Turnovsky to introduce seasonal dummies into the numerical equations for Canada because in this case the time series used in the estimation had been seasonally adjusted.

3.5   The Expectational Model: Solow

The test discussed in the previous section relates to a group of three models which can be properly labelled 'expectational' even though they differ slightly from the basic, prototype expectational model presented in (3.1)–(3.3). Yet another model which differs from the prototype but which can nevertheless be placed legitimately in the expectational class is the following:

$$p = w - r + p^e \tag{3.31}$$

$$w = g(u) \tag{3.32}$$

$$\Delta p^e = \theta(p - p^e) \tag{3.33}$$

Comparing these relationships with (3.1)–(3.3), we see that the difference between the present model and the prototype is that, in the prototype model, the 'shift factor', p^e, is attached to the *wage* equation, whereas in the present model it is attached to the price equation. Thus the view underlying the prototype is that, in formulating their wage demands, wage-earners anticipate *price* increases and that, as a result, the rate of increase of many wage-earnings per man is raised by one percentage point, at any given level of unemployment, for each one-point increase in the expected rate of inflation. On the other hand, the view underlying the present model is that, in setting prices, price-makers anticipate *cost* increases, with the result that the rate of price increase is raised by one percentage point, at any given *actual* rate of increase of unit labour cost (value of $w-r$), for each one-point increase in the *expected* rate of cost increase, as proxied by the expected rate of inflation. Of course these two views are not mutually exclusive and it would be easy (and sensible) enough to embody them both in the one set of relationships.

One way of testing the present model (more precisely the price equation of the model), the logic of which will be clear to the reader who has worked through the earlier sections of the chapter, is to estimate a price equation in which the variables on the right-hand side of (3.31) appear as independent variables, and see whether the estimate of the coefficient of p^e is approximately equal to the value predicted by the model, that is unity. A test of this kind has been performed on both quarterly U.S. data and annual U.K. data by Solow.[11]

The equation which Solow estimates from the U.S. data is:

$$p_t = \alpha_0 + \alpha_1 w_t + \alpha_2 \bar{r}_t + \alpha_3 p_t^f + \alpha_4 D_t + \alpha_5 K_t + \alpha_6 G_t + \alpha_7 p_t^e, \tag{3.34}$$

where p, p^e and w have their usual meanings, $\bar{r}$ is the percentage rate of increase of labour requirements per unit of output (reciprocal of output per man), p^f the percentage rate of increase of farm prices, D a measure of demand pressure, K and G two 'dummy' variables designed to take care of the distortions in the data attributable, respectively, to the Korean War and the incomes policy carried on in the United States since 1962 and the αs are a set of constants.† Altogether eleven numerical versions of (3.34) are presented,[12] corresponding to eleven different series for p^e. The eleven different p^e series are artificial series generated by the method explained earlier in connection with Toyada's study (see p. 58) and correspond to eleven different values of the constant θ. Examination of this series of numerical equations show that, regardless of the value of θ used to generate the p^e series, the coefficient of p^e is well below unity; in fact the coefficient is never greater than 0.5477 and it falls as low as 0.3734. Thus it would appear that the price equation of the expectational model being tested by Solow is clearly refuted by the U.S. data.

The equation estimated from the annual British data is:

$$p_t = \alpha_0 + \alpha_1 n_t + \alpha_3 m_t + \alpha_4 C_t + \alpha_5 L_t + \alpha_6 p_t^e, \qquad (3.35)$$

where n denotes the percentage rate of increase in the index of unit labour cost, m the percentage rate of increase in the index of the prices of imported raw materials, C and L two 'dummy' variables introduced to deal with the distorting effects of U.K. incomes policy and the αs are a set of constants.‡

Solow presents a total of nine numerical versions of this equation[13] corresponding to nine different series for p^e — ultimately to nine different values of θ. The highest value of the coefficient of p^e in these nine equations is 0.2109 whilst the lowest is 0.0034. Thus Solow's U.K. equations refute the particular expectational model under test even more clearly than do his U.S. equations.

---

†(3.34) corresponds much more closely to (3.31) than it appears to do at first sight. Putting aside the two 'trick' variables, K and G, and noting that $\bar{r}$ is effectively the rate of increase of output per man, if not actually so, we see that the only two explanatory variables which appear to be extraneous to the right-hand side of (3.31) are p^f and D. It must be remembered, however, that (3.31) is just a simplified version of (2.5) (see p. 30 above); and it must be recognised that p^f and D are closely related to the variables s and m which appear with w and o on the right-hand side of that equation. The variable s is the rate of increase in the index of unit non-labour cost in the mark-up sector; and since the output of the farm sector is an important (non-labour) input to the mark-up sector in the case of the U.S. economy, p^f is likely to be a good representational ('proxy') variable for s. Likewise it can be argued that D is probably an effective proxy variable for m, the rate of increase of the index of mark-up factors, since in the U.S. case there is a close correlation between variations in the pressure of demand and variations in profit margins.

‡Again there is quite close correspondence between (3.35) and (3.31) despite appearances to the contrary. Leaving aside the two dummy variables, we find that there are two variables which do not appear to fit in with the right-hand side of (3.31). In fact, however, n is equivalent to w *minus* r, that is the rate of increase of the index of unit labour cost can be expressed (approximately) as the rate of increase of the index of wage-earnings per man *minus* the rate of increase of the index of output per man (see above p. 30). Further, since imported raw materials constitute the most important non-labour input to the mark-up sector of the U.K. economy, m is likely to be a very satisfactory proxy variable for s (see previous footnote).

To complete the chapter we shall now briefly summarise the results of the various tests of the expectational model that have been described. Data relating to four different economies – the U.S. economy, the U.K. economy, the Japanese economy and the Canadian economy – have been used in these tests. Tests using *U.S. data* have been performed by Turnovsky and Solow. The expectational model is clearly refuted, in whole or in part, by the U.S. data on the basis of both of these tests. Two tests have been performed using *U.K. data* – by Solow and Parkin. Again the model is refuted by the data on the basis of both tests. The model has been tested against *Japanese data* by Toyoda, and in this case, too, is clearly refuted. Thus there are strong grounds for saying that the expectational model is not a useful model for the U.S. and U.K. economies, and some grounds, at least, for making the same statement in relation to the Japanese economy.

The tests using *Canadian data* comprise two distinct tests by Turnovsky and one by Donner and Lazar. In all three tests the model is strongly supported by the data. Thus it may well be that the expectational model captures the essence of the inflationary process in the case of the Canadian economy, in contrast to the U.S., U.K. and Japanese economies.

4

EMPIRICAL STUDIES OF THE PRICE EQUATION

4.1 Central Relationships of Inflation Theory

From the survey of models of the inflationary process given in Chapter 2 it will be clear that there are two relationships which play a dominant role in the modern theory of inflation. One of these is the 'price equation' – a relationship which sets out to explain either the level of prices, or the rate of increase of prices, in the mark-up sector as a whole or in some sub-sector of the mark-up sector. The other is the 'wage equation', which is a relationship purporting to explain either the level, or the rate of increase of money wages per man or per man-hour in the mark-up sector or in some part of that sector. While it is certainly possible to explain inflation without recourse to a price and/or wage equation (witness the Keynesian model of Section 2.2), inflation theorists have come to rely increasingly on these two relationships and they now occupy the same central position in models of the inflationary process as the consumption function occupies in Keynesian models of real-income determination.

Not surprisingly the price and wage equations have been the subject of extensive empirical investigation in recent years, and the purpose of this chapter and the next is to give an account of some of the more important empirical studies in this field. In the present chapter we shall consider price-equation studies and in the next chapter studies of the wage equation.

Before proceeding, however, we must explain the relationship between the empirical work to be discussed in this chapter and the next and that discussed in Chapter 3. Several of the studies dealt with in the last chapter could be properly described as empirical studies of the wage equation, for example those of Turnovsky, Toyoda, Parkin, while Solow's study would certainly rate as an empirical study of the price equation. In what way, then, do the studies which belong in this chapter and Chapter 5 differ from those which belong in Chapter 3?

A good way of approaching this question is to begin by distinguishing between two different, though closely related, tasks which are performed by the empirical investigator in the field of inflation and, indeed, in all branches of macro-economics. The first task, which forms part of the work of *building* a model of the inflationary process, consists of estimating a series of, let us say, wage equations and then deciding on a 'best' wage equation by applying certain simple econometric criteria to the results yielded by this series of estimations. The second task, which is concerned with *testing* the model once it has been built, is that of formulating the testable predictions of the model or of some part of the model and then confronting these predictions with the facts to determine whether or not the model constitutes a useful simplification of the inflation phenomenon.

Having made this distinction we can proceed immediately to explain how the empirical studies of the wage and price equation to be dealt with in this chapter and the next differ from those discussed in the previous chapter. The studies to be dealt with now are studies in which the author has addressed himself to the first of the two tasks distinguished above, whereas the studies considered in Chapter 3 are studies in which it is the second task that has been undertaken.

The approach followed in the studies which belong in the present chapter and in Chapter 5 has been described in a very general way in the paragraph before last. Before beginning our discussion of these studies, however, we propose to give a much more detailed account of this approach mainly for the benefit of the reader who has no, or little, knowledge of the econometric techniques that are nowadays widely employed in empirical work in economics generally and in the field of inflation in particular.

The first point to note is that the various equations experimented with may differ one from the other as regards: (i) the character of the dependent or explained variable; and/or (ii) the list of independent or explanatory variables; and/or (iii) mathematical form. For example, in a study of the wage equation the *dependent variable* could vary from equation to equation between the following: (i) the index of standard wage rates per man in the current period; (ii) the absolute change in the index from the previous period; (iii) the percentage change in the index from the previous period; (iv) the percentage change in the index from the corresponding period (quarter, say) a year earlier; (v) the same as (i) to (iv) but in terms of the index of wage-*earnings* per man rather than wage *rates* per man. The *independent variables* could vary from equation to equation between any combination of the following: (i) the unemployment percentage in the current period; (ii) the absolute change in the unemployment percentage from the previous period; (iii) the percentage change in the price index from the previous period; (iv) the level of profits in the current period; (v) the degree of trade-union militancy in the current period; (vi) any combination of (i) to (v) but for one or more past periods as well as for the current period. Finally, the *mathematical form* of the equation could vary between: (i) linear; (ii) linear in terms of some variables and in terms of the reciprocals of others; (iii) linear in terms of some variables and of second degree in others.

The method used to estimate the set of trial equations is usually the simplest of the methods which constitute the econometrician's tool kit, namely ordinary least squares (O.L.S.), though sometimes one finds a more refined estimation procedure being employed. As for the decision about the 'best' or 'preferred' equation, this is usually made by applying certain standard econometric criteria to each estimated equation in turn. The basic criterion may be briefly described as the '*signs*' *criterion*. For any particular equation the investigator will have certain preconceptions, suggested by economic theory, as to the signs of the coefficients of the various independent variables and perhaps as to the sign of the intercept term as well. For example, in the case of a wage equation of the form:

$$w_t = \alpha_0 + \alpha_1 u_t^{-1} + \alpha_2 p_{t-1},$$

he will expect α_0 to be negative and α_1 to be positive, these being the signs needed to produce a proper 'Phillips curve' (cf. above, p. 56). He will also expect α_2 to be positive, that is he will expect the rate of increase of money wage-earnings per man to be higher, at a given unemployment percentage, the higher has been the rate of inflation in the immediate past. According to the signs criterion, the estimated version of an equation should exhibit the investigator's preconceived or *a priori* signs if the equation is to qualify as a good one.

A second commonly used criterion is the 'R^2' *criterion*. R^2 measures the 'goodness-of-fit' of an estimated equation in the sense of the closeness with which the *actual* observations on the dependent variable in some past period of time are approximated by the *computed* observations – the observations which are generated by an estimated version of the equation; perfect fit occurs when R^2 equals unity and total absence of fit when R^2 equals zero. An equation is good on the R^2 criterion if its estimated version produces an R^2 figure close to unity – say 0.9 or more.†

A third criterion is the '*t-ratio*' *criterion*. The t ratio associated with any independent variable measures the 'strength' of that variable; the higher, numerically, is the t ratio the smaller is the probability of obtaining the actual (O.L.S.) coefficient estimate if the true value of the coefficient is zero, that is the more confidently we can rule out the hypothesis of a true coefficient value of zero, or, less precisely, the stronger is the variable in question. To be a good equation on the t-ratio criterion, all the t ratios associated with the estimated version of the equation should be 'high' – a conventional figure is 2 or more in absolute value.

Finally, there is the *Durbin–Watson statistic (DW)* criterion. DW supplements the t ratios; a value of DW close to zero (DW cannot be negative) indicates that the above interpretation of the t ratios is not strictly legitimate. A good equation on the DW criterion, then, is one whose estimated version has associated with it a high DW – say a DW of about 1.75 or more.

These, then, are the criteria which the investigator commonly uses to determine, say, the best wage equation from the set of equations tried out. In arriving at his decision as to the best equation he will be looking for an equation whose estimated version exhibits the 'right' signs, has an R^2 close to unity, high t ratios (certainly in excess of 2) all round and a DW not far short of 2 – or higher.

---

†Sometimes $\bar{R}^2$ ('adjusted' R^2) is used instead of R^2, that is the criterion runs in terms of a figure near unity for $\bar{R}^2$.

Having described the general approach followed in the empirical studies which are the concern of this chapter and the next, we turn to the studies themselves, beginning, in this chapter, with studies of the price equation. These are too numerous for us to be able to treat them all, and we shall confine our attention, therefore, to the comparatively small group which have been influential, or, in the case of very recent studies, which have novel features that are likely to make them so in the future.

As in the previous chapter we shall use a uniform notation, conforming as closely as possible with the notation of Chapter 2 throughout. The reader who decides to work through the original studies after completing the present chapter should keep in mind, therefore, that the original notation may not always be the same as the one used here.

4.2   Price Determination in U.K. Manufacturing: Neild

The first price-equation study to be discussed is an important U.K. study undertaken some years ago by Neild.[1] Neild's study relates to U.K. manufacturing, other than food, drink and tobacco. Its purpose is to discriminate between three competing price equations for this sector, using the standard econometric criteria discussed in the previous section. The three price equations in question are derived by setting up a general price equation which has the index of unit labour cost, L, as one of its five independent variables, then writing three different formulae for L, and finally substituting these three formulae, in turn, into the general equation. This procedure will now be explained in more detail.

First, let us consider the general price equation. This is:

$$P_t = b_0 + b_1 L_t + b_2 S_t + b_3 S_{t-1} + b_4 S_{t-2} + b_5 P_{t-1}, \qquad (4.1)$$

where P denotes the index of prices, L the index of unit labour cost, S the index of unit material cost and the bs are a set of constants. Neild arrives at (4.1) by postulating that the current level of P depends, in a precisely specified way, on the current levels of L and S and on all past levels of these indexes and then by manipulating the resulting, somewhat complicated, expression in such a way that all past levels of L, and all past levels of S, except S_{t-1} and S_{t-2}, disappear from the right-hand side, to be replaced by a single past level of P, namely P_{t-1}. Underlying (4.1), then, is the idea that the current movement in the price index is determined not only by the *current* movement of the index of unit labour cost and the index of unit materials cost but also by what happened to those indexes in the past – in principle, the whole of their past history is relevant to what is happening now to the price index.

Turn now to the three formulae for L_t which are as follows:

$$L_t = W_t/O_t \qquad (i)$$

$$L_t = W_t/O_t^{Tr} = W_t/(1.025)^t \qquad (ii)$$

$$L_t = W_t/O_t^{Tr} = W_t/(1+\rho)^t \qquad (iii)$$

In these expressions W denotes the index of wage-earnings per man, O the index of output per man, O^{Tr} the trend value of the index of output per man and ρ some positive constant.

The index of unit labour cost defined by formula (i) responds to *all* movements in output per man whether they be short term or long term in character. By contrast, the unit labour cost indexes defined by formula (ii) and formula (iii) reflect only long-term or trend movements in output per man; there is no response to purely short-term productivity movements in these two cases. For example, it is well known that firms are reluctant to reduce their labour force when faced with a fall in output which they believe to be of a temporary character – in the short run they are inclined to 'hoard' labour and use it at less than full capacity. As a result, when there is a fall in aggregate demand, and hence in output, output per man is likely to fall also. However, this fall in output per man will be reversed when aggregate demand and output recover to their original levels. In other words, output per man typically behaves in the same way, in the short run, as output itself, falling in the 'recession' phase of the cycle and rising in the 'recovery' phase. Now these purely short-run or 'cyclical' movements in output per man would be fully reflected in the index of unit labour cost defined by formula (i). On the other hand, they would not show up in the indexes defined by formulae (ii) and (iii), since these involve the trend value of the index, not its actual value.

This difference between formula (i), on the one hand, and formulae (ii) and (iii) on the other, is clearly quite fundamental. By contrast, the difference between formula (ii) and formula (iii) is a comparatively minor one. In the case of formula (ii) the trend movement of the index of output per man is defined by a path of exponential growth at the rate of 2½ per cent per period, whereas in the case of formula (iii) it is defined by a path of exponential growth at some unspecified rate, namely 100ρ per cent per period.

As indicated earlier, Neild's three competing price equations are derived by substituting the above three formulae in turn into equation (4.1). Hence they are as follows:

$$P_t = b_0 + b_1 \frac{W_t}{O_t} + b_2 S_t + b_3 S_{t-1} + b_4 S_{t-2} + b_5 P_{t-1} \tag{4.2}$$

$$P_t = b_0 + b_1 \frac{W_t}{(1.025)^t} + b_2 S_t + b_3 S_{t-1} + b_4 S_{t-2} + b_5 P_{t-1} \tag{4.3}$$

$$P_t = b_0 + b_1 \frac{W_t}{(1+\rho)^t} + b_2 S_t + b_3 S_{t-1} + b_4 S_{t-2} + b_5 P_{t-1} \tag{4.4}$$

To simplify the estimation of (4.4), Neild replaces the non-linear term:

$$\frac{W_t}{(1+\rho)^t} = W_t(1+\rho)^{-t}$$

by a linear approximation. It can be shown that provided p is close to zero[†] the term $(1 + \rho)^{-t}$ is given, approximately, by: [‡]

$$(1 + \rho)^{-t} = 1 - \rho t.$$

Hence, for small ρ, $W_t/(1 + \rho)^t$ can be approximated by $W_t - \rho W_t t$. Hence, in turn, $b_1(W_t/(1 + \rho)^t$ can be approximated by $b_1 W_1 - \rho b_1(W_t t)$. Thus the final form of Neild's third equation is:

$$P_t = b_0 + b_1 W_t + b_1'(W_t t) + b_2 S_t + b_3 S_{t-1} + b_4 S_{t-2} + b_5 P_{t-1}, \qquad (4.5)$$

where $b_1' = -\rho b_1$. We assume that ρ is positive.

From the discussion of the last few pages, it will be clear that all of the above three price equations embody the idea that the price index adjusts gradually to a change in unit cost and that it may take a long while before the full adjustment occurs. It will also be clear that the second and third equations embody a further important idea — that the price index does not adjust at all to changes in unit cost which are due solely to short-run movements in output per man. This idea is absent from the first equation.

The restrictions which Neild imposes on his original price equation — the relationship from which (4.1) is derived — enable us to say something about the *a priori* signs of the *b*s in (4.2), (4.3) and (4.5). Specifically, one can say, on the basis of these restrictions, that the intercept b_0 must be positive and that the coefficients b_1, b_2 and b_5 must also be positive. Further, since $b_1' = -\rho b_1$, and since ρ is assumed to be positive, the *a priori* sign of the coefficient b_1' must be negative. This leaves b_3 and b_4 with indeterminate signs; unfortunately the restrictions imposed in the original price equation are insufficient to permit us to deduce the signs of these two coefficients.

Turn now to Neild's results. For each of his three equations Neild derived two numerical versions — one based on quarterly information for the years 1953–60 and the other based on quarterly information for the years 1950–60. These six numerical equations are shown in Table 4.1,[2] together with the associated R^2s.

[†]ρ is the (constant) trend rate of increase in the index of output per man in *proportional* terms. Hence it can be taken to be some very small positive figure, such as 0.025.

[‡]The mathematically inclined reader may like a little detail on this point. The first two terms in the Taylor's series expansion of $(1 + \rho)^{-t}$, regarded as a function of ρ, are:

$$(1 + \rho)_a^{-t} + \rho \left[\frac{d}{d\rho}(1 + \rho)^{-t} \right]_a,$$

where the '*a*' subscript denotes that the expression concerned is evaluated at $\rho = a$, *a* being the fixed value of ρ around which the expansion is assumed to apply. Thus with $a = 0$ we have

$$(1 + \rho)^{-t} \simeq 1 - \rho t.$$

Table 4.1

Equation	Estimate of							
	b_0	b_1	b_2	b_3	b_4	b_5	b_1'	R^2
(4.3), 1953–60	−0.038	0.026	0.124	0.033	−0.096	0.939		0.997
	(0.042)	(0.046)	(0.039)	(0.059)	(0.042)	(0.068)	−	
(4.4), 1953–60	0.099	0.197	0.054	0.049	−0.011	0.633		0.999
	(0.028)	(0.031)	(0.027)	(0.037)	(0.028)	(0.055)	−	
(4.6), 1953–60	0.147	0.153	0.051	0.056	*	0.611	−0.203	0.999
	(0.037)	(0.031)	(0.026)	(0.031)		(0.047)	(0.146)	
(4.3), 1950–60	−0.018	0.009	0.126	0.054	−0.108	0.929		0.997
	(0.019)	(0.029)	(0.019)	(0.029)	(0.020)	(0.054)	−	
(4.4), 1950–60	0.044	0.141	0.106	0.065	−0.037	0.683		0.998
	(0.016)	(0.025)	(0.014)	(0.021)	(0.019)	(0.048)	−	
(4.6), 1950–60	0.154	0.059	0.105	0.052	*	0.633	0.129	0.999
	(0.019)	(0.018)	(0.027)	(0.012)		(0.027)	(0.089)	

*Neild does not give the estimate of b_4 for equation (4.6).

No t ratios are shown in the table, but the t ratio associated with any intercept estimate or coefficient estimate can be calculated by expressing the estimate as a ratio of the figure which appears in brackets below the estimate. No DWs are given since none were given by Neild.

Examination of this table shows that equation (4.2) performs rather badly on the econometric criteria presented in the opening section of the chapter. In both estimations of (4.2) the estimate of b_0 has the wrong sign while the only t ratios which are in excess of 2 are those associated with b_2, b_4 and b_5. By contrast, equation (4.3) performs quite well. In both estimations the signs are correct without exception and, with only four exceptions (three in the 1953–60 equation and one in the 1950–60 equation), the t ratios are well in excess of 2. Finally, R^2 is very close to unity for both estimations. Equation (4.5) also performs reasonably well, the only deficiencies being that the estimate of b_1' has the wrong sign in the 1950–60 equation and that three of the t ratios are too small – two in the 1953–60 equation and one in the 1950–60 equation.

To sum up, it would appear that there is little to choose between equations (4.3) and (4.5) and that both are better than (4.2).

4.3 Price Determination in U.S. Industry: Schultze and Tyron

We turn next to a study based on U.S. data which was undertaken by Schultze and Tyron at about the same time as Neild's U.K. study.[3] Of the two studies, the Schultze–Tyron (ST) study is by far the more comprehensive. As we have seen, in Neild's study only three distinct equations are tried out and then only on one set of data — that for U.K. manufacturing other than food, drink and tobacco. In the ST study, on the other hand, some sixty[4] different equations are experimented with and many of these are estimated from more than one set of industrial data.

We shall begin our account of the ST study by discussing the general character of the price equations which are estimated in the study and relating them to the equations estimated by Neild. Obviously the number of equations covered in the ST study is so large that it is not practicable to treat them individually. In any case a discussion of the equations one by one would be highly repetitive since their range of variation is not great. Accordingly, we shall limit ourselves to discussing the ST equations as a whole with the aim of giving a broad picture of the ways in which they differ one from the other and from those tested by Neild.

The first point to note in this connection is that the equations fall into two groups according to the nature of the dependent or explained variable. In ten of the equations the dependent variable is the level of the price index in quarter t *less* its level four quarters earlier, that is in quarter $t-4$. In the remaining equations, on the other hand, the dependent variable is simply the level of the price index in quarter t, as in Neild's three equations.

Within each of these two groups of equations, one equation differs from another only in having a different set of *independent* or explanatory variables; there is no difference in the mathematical form of the equations, which, like Neild's equations, are all strictly linear in form. The complete list of independent variables, from which the set for any particular equation is drawn, is presented below.

ULC — Unit labour cost (labour cost per unit of output)
ULC^N — Normal labour cost
$ULC^N + UCCA^N$ — Normal unit labour cost *plus* normal unit capital consumption allowances
$ULC - ULC^N$ — Excess of unit labour cost over normal unit labour cost
PR — Index of raw-materials price
PR^N — Index of normal raw-materials price
ED — Excess demand for output in current prices
ED^C — Excess demand for output in constant prices
ED^{C+} — Positive excess demand for output in constant prices
ED^{C-} — Negative excess demand for output in constant prices
EDS^{C+} — Positive excess demand for output in constant prices in the supplying industries
EDS^{C-} — Negative excess demand for output in constant prices in the supplying industries

As pointed out above, each of the ten equations which have the *change* in the price index as dependent variable differ one from another in having a different sub-set of the above variables as their independent or explanatory variables; and similarly for the group of fifty or so equations which have the *level* of the price index as dependent variable. As an example, two of the equations from the first group are those shown as (4.6) and (4.7) below,† while three of the equations from the second group are (4.8)–(4.10):

$$P_t - P_{t-4} = \beta_0 + \beta_1 \ ULC_t^N + \beta_2 (ULC - ULC^N)_t + \beta_3 \ ED_{t-1} \tag{4.6}$$

$$P_t - P_{t-4} = \beta_0 + \beta_1 \ ULC_t^N + \beta_2 (ULC - ULC^N)_t + \beta_3 \ PR_t + \beta_4 \ ED_t^C + \beta_5 \ ED_{t-1}^C \tag{4.7}$$

$$P_t = \beta_0 + \beta_1 \ ULC_t^N + \beta_2 (ULC - ULC^N)_t + \beta_3 \ ED_t^{C+} + \beta_4 \ ED_t^{C-} \tag{4.8}$$

$$P_t = \beta_0 + \beta_1 \ ULC_t^N + \beta_2 (ULC - ULC^N)_t + \beta_3 \ PR_t^N \tag{4.9}$$

$$P_t = \beta_0 + \beta_1 (ULC^N + UCCA^N)_t + \beta_2 (ULC - ULC^N)_t + \beta_3 \ ED_t^{C+} + \beta_4 \ ED_t^{C-} + \beta_5 \ EDS^{C+} + \beta_6 \ EDS_t^{C-} \tag{4.10}$$

It will be observed that all of the above equations have either ULC^N or $ULC^N + UCCA^N$ as one independent variable and $ULC - ULC^N$ as another, which suggests that these are the central independent variables in the group of ST equations. This, indeed, is the case. In fact every equation has either ULC^N or $ULC^N + UCCA^N$ as an independent variable and all but two have $ULC - ULC^N$. Thus it is not too much of a simplification to say that all equations have ULC^N and $ULC - ULC^N$ as independent variables and that, as regards the independent variables, variation between equations arises because different sub-sets of the remaining variables in the above list are added to these two.

This is a convenient point at which to compare the ST equations with those of Neild. As regards the *dependent* variables, the only point to note is that whereas the level of the price index is the dependent variable in all of Neild's equations, as we have seen there is a small group of the ST equations which has the change in the index over the preceding twelve months, rather than its current level, as dependent variable.

There is a good deal more to be said in relation to the *independent* variables.

When discussing Neild's study, we saw that in one of his three equations ((4.2) above) the unit labour cost variable (L_t) is taken to be W_t/O_t, whereas in the other two equations ((4.3) and (4.4)) it is taken to be W_t/O_t^T. Now Neild's W_t/O_t is virtually the same as ST's ULC_t, the only difference being that Neild's variable is an index of unit labour cost while ST's variable is the dollar value of unit labour cost. Likewise, Neild's W_t/O_t^T is virtually identical with ST's ULC_t^N. By the 'normal' unit labour cost of quarter t, ST mean the labour cost per man-hour of quarter t divided by a twelve-term moving average of the output per man of quarter t and the eleven preceding quarters.[5] Thus the numerator of ST's ULC_t^N is essentially the same as Neild's W_t, while the denominator of their variable is essentially the same as his O_t^T,‡ that is ULC_t^N can be identified with

---

† In these equations, P denotes the price index and the βs are a set of constants.
‡ Recall that a moving average is possibly the simplest device for estimating the trend component of a time series.

W_t/O_t^T. Recalling that the ST equations include both ULC_t^N and $ULC_t - ULC_t^N$ as independent variables (see above, p. 79), we see, then, that the ST equations incorporate both of the ideas about the role of unit labour cost in price determination which enter separately into Neild's equations — the idea underlying (4.2) being captured by $(ULC - ULC^N)_t$ and the idea underlying (4.3) and (4.4) by ULC_t^N. This is the first point to be made by way of comparison between the two sets of equations.

The second point concerns the materials-cost variable. It will be recalled that all three of Neild's equations contain the index of (actual) unit material cost as an independent variable. Some of the ST equations also include such a variable, for example (4.7). However, many do not. Of the latter group, some include an index of *normal* rather than actual raw-materials price, for example (4.9). Others include one or more excess-demand variables relating to the principal supplying industry as substitutes for an index of an actual raw-materials cost, for example (4.10), while others include no materials-cost variable of any sort, for example (4.6) and (4.8).

Third, in the case of the ST equations neither the labour-cost variables nor the materials-cost variables enter with a lag — the only lagged variables among the independent variables are the excess-demand variables, which in some equations are lagged one quarter behind the dependent variable, for example (4.6) and (4.7). In the case of Neild's equations, on the other hand, both the labour-cost variable and the materials-cost variable are lagged. Only the materials-cost variable is lagged explicitly. However, both variables are lagged implicitly. Indeed the presence of the lagged value of the *dependent* variable among the independent variables means that both the labour- and materials-cost variables enter as independent variables with an *infinite* distributed lag (see the discussion on p. 74 above).

Finally, it is important to note that many of the ST equations include one or more excess-demand variables among the independent variables, whereas excess demand plays no part in Neild's equations. We can interpret this difference between the two sets of equations as a difference of approach to the question of the variability of the profit margin. In Neild's equations it is assumed, tacitly, that there is *no* variation in the profit margin (cf. Section 4.2 above). In the ST equations, on the other hand, there is no such assumption; here the profit margin is permitted to vary from quarter to quarter. Moreover, the key determinant of the variability of the profit margins is taken to be the state of demand for the commodity in question. Specifically, it is assumed that the profit margin will rise as excess demand rises and fall as excess demand falls. On this view excess demand should appear as an independent variable in the price equation because, *ceteris paribus*, movements in excess demand will cause movements in price by producing changes in the profit margin.

The excess-demand variable which appears in the ST equations is sometimes a current-price variable, for example (4.6), and sometimes a constant-price variable, for example (4.7). Also, in some equations the constant-price excess-demand variable is split into two separate variables — positive excess demand in constant prices and negative excess demand in constant prices.† The idea behind this particular treatment of the excess-demand variable is that the upward effect on price when excess demand becomes more positive by $x m. (when it rises, say, from $10m. to $15m.) will be greater than the upward effect on prices when excess demand becomes less negative by $x m. (when it rises from, say, − $8m. to −$3m.). Similarly, the downward effect on price when excess demand becomes less positive by $x m. (when it falls, say, from $15m. to $12m.) will be greater than the downward effect when it falls, say, from −$3m. to −$6m. In short, on this view, price is more responsive to upward and downward movements of excess demand in the *positive* range than it is to upward and downward movements of excess demand in the *negative* range. But if this is so, it follows that positive excess demand and negative excess demand should appear in the price equation as distinct explanatory variables.

Having given this general account of the numerous equations covered in the ST study and compared them with Neild's equations, we turn now to the question of the assessment of the equations on the basis of the econometric criteria presented in the opening section of the chapter. It goes without saying that ST were not able to make an equation-by-equation assessment of the type undertaken by Neild. This would have been impracticable for them even if each equation had been estimated only once. In fact, however, many of the equations were estimated several times. This was possible because the data required for estimation were available to ST for six broad production sectors, namely durable manufacturing, non-durable manufacturing, wholesale and retail trade, regulated industries, contract construction and residual industries, and for twenty-one individual industries, for example primary metals, electrical machinery, mining, finance and insurance. Thus, for example, one finds in the ST study an estimated version of (4.8) for two of the six broad production sectors and for every one of the twenty-one individual industries. The volume of empirical results presented in the ST study was far too large, then, to permit an assessment equation by equation. However, several points of a general kind, which are relevant to the question of which of the sixty or so price equations estimated is 'best', emerge quite clearly from the ST tables.[6]

The first point relates to the equations which have no independent variables apart from ULC^N and $ULC - ULC^N$. These equations did not perform particularly well in terms of our criteria. An equation with ULC^N and $ULC - ULC^N$ as independent variables, and the *level* of the price index as dependent variable, was estimated seven times, and one with these independent variables, and the change in the price index as dependent variable, three times. In only three of the seven estimations of the *first* equation do we find both ULC^N and $ULC - ULC^N$ with

---

†Since the excess demand for the output in a particular industry or group of industries in constant prices is by definition the quantity demanded *less* the quantity available, it follows that ED^C can be either positive or negative in any quarter.

coefficients of the 'right' sign (positive), with high t ratios and with an $\bar{R}^2$ reasonably close to unity. In the remaining four cases we find a low $\bar{R}^2$ and/or low t ratios and/or coefficient estimates with a negative sign. As for the *second* equation, we find that all three estimations are faulty on one or more of our criteria.

Second, there appears to have been little improvement in performance with the addition of PR^N to ULC^N and $ULC - ULC^N$. An equation with ULC, $ULC - ULC^N$ and PR^N as independent variables, and the level of the price index as dependent variable, was estimated three times in the study, and an equation with these three independent variables, and the rate of change of the index as dependent variable, once. In only one of the three estimations of the first equation were all criteria met and they were not met in the single estimation of the second equation.

On the other hand, the addition of PR to ULC^N and $ULC - ULC^N$ resulted in a distinct improvement. An equation with this list of independent variables and the level of the price index as dependent variable was estimated twice and our criteria for success were met in both cases. There was also a single estimation of an equation with ULC^N, $ULC - ULC^N$ and PR as independent variables and the change in the index as dependent variable. While the criteria were not fully met in this estimation, inasmuch as the coefficient of PR had a t ratio of less than two, it was nevertheless reasonably successful.

Fourth, it would seem that the equations which include a straight excess-demand variable with the two unit cost variables were also unsatisfactory. An equation with ULC, $ULC - ULC^N$ and ED as independent variables and the level of the price index as dependent variable was estimated three times while one with the same dependent variable but with ULC, $ULC - ULC^N$ and ED^C as independent variables was also estimated three times. The criteria were met in two of the three estimations of the first equation but were met in only one of the three estimations of the second equation. The corresponding equations with the change in the price index as dependent variable were each estimated once and in neither case were the criteria fully met.

The equations which include one or other of the straight excess-demand variables with the two unit cost variables and one or other of the raw-materials price variables had an even worse record. There were fourteen estimations of equations of this type (including some repetitions) and in only one case were the criteria fully met.

Finally, equations which include the 'twin' excess-demand variables, ED^{C+} and ED^{C-}, with some combination of the remaining independent variables, also show up badly. The ST study includes some forty estimations of equations of this type, including repeat estimations of some equations. In all but three cases some part of the set of econometric criteria is not satisfied.

We can sum up this discussion of the empirical results presented in the ST study by saying that, on the basis of the econometric criteria presented in Section 4.1, the best of the many different price equations considered in the study appears to be one which has the level of the price index as dependent variable and ULC^N, $ULC - ULC^N$ and PR as explanatory variables. This conclusion must be qualified, however. For while it is true that the equation in question has an unblemished record in the ST study, it is also true that, having been estimated only twice, it had less opportunity to fail than many of the other equations which were considered. In conclusion it is interesting to note that, of the ST equations, the one which we are inclined to prefer is the one which resembles Neild's preferred equation (4.3) most closely. The essential difference between the two is that, whereas the independent variables are unlagged in the ST equation, they enter with an infinite distributed lag in Neild's equation.

4.4   Price Determination in U.S. Industry: Eckstein and Fromm

The third major study of the price equation to be considered is the study undertaken by Eckstein and Fromm[7] – to be abbreviated henceforth by EF. Like the ST study the EF study was based on U.S. data. Altogether twenty-three distinct price equations were tried out, ten of these being estimated from quarterly data relating to U.S. manufacturing as a whole, five from quarterly data relating to the durable manufacturing sub-sector of U.S. manufacturing and eight from quarterly data relating to the non-durable sub-sector. Four of the twenty-three distinct equations were estimated twice – both for manufacturing as a whole and for durable manufacturing – while the rest were estimated once only, either for manufacturing as a whole, or for durable manufacturing or for non-durable manufacturing. Thus twenty-seven estimations were performed altogether.[8] As regards comprehensiveness, therefore, the EF study falls somewhere between Neild's study and the study of ST.

Our discussion of the EF study will follow the same sort of pattern as was used in dealing with the ST study; that is, we shall begin by giving a broad account of the equations experimented with, the equations being too numerous and not sufficiently varied for an examination of them one by one to be feasible. We shall then provide a brief summary of the conclusions which emerge from the study when the econometric criteria of Section 4.1 are applied.

As regards the general character of the twenty-three equations which EF consider, we first point out that, like the ST equations, the EF equations can be grouped according to the nature of the dependent variable. Specifically there are three groups on this basis. The first group, containing nine of the twenty-three equations, has the *level* of the price index as dependent variable, the second group (ten equations) has the *absolute change* of the index from the *preceding quarter* as dependent variable while the third group (four equations) has as dependent variable the *proportional* change in the index from the *corresponding quarter a year earlier*. Again like the ST equation, the members of each of these groups differ one from the other only as regards the set of independent variables which is introduced – there are no differences of mathematical form, all equations being linear. The complete list of independent variables, from which the set for any one equation is drawn, is set out below.

In examining this list, the reader should recall that by 'normal unit labour cost' is meant the unit labour cost associated with 'normal output' and that 'normal output' is the long-term trend level of output as distinct from the actual level (see above, pp. 79–80). He should also be warned that some writers describe the long-term trend level of output as 'standard output' rather than as 'normal output'. Since both EF and the authors of the fourth and final study to be examined (Ball and Duffy) adopt this practice, we shall now use the terms 'standard output' and 'standard unit labour cost' ourselves from time to time and ask the reader to bear in mind whenever he sees these terms that they convey the same ideas as ST's 'normal output' and 'normal unit labour cost'.

ULC —   Unit labour cost

ULC^N —   Normal unit labour cost

$ULC - ULC^N$ —   Excess of unit labour cost over normal unit labour cost

PR —   Index of raw-materials price

IOR —   Industrial operating rate (actual production as a ratio of capacity, or maximum production)

ΔU —   Change from previous period in unfilled orders as a ratio of sales

P —   Price index (dependent variable)

The above is really no more than a skeleton list because each of the listed variables appears in the equations in several different guises. For example, ULC^N appears in one equation as a current level and as a level lagged one quarter, in another equation as a current change from the previous quarter and as a change from the previous quarter lagged one quarter, and in yet another equation as a proportional increase over the corresponding quarter one year earlier. As a second example, $ULC - ULC^N$ appears in one equation as a current level and in another as a change from the previous quarter. Again, P appears in one equation as a level lagged one quarter and in another as a change from the previous quarter lagged one quarter, while ULC appears in one equation as a change from the previous quarter and in another as a proportional rate of change from the corresponding quarter one year earlier.

To help make the above discussion more concrete we now present three of the twenty-three EF equations — one from each group. These have been chosen at random and serve to illustrate the ways in which the various equations differ, one from the other, both as regards the dependent variable and as regards the set of independent variables employed.[†]

$$P_t = \beta_0 + \beta_1\ ULC_t^N + \beta_1\ ULC_{t-1}^N + \beta_2(ULC - ULC^N)_t + \beta_3\ PR_t$$
$$+ \beta_4\ IOR_t + \beta_5 \Delta U_{t-1} + \beta_6\ P_{t-1} \qquad \text{(First group)} \qquad (4.11)$$

†The βs in these equations are a set of constants.

$$P_t - P_{t-1} = \beta_0 + \beta_1(ULC_t - ULC_{t-1}) + \beta_2(PR_t - PR_{t-1}) + \beta_3\,IOR_t$$
$$+ \beta_4\Delta U_{t-1} \qquad \text{(Second group)} \qquad (4.12)$$

$$\frac{P_t - P_{t-4}}{P_{t-4}} = \beta_0 + \beta_1\frac{ULC_t^N - ULC_{t-4}^N}{ULC_{t-4}^N} + \beta_2\frac{PR_t - PR_{t-4}}{PR_{t-4}}$$

$$\text{(Third group)} \qquad (4.13)$$

With this account of the various price equations experimented with in the EF study in mind, let us now consider the results which emerge when the numerical price equations derived in the study are examined from the standpoint of the econometric criteria discussed in the opening section of this chapter.

As mentioned at the outset of the present section twenty-three different equations were estimated in the EF study, four of them twice, giving a total of twenty-seven numerical price equations to be considered. These are set out in tables 2–4 of the study[9] together with $\bar{R}^2$, the t ratios and DW for each equation.†

Examination of these tables shows that none of the equations can be faulted on the basis of signs of coefficient estimates. We would expect all the independent variables in the EF list (see above, p. 84) to have positive coefficients in a macro price equation, and in every equation all coefficient estimates have this expected sign.

It is also clear from the tables, however, that with two exceptions, all of the equations fail to satisfy one or more of the remaining criteria in that one or more of the t ratios falls short of 2 in absolute value and/or $\bar{R}^2$ is well below unity and/or DW is well below the desirable figure of 1.75, or thereabouts. The two equations to which this remark does not apply are reproduced below in estimated form[10] with the relevant t ratio appearing in parentheses underneath the coefficient estimate:

$$P_t = -0.097 + 0.212ULC_t^N + 0.167(ULC - ULC^N)_t + 0.080PR_t$$
$$(3.23) \qquad\quad (3.30) \qquad\qquad\quad (4.91)$$
$$+ 0.0010(IOR)_t + 0.151\Delta U_{t-1} + 0.789P_{t-1} \qquad (4.14)$$
$$(5.94) \qquad\qquad (2.58) \qquad\quad (13.22)$$
$$\bar{R}^2 = 0.995 \qquad DW = 1.59$$

$$P_t = -0.108 + 0.179ULC_t^N + 0.079PR_t + 0.0010(IOR)_t$$
$$(3.79) \qquad\quad (4.89) \qquad (7.40)$$
$$+ 0.162\Delta U_{t-1} + 0.819P_{t-1} \qquad (4.15)$$
$$(2.70) \qquad\quad (19.16)$$
$$\bar{R}^2 = 0.995 \qquad DW = 1.64$$

†The t ratio associated with a particular coefficient estimate is shown in parentheses underneath that estimate.

It will be seen that both of these equations stand up well on our four econometric criteria. In both cases all coefficient estimates have the 'correct' (positive) sign, all t ratios are considerably in excess of 2, $\bar{R}^2$ is bordering on unity, and DW, while possibly a little on the low side, is at least in the vicinity of the minimum desirable figure.† There is little to choose between them, and either one might be regarded as the 'preferred' EF equation.

4.5   Price Determination in European Economies: Ball and Duffy

We turn now to the last of the price-equation studies to be considered, namely the recent study by Ball and Duffy[11] – henceforth to be abbreviated to BD. All of the studies so far examined in this chapter are single-country studies – Neild's relates to the United Kingdom and the ST and EF studies to the United States. Also, all three are based on quarterly data and relate to the manufacturing sector of the countries concerned or to some part of that sector. By contrast, the study to be examined now is an international study in the sense that all of the price equations experimented with were estimated for all or several of twelve different countries consisting of nine European countries, the United States, Canada and Japan. Moreover, the data used in estimating the equations were *annual* data relating to the *economy as a whole* rather than quarterly data relating to manufacturing.

We shall begin by listing the price equations with which BD experimented. Altogether five different equations were considered, namely:

$$p_t = \alpha_1 w_t + \alpha_2 o_t + \alpha_3 m_t \tag{4.16}$$

$$p_t = \alpha_1 w_t^* + \alpha_2 o_t + \alpha_3 m_t^* \tag{4.17}$$

$$p_t = \alpha_1 (w - o)_t^* + \alpha_2 m_t^* + \alpha_3 d_t \tag{4.18}$$

$$p_t = \alpha_1 w_t + \alpha_2 o_t + \alpha_3 r_t + \alpha_4 m_t \tag{4.19}$$

$$p_t = \alpha_1 (w - o)_t^* + \alpha_2 r_t + \alpha_3 m_t^* \tag{4.20}$$

In these expressions, p denotes the percentage rate of increase in the price index, w the percentage rate of increase in the index of wage-earnings per man, o the percentage rate of increase in the index of output per man, m the percentage rate of increase in the index of the prices of imported materials, r the percentage rate

---

†The requirement that DW should be not less than about 1.75 is no more than a rough guide since the precise 'cut-off' for DW varies from case to case depending on the number of explanatory variables in the equation and on the number of observations used in estimating it. Unfortunately EF give no information about the number of observations used in estimating their equations, and in the absence of this it is impossible to say precisely what the minimum desirable DW is for equations (4.14) and (4.15).

of increase from the previous period in the ratio of standard unit labour cost to actual unit labour cost, d an indicator of demand pressure and the αs are a set of constants. An asterisk superscript attached to an independent variable indicates that the variable in question is lagged; we have thought it unnecessary to spell out the precise form of the lags which BD have imposed, especially since these are somewhat complicated.

We turn now to a discussion of the conclusions which emerge from the BD study when the econometric criteria outlined in the opening section of this chapter are applied to the estimated versions of these equations.

Each of the five equations was estimated by BD for all of the twelve countries covered in the study, with the exception of (4.17) which was estimated for eight of the twelve only.† Thus to determine a preferred equation it was necessary to apply the criteria to eight different numerical versions of (4.17), and twelve different versions of each of the other four equations. BD do not attempt to do this but in their table 1^{12} they give all information (estimated coefficients, t ratios, $\bar{R}^2$ and DW) required to enable it to be done. Examination of this information shows that (4.19) is clearly the least satisfactory of the five equations on the familiar criteria. In the case of equations (4.16), (4.17), (4.18) and (4.20), at least one of the estimations is completely satisfactory, and the others are on the borderline. In the case of (4.19), on the other hand, none of the estimations is satisfactory on all counts. Moreover, none comes close to this standard. For example, in all twelve estimations at least two of the four t ratios are less than 2 and the coefficient of r has the wrong sign in all but two of the twelve estimations.

The other four equations are not so easily ranked. In the case of (4.17) there are two estimations (those for Belgium and France) which are satisfactory on all criteria, and another two (those for Canada and Italy) which are very nearly so. For (4.18) the record is much the same; here there are two estimations which are satisfactory on all counts and another four which fall just short of this standard. In the case of (4.16) there is only one completely satisfactory estimation, though there are three or four others which are not far behind. Much the same applies in the case of (4.20). It would appear, therefore, that (4.17) and (4.18) are slightly better than (4.16) and (4.20), though there is not a great deal to choose between them. In view of the fact that there are only eight estimations of (4.17) and twelve of all the rest, it would seem reasonable to place (4.17) first followed by (4.18) in second place with (4.16) and (4.20) equal third and (4.19) a clear last.

This ranking is by no means clear-cut and is certainly open to argument. On the other hand, it seems reasonably clear that the first three equations as a whole are superior to the last two as a whole, on the usual econometric criteria. Thus while

†In writing the second equation we have shown *both* w and m as lagged variables. In fact both variables were lagged in only three of the eight estimations of this equation; in the remaining five estimations only one of the two was lagged. Similar remarks apply to the third and fifth equations.

the BD study is somewhat inconclusive as to the relative merits of the five equations which are tried out in the study, it does provide a fairly definite ranking of the two broad groups into which these five equations fall.

4.6   Consensus of the Four Studies

In the opening section of this chapter we distinguished two tasks which fall to the lot of the empirical investigator in the field of inflation. The first task is to 'try out' various price equations, say, with a view to finding a 'preferred equation'. The aim of work of this type is to assist in the construction of a model of the inflationary process which appears to have some prospect of success, and which is therefore worth pursuing. The second task consists of taking a model which is believed to have some prospect of success, deriving testable predictions from the model and then testing the model by confronting these testable predictions with the facts. The ultimate purpose of work of this second type is to determine whether the promise shown by the model is, in fact, realised when the model is placed under test. Put briefly (and crudely) the distinction between the two tasks is between finding a model which is worth pursuing, on the one hand, and actually pursuing it on the other.

In Sections 4.2–4.5 we have given an account of four recent price-equation studies which are of the 'trying-out' type rather than the 'testing' type, that is in which the authors have addressed themselves to the first task rather than to the second. We would hope to come away from these studies with a reasonably clear picture of the sort of price equation that a 'worth-pursuing' model of the inflationary process might contain. Does such a clear picture, in fact, emerge? Is there a broad consensus to be found in the studies which permits us to delineate the essential features of a satisfactory price equation? We shall consider these questions in this final section.

It will be convenient to begin with the Neild, ST and EF studies in which the preferred equation is an equation explaining the *level* of the price index. Having searched for, and hopefully found, a consensus in these three studies we shall then bring in the BD study, in which the preferred equation has the *rate of increase* of the price index as the explained variable, and see whether the consensus found in the three earlier studies extends to the BD study also.

One point on which the Neild, ST and EF studies are unanimous is that the variables, wage-earnings per man and output per man, are symmetrical as regards their effect on the price index, in the sense that a 1 per cent increase in wage-earnings per man has precisely the opposite effect on the price index of a 1 per cent increase in output per man.

That the three studies are unanimous in support of this view is indicated by the fact that, in all three, unit labour cost (dollar value or index) appears in the preferred price equation as an independent variable but not wage-earnings per man or output per man. (See above, pp. 77, 82, 83 and 85, for details of the preferred equations of the Neild, ST and EF studies, respectively.) For if the above symmetry property holds, a given increase in wage-earnings per man, accompanied by the same proportionate increase in output per man, will leave the price index unchanged; only if the increase in wage-earnings per man is more than in proportion to the increase in output per man, that is only if the wage-earnings per man/output per man ratio increases, will there be an increase in the price index. Thus to subscribe to the above symmetry view is, in effect, to subscribe to the view that it is the ratio of wage-earnings per man to output per man, that is *unit labour cost*, which should appear as an independent variable in the price equation, not the wage-earnings and output variables themselves.

A second point on which there is complete agreement is that the unit labour cost variable which is relevant for the price equation is standard (or normal) unit labour cost, that is to say, that the output variable which constitutes the denominator of the unit cost variable should be standard (or normal) output, not actual output. Thus the preferred equations of the ST and EF studies include labour cost per man (in dollars) divided by the trend level of output per man (in dollars) as an independent variable while Neild's preferred equation includes the index of labour cost per man divided by the trend level of the index of output per man. Clearly, the only changes in output per man which can affect the price index *via* the standard unit labour cost variable are trend-level, or long-run changes. The unanimity of the studies in favour of standard unit cost as the relevant unit cost variable amounts, therefore, to a consensus that short-run productivity changes should be played down as a possible determinant of changes in the price index.†

Third, there is complete agreement that changes in the price index flow from changes in unit materials cost as well as from changes in unit labour cost. This is evident from the appearance in the preferred equations of all studies either of a unit materials cost variable or of a price of materials variable, the latter being equivalent to the former provided the usage of materials per unit of output remains fixed.‡

A fourth point on which there is near, if not complete unanimity is that the level of excess demand has no *direct* influence on the price index. This is indicated by the fact that no excess-demand variable nor any proxy for an excess demand appears in any one of the preferred equations. A possible exception are the EF equations in which *IOR* (industrial operating rate), which could be regarded as a proxy for excess demand, appears among the independent variables. Of course, excess demand may well have an effect on the price index, even if it has no direct

---

†It would be going too far to say that the studies agree in dismissing short-run productivity changes as completely irrelevant because the variable, $ULC - ULC^N$, appears in the preferred ST equation and in one of the (equally) preferred EF equations, and this variable can be moved by short-run productivity changes (through ULC) as well as by long-run changes.

‡Cost of materials per unit of output = Usage of materials/Output x Price of materials.

effect. For example, it could well be the case that the level of wage-earnings per man is an increasing function of the level of excess demand, in which case excess demand could help to determine the price index *via* the unit labour cost variable.

We turn now to the BD study and enquire whether the consensus which we have found in the Neild, ST and EF studies extends to this study also. The reason for proceeding in this way is that the BD preferred equations differ from those of the other three studies in having the percentage rate of increase of the price index, rather than its level, as the dependent variable.

It will be recalled that, after examining the results of the BD study, we concluded that one of the five equations tried out in the study was noticeably inferior to the rest, but that there was little to choose between the other four. Consequently, it was difficult to pick one equation or even two that could be clearly labelled 'preferred'. On the other hand, there appeared to be good reason to say that the first three equations as a group were to be preferred to the last two as a group. To the extent that this is so, the BD study is not entirely at one with the other three.

The reason for this is that the first three equations all derive from the 'rate-of-increase' equation:

$$p_t = \alpha_1 (w - o)_t + \alpha_2 m_t,$$

while this derives, in turn, from a 'level' equation of the form:[13]

$$P_t = (1 + \beta)(1 + \mu)\frac{WL}{V^c} + (1 + \beta)(1 + \mu)\gamma M.$$

Thus the 'level' equation underlying BD's first three equations is a linear relationship (β, μ and γ are all constants) with *actual* unit labour cost (WL/V^c) and the price level of imported materials (M) as independent variables. On the other hand, as we have seen, the other three studies suggest a 'level' equation in which *standard* unit labour cost and the materials price index are the decisive independent variables. Thus while the results of the BD study are broadly in line with those of the other three, there is one important point at least at which it is somewhat at odds with them.

To sum up, there is a consensus in the studies that the price-*level* equation should have as its key independent variables unit labour cost and an index of materials prices. If we assume that the 'level' equation is linear in form, this would imply a 'rate-of-increase' equation giving the rate of increase of the price index as a linear combination of: (i) the rate of increase of wage-earnings per man *less* the rate of increase of output per man; and (ii) the rate of increase of the materials price index. Beyond this point, however, the Neild, ST and EF studies are somewhat at variance with the BD study. For while the former suggest fairly strongly that the rate of increase of output per man which should appear in the 'rate-of-increase' equation is the rate of increase of *standard* output per man, the latter suggests that it is the rate of increase of *actual* output per man which is appropriate.

At all events it seems reasonable to say that the four studies we have examined in this chapter do provide us with a fairly definite picture of the sort of price equation that might feature in a model of the inflationary process that is 'worth pursuing'; in its 'rate-of-increase' form it would be an equation rather like (2.5) — the price equation of the mark-up model of Chapter 2 — with the final term put at zero† and possibly with the variable o being defined as the rate of increase of standard output per man rather than actual output per man.

†Recall that in (2.5) m denotes the rate of increase of profit margins, not the rate of increase of materials prices. The variable s in (2.5) (the rate of increase of unit non-labour cost) could be interpreted as the rate of increase of materials prices, that is as being equivalent to the m of the present chapter.

5

EMPIRICAL STUDIES OF THE WAGE EQUATION

5.1 The Phillips–Lipsey Hypothesis

In this chapter we turn from the price equation to the second of the two relationships which play a key role in contemporary models of the inflationary process – the wage equation. As in Chapter 4, our purpose will be to give an account of the more important of the empirical studies of this relationship which have been undertaken in recent years. The famous studies of Phillips and Lipsey[1] form a convenient starting-point. Phillips described the purpose of his study in the following way:

> The purpose of the present study is to see whether statistical evidence supports the hypothesis that the rate of change of money wage rates in the United Kingdom can be explained by the level of unemployment and the rate of change of unemployment, except in or immediately after those years in which there was a very rapid rise in import prices, and if so to form some quantitative estimate of the relation between unemployment and the rate of change of money wage rates.[2]

The statistical evidence which Phillips examined consisted of U.K. annual time series for the relevant variables for the years 1862–1957, and the conclusion which he reached was:

> statistical evidence . . . seems in general to support the hypothesis . . . that the rate of change of money wage rates can be explained by the level of unemployment and the rate of change of unemployment except in or immediately after those years in which there is a sufficiently rapid rise in import prices to offset the tendency for increasing productivity to reduce the cost of living.[3]

The purpose of Lipsey's paper was 'to reconsider Phillips' work in some detail'.[4] More specifically he set out to confront the same hypothesis with the same data but to do so by using standard econometric techniques in place of the somewhat crude subjective methods which Phillips had employed.† Lipsey concluded from

---

†While this was the main purpose of the Lipsey study, it was not the only one. Perhaps the most important of his secondary tasks was to construct a model that

his re-examination of Phillips's work that there 'is a significant relation between the rate of change of money wage rates on the one hand and the level of unemployment and its rate of change on the other. Over 80 per cent of the variance in money wage rates over the period 1862–1913 can be associated with these two variables', and, further, that there is 'some evidence in favour of a simple (but rather weak) relation between changes in the cost of living and changes in money wage rates'.[5] Thus, using more refined techniques, Lipsey reached essentially the same conclusions as Phillips.

The Phillips–Lipsey studies gave an extraordinarily powerful impetus to empirical studies of the wage equation, and, in the fifteen years or so since their publication, wage-equation studies, based in some way or other on them, have been undertaken for all of the leading countries of the non-Communist world, including the United Kingdom, the United States, Canada, New Zealand and several Western European countries. It is these post-Phillips studies that we shall be concerned with in the present chapter, though, of course, we shall not be attempting to cover them all.

In general these studies resemble the price-equation studies discussed in Chapter 4 in that, typically, the objective of the study is to experiment with the several different forms of the wage equation and then to select the most satisfactory form by applying the econometric criteria discussed in Section 4.1. They also resemble the price-equation studies in that, typically, the data used relate to the post-war period – usually the post-1950 period. In both these respects the wage-equation studies to be discussed here have little in common with the original Phillips–Lipsey studies. In other respects, however, their link with the work of Phillips and Lipsey is very close indeed. In the first place, in the studies to be discussed the dependent variable is invariably the percentage rate of change of some wage index, as in the original studies. Second, the list of independent variables from which the independent variables for any one equation are drawn, however extensive it may be, invariably includes the key Phillips–Lipsey variable – the level of unemployment as a percentage of the labour force or the unemployment rate – and more often than not the subsidiary Phillips–Lipsey variables – the rate of change of unemployment and the rate of change of prices – as well. Third, the studies to be discussed almost always experiment with a non-linear relationship between the rate of change of money wages and the level of unemployment of the type envisaged in the original studies. Phillips himself suggested that the relationship was likely to be of the form shown in Figure 2.1 (p. 31) for fixed values of any additional explanatory variables that might be included along with the unemployment rate. Lipsey formalised this suggestion by

---

would account for the relationship which Phillips believed he had discovered. This, in fact, has proved to be the most enduring part of Lipsey's work and we shall return to it in Chapter 6.

postulating a relationship of the form:

$$w = a + bu^{-1} + cu^{-2},\qquad(5.1)$$

where w denotes the rate of change of money wage rates, u the unemployment rate and a, b and c three constants, the first being negative and the second and third being positive.[6]†

The early post-Phillips studies were patterned very closely on the Lipsey study, and in most cases virtually repeated the Lipsey study for some other economy.[7] In particular, the early studies were concerned with what we shall call 'the straight Phillips–Lipsey relationship', by which we mean a relationship having the rate of change of some wage index as dependent variable, having as independent variables some combination of u, $\dot{u}$ and p, the three variables canvassed in the original studies, and featuring a non-linear association between the dependent variable and the unemployment rate, u. By contrast, the studies which appeared after about the mid-1960s were invariably concerned with what, henceforth, will be labelled 'the extended Phillips–Lipsey relationship', this being a relationship in which the first and third features of the straight relationship appear but in which the independent variables go beyond the three involved in the straight relationship. The first major study of the extended relationship, and one of the most influential, was that undertaken by Perry for the United States[8] and we shall devote the next section to a discussion of Perry's work.

5.2   The Level and Rate of Change of Profits: Perry

All of the equations experimented with in Perry's study have the same general form, and as this is of some interest we shall present the general relationship and explain how it was developed before discussing the individual equations in detail.

As regards the general relationship there are three points to be noted. The first concerns the *dependent* variable. In the general relationship the dependent

---

†It is easy to see that the curve of (5.1) has the same form as the curve shown in Figure 2.1. From (5.1) we obtain:

$$\frac{dw}{du} = -(bu^{-2} + 2\,cu^{-3}).$$

With b and c both positive this expression is negative for all values of u. (u is necessarily positive of course.) Furthermore it tends to zero as u tends to infinity. Thus (5.1) implies that the curve linking w and u has a negative slope at all points and that the slope decreases numerically as one moves to the right along the u axis. Finally since $(bu^{-1} + cu^{-2})$ becomes less and less positive as u increases, there must be some level of u at which this term is equal to $-a$ (recall that a is negative). At this level of u, w will be zero and for all higher values of u, w will be negative. Taking these three points together we see that the curve of (5.1) has exactly the properties of the 'Phillips curve' shown in Figure 2.1.

variable is the percentage change in the index of negotiated wage rates between quarter t and the corresponding quarter one year earlier.† Thus if we denote the *level* of the index of negotiated wage rates by W and the dependent variable in the general Perry relationship by $\tilde{w}$, the dependent variable is given by:

$$\tilde{w}_t = 100 \left(\frac{W_t - W_{t-4}}{W_{t-4}} \right). \tag{5.2}$$

The second point concerns the *independent* variables. All the independent variables take the form of an average over the four quarters up to and including quarter t. Take the unemployment rate as an example. When the unemployment rate is included as an independent variable, it appears as $\bar{u}_t$, defined by:

$$\bar{u}_t = \tfrac{1}{4}(u_t + u_{t-1} + u_{t-2} + u_{t-3}), \tag{5.3}$$

where u_t is the unemployment rate of quarter t, u_{t-1} the unemployment rate of the quarter prior to period t, and so on. The third point concerns the mathematical form of the relationship. The general relationship is a linear relationship between $\tilde{w}_t$ (defined by (5.2)) as dependent variable and the various independent variables (defined as in (5.3)).

Let us now see how this general form of wage relationship was derived. Perry's first step was to make three simplifying assumptions: (i) that each firm negotiates a new wage contract once a year; (ii) that one-quarter of all wages are renegotiated in each quarter, that is to say, that wage negotiations are spread evenly throughout the year; and (iii) that the relative size of the wage increase which is negotiated for the workers of a particular firm depends linearly on certain macro variables, $x_1, \ldots, x_m$.

Consider a firm whose wage rates are renegotiated in quarter t — call it firm i. Using assumption (iii) above, Perry argued that the percentage change in the negotiated wage rates of firm i as between quarter $t-1$ and quarter t, denoted by w_{it}^*, will be given by:

$$w_{it}^* = {}_i\gamma_0 + {}_i\gamma_1 x_{1t} + {}_i\gamma_2 x_{2t} + {}_i\gamma_m x_{mt}, \tag{5.4}$$

† By 'negotiated wage rates' we mean the wage payments per man which emerge from collective bargaining between the organisations of employers and the trade unions or the agreed minimum wage payments per man. Employers may for various reasons pay some workers more than they are obliged to do under the collective bargaining agreement, and as a result the index of average earnings (the index of actually received wage payments per man or per man-hour) may move differently from the index of negotiated wage rates. When it comes to empirical work with the wage equation, therefore, one must be careful to specify which of these two indexes is being explained by the equation and avoid ambiguous terms such as 'wage index'. We shall mostly use the full expressions, 'index of negotiated wage rates' and 'index of wage-earnings per man', to distinguish the two indexes, but where there is no possibility of confusion we shall sometimes use the shorter terms, 'index of wage rates' and 'index of wage-earnings'.

where the $_i\gamma$s are a set of constants. Now consider the firms whose wage rates are renegotiated in quarter t, *as a whole*. According to Perry the (weighted arithmetic) *average* percentage change in the negotiated wage rates of these firms, as between quarter $t-1$ and quarter t, denoted by w_t^* cant be found by applying a weight $_ik$ to each of the individual-firm expressions (5.4), and summing; it being assumed, of course, that the weights sum to unity. Thus he argues that average percentage change between quarter $t-1$ and quarter t in the negotiated wage rates of *those firms which renegotiate in quarter* t is given by:

$$w_t^* = \sum_i (_ik_iw_t^*) = \sum_i (_ik_i\gamma_0) + \left\{\sum_i (_ik_i\gamma_1)\right\} x_{1t} + \ldots + \left\{\sum_i (_ik_i\gamma_m)\right\} x_{mt},$$

or more simply by:

$$w_t^* = \gamma_0 + \gamma_1 x_{1t} + \ldots + \gamma_m x_{mt}, \tag{5.5}$$

where $\gamma_0 = \sum_i(_ik_i\gamma_0)$, $\gamma_1 = \sum_i(_ik_i\gamma_1)$, and so on. The γs are, of course, a set of constants. The average percentage change between quarter $t-1$ and quarter t in the negotiated wage rates of *all other firms* is, of course, zero. Since by assumption (ii) these constitute three-quarters of all firms, Perry concludes that the percentage change in the index of negotiated wage rates between quarter $t-1$ and quarter t will be $w_t^*/4$. By a similar argument he shows that the percentage change in the index of negotiated wage rates between quarter $t-2$ and quarter $t-1$ will be $w_{t-1}^*/4$ where w_{t-1}^* is given by:

$$w_{t-1}^* = \beta_0 + \beta_1 x_{1(t-1)} + \ldots + \beta_m x_{m(t-1)}, \tag{5.6}$$

the βs being a set of constants corresponding to the γs of (5.5). Likewise the percentage change in the index of negotiated wage rates between quarter $t-3$ and quarter $t-2$ and quarter $t-4$ and quarter $t-3$ will be $w_{t-2}^*/4$, and $w_{t-3}^*/4$, respectively, where w_{t-2}^* and w_{t-3}^* are given by (5.7) and (5.8), respectively:

$$w_{t-2}^* = \pi_0 + \pi_1 x_{1(t-2)} + \ldots + \pi_m x_{m(t-2)} \tag{5.7}$$

$$w_{t-3}^* = \delta_0 + \delta_1 x_{1(t-3)} + \ldots + \delta_m x_{m(t-3)} \tag{5.8}$$

where the πs and the δs are constants corresponding to the γs of (5.5) and the βs of (5.6).

Now the percentage change in the index of negotiated wage rates between quarter $t-4$ and quarter t (denoted by $\tilde{w}_t$) must be the sum of: (i) the percentage change between quarter $t-4$ and quarter $t-3$; (ii) the percentage change between quarter $t-3$ and quarter $t-2$; (iii) the percentage change between quarter $t-2$ and quarter t; and (iv) the percentage change between quarter $t-1$ and quarter t. Hence:

$$\tilde{w}_t = \frac{1}{4}(w_t^* + w_{t-1}^* + w_{t-2}^* + w_{t-3}^*),$$

or

$$\tilde{w}_t = \frac{(\gamma_0 + \beta_0 + \pi_0 + \delta_0)}{4} + \frac{\gamma_1 x_{1t} + \beta_1 x_{1(t-1)} + \pi_1 x_{1(t-2)} + \delta_1 x_{1(t-3)}}{4}$$

$$+ \ldots + \frac{\gamma_m x_{mt} + \beta_m x_{m(t-1)} + \pi_m x_{m(t-2)} + \delta_m x_{m(t-3)}}{4}. \tag{5.9}$$

Finally it is assumed by Perry that: $\gamma_1 = \beta_1 = \pi_1 = \delta_1$; $\gamma_2 = \beta_2 = \pi_2 = \delta_2$; and so on. If we denote the intercept in (5.9) by α_0, the common value of γ_1, β_1, π_1 and δ_1 by α_1, and so on, we can rewrite (5.9), with the help of this assumption, as:

$$\tilde{w}_t = \alpha_0 + \alpha_1 \bar{x}_{1t} + \alpha_2 \bar{x}_{2t} + \ldots + \alpha_m \bar{x}_{mt}, \tag{5.10}$$

where $\bar{x}_{1t} = \frac{1}{4}\{x_{1t} + x_{1(t-1)} + x_{1(t-2)} + x_{1(t-3)}\}$, and similarly for $\bar{x}_{2t}, \ldots, \bar{x}_{mt}$.

In (5.10) we have a general wage equation which possesses the three characteristics mentioned earlier: the dependent variable is the percentage change in the index of negotiated wage rates between quarter $t - 4$ and quarter t; the independent variables are averages over the four quarters up to and including quarter t; and finally, the dependent variable depends linearly on the independent variables.

We turn now to the individual equations experimented with in Perry's study. Subject to the qualification that in some equations one or more of the $\bar{x}$s is lagged, and one other qualification noted later, Perry's equations are all of the form (5.10). That is, they differ, one from the other, only as regards the set of $\bar{x}$s which constitute the independent variables.

The equations in question are as follows:

$$\tilde{w}_t = \alpha_0 + \alpha_1 (\bar{u}_t)^{-1} + \alpha_2 (\bar{u}_t)^{-2} \tag{5.11}$$

$$\tilde{w}_t = \alpha_0 + \alpha_1 (\bar{u}_t)^{-1} + \alpha_2 (\bar{u}_t)^{-2} + \alpha_3 \bar{p}_{t-1} \tag{5.12}$$

$$\tilde{w}_t = \alpha_0 + \alpha_1 (\bar{u}_t)^{-1} + \alpha_2 \bar{p}_{t-1} + \alpha_3 \bar{R}_{t-1} \tag{5.13}$$

$$\tilde{w}_t = \alpha_0 + \alpha_1 (\bar{u}_t)^{-1} + \alpha_2 \bar{p}_{t-1} + \alpha_3 (\bar{R}_t - \bar{R}_{t-1}) \tag{5.14}$$

$$\tilde{w}_t = \alpha_0 + \alpha_1 (\bar{u}_t)^{-1} + \alpha_2 (\bar{u}_t)^{-2} + \alpha_3 \bar{p}_{t-1} + \alpha_4 \bar{R}_{t-1} + \alpha_5 (\bar{R}_t - \bar{R}_{t-1}) \tag{5.15}$$

$$\tilde{w}_t = \alpha_0 + \alpha_1 \bar{u}_t + \alpha_2 \bar{p}_{t-1} + \alpha_3 \bar{R}_{t-1} + \alpha_4 (\bar{R}_t - \bar{R}_{t-1}) \tag{5.16}$$

$$\tilde{w}_t = \alpha_0 + \alpha_1 (\bar{u}_t)^{-1} + \alpha_2 \bar{p}_t + \alpha_3 \bar{R}_t + \alpha_4 (\bar{R}_t - \bar{R}_{t-1}) \tag{5.17}$$

In these equations u denotes the unemployment rate, p the proportional change from the preceding quarter in the price index and R the annual profit rate, while the bar at the top of a variable indicates that the variable is an average over from quarters up to and including the quarter in question.[9]†

Each of the equations listed above was estimated for the manufacturing sector as a whole from quarterly U.S. data for the years 1947 to 1960. In addition, equations (5.11), (5.12), (5.13), (5.14) and (5.17) were estimated separately for the durable and non-durable sub-sectors of the manufacturing sector. Finally, equation (5.14) was re-estimated for each of the two sub-sectors using data for the manufacturing sector as a whole for the variable $\dot{u}$, rather than the appropriate sub-sectoral data. Thus the Perry study presents five numerical versions of equation (5.14), three of each of equations (5.11), (5.12), (5.13) and (5.17), and one of each of equations (5.15) and (5.16).

Examination of these estimations in the light of the econometric criteria presented in Section 4.1 suggests that equation (5.14) is the best of the seven equations experimented with in the study. From the argument of Section 5.1 (see above, p. 94) we see that, in all the Perry equations, except equation (5.16), the *a priori* sign of the intercept is negative while those of $(\bar{u}_t)^{-1}$ and (if it appears) of $(\bar{u}_t)^{-2}$ are positive. In all five estimations of equation (5.14)[10] these *a priori* signs are confirmed. Moreover, in all five estimations the coefficients of $\bar{p}_{t-1}, \bar{R}_{t-1}$ and $\bar{R}_t - \bar{R}_{t-1}$ all have the expected (positive) signs. Thus equation (5.14) cannot be faulted on the 'signs' criterion. Nor can it be faulted on the R^2 and t-ratio criteria; all five estimations show an R^2 well in excess of 0.8 and in all five every t ratio is well in excess of 2.‡ Perry gives no information about DW except to say that the estimation of equation (5.14) for manufacturing as a whole gives a DW of 1.2. While this is on the low side, it would appear that the DW figures for the other equations are lower still.[11] In short equation (5.14) stands up very well on the signs, R^2 and t-ratio criteria and apparently does better than its competitors on the DW criterion, though it does not do well in terms of DW.

The only other equations with comparable records are equations (5.13) and (5.16). In all three estimations of equation (5.13), the *a priori* signs are confirmed throughout,[12] all t ratios are well in excess of 2 and R^2 exceeds 0.8. However, equation (5.14) is to be preferred to equation (5.13) because each of the three estimations of equation (5.13) has a significantly lower R^2 then the corresponding estimation of equation (5.14) and also because equation (5.13) appears to be inferior to equation (5.14) in terms of the DW criterion, as pointed out above. In the single estimation of equation (5.16) the *a priori* signs are confirmed throughout,¶ all t ratios are well in excess of 2 and R^2 exceeds 0.8. But the R^2 figure is substantially less than that for the corresponding estimation of equation

---

†Actually this is not strictly true of p, which is a four-quarter *sum* not a four-quarter average.

‡The t ratios are not shown by Perry but they can be derived by dividing the coefficient estimates by the figures which appear in brackets underneath.

¶In the case of equation (5.16) the *a priori* signs of the intercept and the coefficient of u_t are positive and negative, respectively. Cf. p. 63.

(5.14), and for this reason (and also because it does better in terms of DW) equation (5.14) is to be preferred.

All of the other equations are decidedly inferior to equation (5.14). Equation (5.11) falls down badly on the signs criterion, with a negative sign for $(\bar{u}_t)^{-2}$ in all three estimations and a positive sign for the intercept in one of the three, and also on the R^2 criterion with all three R^2s being less than 0.5. Equation (5.12) also falls down on the signs criterion, $(\bar{u}_t)^{-2}$ having a negative sign in all three estimations. Moreover, it performs badly on the t-ratio criterion in that four of the t ratios are less than 2. Equation (5.15) fails on both the signs and t-ratio criteria — in the single estimation of this equation, $(\bar{u}_t)^{-2}$ has the 'wrong' sign and one t ratio is only a little over one-half. Finally, equation (5.17) also falls down on the signs and t-ratio criteria, the sign of the coefficient of $\bar{R}_t - \bar{R}_{t-1}$ being negative, contrary to expectations, in two of the three estimations and two t ratios falling well short of 2.

The conclusion which emerges, then, is that of the seven wage equations experimented with in the Perry study, equation (5.14) is the preferred equation. This equation is marginally superior to two, and clearly superior to four of the remaining six equations, on the econometric criteria presented in Section 4.1.

The special feature of Perry's study which separates it from the work of Phillips and Lipsey, and which justifies our describing it at the outset as a study of 'the extended Phillips relationship', is the inclusion in the list of independent variables experimented with of $\bar{R}_t$, $\bar{R}_{t-1}$ and $(\bar{R}_t - \bar{R}_{t-1})$ — variables which were not considered in the original studies. Following the lead given by Perry, other authors have undertaken studies of the extended Phillips–Lipsey relationship in which one or more profit variables are included in the list of independent variables, along with the three original variables, u, $\dot{u}$ and p, and the reader is urged to follow these up.[13]

5.3 Price Expectations: Vanderkamp

At the beginning of the previous section we introduced the notion of the extended Phillips–Lipsey relationship — a wage equation in which the percentage rate of increase of a wage index depends non-linearly (in the Phillips manner) on the unemployment rate and in which the remaining independent variables include one or more that were not considered in the original studies. We then considered a study which qualified as a study of the extended Phillips–Lipsey relationship because of the inclusion of one or more *profit variables* among the independent variables. In the present section we shall consider another study in which 'new' independent variables are tried out, and which can therefore be regarded as a study of the extended relationship. The most interesting of the new variables in question is the *expected rate of increase of prices*. This variable, like the profit variables discussed in the preceding section, was not considered in the original studies which embraced only the unemployment rate, the rate of change of unemployment rate and the *actual* rate of increase of prices, as distinct from the expected rate.

The study to be considered is a Canadian study undertaken by Vanderkamp.[14] The dependent variable in Vanderkamp's equations is the percentage rate of increase in the index of average wage-earnings between the current quarter and the corresponding quarter a year earlier; we shall denote it by $\tilde{w}_t^a$.[15]

Altogether four distinct equations are investigated in the study. These fall into two groups of two. The first group takes the form:

$$\tilde{w}_t^a = \alpha_0 + \alpha_1 \bar{u}_t^{-1} + \alpha_2 (\bar{u}_t^{-1} - \bar{u}_{t-1}^{-1}) + \alpha_3 \bar{L}_t + \alpha_4 \bar{p}_t^e \tag{5.18}$$

$$\tilde{w}_t^a = \alpha_0 + \alpha_1 \bar{v}_t + \alpha_2 (\bar{v}_t - \bar{v}_{t-1}) + \alpha_3 \bar{L}_t + \alpha_4 \bar{p}_t^e \tag{5.19}$$

In these equations L_t denotes:

$$100 \left[\frac{O_t - O_t^{Tr}}{O_t^{Tr}} \right],$$

where O is output per person employed (in constant dollars) and O^{Tr} is the linear trend value of O. That is, L_t is the current level of output per employee expressed as a percentage deviation from its (linear) trend value.[16] Apart from L, the only variable which has not been introduced previously is v, which is the level of unfilled vacancies expressed as a percentage of the labour force. This variable is used in (5.19) in place of u^{-1}; it is a genuine alternative to u^{-1} because the vacancy rate is observed to be very highly correlated with the reciprocal of the unemployment rate wherever both variables are measured. As in the discussion of Perry's study, the bars over an independent variable indicates that the variable in question is a quarterly average — in this case a *weighted* average, over the *five* quarters from quarter $t - 4$ to quarter t inclusive.[17]

The second group of equations are identical with (5.18) and (5.19), except that they contain an additional independent variable, namely the number of quarters in the four years (sixteen quarters) preceding quarter t in which the rate of increase of prices exceeded 2 per cent.

If we consider the list of independent variables used in the four equations just described, we see that it includes the three original variables — the unemployment (or vacancy) rate, the (absolute) rate of change in the unemployment (or vacancy) rate and the (past) rate of price increase, the latter taking the special form of the number of quarters in the preceding four years in which a price increase of more than 2 per cent was observed. We also see, however, that the list contains two independent variables which were not covered in the original studies. These are the expected rate of price increase (mentioned previously) and the per cent deviation of labour productivity from trend. It has been observed that recorded labour productivity falls in the recession phase and rises in the boom phase. This being so, the productivity variable included in the four Vanderkamp equations is likely to be highly correlated with profits, and can be regarded as performing much the same role in these equations as that performed by the profit variables in the equations of the Perry study.

We next consider the *a priori* signs of the intercepts and coefficients in Vanderkamp's equations. This will assist us when we come to examine the numerical versions of these equations from the standpoint of our four econometric criteria.

Take (5.18) to begin with. As noted on a number of previous occasions, we would expect the intercept in this equation to be negative and the coefficient of u^{-1} to be positive, these being the signs that are required to produce a wage-earnings/unemployment curve of the Phillips type. The expected sign of the variable $u_t^{-1} - u_{t-1}^{-1}$ is positive since $\tilde{w}^a$ will be higher, *ceteris paribus*, the more rapidly unemployment is falling, that is the higher is $u_t^{-1} - u_{t-1}^{-1}$.† Since the productivity variable L is highly correlated with profits, and since $\tilde{w}^a$ will be higher, *ceteris paribus*, the higher is profits, we would expect the coefficient of L to have a positive sign. The same is true, of course, of the price-expectations variable, p^e.

Turn now to (5.19). Here again we would expect α_1 to be positive and the intercept, α_0, to be negative. The reason for expecting α_1 to be positive is clear enough – the higher the vacancy rate the stronger the pressure of demand in the labour market and the stronger the pressure of demand in the labour market the higher, *ceteris paribus*, ought the rate of increase of money wages to be. The reason for expecting α_0 to be negative is that, otherwise, the implication would be that, no matter how low the vacancy rate, money wages would always be rising ($\tilde{w}^a$ always positive), which does not seem reasonable. That is, we need a negative intercept in (5.19) to guarantee that money wages will fall if the vacancy rate is sufficiently low, just as we need a negative intercept in (5.18) to guarantee that money wages will fall if the unemployment rate is sufficiently high.‡ As for the remaining coefficients, the *a priori* sign of α_2 is positive because the more rapidly vacancies are increasing, the higher, *ceteris paribus*, ought the rate of increase of money wages to be, while the *a priori* signs of α_3 and α_4 are positive for the same reasons as those which apply in the case of (5.18).

As mentioned previously, the third of Vanderkamp's four equations is identical with (5.18) except that an additional explanatory variable (the number of quarters in the preceding four years in which the inflation rate has exceeded 2 per cent) is added. Similarly, the fourth equation is identical with (5.19) except for the addition of this explanatory variable. It follows that to deal with the question

---

†To see that high values of $u_t^{-1} - u_{t-1}^{-1}$ correspond to rapidly falling unemployment, it is only necessary to write it as

$$\frac{u_{t-1} - u_t}{u_t u_{t-1}}.$$

‡Cf. footnote on p. 94 above where it is shown that this is indeed, the function of the negative intercept in (5.18).

of *a priori* signs for the third and fourth equations we have only to specify the expected sign of the coefficient of this new explanatory variable. The expected sign is positive, that is, *ceteris paribus*, we would expect the rate of increase of money wages to be higher the more common the experience of inflation rates in excess of some prescribed level in the immediate past.

Our next task is to apply the econometric criteria outlined in Section 4.1 to the estimated versions of Vanderkamp's four equations. Before undertaking this task, however, there is one preliminary point which we must consider. It will be evident that, to estimate his equations, Vanderkamp required, among other information, a time series for the variable p^e. Now, broadly speaking, there are two ways of obtaining such a series. One is to observe the variable in the same way as other variables such as $\tilde{w}^a$ and u. The other is to set up an expectations-formation equation and use this, in association with a time series for p (that is the *actual* rate of increase of prices), to generate an artificial series for p^e. Vanderkamp chose the second of these two approaches and proceeded to generate two distinct artificial p^e series, each corresponding to a particular expectations-formation equation. The first series was generated by using an expectations-formation equation of the form:

$$p_t^e = \lambda p_t + (1 - \lambda)p_{t-1}^e, \qquad (5.20)$$

with a value of λ of 0.7.† The second series was generated by using an expectations-formation equation of the form:

$$p_t^e = 12/42p_t + 10/42p_{t-1} + 8/42p_{t-2} + 6/42p_{t-3} + 4/42p_{t-4} + 2/42p_{t-5}.$$
$$(5.21)$$

That is, the observation on p^e for quarter t was taken to be a weighted arithmetic average‡ of the observations on p for quarter t and the five preceding quarters.¶

---

†It will be observed that (5.20) is identical with (3.8) except that p_t replaces p_{t-1} on the right-hand side. Accordingly the way in which (5.20) was used to generate a p^e series will be clear from a reading of pp. 58–9 above.

‡Note that the weights sum to unity.

¶(5.21) gives p_t^e as a weighted arithmetic average of the current, and a *finite* number of past values of p, in which the weights decline *linearly*. By contrast (5.20) gives p_t^e as a weighted arithmetic average of the current, and an *infinite* number of past, values of p, in which the weights decline *geometrically*. That this is the case can be seen by the following argument:

$$p_t^e = (1 - \lambda)p_t + \lambda p_{t-1}^e.$$

Therefore,

$$\lambda p_{t-1}^e = (1 - \lambda)\lambda p_{t-1} + \lambda^2 p_{t-2}^e.$$

Therefore,

$$p_t^e = (1 - \lambda)p_t + (1 - \lambda)\lambda p_{t-1} + \lambda^2 p_{t-2}^e.$$

Having generated these two distinct p^e series, Vanderkamp estimated each of his four equations twice – once using the p^e series generated by (5.20) and once using the p^e series generated by (5.21). There are therefore eight numerical equations to be looked at from the familiar econometric standpoint.†

Examination of these numerical equations shows that all signs are correct except for the intercept, which is positive in all cases, and that all DW are acceptable. The four equations must be weeded out, therefore, on the basis of the t-ratio and R^2 criteria. As regards the first, there are only two estimated equations which have acceptable t ratios throughout,‡ and one of these has a slightly higher R^2 than the other. The equation in question is:¶

$$\tilde{w}_t^a = 0.761 + 1.655\bar{v}_t + 5.653(\bar{v}_t - \bar{v}_{t-1}) + 0.319\bar{L}_t + 0.651p_t^e + 0.099Z_t,$$

where Z denotes the number of quarters in the sixteen quarters prior to quarter t in which the rate of inflation has exceeded 2 per cent. The equation which

---

But

$$\lambda^2 p_{t-2}^e = (1 - \lambda)\lambda^2 p_{t-2} + \lambda^3 p_{t-3}^e.$$

Therefore,

$$p_t^e = (1 - \lambda)p_t + (1 - \lambda)\lambda p_{t-1} + (1 - \lambda)\lambda^2 p_{t-2} + \lambda^3 p_{t-3}^e.$$

Continuing in this way we find:

$$p_t^e = (1 - \lambda)p_t + (1 - \lambda)\lambda p_{t-1} + (1 - \lambda)\lambda^2 p_{t-2} + \ldots + (1 - \lambda)\lambda^i p_{t-i}$$
$$+ \lambda^{i+1} p_{t-(i+1)}^e$$

As $i \to \infty$ the final term $\to 0$, since $0 < \lambda < 1$.

Hence (5.20) implies:

$$p_t^e = \sum_{i=0}^{\infty} (1 - \lambda)\lambda^i p_{t-i}.$$

Now

$$\sum_{i=0}^{\infty} (1 - \lambda)\lambda^i = \frac{(1 - \lambda)}{(1 - \lambda)} = 1.$$

Hence (5.20) gives p_t^e as a weighted arithmetic average of the current, and an infinite number of past, values of p in which the weights decline geometrically.

†See Vanderkamp's tables II A and III A. We shall ignore the eight numerical equations presented in Tables II and III because Vanderkamp obviously regards these as having been superseded by the equations in Tables II A and III A.

‡The figures in brackets in tables II A and III A are the denominators of the t ratios, cf. the last sentence on p. 67 in Vanderkamp's article.

¶This is the equation designated by 3A.1 in table III A. Like all Vanderkamp's equations it has been estimated from quarterly Canadian data.

emerges as preferred equation is, then, an equation of the form:

$$\tilde{w}_t^a = \alpha_0 + \alpha_1 \bar{v}_t + \alpha_2 (\bar{v}_t - \bar{v}_{t-1}) + \alpha_3 \bar{L}_t + \alpha_4 p_t^e + \alpha_5 Z_t. \qquad (5.22)$$

5.4   Trade-Union Militancy: Hines

All of the wage relationships which have been explored in the studies dealt with so far have one striking common characteristic, namely that they make no explicit reference to trade-union activity. At first sight this appears to be a serious weakness. One of the main objectives of the trade unions is to see that the money wages of their members advance as rapidly as possible. Furthermore, there is no denying that the power of the unions to achieve this, and other objectives, is immense. Surely, then, variations in trade-union 'pushfulness' must play a major part in determining variations in the rate of increase of money wages and should not be ignored in framing an equation which is designed to explain these variations.

The authors of the wage equations dealt with in earlier sections would not disagree with this view. In defence of their efforts, however, they would say that trade-union influence has *not* been overlooked despite the fact that it does not appear in their equations. To support this claim they would argue that, in framing a wage equation, one can either introduce the *immediate* determinants of the rate of increase of money wages (the degree of trade-union pressure and the degree of employer resistance to that pressure) as the independent variables or one can go behind these immediate determinants and introduce the variables which ultimately govern the degree of trade-union pressure and the degree of employer resistance – variables such as the extent of excess demand in the labour market, as represented by the unemployment percentage, the rate of price increase in the immediate past, the expected rate of price increase, the level of profits and productivity, and so on. It is the second alternative, they would say, which has been chosen. Thus it is not the case that trade-union influence on the rate of increase of money wages has been ignored. Rather it has been 'taken care of' by the independent variables already included.

Some investigators of the money wage relationship are not convinced by this defence. While admitting that the unemployment rate, the past rate of price increase, and so on, may play a considerable part in determining the degree of trade-union pressure for money wage increases, they are not willing to accept that it is completely, or even largely, determined by these variables, and hence are not easily assured that including them as independent variables really does take care of variations in union pushfulness. For this reason they believe it desirable to include trade-union influence explicitly, that is to experiment with an independent variable which represents, so to speak, the residual element of trade-union pushfulness – the element that cannot be explained in terms of the unemployment percentage, and so on.

Perhaps the foremost protagonist of this point of view is Hines, who has undertaken several empirical studies of the money wage equation in which it is clearly expressed. In this section we shall consider the most comprehensive of these studies,[18] which, like all of Hines's work, is based on annual U.K. data.

A notable feature of Hines's study is that it is disaggregated in the sense that the competing wage equations are framed and estimated not for a single comprehensive industry aggregate (manufacturing industry for example), as in most of the other studies considered so far, but for each of twelve individual industries, including the primary industries and some tertiary industries as well as the usual manufacturing industries.

To assist in presenting the competing equations – there are six of them – we shall refer to a typical industry in the list of twelve as industry i. Where we wish to indicate that a particular variable relates to industry i we shall insert a subscript i before the time subscript. Thus, for example, w_{it} will be used to denote the percentage rate of increase in the index of negotiated wage rates for industry i between the last period and the current period. On the other hand, to indicate that a variable refers to the industry aggregate to which the twelve individual industries belong, we shall insert a subscript A before the time subscript. Thus p_{At} will denote the percentage rate of increase of the price index for the industry aggregate between the last period and the current period. Using these notational devices, the six equations which Hines tries out for each of the twelve industries can be presented as follows:

$$w_{it} = \alpha_0 + \alpha_1 u_{it} + \alpha_2 \pi_{it} + \alpha_3 z_{it} \tag{5.23}$$

$$w_{it} = \alpha_0 + \alpha_1 u_{it} + \alpha_2 z_{it} \tag{5.24}$$

$$w_{it} = \alpha_0 + \alpha_1 u_{it} + \alpha_2 w_{jt} + \alpha_3 z_{it} \tag{5.25}$$

$$w_{it} = \alpha_0 + \alpha_1 u_{it} + \alpha_2 p_{At} + \alpha_3 z_{it} \tag{5.26}$$

$$w_{it} = \alpha_0 + \alpha_1 u_{it} + \alpha_2 p_{At} + \alpha_3 w_{jt} + \alpha_4 z_{it} \tag{5.27}$$

$$w_{it} = \alpha_0 + \alpha_1 p_{At} + \alpha_2 z_{it} \tag{5.28}$$

In these expressions w_i denotes the percentage rate of increase in the index of negotiated wage rates in industry i, u_i the unemployment percentage in industry i, π_i the ratio between aggregate profits in industry i and aggregate wages and salaries, z_i the percentage rate of increase in the ratio of union members to labour force (membership ratio) in the ith industry, p_A the percentage rate of increase in the price index relating to the industry aggregate and w_j the percentage rate of increase in the index of negotiated wage rates in the 'leading' industry, that is the industry which traditionally 'sets the pace' as regards money wage increases.

Several features of these relationships are worth noticing. To begin with, Hines's dependent variable is a percentage rate of increase *between the last period and the current period*. Second, one of the independent variables of the original Phillips–Lipsey relationship (the unemployment rate, u) appears in all five relationships and another (the rate of increase of prices) in three of the five. Third, the unemployment rate enters linearly whereas in the other studies considered so far it enters linearly in terms of the reciprocal. Fourth, the list of independent variables experimented with contains three that were not considered in the original Phillips—Lipsey studies, namely the profit variable π, the trade-union variable z and the leading-industry variable w_j. Thus Hines's study is clearly a study of the extended Phillips—Lipsey relationship as we have defined that term.† Finally, the trade-union variable z is introduced to represent the residual element of trade-union pushfulness (see above, p. 104). The ideal variable for this purpose would be 'the degree of trade-union militancy'. But since the degree of militancy is not measurable, some 'proxy variable' that is some measurable variable which is highly correlated with degree of militancy) must be used instead. Hines's choice for the role of proxy is z, the percentage rate of change in the membership ratio. This variable is measurable and is likely to be highly correlated with the degree of militancy since, when they are in a militant mood, 'unions increase their membership as a proportion of the labour force, i.e. they run successful membership campaigns'.[19] Moreover, the determinants of z do not include the other independent variables in Hines's relationships.[20] This is essential because otherwise z would be little more than a repetition of these variables, and hence would not capture the residual trade-union influence, as it is meant to do.

We turn now to the econometric assessment of Hines's relationships. As already indicated, all six were estimated for each of twelve U.K. industries using annual data. Thus altogether there are seventy-two numerical relationships to be considered. Hines does not present these numerical relationships but he does give the t ratio, R^2 and DW associated with each[21] so that all four of our econometric criteria can be applied. ‡ In the case of three of the twelve industries (industries 3, 5 and 7), all four relationships perform so badly in terms of these criteria that one can hardly talk of a 'preferred relationship' for these industries — the preferred relationship is to be thought of as the best of a set of good performers not the least bad of a set of bad performers. In the case of the remaining nine industries, the preferred relationship is fairly easy to identify. Let us take them in turn.

For industry 1 the preferred relationship is (5.28). The numerical version of this relationship has the right signs¶ for both estimated coefficients, has both t ratios in excess of 2 and has a DW of 2.18. Econometrically, the only unsatisfactory feature is a comparatively low R^2 (0.603). Each of the other five

---

†This is subject to the qualification that the relationship between the rate of wage increase and unemployment is linear whereas in the extended Phillips—Lipsey relationship, as we have defined it, the relationship is non-linear.

‡The signs criterion can be applied so long as the t ratios are known since the t ratio associated with a particular independent variable always has the same sign as the estimated coefficient of that variable.

¶In all relationships the *a priori* sign of u_i is negative (cf. the discussion of p. 63 above) while that of all other variables is evidently positive.

relationships is neither better nor worse as regards R^2, and in addition is unsatisfactory as regards signs and/or t ratios and/or DW.

Relationship (5.23) is the preferred relationship for industry 2. Again the only deficiency is a too low R^2 (only 0.642). Some of the other relationships show a significantly higher R^2 but all of these are decidedly inferior on one or more of the other three criteria.

In the case of industry 4 relationship (5.28) is satisfactory on all counts. Both signs are right, the t ratios are 6.07 and 9.21, respectively, R^2 is 0.865 and DW is 1.84. The only other relationship which is wholly satisfactory is (5.24); but since the two t ratios are a good deal smaller, and R^2 is slightly smaller for this relationship than for (5.28), the latter must be regarded as the preferred relationship for this industry.

Relationship (5.28) is satisfactory in all respects for industry 6 also. Moreover, in this case it is the only relationship which is so. Thus (5.28) is the obvious candidate for the preferred equation in the case of industry 6.

The same is true of industry 8. The position here is that (5.28) is satisfactory in all respects except that R^2 is only 0.646. However, none of the other relationships is noticeably better in this respect, and all are decidedly worse from the point of view of the signs and t-ratio criteria.

Relationship (5.28) is the obvious choice for industry 9 also. As in the case of industry 6, (5.28) satisfies all four criteria and is the only relationship which does so.

For industry 10, (5.26) appears to be the best performer. This relationship fails on the t-ratio criterion since one of the t ratios is only 1.01. However, all of the other relationships have at least one unacceptable t ratio; and the only one with a comparable R^2, namely (5.27), has three.

Relationship (5.26) is the preferred relationship for industry 11 also, though in this case the choice is not quite so clear-cut. None of the relationships, including (5.26), meets the t-ratio criterion. But (5.26) stands out on the other three criteria, being the only relationship to meet all three, and hence deserves the top ranking.

Finally, (5.28) again emerges as the preferred relationship for industry 12, being the only relationship which is satisfactory in all respects.

To sum up, of the nine industries for which a preferred equation can be identified, six have (5.28) as preferred relationship, two have (5.26) and one has (5.23).

5.5   Unemployment Dispersion: Archibald

In the last three sections we have dealt with three empirical studies of the extended Phillips–Lipsey relationship, this being a wage equation which exhibits the 'original' non-linear dependence of the rate of wage increase on the unemployment percentage but in which one or more 'new' independent variables appear. In the first of the three studies in question, a profit variable appeared as the new independent variable, in the second a price-expectation variable and in the third a variable designed to act as a proxy for trade-union pushfulness. We come now to a fourth and final study of the extended relationship in which the new independent variables comprise one or more 'dispersion' variables. The precise character of these variables will be explained at a later stage but they may be defined broadly as variables which attempt to capture the influence on the rate of increase of money wages, not of changes in the over-all unemployment rate, but of changes in the extent to which the unemployment rates of individual labour markets are scattered around the over-all unemployment rate.

The study to be considered is a study undertaken some five years ago by Archibald.[22] We begin by listing the equations tried out in Archibald's study.† They are:

$$w_t = \alpha_0 + \alpha_1 u_t^{-1} + \alpha_2 p_t + \alpha_3 \dot{u}_t \tag{5.29}$$

$$w_t = \alpha_0 + \alpha_1 u_t^{-1} + \alpha_2 p_t + \alpha_3 \sigma_t^2 \tag{5.30}$$

$$w_t = \alpha_0 + \alpha_1 u_t^{-1} + \alpha_2 p_t + \alpha_3 \sigma_t^2 + \alpha_4 D_t \tag{5.31}$$

$$w_t = \alpha_0 + \alpha_1 u_t^{-1} + \alpha_2 p_t + \alpha_3 \sigma_t^2 + \alpha_4 \gamma_t \tag{5.32}$$

$$w_t = \alpha_0 + \alpha_1 u_t^{-1} + \alpha_2 p_t + \alpha_3 \dot{u}_t + \alpha_4 \sigma_t^2 \tag{5.33}$$

$$w_t = \alpha_0 + \alpha_1 u_t^{-1} + \alpha_2 p_t + \alpha_3 \dot{u}_t + \alpha_4 \sigma_t^2 + \alpha_5 \gamma_t \tag{5.34}$$

The only new symbols in these six relationships are σ^2, γ and D. The variable σ^2 is Archibald's dispersion variable. It is defined by:

$$\sigma_t^2 = \sum_{i=1}^{n} \alpha_{it}(u_{it} - u_t)^2,$$

where n denotes the number of labour markets, α_i the proportion of the total labour force to be found in market i, and u_i the unemployment rate in that market. Thus σ^2 is just a weighted arithmetic average of the squared deviations of the individual unemployment rates from the over-all unemployment rate, and so measures the degree of dispersion of the individual unemployment rates around the over-all figure.

Turn now to γ. This variable is defined by:

$$\gamma_t = \frac{\sum_{i=1}^{n} \alpha_{it}(u_{it} - u_t)^3}{\left[\sum_{i=1}^{n} \alpha_{it}(u_{it} - u_t)^2 \right]^{3/2}}.$$

†We refer to the equations tested against U.K. data and shown in numerical form in tables 2 and 4 of Archibald's study, pp. 129–30. The slightly different equations which were tried out on U.S. data will not be discussed.

Recalling that a familiar measure of the degree of skewness in a frequency distribution is $m_3/(m_2)^{3/2}$, where m_3 and m_2 are, respectively, the third and second moments of the distribution, we see that while σ^2 measures the degree of *dispersion* in the distribution of the individual unemployment rates around the over-all rate, γ measures the degree of *skewness* in that distribution.

Finally, we have the variable D. As the symbol suggests, this is a 'dummy variable' – a variable introduced into a relationship to enable estimation to proceed satisfactorily despite some known deficiency in the data on which estimation is to be based.† Thus D is a 'trick' variable with statistical significance but with no economic significance whatsoever.

It will be observed that the dependent variable in Archibald's equations is identical to that used by Hines, that is it is the rate of increase between the last period and the current period in the index of negotiated wage rates.‡ It will be noticed, too, that (5.29) is a 'straight' Phillips–Lipsey relationship – only the three original independent variables appear in this equation. By contrast, the other five are to be regarded as extended relationships since in each case the independent variables comprise not only the original variables but one or more new variables as well. In particular, the dispersion variable σ^2 appears as an independent variable in all five equations.

Our next task is to examine the numerical versions of (5.29)–(5.34) from the standpoint of our four econometric criteria with a view to selecting a preferred equation. Before embarking on this task, however, we shall consider the *a priori* sign of the coefficient of the dispersion variable – we are already familiar, of course, with the *a priori* signs of the intercept and the coefficient of u^{-1}, $\dot{u}$ and p.

The *a priori* sign of the coefficients of the dispersion variable is usually taken to be positive, that is it is usually assumed that a reduction in the dispersion variable will lead to a reduction in the rate of increase of money wages, given that u and all other independent variables are held fixed. This particular sign specification can be justified along the following lines.

Let us suppose that there are two labour markets only. Designate them market 1 and market 2. Denote the unemployment rate in market 1 by u_1. Thus u_1 is the number of unemployed persons in market 1 as a percentage of the labour force in market 1. Similarly denote the unemployment rate in market 2 by u_2. Let the values of u_1 and u_2 in the initial situation be, respectively, u_{10} and u_{20}, as shown in Figure 5.1. Suppose, further, that the total labour force is split evenly between the two markets. Then, in Figure 5.1, the over-all unemployment rate in

---

†The interested reader can find details of the particular data deficiency leading to the use of a dummy variable in this case in Archibald's study, p. 128.

‡The dependent variable and all rates of change included among the independent variables are expressed in the 'first central difference' form.

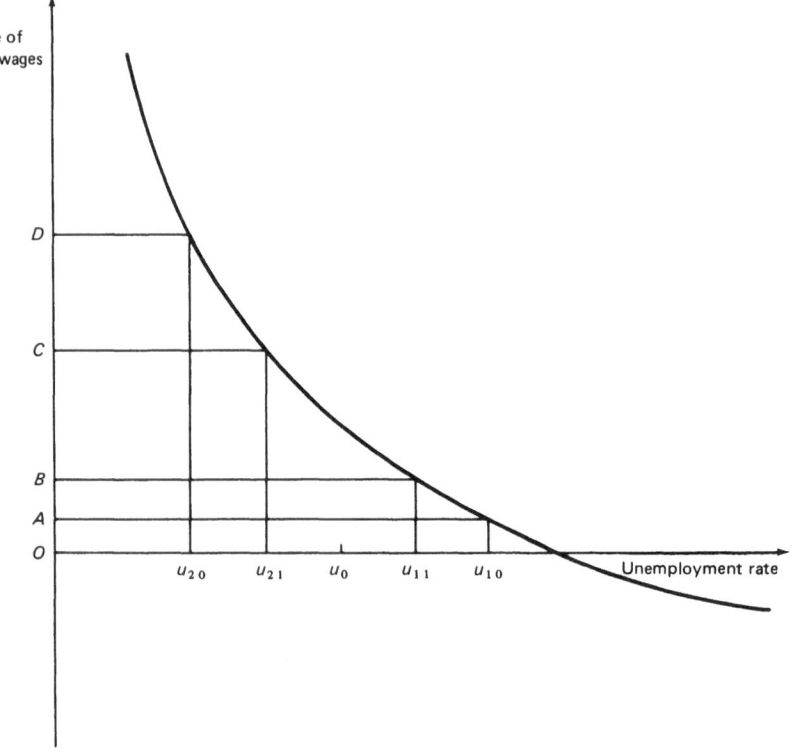

Fig. 5.1

the initial situation (u_0) will lie midway between u_{20} and u_{10}.† As a final simplication, assume that the wage equations in the two markets are identical and of the form:

$$w_{it} = \alpha_0 + \alpha_1 u_{it}^{-1} + K_t, \qquad i = 1, 2$$

where K denotes some linear combination of 'national' variables, that is variables,

---

†Using obvious abbreviations we can say that:

$$u = \frac{\text{total unemployment}}{\text{total labour force}} = \frac{\text{unemployment in 1} + \text{unemployment in 2}}{\text{total labour force}}$$

$$= \frac{(u_1 \times \text{labour force in 1}) + (u_2 \times \text{labour face in 2})}{\text{total labour force}} = \tfrac{1}{2}(u_1 + u_2).$$

Hence:

$$u_1 - u = u_1 - \tfrac{1}{2}u_1 - \tfrac{1}{2}u_2 = \tfrac{1}{2}u_1 - \tfrac{1}{2}u_2 = \tfrac{1}{2}u_1 + \tfrac{1}{2}u_2 - \tfrac{1}{2}u_2 - \tfrac{1}{2}u_2 = u - u_2.$$

That is, u is half-way between u_1 and u_2.

such as the rate of change in the aggregate price index, which always assume an identical value in both wage equations. This common wage equation is represented by the downward-sloping 'Phillips' curve in Figure 5.1, for fixed values of the variables entering into K.

Let us now take Figure 5.1 and reduce the dispersion of the two individual unemployment rates around the over-all unemployment rate while holding the over-all rate fixed at u_0. This procedure will enable us to use the diagram to deduce the direction of change in the over-all rate of wage increase consequent on a reduction in dispersion, for a *given* value of the over-all unemployment rate and for given values of all the other independent variables in the over-all wage equation, that is those entering into K. This, of course, is what we are trying to discover.

To reduce the dispersion of the individual unemployment rates while holding the over-all unemployment rate fixed, we must shift u_1 to the left – say to u_{11} – and u_2 an equal distance to the right – say to u_{21}.† Evidently the *reduction* in the rate of wage increase in market 1, conequent on this reduction in dispersion, is larger than the *increase* in the rate of wage increase in market 2, the former being DC and the latter AB.

Finally, if we define the 'over-all rate of wage increase' so that it is consistent with the 'over-all unemployment rate' (that is as a weighted arithmetic average of the rates of increase in the two individual markets with labour-force proportions as weights),‡ we have:

$$w_t = \tfrac{1}{2}(w_{1t} + w_{2t}),$$

where w is the over-all rate of wage increase and w_1 and w_2, respectively, the rates of increase in market 1 and market 2. From this expression it is clear that if, as shown, the reduction in w_1 consequent on the decrease in dispersion is greater than the increase in w_2, the result of the decrease in dispersion must be a decrease in w, the over-all rate of wage increase.

The above, then, is the argument normally used to support the view that a reduction in the dispersion variable, all other independent variables in the macro wage equation being held fixed, will lead to a reduction in the rate of increase of

---

†Since $u = \tfrac{1}{2}(u_1 + u_2)$ (see previous footnote) we have:

$$u_1 - u_0 = \tfrac{1}{2}[(u_{11} + u_{21}) - (u_{10} + u_{20})].$$

Putting $u_1 - u_0 = 0$ in this expression we obtain:

$$u_{11} + u_{21} = u_{10} + u_{20}.$$

Therefore

$$u_{21} - u_{20} = u_{10} - u_{11}.$$

Thus if u is to remain fixed, the increase in u_2 must be equal to the decrease in u_1.

‡See footnote on p. 110 where it is shown that $u = \tfrac{1}{2}u_1 + \tfrac{1}{2}u_2$.

money wages, that is to support an *a priori* sign specification of positive for the dispersion variable. Having dealt with this point, we can now turn to the task of assessing Archibald's six equations by application of our four econometric criteria.

The Archibald study makes use of two different series for the dispersion variable, σ^2. In constructing the first of these two series, Archibald takes the n individual labour markets, in terms of which σ^2 is defined (see above, p. 108), to be geographical regions, while in constructing the second he takes the n individual labour markets to be industrial groupings. Each of the equations in which σ^2 appears as an independent variable is then estimated twice – once using the geographical series for σ^2 and once using the industrial series. Thus (5.29) is estimated once, and each of the other five equations twice. Annual U.K. data for the post-war period are used in all estimations.

Examination of these numerical equations shows that equation (5.29) is not a serious contender since in the single estimation of this equation the intercept has the wrong sign (positive instead of negative), three of the four t ratios are less than 2, $\bar{R}^2$ is only 0.64 and DW is only 1.16, that is the equation fails on all four criteria. Of the remaining five equations, (5.30) is clearly the best on the t-ratio criterion. In the first (geographical) estimation of this equation none of the t ratios is less than 2, whereas there is at least one unacceptable t ratio in the first estimation of each of the rest. In the second (industrial) estimation of (5.30) there is one unacceptable t ratio but there are at least two in the remaining second estimations. As well as standing out on the t-ratio criterion, (5.30) is unexceptionable on the signs criterion. The dispersion variable has the required (positive) sign in both estimations and all other signs are likewise correct throughout. The $\bar{R}^2$ values for (5.30) are 0.78 for the first estimation and 0.71 in the second. While these figures are on the low side, the highest $\bar{R}^2$ in the first estimations of (5.30)–(5.34) is only 0.81 and the highest for the second estimations only 0.76, so that none of the equations (5.31)–(5.34) is clearly superior to (5.30) on the $\bar{R}^2$ criterion. As for DW, none of the equations are satisfactory on this criterion, the highest DW for the first estimations being only 1.53 and the highest for the second being only 1.62. Taking the criteria as a whole, then, it seems clear that (5.30) is the preferred equation for the Archibald study.

5.6   Consensus of the Studies

In the preceding sections of this chapter we discussed several recent empirical studies of the wage equation in which certain simple econometric criteria were applied to the numerical versions of a set of competing wage equations with the object of selecting the best, or preferred, equation. We must now try to define the area of agreement which emerges from these studies. Hopefully, this will be substantial enough to permit us to specify the main features, if not the detail, of a satisfactory wage equation. The price-equation studies examined in Chapter 4 contributed a fairly clear picture of a satisfactory *price* equation. If we can now obtain a similarly clear picture from our wage-equation studies we shall have the main ingredients of a potentially successful model of the inflationary process – a model which promises to perform well under test in the sense of generating testable predictions which square up well with known facts.

We shall begin our search for the consensus of the studies by listing the preferred equations which have emerged. These are as follows:

Perry

$$\tilde{w}_t = \alpha_0 + \alpha_1 (\bar{u}_t)^{-1} + \alpha_2 \bar{p}_{t-1} + \alpha_3 \bar{R}_{t-1} + \alpha_4 (\bar{R}_t - \bar{R}_{t-1}).$$

Vanderkamp

$$\tilde{w}_t^a = \alpha_0 + \alpha_1 \bar{v}_t + \alpha_2 (\bar{v}_t - \bar{v}_{t-1}) + \alpha_3 \bar{L}_t + \alpha_4 p_t^e + \alpha_5 Z_t.$$

Hines

$$w_{it} = \alpha_0 + \alpha_1 p_{At} + \alpha_2 z_{it}. \qquad \text{(six industries)}$$

$$w_{it} = \alpha_0 + \alpha_1 u_{it} + \alpha_2 p_{At} + \alpha_3 z_{it}. \qquad \text{(two industries)}$$

$$w_{it} = \alpha_0 + \alpha_1 u_{it} + \alpha_2 \pi_{it} + \alpha_3 z_{it}. \qquad \text{(one industry)}$$

Archibald

$$w_t = \alpha_0 + \alpha_1 u_t^{-1} + \alpha_2 p_t + \alpha_3 \sigma_t^2.$$

Examination of these preferred equations reveals a wide area of agreement on the general shape of the post-war wage equation. In the first place, the studies are virtually unanimous in their support of the unemployment rate as a key determinant of the rate of increase of money wages; the only one of the preferred equations which does not contain the unemployment rate (or its equivalent, the vacancy rate) as an independent variable is the first of the three Hines equations.

Second, there is a consensus that the dependence of the rate of increase of money wages on the unemployment rate is of the particular non-linear form depicted by the Phillips curve of Figure 2.1 (p. 31). It will be seen that a non-linear dependence of this type is incorporated in every one of the preferred equations listed above except that of Hines.†

Third, there is universal agreement that the rate of increase of money wages cannot be satisfactorily explained by the unemployment rate alone; in every preferred equation at least one independent variable appears in addition to the unemployment rate.

Fourth, there is unanimity of view that one of the 'supporting' explanatory variables must be a price variable – either the *actual* rate of increase of prices or

†Since the vacancy rate is highly correlated with the reciprocal of the unemployment rate, the linear term in $\bar{v}_t$ in the Vanderkamp equation can be regarded as being equivalent to a linear term in the reciprocal of the unemployment rate such as appears in several of the other preferred equations.

the *expected* rate of increase of prices. It will be noted that one or other of these variables appears in every one of the preferred equations.

Finally, there is agreement that the list of supporting explanatory variables extends beyond the two suggested in the original Phillips–Lipsey studies, that is the rate of increase of the unemployment rate and the current, or past rate of increase of prices. All of the preferred equations are extended Phillips–Lipsey relationships in the sense that they incorporate independent variables other than those envisaged by Phillips and Lipsey in their seminal studies.

Here, then, is the consensus of the studies examined in this chapter; evidently it is quite substantial. There appear to be only two matters of any importance on which the studies are not at one. One of these relates to the dependent variable in the wage equation. In three of the preferred equations, the dependent variable is the rate of increase of negotiated wage rates, while in the fourth it is the rate of increase of wage-earnings per man which is explained by the relationship. The other matter on which unanimity has not yet been reached concerns the independent variables which are needed to support the unemployment rate. As we have seen, there is complete agreement that a price variable (actual or expected) is needed and that this variable will not do the job on its own; but there is little agreement as to what other variables should be included. The strongest candidates for inclusion are: some form of profit variable, the dispersion of unemployment rates (in combination with the over-all unemployment rate) and trade-union pushfulness.

To sum up, one can say that these points of disagreement notwithstanding, the wage-equation studies discussed in the present chapter have gone a long way towards clarifying the wage-equation element of a worthwhile model of the inflationary process — worthwhile in the sense of promising good test performance. It is a relationship in which either the rate of increase of negotiated wage rates or the rate of increase of wage-earnings per man appears as the dependent variable (one cannot be more definite than this) and .in which two of the independent variables are the unemployment rate and either the actual rate of price increase or the expected rate of price increase. Further, the unemployment rate enters the relationship non-linearly — in a manner that will produce a Phillips curve. Finally, the unemployment rate and the price variable are not the only independent variables in the relationship, though what the others are cannot be stated with any certainty.

Thus the wage equation of a worthwhile model of the inflationary process could look like equation (2.6) (the wage equation of the mark-up model) after certain additional independent variables had been included. Alternatively it could take the form:

$$w_t^a = \alpha_0 + \alpha_1 u_t^{-1} + \alpha_2 p_t^e + \beta_1 x_{1\,t} + \ldots + \beta_m x_{m\,t}, \qquad (5.35)$$

where $x_1, \ldots, x_m$ are various 'supporting' independent variables which remain to be specified. Other wage equations which would meet the broad requirement laid down in the preceding paragraph could, of course, be suggested.

6

MICROECONOMIC FOUNDATIONS OF THE PHILLIPS RELATIONSHIP

6.1 Reasons for Investigating the Micro Foundations

Suppose that, having developed a certain macroeconomic relationship, we were then to try it out against possible rivals, using econometric criteria of the type applied throughout the two preceding chapters as sorting-out devices. Suppose further that our relationship proved to be an excellent performer, in econometric terms, for many different economies and for many different periods of time. Finally, let us say that, having deduced the testable implications of the relationship (or of some wider system of relationships of which it formed a part) we found that it performed well under test, again for different economies and different periods of time. Would we then know all that we needed to know about the relationship and be justified in saying that further research was unnecessary? The answer is 'No' because as well as knowing that a macro relationship exists we need to know *why* it exists, that is what are the more basic, less aggregative relationships which combine to produce it. An investigation of this latter question typically involves an analysis in terms of individual decision-making units — households and firms — and for this reason is often described as an investigation of the microeconomic foundations of the macro relationship in question. Using this terminology, then, we can sum up the position by saying that we need to know something about the microeconomic foundations of a macro relationship before we can be satisfied that there is nothing of importance still to be learned about the relationship.

There are at least four reasons why it is desirable to know something about the micro foundations of a macro relationship. In the first place, until we have satisfied ourselves that the relationship is indeed the logical consequence of particular micro (less aggregative) relationships, we cannot be fully confident that it really does exist, an impressive econometric and test performance notwithstanding. Second, a knowledge of the micro foundations of the relationship will help us to understand the sources of shifts in the relationship and will indicate the types of action that will be required to *produce* shifts of particular kinds should we wish to do so. A third reason for investigating the micro foundations of a macro relationship is that the knowledge gained is likely to help in devising appropriate tests of the relationship. Finally, knowledge of the micro foundations of a macro relationship may enable us to improve the formulation of the relationship.

At the end of Chapter 4 we outlined a macro price equation whose existence has been fairly well established, we believe, by the empirical studies reviewed in that chapter. Similarly at the end of Chapter 5 we presented an outline of a Phillips-type macro wage equation, believing its existence to be clear beyond reasonable doubt from the long line of empirical studies initiated by the original studies of Phillips and Lipsey. The argument of the previous paragraphs suggests that we should not be content now to let the matter rest. Having satisfied ourselves that a price equation and a wage equation of the general forms outlined do, indeed, exist, we should press on to find out *why* they exist.

Some discussion of the micro foundations of the price equation has been presented already in Section 2.3, and we do not propose to add to that discussion in the present chapter. On the other hand, further discussion of the theoretical basis of the wage equation is called for, both because this matter has been extensively investigated in recent years, and also because most of the important work has been done independently of empirical study of the wage equation and so has not been touched on already in Chapter 5. To this further discussion we now turn.

6.2   The Contribution of Phillips and Lipsey

In their original studies both Phillips and Lipsey were primarily concerned with the question of the existence of a wage equation of the type outlined at the end of the previous chapter and only incidentally with its theoretical foundations. Nevertheless, both (and especially Lipsey) had something to say on the latter question, and, as their contributions set the direction for future work for several years, it is appropriate to take them as our starting-point.

Phillips's remarks on the question of the micro foundations of a Phillips-type, macro wage equation were sketchy but nevertheless extremely stimulating. They are contained in the following passage:[1]

> When the demand for a commodity or service is high relatively to the supply of it we expect the price to rise, the rate of rise being greater the greater the excess demand. Conversely when the demand is low relatively to the supply we expect the price to fall, the rate of fall being greater the greater the deficiency of demand. It seems plausible that this principle should operate as one of the factors determining the rate of change of money wage rates, which are the price of labour services. When the demand for labour is high and there are very few unemployed we should expect employers to bid wage rates up quite rapidly, each firm and each industry being continually tempted to offer a little

above the prevailing rates to attract the most suitable labour from other firms and industries. On the other hand it appears the workers are reluctant to offer their services at less than the prevailing rates when the demand for labour is low and unemployment is high so that wage rates fall only very slowly. The relation between unemployment and the rate of change of wage rates is therefore likely to be highly non-linear.

Lipsey's analysis of the problem of the micro foundations of the macro wage equation was a good deal more detailed and rigorous than that of Phillips. His first and main contribution was to provide a theoretical foundation for a wage–unemployment relationship of the Phillips-curve type at the level of the individual labour market.

To this end, he took up the key idea in the passage just quoted from Phillips's paper, namely:

> When the demand for a commodity or service is high relatively to the supply of it we expect the price to rise, the rate of rise being greater the greater the excess demand. . . . It seems plausible that this principle should operate as one of the factors determining the rate of change of money wage rates, which are the price of labour services.

This idea Lipsey formalised as follows:

$$w_{it} = \gamma x_{it}, \tag{6.1}$$

where, as before, w_i is the percentage rate of increase from the previous period in the level of money wage rates in the ith labour market, x_i is the excess demand for labour in the ith market, expressed as a percentage of the supply of labour to that market (relative excess demand) and γ is some positive constant. The implication of (6.1) is that money wages will remain constant in the ith market when the relative excess demand for labour in that market is zero ($w_{it} = 0$ when $x_{it} = 0$), will rise when excess demand is positive ($w_{it} > 0$ when $x_{it} > 0$, since $\gamma > 0$) and will fall when excess demand is negative ($w_{it} < 0$ when $x_{it} < 0$). Moreover, the rate of increase of money wages in the ith market will be greater the more positive is excess demand in that market and the rate of decrease greater the more negative is excess demand.

Lipsey's next step was to consider the relationship between u_i and x_i, that is between the unemployment rate in the ith market and the relative excess demand for labour in that market. This part of his argument can be conveniently presented in terms of Figure 6.1.

Suppose that x_i is zero. This means that there are just enough jobs available for all those who are prepared to work at the going wage rate. Hence if there were no frictions of any sort in the market, that is if an unemployed worker could be matched with an unfilled vacancy the instant he became unemployed, $x_i = 0$ would imply $u_i = 0$. In fact, however, frictions exist – it takes time for an unemployed worker to find a suitable vacancy even if there is no shortage of

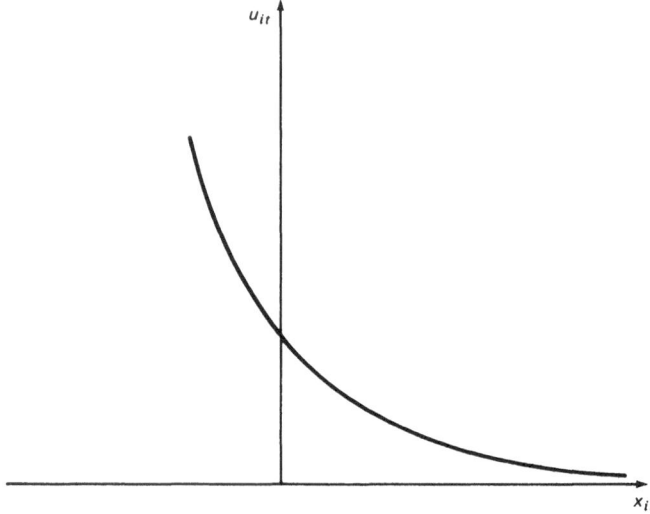

Fig. 6.1

vacancies. Consequently u_i will be *positive* when $x_i = 0$; in terms of Figure 6.1 the curve of u_{it} against x_{it} will cut the vertical axis above the origin.

When excess demand is positive there are more than enough jobs available for those who are prepared to work at the going wage. It is to be expected, therefore, that as excess demand becomes more and more positive (as the surplus of jobs increases) the average time taken to move between jobs will decline. Hence u_i will decline as x_i becomes increasingly positive. However, u_i will remain positive (there will be *some* frictional unemployment) however large x_i becomes. Accordingly, to the right of the vertical axis the curve u_{it} against x_{it} will have the form shown in Figure 6.1.

On the other hand, when excess demand is negative there are less than enough jobs available, and hence it is to be expected that the average time taken to move between jobs will increase as x_i becomes more and more negative (as the shortage of jobs grows). Thus to the left of the vertical axis the curve of u_{it} against x_{it} will rise steadily as shown in Figure 6.1.

Figure 6.1 shows the curve of u_{it} against x_{it}. The curve of x_{it} against u_{it} can be obtained in the following way. Take hold of the page on which Figure 6.1 appears at the bottom left-hand corner and turn the page through $90°$ in a clockwise direction. Then take hold of the page by the left-hand edge and turn it over. The curve which then shows through the page will be the curve of x_{it} against u_{it}. Evidently it takes the form of the unbroken curve which appears in Figure 6.2.

The final step in Lipsey's argument was to combine the first step, represented by equation (6.1), with the second, represented by the unbroken curve of Figure

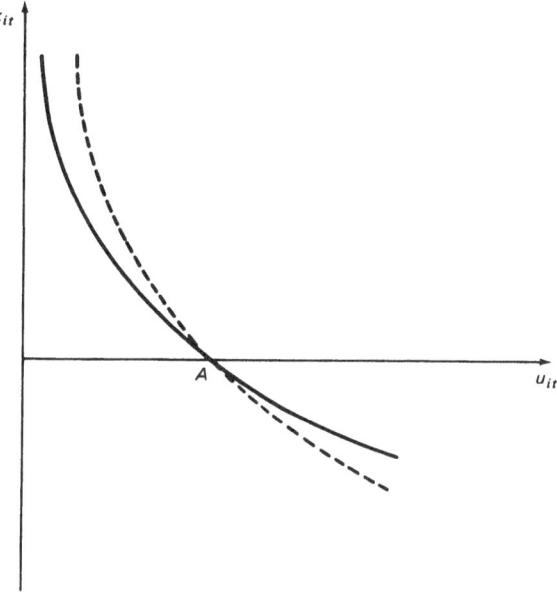

Fig. 6.2

6.2. Suppose that we wish to draw the curve of w_{it} against u_{it}. From equation (6.1) we know that we can do so by taking the curve of x_{it} against u_{it} and applying a constant positive factor to every ordinate of that curve. So to obtain the curve of w_{it} against u_{it} we have merely to take the unbroken curve of Figure 6.2, raise it at all points to the left of A by some fixed proportion and lower it to the right of A by this same fixed proportion. Evidently we shall finish up with a curve resembling the broken curve shown in Figure 6.2, that is we shall finish up with a Phillips curve.

According to Lipsey, then, a wage—unemployment relationship of the Phillips-curve type will exist at the level of the individual labour market because of the existence of two more basic relationships – a wage—excess-demand relationship of the form given by equation (6.1) and an excess-demand—unemployment relationship of the form given by the unbroken curve of Figure 6.2.

The above analysis represents a significant contribution to the problem in hand – the problem of deriving the micro foundations of a macro wage equation of the type thrown up by the empirical studies reviewed in Chapter 5. But it is by no means the last word. For one thing, the analysis is confined to the individual labour market. It has not been shown that the existence of a wage—unemployment relationship of the Phillips-curve type in each individual labour market implies the existence of a macro wage equation of the type revealed by the empirical studies.† And as well as being incomplete, the analysis is faulty in at least one important respect. As we have seen, in deriving the relationship between u_{it} and x_{it}, Lipsey argues that u_i will decline as x_i becomes increasingly positive because the average time taken to move between jobs will decline as x_i becomes increasingly positive. While this is no doubt true, it is also probably true that the number of people moving from one job to another in search of advancement will *increase* as x_i becomes increasingly positive. If this is so we cannot say with any certainty that u_i will decline as x_i increases because we have no reason to think that the first effect of increasing x_i (the one stressed by Lipsey) will more than offset the second (opposite) effect which Lipsey neglects.‡[2]

6.3   The New Microeconomics

In recent years the problem of the microeconomic foundations of a Phillips-type macro wage equation has been investigated afresh by the proponents of the so-called New Microeconomics and we shall discuss two of their more important contributions in Sections 6.4 and 6.5. In this section we shall prepare the way by explaining the special characteristics of the New Microeconomics — what it is that makes it 'new' — and then relating the new work, which is best regarded as a direct application of the New Microeconomics, to the older, better-known and more traditional work discussed in the preceding section.

The New Microeconomics is not 'new' in the sense that it studies new problems — the New Microeconomics is concerned, like the old, with 'the age-old problems of economic analysis: What are optimal prices, wages, employment, output, and so forth.'[3] Nor is it 'new' in the sense that it employs unfamiliar analytical techniques. Its 'newness' lies rather in the special character of its assumptions.

In what way do these differ from the assumptions of the more traditional microeconomics of the textbooks? Again, the question is best answered negatively in the first instance. The New Microeconomics does not differ from the old in rejecting the all-pervading assumption of rationality; firms are profit, or net worth maximisers and householders are utility-maximisers every bit as much in the New Microeconomics as they are in the old. As Phelps, one of the leading architects of

† In fairness to Lipsey, it should be said that he was well aware of this point and, moreover, that he presented a preliminary discussion of the aggregation question which has formed the basis for most later work of a more rigorous kind, for example that of Thomas and Stoney mentioned in the preceding chapter. See Lipsey's study, pp. 17–19.

‡ Again, it must be pointed out that Lipsey was well aware of the second effect. However, he was not able to accommodate it within the framework of his analysis.

the new development, puts it: 'The theory ... sticks doggedly to the neoclassical postulates of lifetime expected utility maximization and net worth maximization.'[4] The essential difference between the new and the old as regards assumptions lies in an altogether different direction. Phelps states the difference in the following way: 'The theoretical departure that is common to this *otherwise neoclassical* analysis is the removal of the Walrasian postulate of complete information.'[5] Nordhaus uses similar language: 'the "new" theory accepts the neoclassical analysis except the assumption of perfect and costless information structure.'[6]

The following passage from Nordhaus is also illuminating:

The Walrasian paradigm which is usually the starting point for most microeconomic reasoning assumes that products are homogeneous and that all economic agents have full information about both the quality and price of relevant goods ... there are no costs of obtaining information about characteristics of goods or about states of the world .... Under conditions of uncertainty, markets are imperfect, reliable information is costly and the economic agent has a quite different task. It is now possible that he will spend a good deal of his time engaged in searching for goods that suit his tastes, determining the cost and characteristics of products, and hedging himself against risks that he cannot market.

It is instructive to consider 'information' as an additional commodity. Especially where goods are heterogeneous, indivisible, infrequently purchased, or immovable, it costs real resources to gather information about the different dimensions of a good. This information is an intermediate good since it does not yield satisfaction directly. There are several consequences of this added complication. Often, workers will decide to spend time searching for a better job ('unemployment'), goods will wait for potential customers ('inventories'), and in certain cases specialists in information ('brokers') will help facilitate transactions.

This passage elaborates the two shorter passages quoted above in a helpful way. Phelps is being too negative, perhaps, when he refers to the characteristic feature of the 'new' analysis as the 'removal of the Walrasian postulate of complete information'. There is rather more to it than that. What gives the New Microeconomics its special flavour is not merely that the model-builder dispenses with the perfect-information assumption — but rather that, having done so, he typically goes on to construct a set of relationships which clearly reflects the imperfection and costliness of information and which incorporates its consequences (such things as are mentioned by Nordhaus) into the analysis in an essential way.

As mentioned earlier, the next two sections will contain a discussion of two important recent contributions to inflation theory in which the New Microeconomics is applied to the problem with which this chapter is concerned — the problem of the microeconomic foundations of Phillips-type macro wage equation.

Before presenting this work, however, it may be helpful to explain its relationship to the work on this problem in Section 6.2.

The new work which we are about to discuss differs from the 'old' in two main ways. In the first place, the micro foundations which are finally revealed are much more truly 'microeconomic' in the case of the new work than in the case of work in the Phillips–Lipsey vein. In the latter, the analysis rarely digs deeper than the individual labour market; in the former it gets right down to the individual firm and the individual supplier of labour. In the second place, as will be expected from our earlier discussion of the hallmark of the New Microeconomics, there is a great deal more emphasis on information deficiencies and information costs in the new work than there is in the old. Such considerations are not entirely neglected in analysis of the Phillips–Lipsey type but they are not given a central position as they are in the analysis of the New Microeconomists.

6.4   Application of the New Microeconomics: Phelps

In this section we give an account of an important contribution by Phelps in which he applies the tools of the New Microeconomics to the problem of the present chapter.[7]

Like the analysis of Section 6.2 Phelps's analysis is directed towards establishing certain basic relationships which are then put together to yield a macro wage equation with the required properties. The basic relationships in question are three in number. They are: (i) a relationship which explains the *average desired wage differential* (the 'wage-differential relationship'); (ii) a relationship which explains *the absolute rate of change of aggregate employment* (the 'employment-change relationship'); and (iii) a relationship which explains the *percentage rate of change of average money wage rates* (the 'wage-change relationship'). We shall now present these three relationships and briefly explain how each is derived. We shall then show that, together, the relationships do indeed imply a macro wage equation of the required type.

The three relationships are:

Wage-differential relationship

$$\Delta^* = m(u, v) \tag{6.2}$$

Employment-change relationship

$$z = f(u, v) \tag{6.3}$$

Wage-change relationship

$$w = \lambda\Delta^* + \Pi \tag{6.4}$$

Here Δ^* denotes the average desired wage differential (a concept which will be explained in a moment), z the absolute rate of change in employment per unit of the labour force, w the proportional rate of change of the *actual* money wage rate, u the unemployment rate, v the vacancy rate, Π an autonomous component of the proportional rate of change of the *expected* money wage rate, λ a constant satisfying the requirement $0 < \lambda < 1$, and f and m 'function of'.

The above set of three relationships is thought of as determining Δ^*, z and w on the basis of given values for u, v and Π.

To develop his *wage-differential relationship* Phelps starts with a typical firm — the ith firm. At any instant of time this firm will have a certain desired (optimal) money wage rate which we denote by W_i^*. The firm will also have some expectation regarding the average money wage rate that will be paid by other firms. We denote this by W_i^e. Then the firm's *desired wage differential* at time t is given by:

$$\Delta_i^* = \frac{W_i^* - W_i^e}{W_i^e} \, .$$

That is, the desired wage differential of firm i at instant t is the excess of the money wage rate which it desires to pay over the average money wage rate which it expects other firms to pay, as a proportion of the latter. Δ_i^* can, of course, be either positive or negative.

To simplify the analysis, Phelps assumes that all firms have the same expectation of the future wage level. This makes it unnecessary to attach a 'firm i' subscript to the variable W^e and so enables us to write the definition of the desired wage differential more simply as:

$$\Delta_i^* = \frac{W_i^* - W^e}{W^e} \, . \tag{6.5}$$

Phelps argues that one of the main determinants of Δ_i^* will be V_i, the size of the firm's stock of vacancies. More specifically, he argues that Δ_i^* will vary directly with V_i since the larger the firm's stock of vacancies the more likely it is to increase its wage differential as a means of retaining its present employees and attracting new workers from other firms.

A second determinant of Δ_i^* will be the number of unemployed in the economy as a whole. It is argued that Δ_i^* will vary inversely with the number of unemployed. There are two reasons for this. In the first place, since unemployed workers are able to 'sample' wage opportunities more intensively than employed workers,[†] the higher is the number of unemployed workers, the larger will be the number of workers who will contact firm i with a view to obtaining employment, and hence the lower the wage differential that it will need to maintain to reduce

---

†The notion of the sampling of wage and employment opportunities by suppliers of labour is one which presupposes that information relating to these opportunities is both incomplete and costly to obtain. Thus it is a characteristic notion of the New Microeconomics: cf. Section 6.3.

V_i to an acceptable level. Second, the higher is the number of unemployed the longer is the time that workers already employed by firm i will expect to have to spend in the unemployment pool if they leave in search of a better job,† and hence the smaller the probability that they will actually do so. But the smaller the probability of quitting, the smaller the wage differential that will be required to keep quitting at a level which is acceptable, having regard to the figure desired for V_i.

It is argued that the number of vacancies in the economy as a whole will be a third determinant of Δ_i^*. In this case the association will be a direct one because the higher is the over-all vacancy level, the larger will be the number of job openings facing potential quitters from firm i, and hence the shorter the time they will expect to have to spend in the unemployment pool if they actually do quit to look for a better job. But the less the discouragement to quitting in the shape of transitional unemployment, the higher will the wage differential need to be to keep it to an acceptable level.

If we denote the labour force (labour supply) at time t by L and use u and v to denote the unemployment rate and the vacancy rate, respectively, as in earlier chapters, we can sum up the argument of the preceding paragraphs by means of the following:

$$\Delta_i^* = f(V_i, uL, vL) \qquad \frac{\partial \Delta_i^*}{\partial V_i} > 0; \frac{\partial \Delta_i^*}{\partial (uL)} < 0; \frac{\partial \Delta_i^*}{\partial (vL)} > 0. \qquad (6.6)$$

The wage-differential relationship (6.2) is the macro counterpart of the micro relationship (6.6). Corresponding to Δ_i^* and V_i we have Δ^*, the average desired wage differential of all firms and vL, the total stock of vacancies, respectively. The other two explanatory variables in (6.6), being macro variables, appear in the same form in the aggregate relationship. Hence the aggregate relationship corresponding to (6.6) is one which has Δ^* as the left-hand variable and uL and vL as the two right-hand variables.‡ Thus we have:

$$\Delta^* = \phi(uL, vL), \qquad (6.7)$$

where ϕ denotes 'function of'.

Finally, it is assumed that L is a given constant.[8] This means that uL is a function of u only and that vL is a function of v only. This means, in turn, that Δ^* can be written as a function of u and v alone, say:

$$\Delta^* = m(u, v), \qquad (6.8)$$

which is the wage-differential relationship.

---

†'Search unemployment' is another characteristic concept of the New Microeconomics in the sense that it presupposes imperfect information.

‡We need only two right-hand variables in the aggregate relationship, of course, because the aggregate counterpart of V_i is vL and we do not want the variable vL to appear twice.

Turn now to the *employment-change relationship*. Phelps's starting point for the development of this relationship is a macro identity which states that the absolute change in aggregate employment per unit of time is equal to R minus the sum of D and Q, where R is the total number of persons hired from the unemployment pool per unit of time, D is the total number of persons departing from the labour force per unit of time, and Q is the number of persons quitting employment to search for a new job, per unit of time. Dividing this expression through by L we get an identity in z, namely:

$$z = R/L - D/L - Q/L. \tag{6.9}$$

Phelps's next step is to lay down relationships governing R, D and Q. These are:

$$R = \phi(U, V, L) \tag{6.10}$$

$$D = \delta N \tag{6.11}$$

$$Q = \psi(U, V, L) \tag{6.12}$$

Here U and V denote, respectively, the *number* of unemployed persons and the number of vacancies, δ is a constant and ϕ and ψ denote 'function of'.

Next it is assumed that the functions ϕ and ψ are homogeneous of degree one, in which case (6.10) and (6.12) imply:

$$R/L = g(U/L, V/L) = g(u, v) \tag{6.13}$$

and

$$Q/L = h(U/L, V/L) = h(u, v). \tag{6.14}$$

where g and h denote 'function of'. Also (6.11) implies:

$$D/L = \delta(N/L) = \delta\{(L - U)/L\} = \delta(1 - U/L) = \delta(1 - u). \tag{6.15}$$

Finally, (6.13), (6.14) and (6.15) are substituted into (6.9) to obtain:

$$z = g(u, v) - \delta(1 - u) - h(u, v) = f(u,v), \tag{6.16}$$

which is the employment-change relationship.

This brings us to the third and final relationship — the *wage-change relationship*. The starting point for the development of this relationship is the same as for the wage-differential relationship, namely the desired wage differential of the ith firm, denoted by Δ_i^*. To this is added the related concept of the *actual* wage differential, defined by:

$$\Delta_i = \frac{W_i - W^e}{W^e}, \tag{6.17}$$

where Δ_i is the actual wage differential, W_i is the actual wage rate of firm i and W^e is the expectation of the wage rate (assumed to be held in common by all firms).†

It is now assumed that the actual wage differential is adjusted towards the desired wage differential by means of a so-called 'partial-adjustment' mechanism, that is to say, that the change per unit of time in Δ_i is some positive fraction (say μ_i) of Δ_i^* *minus* Δ_i — the excess of the desired over the actual wage differential. Using this assumption and the expression defining Δ_i^* and Δ_i, Phelps derives the following expression for w_i the proportional rate of increase in the actual wage of firm i:

$$w_i = \mu_i \left(\frac{\Delta_i^* - \Delta_i}{1 + \Delta_i} \right) + w^e, \qquad (6.18)$$

where w^e is the proportional rate of increase in the *expected* wage. (We omit the details of this derivation, which are complicated.) Assuming that the adjustment coefficient, μ_i, is the same for all firms, we can say that the macro counterpart of (6.18) is:

$$w = \mu \left(\frac{\Delta^* - \Delta}{1 + \Delta} \right) + w^e, \qquad (6.19)$$

where μ is the common value of the μ_i.

The final major assumption which is used in the development of the wage-change relationship relates to the process by which W^e is revised. This may be stated symbolically as follows:

$$w^e = \lambda \left(\frac{W - W^e}{W^e} \right) + \Pi, \qquad (6.20)$$

where λ is a constant satisfying the requirement $0 < \lambda < 1$, and Π is an exogenous variable (datum) which assumes only positive values. According to this relationship the proportional rate of change in the expected wage rate at time t consists of two components: (i) a component (Π) which is autonomous or exogenous, in the sense that it is not influenced in any way by what actually happens to money wage rates; and (ii) a component, $\lambda (W - W^e/W^e)$ which is induced, that is which reflects actual wage-rate behaviour.

Now reference to (6.17) shows that the bracketed expression on the right-hand side of (6.20) is simply Δ. Hence (6.20) may be written as:

$$w^e = \lambda \Delta + \Pi. \qquad (6.21)$$

---

†Phelps refers to $(W_i - W^e)/W^e$ as the 'expected wage differential' (p. 141 of his study), and denotes it by Δ_i^e. However, since the only difference between this magnitude and the *desired* wage differential is that the *actual* wage rate replaces the desired wage rate, the term 'actual wage differential' appears to be more appropriate.

Substituting this expression in (6.19) we obtain:

$$w = \mu \left(\frac{\Delta^* - \Delta}{1 + \Delta} \right) + \lambda \Delta + \Pi. \tag{6.22}$$

Finally (6.22) is approximated by:

$$w = \lambda \Delta^* + \Pi. \tag{6.23}$$

The approximation is likely to be a good one if μ is close to λ (recall that they are both positive fractions) and if Δ is small.

As indicated at the outset of our discussion of his work, Phelps's ultimate purpose is to derive a possible micro foundation for the macro wage equation which recent empirical wage-equation studies have shown to exist — the equation outlined at the end of Chapter 5. He achieves this purpose by showing that the three relationships just discussed together imply a macro wage equation with the required properties when certain restrictions which he imposes on the wage-differential and employment-change relationships are taken into account. We shall now consider this final stage of Phelps's analysis.

The first step is to note that the employment-change relationship can be 'twisted round' to show v as a single-valued function of u and z:

$$v = \psi(u, z), \tag{6.24}$$

where ψ denotes 'function of'. This is possible because one of the restrictions imposed on the employment-change relationship is to the effect that, with u fixed, z *rises continuously with* v. Thus with u fixed there is one, and only one, v value associated with any given z value. Moreover, this is true whatever value is alloted to u. Hence for *any* given u value and *any* given z value there is one, and only one, v value, which amounts to saying that v can be regarded as a single-valued function of u and z as stated in (6.24).

The next step is to replace the variable v in the wage-differential relationship by $\psi(u, z)$, using (6.24). In this way the first two of Phelps's three relationships are reduced to one as follows:

$$\Delta^* = m[u, \psi(u, z)], \tag{6.25}$$

which says that Δ^* is a function of u and v where v is a function of u and z.

Finally, substituting the expression given for Δ^* by (6.25) into the wage-change relationship we obtain:

$$w = \lambda m[u, \psi(u, z)] + \Pi. \tag{6.26}$$

Since λ is a constant, (6.26) effectively gives w as a function of u, z and Π. Thus the three basic relationships can be combined to give the following:

$$w = f(u, z, \Pi), \tag{6.27}$$

which says that the proportional rate of change in the average wage rate is some function of the unemployment rate, with the absolute rate of change of employment per member of the labour force and the (autonomous) proportional rate of change in the expected wage rate as additional independent variables.

It is clear without further analysis that in (6.27) we have a macro wage equation which possesses several of the features that we require. In the first place, the unemployment rate appears as an independent variable. But, second, it is not the only independent variable — z and Π appear as well. Third, one of the supporting independent variables is effectively, if not actually, a price variable. We refer to Π, which is likely to be a close substitute for p^e, the expected rate of increase of prices.† Finally, the equation is an extended Phillips—Lipsey relationship since the list of independent variables includes the employment variable z, which was not one of the independent variables contemplated by Phillips and Lipsey in their original studies.

However, it is not clear without further analysis that (6.27) possesses the special 'Phillips-curve' properties, that is it is not immediately obvious that, given z and Π, w will fall continuously as u increases and that the decline in w per one-point fall in u is smaller the larger is u. Nevertheless it can be shown by a fairly complicated mathematical argument, which we shall not reproduce, that (6.27) does indeed possess these further properties, provided the restrictions imposed on (6.2) and (6.3) apply.

6.5   Application of the New Microeconomics: Holt

In the present section we shall present yet another rationalisation of the Phillips-type macro wage equation outlined at the end of Chapter 5, using ideas developed by Holt.[9] As we shall see, Holt's work, like Phelps's, is a direct application of the New Microeconomics in the sense that it highlights job search and other manifestations of imperfect information in the labour market.

Holt's broad strategy is the same as that of Phillips—Lipsey and Phelps. That is, his approach is to develop certain basic relationships and then fit them together to produce a macro wage equation with the required properties. The most important of these basic relationships is one which determines the percentage rate of increase in average money wage rates in the absence of trade-union influence on money wages, and we shall begin by considering the development of this relationship. We

---

†Taking (2.9) as our price equation we find that the expected rate of price increase is equal to the expected rate of increase of money wage rates per man *less* the expected rate of increase of output per man. We shall probably not go far wrong if we take the latter to be constant. In this case w^e, the expected rate of increase of money wage rates per man, will vary closely with p^e, and hence can be regarded as a good proxy for p^e. Further, provided the constant λ in (6.23) is close to zero, Π will vary closely with w^e, and hence can be regarded as a close substitute for w^e and, in turn, for p^e.

shall then consider the way in which Holt adds to the relationship in question to take care of the hitherto neglected trade-union influence and finally show how he demonstrates that the full set of relationships does indeed imply a macro wage equation of the required type.

The key relationship referred to in the previous paragraph is itself a combination of three subsidiary relationships. These are (i) a relationship which explains the percentage rate of increase at time t in the money wage rates of workers who become unemployed at that time; (ii) a relationship which explains the percentage rate of increase at time t in the money wage rates of workers who change jobs subsequent to time t without intervening unemployment; (iii) a relationship which explains the percentage rate of increase at time t in the money wage rates of all other workers, that is those who neither become unemployed nor subsequently change jobs. We shall discuss each of these three relationships in turn.

Relationship (i) relies heavily on the notion of the 'wage aspiration level of the unemployed worker'. Consider a worker who joins the unemployed pool at time t, either voluntarily, to look for a better job, or because he is laid off. Let his wage at the end of his last job (at time t) be $W_i(t)$ where the i subscript indicates that we are talking about an individual unemployed worker, and the t in parenthesis, that we are talking about time t. At time t this worker will begin searching for a new job and will have in mind a particular minimum wage that he would be prepared to accept. We call this particular wage his *wage-aspiration level* at time t. Presumably, the wage-aspiration level at time t will be closely related to $W_i(t)$ since this is the most recently experienced wage. We say that:

$$W_i^*(t) = a_i \times W_i(t), \tag{6.28}$$

where $W_i^*(t)$ is the wage-aspiration level at time t and a_i is a constant. We assume that a_i is not less than unity, that is to say, that the worker in question will hope, initially, to secure a new job offering a wage at least as high as his last one.

The end of the unemployment period can be designated time $t + T$, where T is any positive number of time units. For example, if time is measured in days, $t + T$ would be $t + 1/24$ if the worker is unemployed for one hour, $t + 1$ if he is unemployed for one day and $t + 7$ if he is unemployed for one week. Designate the wage-aspiration level at time $t + T$ by $W_i^*(t + T)$. How will $W_i^*(t + T)$, the wage-aspiration level which applies at the end of the unemployment period, be related to $W_i^*(t)$, the wage-aspiration level which applies at the beginning?

On the one hand, we would expect the wage-aspiration level to rise in proportion to the general level of money wages. Thus, if the general level of money wages rises by 5 per cent between time t and time $t + T$, we would expect the wage-aspiration level to be 5 per cent higher at time $t + T$ than it was initially, *ceteris paribus*. However, this is not the whole story. One would also expect to find the wage-aspiration level falling steadily as T increases, that is as the period of unemployment increases, *ceteris paribus*. There are three main reasons for this which are well stated by Holt[10] as follows:

> With the passage of time unemployed, we expect that the aspiration level would fall for several reasons:
>
>   a. Initially the aspiration level is set high to protect the worker from the risk of selling himself short by accepting the first job that comes along — unless it is a very good one. Then, as knowledge accumulates about the universe being sampled, the aspiration level is lowered.
>
>   b. When the search starts, the better job opportunities are explored first, and the aspiration level is gradually lowered as the search turns toward less attractive occupations, firms, and locations.
>
>   c. Finally, the penalties of continued searching rise with the exhaustion of financial and psychic resources and this tends to lower aspirations. With family capital reduced, income is increasingly attractive.

To incorporate these two considerations, Holt modifies (6.28) as follows:

$$W_i^*(t + T) = a_i \times W_i(t) \times \frac{W(t + T)}{W(t)} \times e^{-d_i T}, \tag{6.29}$$

where W is the index of money wage rates and d_i is a positive constant. This relationship implies that there is a constant percentage rate of decline in the wage-aspiration level of $(100 d_i)$ per cent per time period, throughout the unemployment period, given that the general level of money wages remains constant.

Relationship (6.29) determines the wage-aspiration level at time $t + T$, the end of the unemployment period. The wage which is offered, and accepted, at time $t + T$ cannot be less than the wage-aspiration level because, by definition, the wage-aspiration level is the *minimum* wage that the worker is prepared to accept. A simple relationship which embodies this restriction is:

$$W_i(t + T) = b_i \times W_{(t+T)}^*, \tag{6.30}$$

where $W_i(t + T)$ is the wage actually offered at time $t + T$ and b_i is a constant satisfying the restriction $b_i \geqslant 1$.

To complete the development, Holt assumes that the percentage rate of increase in the general level of money wage rates remains constant over the period $t + T$, that is:

$$\frac{W(t + T)}{W(t)} = e^{\hat{w}(t)T}, \tag{6.31}$$

where $\hat{w}(t)$ is the proportional rate of increase in the general level of money wage rates at time t in the absence of trade-union influence.

From (6.29), (6.30) and (6.31), Holt derives the following relationship to explain the percentage rate of increase at time t in the money wage rates of workers who become unemployed at that time:†

$$\text{Rate of wage increase for all unemployed workers} = \{\hat{w}(t) - d\} + \frac{\ln ab}{T}, \tag{6.32}$$

where d, a and b are constants found by taking the average over all unemployed workers of the d_i, a_i and b_i, and T is now to be regarded as the average length of unemployment experienced by workers who join the unemployment force at time t. ‡

We turn now to the second of the three relationships which Holt combines in order to explain the percentage rate of increase in average money wage rates in the absence of trade-union influence (see above, p. 129). This is a relationship which determines the percentage rate of increase at time t in the wage rates of workers who change jobs at some time after time t, without suffering unemployment in the process.

Consider a particular worker who commences a job at time t and who changes to a better job subsequent to time t. We designate the point of time at which the job change occurs as time $t + T'$, where T' is any positive number of time units. The starting wage on the original job, that is the wage at time t, we denote by $W_j(t)$ and the starting wage on the new job by $W_j(t + T')$. Holt makes the reasonable assumption that the wage advance secured by the change of jobs will be larger the longer the time period involved, that is the larger is T'. Specifically, he assumes that:

$$\frac{W_j(t + T')}{W_j(t)} = e^{c_j T'}, \tag{6.33}$$

where c_j is a constant. From (6.33) it follows that:

$$\text{Rate of wage increase for all job-changing workers} = c, \tag{6.34}$$

where c is a constant found by taking the average, over all job-changing workers, of the c_j.¶

The third of the subsidiary relationships which Holt uses to explain the free-market rate of increase of average money wage rates is one which determines the percentage rate of increase at time t in the wage rates of workers who neither

---

†The steps are as follows. First (6.29) is substituted into (6.30). Then (6.31) is substituted into the resulting expression to get an expression for $W_i(t + T)/W_i(t)$. This expression is then used to get an expression for the rate of wage increase of the ith unemployed worker. Finally, this last expression is aggregated to obtain (6.32).

‡ 'ln' is, of course, shorthand for 'log to the base e'.

¶ (6.34) is derived by using (6.33) to obtain an expression for the rate of wage increase for the jth job-changing worker and then aggregating this expression.

become unemployed at time t nor change jobs subsequent to time t, that is all those workers *not* covered either by (6.32) or by (6.34). The relationship postulated is:

$$\text{Rate of wage increase for all stay-on-the-job workers} = k_1 \left[\hat{w}(t) - d + \frac{\ln ab}{T} \right] + k_2 c, \qquad (6.35)$$

where k_1 and k_2 are positive constants both of which are less than unity. According to this relationship the rate of increase at time t in the money wage rates of the third group of workers is an increasing function of the rates of increase which apply to the other two groups. This makes good sense since the wage increases which are needed to keep workers on the job will be larger the larger the wage increases which can be secured by leaving the job. The constants k_1 and k_2 are specified as less than unity since otherwise (6.35) would make it possible for workers who stay on the job to secure larger wage increases, on the average, than those who quit. This would not be reasonable because the latter group incurs penalties (for example a period of unemployment) which are avoided by the former group.

Having developed (6.32), (6.34) and (6.35), Holt next combines them to form a relationship determining $\hat{w}(t)$. He does this by making $\hat{w}(t)$ a weighted arithmetic average of: (i) the right-hand side of (6.32); and (ii) the sum of the right-hand sides of (6.34) and (6.35), the relative weight attached to (i) being u_t, the proportion of unemployed workers at time t, and that attached to (ii) being $1 - u_t$, the proportion of employed workers at time t. When the relationship in question is tidied up, it takes the simple form:

$$\hat{w}(t) = g_1 + g_2 \frac{\ln ab}{T}, \qquad (6.36)$$

where g_1 is a constant involving c, d, k_1 and k_2, and g_2 is a constant involving only k_1.

Finally, (6.36) is written in terms of $u(t)$, the unemployment rate at time t. Recall that T is the average duration of unemployment at time t, that is T is a certain number of days. Let $F(t)$ equal the flow of workers into the unemployment pool at time t, that is F is a certain number of men per day. Then $U(t)$, the number of unemployed men at time t, will be given by:

$$U(t) = T F(t). \qquad (6.37)$$

For example, if 100 men are flowing into the unemployment pool per day at time t, and each is staying in the pool for ten days on the average, there must be 1000 men actually in the pool at that point of time. Dividing (6.37) through by the labour force at time t we obtain:

$$u(t) = T f(t), \qquad (6.38)$$

where $f(t)$ is the so-called 'turnover rate' at time t, that is the flow of workers from employment into unemployment per member of the labour force. Now the numerator of the turnover rate remains fairly constant in the short run because the numerator is the sum of: (i) the flow of 'quits-to-search'; and (ii) the flow of lay-offs — and these two flows move in opposite directions in response to changes in the level of activity. Likewise the denominator of the turnover rate (the labour force) is effectively constant in the short run. It is not unreasonable, therefore, to treat $f(t)$ as a constant. If this is done we can write (6.36) as:

$$\hat{w}(t) = g_1 + (fg_2 \ln ab)\frac{1}{u(t)},$$

where f is the constant turnover rate, or as:

$$\hat{w}(t) = g_1 + g_3 \frac{1}{u(t)}, \tag{6.39}$$

where g_3 is the constant $fg_2 \ln ab$.

Relationship (6.39) is the relationship which Holt proposes to explain the percentage rate of increase in the general level (index) of money wage rates, in the absence of trade-union influence. Two points should be noted in connection with this relationship.

The first is that it possesses certain, though not all, of the properties of the macro wage equation outlined at the end of Chapter 5.

The second point is that the analysis which underlies (6.39) has a particularly strong flavour of the New Microeconomics. This is especially true of the analysis leading up to (6.32), where the basic notions are those of a wage-aspiration level and of a relationship showing the way in which this is modified as the unemployed worker continues his search of the labour market. These notions make sense, of course, only in the context of a labour market characterised by imperfect information. Were information perfect there would be no such thing as a wage-aspiration level nor would there be a process of modification of the wage-aspiration level through job search because the job-search phenomenon itself would cease to exist.

In the final stage of Holt's analysis the hitherto neglected influence of trade unions on money wages is brought into the picture.

This part of the argument is quite complex, and we shall not enter into the details. However, the general drift is as follows. First, the over-all index of money wage rates is made a weighted arithmetic average of: (i) the index of non-union rates; and (ii) the index of union rates. On this basis, the following expression for w_t, the rate of increase of the index of money wage rates in the *presence* of trade-union influence, is then derived:

$$w(t) = \hat{w}(t) + K(t). \tag{6.40}$$

The second term on the right-hand side of (6.40) is a fairly complicated expression and can be regarded as a function of the variables which determine $x(t)$ and $n(t)$ and their absolute rates of change, x being the proportional excess of union wage rates over non-union wage rates and n the proportion of workers receiving union rates. Finally, the expression already derived for $\hat{w}(t)$, that is (6.39) is substituted into (6.40) to obtain:

$$w(t) = g_1 + g_3 \frac{1}{u(t)} + K(t). \tag{6.41}$$

Thus by combining (6.39) and (6.40) (each of these being, itself, a combination of other relationships), Holt obtains a macro wage equation in which the dependent variable is the percentage rate of increase in money wage rates. Moreover, subject to one minor qualification, this relationship has all of the properties of the wage equation which has been thrown up by the empirical studies discussed in Chapter 5. To begin with, the unemployment rate is one of the independent variables, as required. Second, since g_3 is positive,† the curve of $w(t)$ against $u(t)$, for given $K(t)$, will have a negative, but decreasingly negative, slope at all points, as required. Third, the unemployment rate is not the only independent variable – the determinants of $K(t)$ appear as well. Thus subject to the qualification that the determinants of $K(t)$ include a price variable and at least one variable outside the original Phillips–Lipsey list, (6.41) will have all the properties that we require.

What emerges, then, is the Holt's analysis provides yet another possible microeconomic foundation for our macro wage equation – the wage equation revealed by the empirical work of the last decade and outlined at the end of Chapter 5.

6.6 The Choice Between Alternative Rationalisations

In the three preceding sections of this chapter we have considered three quite distinct answers to the question 'Why does a Phillips-type macro wage equation exist?'

In Section 6.2 we produced an answer based on the work of Phillips and Lipsey. In essence, and shorn of refinements, this answer is as follows. It can be assumed that the rate at which money wages rise in a particular labour market increases as the level of relative excess demand in that market increases. However, since relative excess demand in a particular labour market is the excess of the vacancy rate in the market over the unemployment rate, and since there is an inverse relationship between the vacancy rate and the unemployment rate, there must be an inverse relationship between the level of relative excess demand and the unemployment rate. But if money wages rise more rapidly as excess demand

---

†Recall that $g_3 = fg_2 \ln ab$. Now f is necessarily positive. Also g_2 is positive since $g_2 = k_1/(1 - k_1)$ and k_1 is subject to the restriction $0 < k_1 < 1$ (see above, p. 132). Finally $\ln ab$ is positive so long as either a or b exceeds unity. It follows that g_3 is positive.

increases, and if the unemployment rate *decreases* as excess demand increases, it must be the case that a more rapid rise of money wages is associated with a decline in the unemployment rate, that is there must be an inverse relationship between the rate of increase of money wages and the unemployment rate at the level of the individual market. Moreover, this inverse relationship will persist when the individual market relationships are aggregated and will result in a macro wage equation with the familiar 'Phillips-curve' properties.

In Section 6.4 we discussed the much more detailed and elaborate answer given by Phelps. The fundamental notion here is that of the desired wage differential of the individual firm – the excess of the firm's optimal wage rate over the wage rate which it expects other firms to offer. It is argued that the size of this desired wage differential will depend, directly, both on the number of vacancies which the firm wishes to fill and on the number of vacancies which firms in the aggregate wish to fill, and inversely on the number of unemployed in the economy as a whole. It is then shown that aggregation of the individual wage-differential relationships results in the average desired wage differential appearing as a function of two variables only – the over-all unemployment rate and the over-all vacancy rate – with the association being inverse in the case of the unemployment rate and direct in the case of the vacancy rate.

However, on plausible assumptions as to the way in which the individual firm adjusts its actual wage differential to its desired wage differential and as to the way in which expectations about wage rate changes are revised, the rate of change of aggregate money wage rates turns out to be directly dependent on the average desired wage differential, and hence to be inversely related to the unemployment rate and directly to the vacancy rate, in view of the earlier conclusion as to the determinants of the average desired wage differential.

Finally, it is shown that the vacancy rate can be expressed in terms of the unemployment rate and the absolute rate of change of employment. This permits the elimination of the vacancy rate as a determinant of the rate of change of aggregate money wage rates and its replacement by the unemployment rate and the rate of change of employment. In the event, therefore, the rate of change of money wage rates shows the familiar inverse dependence on the unemployment rate with the rate of change of employment as an additional explanatory variable.

Finally, in Section 6.5, we considered Holt's answer to the question of why there should be a Phillips-type macro wage equation. Holt's analysis resembles Phelps's in being genuinely microeconomic – in both cases the argument is firmly based on the decision-making processes of individual economic agents. There is, however, an important difference between the two approaches. In Phelps's work it is the individual *firm* which occupies the centre of the stage. In Holt's, on the other hand, there is no reference to the firm; rather it is the decision-making of the individual supplier of labour which is given prominence.

The basis of Holt's analysis is the distinction between three types of wage changes: (i) those which occur when there is a job change with intervening unemployment; (ii) those which occur when there is a job change without intervening unemployment; (iii) those which occur when there is no job change. An explanation is proposed for each of these three types of wage change, and these individual explanations are then combined to give an explanation of the rate of increase in money wage rates as a whole. This proves to have the characteristic Phillips-type features – essentially because the rate of increase of money wage rates for those workers who change jobs with intervening unemployment is inversely related to the average duration of their unemployment, and hence, through the stock–flow connection between the average duration of unemployment and the number of unemployed workers, to the unemployment rate.

Faced with these three quite distinct rationalisations of the Phillips-type macro wage equation, we are naturally led to ask how we choose between them and any others that have been, or might be, proposed. The answer to this question becomes clear once we recognise that what we have referred to throughout this chapter as 'a microeconomic foundation' of our macro wage equation, or as 'a rationalisation' of this equation, or as 'an answer to the question of why the equation exists', the thing to which these terms have been applied is simply an economist's model and is to be judged in the same way as any model, that is in terms of predictive success. Thus, if we wished to discriminate between the three pictures of the essential reality behind our macro wage equations that have been presented in Sections 6.2, 6.4 and 6.5, we would need to frame the testable implications of each and devise some way of confronting these testable implications with the relevant facts. Only then would we have a proper basis for the exercise of choice.

7

POLICY AGAINST INFLATION: DEMAND MANAGEMENT

7.1 The Policy Options

In this chapter and the next two we shall be considering anti-inflation policy — the various steps which the economic-policy authorities can take to check inflation — within the context of a developed market economy. Obviously one cannot begin to suggest ways of checking inflation unless one has some idea of how inflation is caused. This being so, the starting-point for the development of anti-inflation policy in a developed economy must be an analysis of the cause of inflation in such an economy.

In political, journalistic, trade-union and business circles one often hears statements to the effect that inflation is caused by such-and-such — by 'the pull of demand', by 'cost-push', by 'too rapid wage increases', by 'excessive profits', by 'too much government spending', by 'too large an increase in the money stock', by 'inflation abroad', and so on. To the economist such single-sentence statements about cause appear hopelessly amateurish and dangerously misleading. As pointed out in Section 2.1, the professional's approach to the question of how inflation occurs is to build a model of the inflationary process — a set of relationships linking the price index chosen to measure inflation, with certain given variables or data — and then to show that the model generates the continuous upward movement in the price index which constitutes inflation if the data behave in a particular fashion. The set of data as a whole, behaving in a certain way, and the set of relationships through which the data impinge on the price variable, this whole complex is then regarded as the 'cause' of inflation since it is necessary to invoke the complex as a whole in order to explain why inflation occurs. This is an entirely reasonable way of looking at the question of cause since, at least in ordinary language, when we say that x causes y, we mean that x must be invoked to account for the occurrence of y.

The economist's approach to anti-inflationary policy develops naturally from his approach to the question of what causes inflation. If one holds that inflation occurs because particular data time paths impinge on the price variable *via* a particular system of relationships, then one naturally holds also that to check inflation (remove its cause) one must take one or both of the following two steps: (i) one must use the available policy instruments to *modify the existing time paths of the data* in such a way that the upward pressure which they are exerting on the price index through the system of relationships is reduced; (ii) one must use the available policy instruments to *modify the system of relationships* which transmits the influence of the data through to the price index in such a way as to lessen the upward pressure which is being exerted on the price index by the existing set of data time paths.

It goes without saying that it is the professional approach just outlined that will provide the framework for the policy discussion of this chapter and the next two. However, we want the discussion to be as specific as possible within this framework, and this requires, of course, that we work with a specific model of the inflationary process in mind. Our first task, then, is to choose our model.

Ideally, the chosen model would be one which had been extensively tested and which had performed well under test. Unfortunately none of the existing models quite live up to this ideal. If we accept the models discussed in Chapter 2 as providing an adequate representation of the available range, then it would appear from Chapter 3 that none of the existing models have been extensively tested apart from those in the expectational group; and the conclusion reached in Chapter 3 is that these models have a rather poor test record except, possibly, in relation to the Canadian economy.

The next best thing to a model with a good test record is one with a good test promise. The empirical price-equation studies surveyed in Chapter 4 give a fairly clear picture of the price-equation component of such a model (see above, p. 90) while the wage-equation studies of Chapter 5 provide quite definite indications as to the nature of the wage-equation component (see above, p. 114). Following these empirical signposts, we have been led to choose the following three-equation system as a basis for discussing anti-inflation policy:

$$p_t = \beta_1(w_t - o_t) + \beta_2 s_t \tag{7.1}$$

$$w_t = \alpha_0 + \alpha_1 u_t^{-1} + \alpha_2 p_t^e + X_t^{\cdot} \tag{7.2}$$

$$p_t^e - p_{t-1}^e = \delta(p_{t-1} - p_{t-1}^e) \tag{7.3}$$

Most of the symbols used in (7.1)–(7.3) will be familiar from earlier chapters, but we shall explain the notation in full just the same. The lower-case symbols, p, w, o and s are, respectively, the percentage rates of increase from the previous period in the index of prices, the index of money wage-earnings per man, the index of standard output per man and the index of the prices of raw materials. All relate to the mark-up sector as a whole. The superscript e denotes 'expected'. We use u to denote the over-all unemployment rate and X to denote one or more terms in independent variables outside the original Phillips–Lipsey list. Finally, $\alpha_0, \alpha_1, \alpha_2$, β_1, β_2 and δ are a group of constants which are subject to the following restrictions: (i) $\alpha_0 < 0$; (ii) $\alpha_1 > 0$; (iii) $0 < \beta_1 \leqslant 1$; (iv) $0 < \beta_2 \leqslant 1$; (v) $0 < \alpha_2 \leqslant 1$; (vi) $0 < \delta < 1$. Thus α_0 is negative, α_1 is positive, β_1, β_2 and α_2 are positive but not greater than unity and δ is positive but less than unity.

We allow the three relationships to determine p, w and p^e and treat the remaining variables, namely, o, s, u and X, as the data of the model.

The above three-equation policy model has the great advantage of simplicity. It is also reasonably familiar. In fact, it would be fair to say that nowadays most professional discussion of anti-inflation policy is based either on a monetary model resembling the prototype presented in Section 2.5, or on an expectational model which is close to, if not identical with, the model of (7.1)–(7.3). Moreover, we know from Chapter 2 that the price equation can be given a quite plausible microeconomic foundation and from Chapter 6 that the same is true of the wage equation. This theoretical support for the price and wage equations, together with the empirical support provided by the discussion of Chapters 4 and 5, justifies our placing a considerable degree of confidence in the model, though much less, of course, than we could place in a model which had been well tested and which had survived all tests with flying colours.

As will be clear from the earlier discussion of this section, in adopting the above model of the inflationary process, we are saying that the 'cause' of inflation is that the time paths of the variables o, s, u and X are such that when they are transmitted by the equation system to the variable p, a positive value of p (inflation) must result. Further, we are saying that if we wish to 'cure' inflation, that is if we wish p to be zero (no inflation) or less positive (less inflation), we must either change the time paths of one or more of the variables o, s, u and X, or change the 'transmission structure' by changing one or more of the constants of the system – the αs, the βs and δ – or adopt both of these approaches.

Of course some of the data, o, s, u and X, are more easily manipulated by the policy authorities than others. Probably the most easily controlled is u, the unemployment rate; in most developed market economies the instruments which are available to the authorities for the management of aggregate demand are powerful enough to give them a high degree of control over this particular variable. For this reason the change-of-data approach to anti-inflation policy is now virtually synonymous with manipulation of the unemployment rate and is commonly referred to as 'demand management' (see p. 217 below for a qualification to this statement). We shall use this term and devote the rest of this chapter to a consideration of this particular approach, which has been very widely discussed ever since the publication of Phillips's famous study of the wage equation. The change-of-structure approach to anti-inflation policy nowadays takes two main forms which go by the names, 'Prices and Incomes Policy' and 'Manpower Policy'. We shall consider the first of these approaches in Chapter 8 and the second in Chapter 9.

7.2 The Short-Run and Long-Run Inflation–Unemployment Curves

The basis analytical tool which we shall use in this chapter to facilitate the discussion of the demand-management approach to anti-inflation policy is the

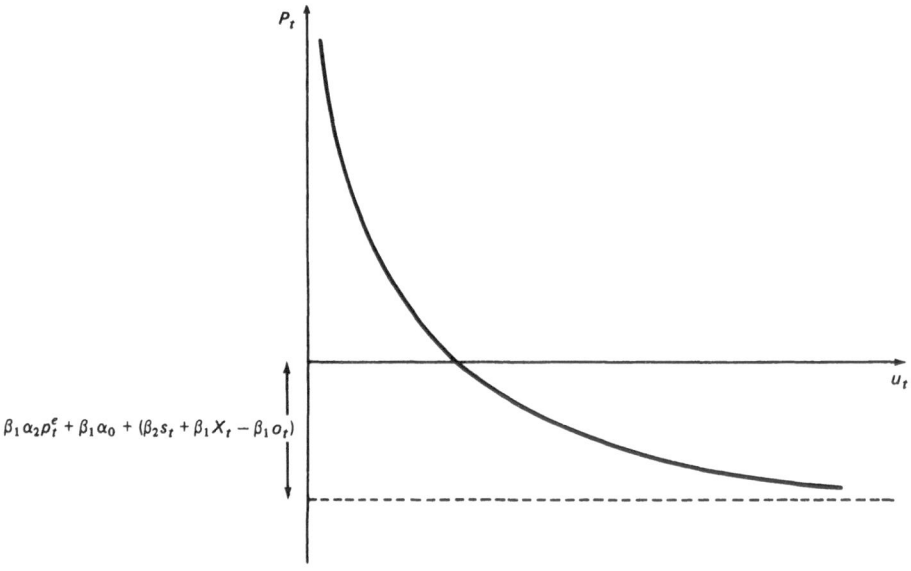

Fig. 7.1

inflation–unemployment curve. We shall introduce this tool in the present section.

If we substitute equation (7.2) into (7.1) we obtain an expression for the inflation rate in terms of the unemployment rate. This expression is as follows:

$$P_t = \beta_1\alpha_1 u_t^{-1} + \beta_1\alpha_2 p_t^e + \beta_1\alpha_0 + (\beta_1 X_t + \beta_2 s_t - \beta_1 o_t). \qquad (7.4)$$

Let us now suppose that values are allotted to p_t^e, to each of the data, o_t, X_t and s_t and to each of the constants α_0, α_1, α_2, β_1 and β_2. We could then use (7.4) to draw a curve showing the way in which the current inflation rate, p_t, varies as the current unemployment rate, u_t, varies. This curve will have the general form of the curve shown in Figure 7.1. That this is so can be seen as follows.

As u_t tends to infinity, the term $\beta_1\alpha_1 u_t^{-1}$ tends to zero. Hence according to (7.4) the inflation rate tends to $\beta_1\alpha_2 p_t^e + \beta_1\alpha_0 + (\beta_1 X_t + \beta_2 s_t - \beta_1 o_t)$. Since β_1 and α_2 are both positive, the first term in this expression will be negative if p_t^e is negative (if prices are expected to fall), zero if p_t^e is zero and positive if p_t^e is positive. The second term is necessarily negative given the restrictions on α_0 and β_1. The term in parentheses can be negative, zero or positive depending on the values allotted to the data X_t, s_t and o_t and the constants β_1 and β_2. Hence the expression as a whole can be either negative, zero or positive.

Examination of (7.4) shows, then, that as u_t tends to infinity the inflation rate levels out at some figure which is determined by the values allotted to p_t^e, to the remaining data and to the constants and which can be negative, zero or positive. It follows that the curve showing the variation of p_t with u_t will be asymptotic either to the horizontal axis or to a line which is parallel to the horizontal axis, above or below. Figure 7.1 shows the case where the line in question is parallel below.

We can also deduce from (7.4) that, as u_t tends to zero, the term $\beta_1 \alpha_1 u_t^{-1}$ will tend to infinity, and hence that the inflation rate will tend to infinity, regardless of the values allotted to p_t^e, the data and the constants. In other words, the curve of p_t against u_t will be asymptotic to the vertical axis, as shown in Figure 7.1.

Finally, since α_1 is positive, the curve will have a negative slope at all points but the slope will become less and less negative as we move to the right – again as shown in Figure 7.1.†

By allowing p_t^e to take on different values while keeping the data, o, s and X fixed, we can generate a whole family of curves of the type shown in Figure 7.1. Five members of this family, corresponding to $p_t^e = -2, -1, 0, 1$ and 2, are shown in Figure 7.2. As will be clear from (7.4), each of these curves is obtained from the one below by shifting it upward at all points by the constant amount, $\beta_1 \alpha_2$.‡

Each of the curves in Figure 7.2 may be described as a 'short-run' inflation–unemployment curve because it shows, for the specified value of p_t^e, the reduction that will occur in the inflation rate *in period* t as a result of a given increase in the unemployment rate *in period* t, that is it shows the *immediate* effect on the inflation rate of a given manipulation of the unemployment rate. We shall use this term. We shall also say that each curve gives the 'short-run trade-off between inflation and unemployment' for the specified expected inflation rate.

We now introduce the 'long-run' inflation–unemployment curve. This is a curve which shows the *steady* inflation rate that will be associated with a given *indefinitely maintained* unemployment rate, provided that all data apart from the unemployment rate are also maintained indefinitely at fixed levels.

To see what this curve looks like we must use the steady-state version of the model, (7.1), (7.2) and (7.3), to derive an expression for the steady-state inflation rate. By 'the steady-state version of the model' we mean the version which applies when every variable continues at some fixed level period after period, indefinitely,

---

†From (7.4) we have:

$$\frac{\partial p_t}{\partial u_t} = -\beta_1 \alpha_1 u_t^{-2},$$

which is negative for all u_t since both β_1 and α_1 are positive. Also:

$$\frac{\partial^2 p_t}{\partial u_t^2} = 2\beta_1 \alpha_1 u_t^{-3},$$

which is positive for all u_t.

‡In drawing these five curves we have assumed that the data, o, s and X, and the constants are set at such levels that the curve corresponding to $p_t^e = 2$ is the only one of the five to be wholly above the horizontal axis.

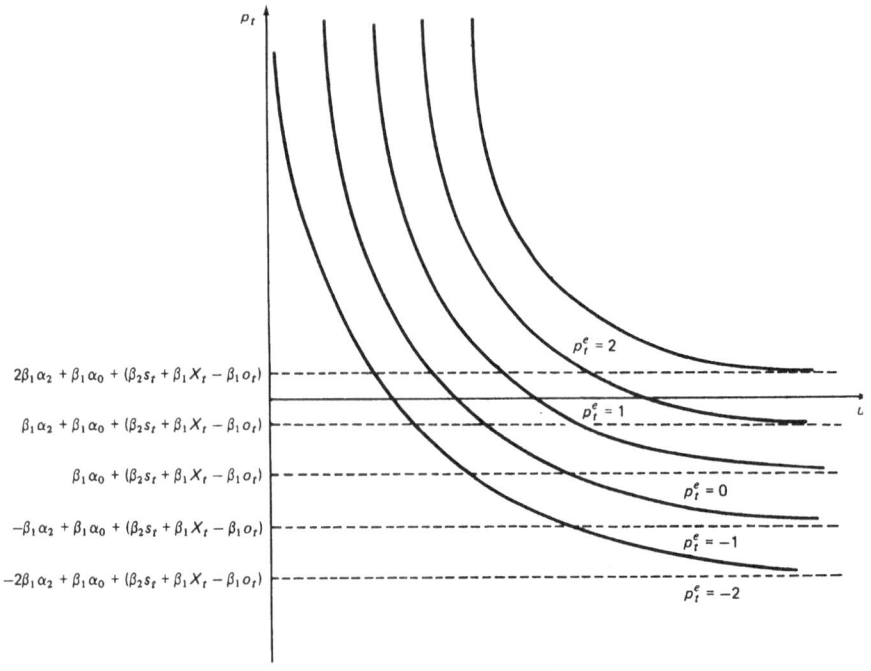

Fig. 7.2

for example when $p_t = p_{t-1} = p_{t-2} = \ldots = \bar{p}$, where $\bar{p}$ is some specified inflation rate, and similarly for all other variables. Thus, the steady-state version of our model is:

$$\bar{p} = \beta_1(\bar{w} - \bar{o}) + \beta_s\bar{s} \tag{7.5}$$

$$\bar{w} = \alpha_0 + \alpha_1\bar{u}^{-1} + \alpha_2\bar{p}^e + \bar{X} \tag{7.6}$$

$$\bar{p}^e - \bar{p}^e = \delta(\bar{p} - \bar{p}^e) \tag{7.7}$$

where the bar over a variable denotes the steady-state level of the variable, that is a specified level which persists period after period. From (7.7) it follows that:

$$\delta(\bar{p} - \bar{p}^e) = 0,$$

or that:

$$\bar{p} = \bar{p}^e. \tag{7.8}$$

Substituting (7.8) into (7.6) and then substituting the resulting expression in (7.5) we obtain:

$$\bar{p} = \beta_1\alpha_0 + \beta_1\alpha_1\bar{u}^{-1} + \beta_1\alpha_2\bar{p} + \beta_1\overline{X} - \beta_1\bar{o} + \beta_2\bar{s}.$$

This, in turn, gives:

$$\bar{p}(1 - \beta_1\alpha_2) = \beta_1\alpha_0 + \beta_1\alpha_1\bar{u}^{-1} + \beta_1\overline{X} - \beta_1\bar{o} + \beta_2\bar{s}. \tag{7.9}$$

Relationship (7.9) is an expression for the steady-state inflation rate in terms of indefinitely maintained levels of the unemployment rate and the other data of the model. Suppose now that we were to allot values to $\overline{X}$, $\bar{o}$ and $\bar{s}$ and to each of the α and β constants. Then we could use (7.9) to draw a curve showing the way in which $\bar{p}$ varies with $\bar{u}$. There are two cases which must be considered separately: (a) the case where one or both of β_1 and α_2 are below their upper limit of unity (see above, p. 138); (b) the case where both are equal to their upper limit of unity.

If at least one of β_1 and α_2 is less than unity, then $\beta_1\alpha_2$ is less than unity and $1 - \beta_1\alpha_2$ is non-zero (actually positive). Consequently we can divide both sides of (7.9) by $1 - \beta_1\alpha_2$ to obtain:

$$\bar{p} = \frac{\beta_1\alpha_0}{1 - \beta_1\alpha_2} + \frac{\beta_1\alpha_1}{1 - \beta_1\alpha_2}\bar{u}^{-1} + \frac{\beta_1}{1 - \beta_1\alpha_2}\overline{X} - \frac{\beta_1}{1 - \beta_1\alpha_2}\bar{o} + \frac{\beta_2}{1 - \beta_1\alpha_2}\bar{s}. \tag{7.10}$$

By applying the same type of analysis to (7.10) as we applied earlier to (7.4) (see above, p. 141) we find that the curve of $\bar{p}$ against $\bar{u}$ will have the general appearance of the curve shown in Figure 7.3. That is, like each of the short-run curves shown in Figure 7.2, the curve of $\bar{p}$ against $\bar{u}$: (i) will be asymptotic to the vertical axis; (ii) will be asymptotic either to the horizontal axis or to a line parallel to it above or below, depending on the values allotted to $\overline{X}$, $\bar{o}$ and $\bar{s}$ and to the α and β constants; (iii) will have a negative slope at all points; (iv) will become less negatively sloped as one moves to the right.

Turn now to the second case, where both β_1 and α_2 are equal to unity. In this case $1 - \beta_1\alpha_2 = 0$ and (7.9) gives:

$$\beta_1\alpha_0 + \beta_1\alpha_1\bar{u}^{-1} + \beta_1\overline{X} - \beta_1\bar{o} + \beta_2\bar{s} = 0. \tag{7.11}$$

Therefore

$$\beta_1\alpha_1\bar{u}^{-1} = -\beta_1\alpha_0 - \beta_1\overline{X} + \beta_1\bar{o} - \beta_2\bar{s}.$$

Therefore

$$\bar{u}^{-1} = \frac{-\beta_1\alpha_0 - \beta_1\overline{X} + \beta_1\bar{o} - \beta_2\bar{s}}{\beta_1\alpha_1}.$$

Therefore

$$\bar{u} = \frac{\beta_1\alpha_1}{-\beta_1\alpha_0 - \beta_1\overline{X} + \beta_1\bar{o} - \beta_2\bar{s}}. \tag{7.12}$$

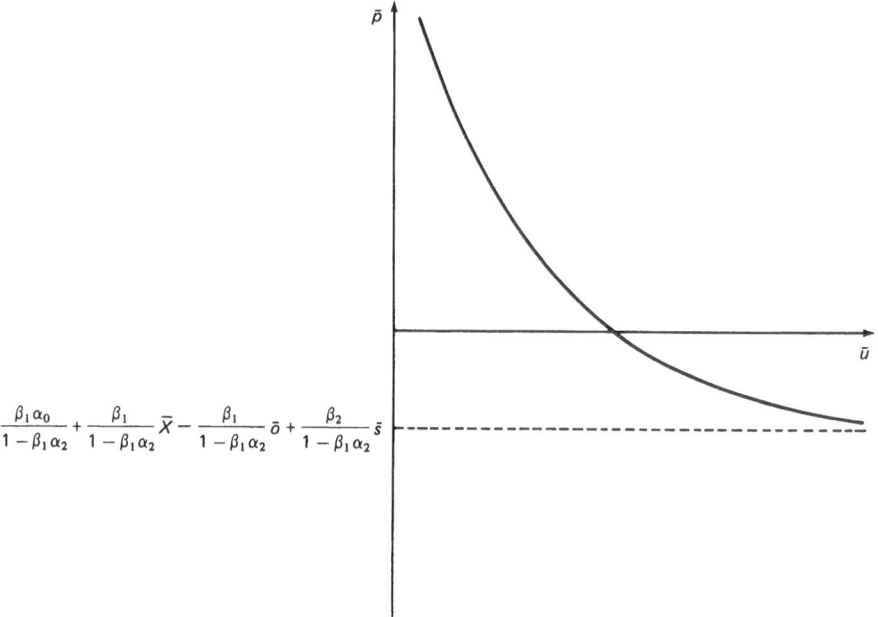

Fig. 7.3

Once values have been allotted to $\overline{X}$, $\overline{o}$ and $\overline{s}$, and to the αs and the βs, the right-hand side of (7.12) reduces to a single figure — say 0.05. Thus our model, (7.1), (7.2), (7.3), implies that there is one and only one unemployment rate which is compatible with the steady-state situation. This unique, steady unemployment rate is usually called the 'natural rate'. We shall employ this term and use the symbol $\overline{u}^*$ to denote the natural rate.

What level of $\overline{p}$ is associated with the natural rate? We can answer this question by putting the expression given by (7.12) for the natural rate in place of $\overline{u}$ in (7.9). If we do this we learn that when $\overline{u} = \overline{u}^*$, $\overline{p}$ must satisfy the following equation:

$$\overline{p}(1 - \beta_1\alpha_2) = 0. \qquad (7.13)$$

But since $1 - \beta_1\alpha_2 = 0$, any value of $\overline{p}$ at all will satisfy (7.13). It follows that when both β_1 and α_2 equal unity the curve of $\overline{p}$ against $\overline{u}$ will take the form of the 'curve' shown in Figure 7.4, that is it will be a vertical line drawn at the natural rate.

The curves of Figure 7.3 and Figure 7.4 may be described as 'long-run' inflation–unemployment curves because they show the *continuing* (year-in, year-out) inflation rate that corresponds to a particular continuing unemployment rate. We shall use this term. We shall also say that the curve of Figure 7.3 gives the

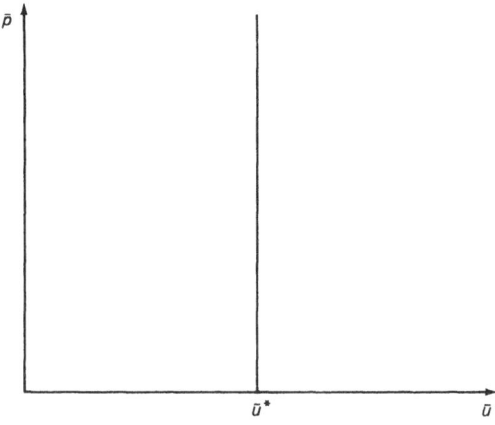

Fig. 7.4

'long-run trade-off between inflation and unemployment' because it permits us to read off the reduction in the (steady) inflation rate that will accompany a specified increase in the unemployment rate from one steady level to a higher steady level. Where the curve of $\bar{p}$ against $\bar{u}$ takes the special form shown in Figure 7.4, we shall say that there exists no long-run trade-off between inflation and employment.

It must be stressed that the long-run inflation–employment curves of Figures 7.3 and 7.4 show the variation of $\bar{p}$ with $\bar{u}$ *for given values of the parameters of the model (the αs and the βs) and for given values of the data of the model* (X, o *and* s). Any change in the parameters or in the fixed values of the data will cause a change in the position and/or slope of the curve of Figure 7.3 and a change in the position of the curve of Figure 7.4. Take the curve of Figure 7.3 first. Any change in β_1, β_2, α_0, α_2, $\bar{X}$, $\bar{o}$ and $\bar{s}$ will change the position of the horizontal asymptote (the dashed horizontal line) and hence cause a shift in the *position* of the curve. This is evident from the expression defining the horizontal asymptote which is shown on the diagram. Any change in β_1, α_1 and α_2 will cause a change in the *slope* of the curve. This follows from the fact that the slope is given, from (7.10), by:

$$\frac{\partial \bar{p}}{\partial \bar{u}} = -\frac{\beta_1 \alpha_1}{1 - \beta_1 \alpha_2} \bar{u}^{-2}.$$

Turning to the 'curve' of Figure 7.4, it is clear, from (7.12), that any change in α_0, α_1, β_1, β_2, $\bar{X}$, $\bar{o}$ and $\bar{s}$ will cause a change in the level of the natural rate and hence shift the vertical inflation–unemployment curve bodily, either to the right or to the left.

Suppose that the long-run inflation–unemployment curve takes the form shown in Figure 7.3, and that because of some change in the parameters or the data, the curve changes position and/or slope in such a way that over a certain range of $\bar{u}, \bar{p}$ is higher for any given $\bar{u}$ than was previously the case. We would then say that the long-run trade between inflation and unemployment has 'become less favourable', or has 'deteriorated', or has 'worsened', because to achieve any given steady inflation rate the authorities would have to maintain a higher steady unemployment rate than was previously necessary.

It can be shown (see Appendix 7.1 for the proof, pp. 163–4) that if $\beta_1 \alpha_2$ is less than unity, so that the long-run inflation–unemployment curve takes the downward-sloping form of Figure 7.3, the economy will move toward the long-run curve from *any* position off that curve so long as the unemployment rate is kept steady by policy action and so long as the other data remain fixed.

7.3   Alternative Routes to a Desired Long-Run Position

Demand management, under which the authorities exercise control over the inflation rate by manipulating the unemployment rate, can take one of two forms. The first form is found when short-run considerations dominate the policy-maker's thinking and consists of a sequence of unemployment-rate manipulations, each of which is designed to move the economy from some short-run position to a different, preferred, short-run position. The second form is found when long-run considerations are uppermost and consists of a sequence of unemployment-rate manipulations aimed at moving the economy from some short-run position to some *long*-run position or from one long-run position to another. We shall now consider this distinction in more detail.

Figure 7.5 helps to clarify the first of the two forms of demand management. This diagram shows three of the family of short-run inflation–umemployment curves, the curves labelled SR_1, SR_2 and SR_3. Also shown is the corresponding long-run inflation–unemployment curve, the curve labelled LR, which has been drawn on the assumption that $\beta_1 \alpha_1$ is less than unity.†

To illustrate the first of the two forms of demand management let us suppose that the economy is at point A on SR_3 with an unemployment rate of u^1 and an inflation rate of p^1. Suppose that short-run balance-of-payments difficulties emerge and that the authorities decide that some improvement in the competitive position of domestic producers is essential in order to deal with these difficulties.

---

†It should be noted that the LR curve in Figure 7.5 has a steeper slope at any unemployment rate than the SR curves. That this is correct is evident from (7.4) and (7.10). From (7.10) we see that the numerical slope of the *long*-run curve at any given unemployment rate is $\beta_1 \alpha_2 / (1 - \beta_1 \alpha_2)$ multiplied by the square of the reciprocal of the unemployment rate in question, while from (7.4) we see that the numerical slope of all members of the short-run family will be $\beta_1 \alpha_1$ multiplied by the same factor. Since by assumption $\beta_1 \alpha_1$ is a positive fraction, $\beta_1 \alpha_1 / (1 - \beta_1 \alpha_2)$ will be greater than $\beta_1 \alpha_1$. Hence the former slope will be greater than the latter.

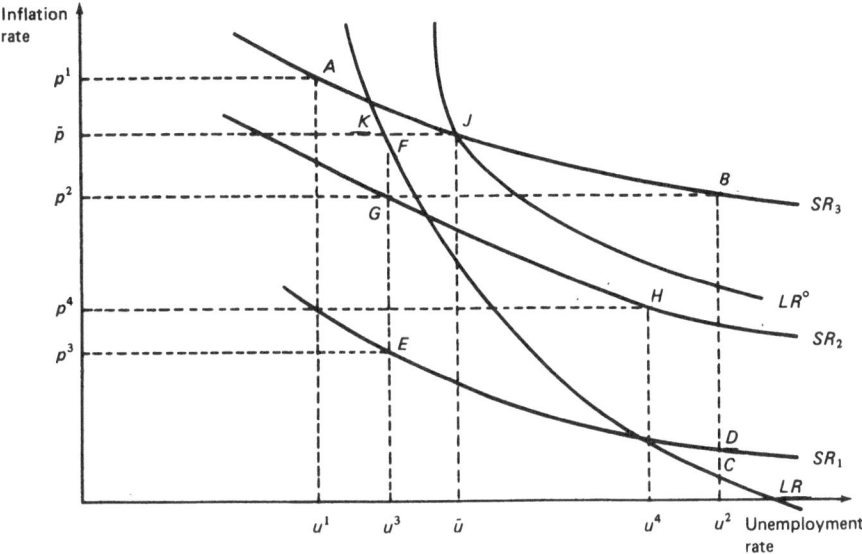

Fig. 7.5

The alternatives, then, are: (i) reduction of the inflation rate; and (ii) exchange devaluation.

Suppose that the latter is ruled out because the country concerned is committed to a regime of fixed exchange rates. Then, under the first form of demand management, the authorities would typically raise the unemployment rate to, say, u^2 and hold it at this level. The *immediate* effect of this action would be to shift the economy along SR_3 to B, that is to reduce the inflation rate to p^2. As pointed out earlier, however, the economy will move towards the long-run curve from any point off that curve so long as the unemployment rate is held fixed (see above, p. 146). Provided the unemployment rate is held at u^2, therefore, the economy will move under its own steam from B towards C so that the inflation rate will fall still further. Suppose that, by the time point D is reached, an election is imminent and that the unemployment rate, u^2, is high enough to be electorally damaging. Then under the first form of demand management the authorities would typically lower the unemployment rate to a more popular figure, u^3, say, and hold it there, at least until the election was over. This would have the immediate effect of bringing the inflation rate back to p^3. However, with the unemployment rate held at u^3, the economy would move towards the point F on the long-run curve, that is the inflation rate would continue to rise beyond p^3. We shall say that by the time G is reached, the inflation rate has risen to a point where the improvement in competitive position achieved by the movement from A to B to D has been undone and that the external difficulties which led to that movement re-appear. The election having been won, we shall say, the authorities' typical behaviour under the first form of demand managemnt would then be to raise the unemployment once again to, say, u^4, and hold it there until the external difficulties disappeared.

In terms of this illustration, then, the first form of demand management would consist of a sequence of unemployment-rate manipulations from u^1 to u^2 to u^3 to u^4, each designed to move the economy from one short-run position to another, preferable, short-run position — from A to B to D to E to G to H.

Turn now to the second form of demand management. In this case, the policy-maker first determines a 'desired' rate of inflation on the basis of strictly long-run considerations, and then sets out to achieve *steady* inflation at this particular rate. Arguments in favour of temporarily reducing the inflation rate, or for allowing it to rise temporarily in order to meet some passing economic or political difficulty, would be given little weight or dismissed altogether.

It might seem inappropriate to describe this particular type of policy behaviour as a form of demand management. The essence of demand management is that the unemployment rate is manipulated as a means of controlling the inflation rate. But with steady inflation as the objective, there would appear to be no call for *manipulation* of the unemployment rate. With a downward-sloping long-run inflation—unemployment curve it would simply be a matter, it seems, of holding the unemployment rate steady at $\bar{u}$, the abscissa of the long-run curve corresponding to $\bar{p}$, the desired inflation rate. With a vertical long-run curve it would simply be a matter, surely, of holding the unemployment rate steady at u^*, the natural rate.

While this argument is sensible it overlooks two points. The first is that the policy-maker may occasionally find it necessary to revise his ideas as to what the target steady inflation rate should be, without backing away from his steady inflation objective. In this case he will be obliged to undertake a sequence of unemployment-rate manipulations designed to move the economy to a new point on the long-run curve, that is he will then be obliged to engage in demand management. The second point is that, as explained earlier, the long-run curve may shift from time to time because of some change in the parameters of the system or in the fixed values of the data. Should such a shift occur, the policy-maker will be obliged once again to engage in demand management, for he will now have to devise a series of unemployment-rate manipulations that will move the economy from its present position which, with the shift in the long-run curve, has become a *short-run* position, to the appropriate point on the new long-run curve. The point can be explained further, for the case of the downward-sloping long-run curve, with the help of Figure 7.5. Let the curve LR° be the original long-run curve and suppose that the desired inflation rate is $\bar{p}$. Thus before the shift in the long-run curve the economy is at point J with a steady unemployment rate of $\bar{u}$ and a steady inflation rate of $\bar{p}$. Suppose that the new long-run curve is the curve LR. Then the policy-maker's problem is to devise a series of unemployment-rate manipulations that will move the economy from J, which is now a short-run position, to K — the point on the new long-run curve with ordinate $\tilde{p}$.

A question which arises quite naturally from this discussion is the following. Suppose that the policy-maker is committed to the second form of demand management. Suppose further that he wishes to shift the economy from one long-run position to another (because he now feels it appropriate to pursue a different steady inflation rate), or from its present short-run position to a particular long-run position (because the long-run inflation—unemployment curve has shifted). What route should he choose? We shall now consider this question. In doing so, we shall confine our attention to the case where the problem is to choose a route from one long-run position to another; the other case, where the problem is to choose a route between a short-run position and some desired long-run position, will be left to the reader. We shall also confine ourselves to the sub-case of the chosen case where the long-run curve is downward-sloping; the other sub-case, where the long-run curve is vertical, will again be left to the reader. Thus the specific question to be answered is: 'What route should the policy-maker choose if he wishes to move the economy from an "old" position on a downward-sloping long-run inflation—unemployment curve to a "new" position on the curve?' In asking this question we imply, of course, that more than one route exists. This is, indeed, the case; and the first, and major, task involved in answering our question is to explore the possibilities. For this purpose we shall begin by using Figure 7.6.

Suppose that the economy is at point A on the long-run curve, that is to say, that the inflation rate is steady at p_0 and the unemployment rate at u_0. Suppose also that the policy-maker wishes to reduce the inflation rate to $\tilde{p}$ and to keep it steady at this lower level, that is to say, that he wishes to shift the economy to the point B, also on the long-run curve. There are a number of routes by which the point B could be reached, and we show two of them (we shall refer to them as route 1 and route 2) in Figure 7.6.

Take route 1. Designate the period in which the policy-maker takes action as period 1. Then route 1 involves lifting the unemployment rate from u_0 to u_1 in period 1. The immediate effect (period 1 effect) of this change can be deduced from the appropriate short-run curve, that is the short-run curve corresponding to an expected inflation rate of p_1^e (cf. p. 141 above). But since, by hypothesis, period 0 was a steady-state situation, we know from (7.3) that $p_0^e = p_0$, and hence that $p_1^e = p_0^e$. Consequently the impact effect of the change in the unemployment rate can be deduced equally well from the short-run curve corresponding to an expected inflation rate of p_0^e. This is the short-run curve SR_1, since A lies on this curve and the expected inflation rate at A is p_0^e.† Our final conclusion, then, is that the inflation rate will be reduced in period 1 to the desired level, $\tilde{p}$.

---

†We assume here and throughout the ensuing analysis that the data X, o and s remain at the levels ruling in period 0.

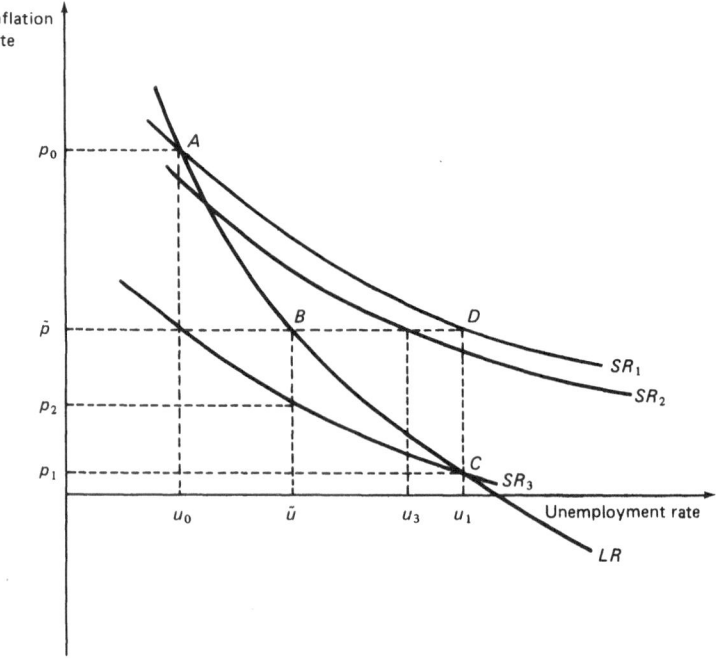

Fig. 7.6

Route 1 now involves keeping the unemployment rate steady at u_1. It follows from the proposition stated at the end of the previous section that, with the unemployment rate steady at u_1, a steady inflation rate of p_1, which is less than the desired level, will eventually be achieved.

Once the inflation rate has steadied at p_1, the next move under route 1 is to lower the unemployment rate to $\tilde{u}$. Once again, the immediate effect of this change can be deduced from the appropriate short-run curve; and by the same reasoning as before this is the curve SR_3 passing through the point C. Thus the immediate effect of the reduction in the unemployment rate to $\tilde{u}$ will be to raise the inflation rate to p_2.

Finally, the unemployment rate is kept steady at $\tilde{u}$. With this steady-unemployment rate a steady inflation rate of the desired level, $\bar{p}$, will eventually be realised. Once again, this follows from the proposition stated at the end of Section 7.2.

Turn now to route 2. Route 2, like route 1, involves lifting the unemployment rate from u_0 to u_1 in period 1 and reducing the inflation rate to the desired level, $\bar{p}$. However, whereas on route 1 the unemployment rate is first kept steady at u_1 and then cut back to $\tilde{u}$ in a single period, on route 2 the unemployment rate is held at u_1 for a single period only and is then reduced, period by period, to $\tilde{u}$, the successive reductions being just sufficient to ensure that the inflation rate stays at the desired level, $\bar{p}$, throughout. To see the implications of the last part of the preceding sentence note that if the actual inflation rate falls from p_0 to $\bar{p}$ in period 1 and remains at $\bar{p}$ in subsequent periods, as it does on route 2, the expected inflation rate will fall steadily from p_0^e towards $\bar{p}$ from period 2 onwards (see Appendix 7.2 for a demonstration). It follows from this that, on route 2, the short-run curve corresponding to the expected inflation rate of period 2 will be SR_2, say — a curve which lies to the left of SR_1, the short-run curve corresponding to the expected inflation rate of period 1. From SR_2 we learn that, to keep the inflation rate at $\tilde{p}$ in period 2, it is necessary to cut the unemployment rate back from u_1 to u_3; and it is this change which is made on route 2. Similarly, the short-run curve corresponding to the expected inflation rate of period 3 will be to the left of SR_2. This curve will show that, to keep the inflation rate steady at $\bar{p}$ in period 3, a further cut in the unemployment rate, bringing it somewhat closer to $\tilde{u}$, will be required; and so on for subsequent periods.

Two other possible routes which we shall designate route 3 and route 4, respectively, are shown in Figure 7.7. Let us consider them in turn.

If route 3 is chosen, the policy-maker's first move is to raise the unemployment rate from the initial level, u_0, to $\tilde{u}$. As will be clear from earlier discussion, the immediate effect of this increase in the unemployment rate is to lower the

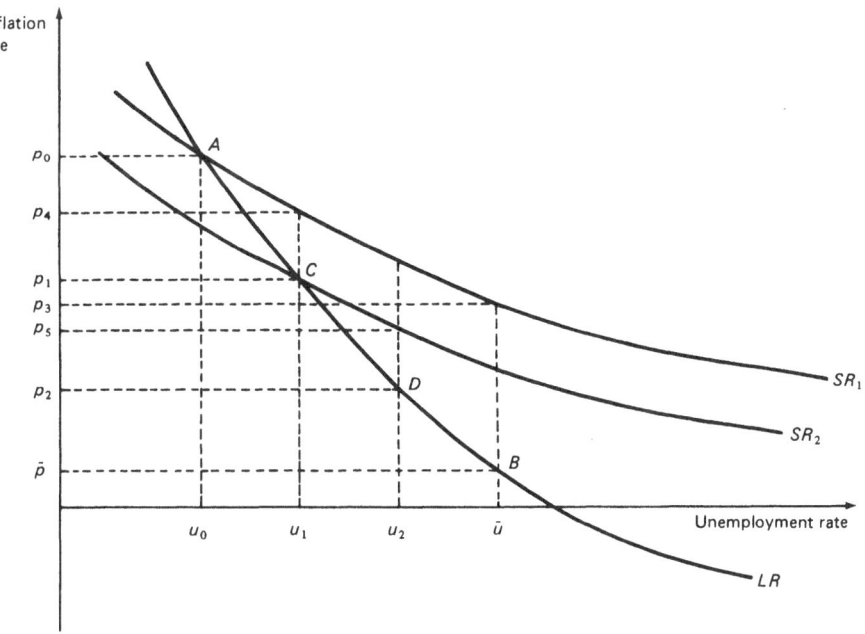

Fig. 7.7

inflation rate to p_3, this being the inflation rate given by SR_1, the short-run curve passing through A, for an unemployment rate of $\bar{u}$. Having reduced the inflation rate part of the way in this fashion, the policy-maker then keeps the unemployment rate steady at $\bar{u}$. This steadying of the unemployment rate guarantees that the inflation rate will eventually fall to the desired level, $\bar{p}$. This we know from the basic proposition stated at the end of the previous section.

In the case of route 4, the policy-maker's first move is to increase the unemployment rate in the direction of, but not as far as, $\bar{u}$ — say to u_1. The immediate effect of this move will be to reduce the inflation rate to p_4, the inflation given by SR_1 for an unemployment rate of u_1. The unemployment rate is then held steady at u_1 until the point C on the long-run curve is reached, as it must be according to our basic proposition. By then the inflation rate will have fallen to p_1. The next move is to increase the unemployment rate a second time while still keeping it below $\bar{u}$ — say to u_2. The impact effect of this move will be to reduce the inflation rate to p_5 — the inflation rate given by SR_2, the short-run curve passing through C, for an unemployment rate of u_2. Again the unemployment rate is held steady until the long-run curve is reached — this time at the point D — by which time the inflation rate will have fallen to p_2. The above procedure is repeated one or more times, the last move being to raise the unemployment rate to $\bar{u}$ and to hold it there until the point B is reached, that is until the inflation rate has fallen to the desired figure of $\bar{p}$.

Thus the essential difference between routes 3 and 4 is that on route 3 the unemployment rate is raised to $\bar{u}$ in a single step, whereas on route 4 it is raised in two or more steps.

Routes 1 and 2 may be described as 'high-unemployment' routes in the sense that, on these routes, the unemployment rate is higher throughout the transition period than the level that will eventually be required, year-in, year-out, to keep the inflation rate at the desired level. On the other hand, routes 3 and 4 are 'low-unemployment' routes in the sense that, on these routes, the unemployment rate is never higher than the level that will ultimately be required. If the high-unemployment routes are re-examined it will be seen that, on these routes, the inflation rate is reduced immediately to the desired level and does not rise above the desired level at any stage. By contrast, on the low-unemployment routes, the inflation rate is above the desired level throughout the transition period. What emerges, therefore, is that the broad choice open to the policy-maker is between: (i) getting the inflation rate down quickly to the desired level and facing 'high' unemployment during the transition period; and (ii) getting the inflation rate down slowly and enjoying 'low' unemployment during the transition. In making his decision as to the route to be followed the policy-maker will have to face this dilemma and weigh the cost of 'high' unemployment against the benefits of a rapid reduction of the inflation rate. Before he can do this, of course, he will need to know, among other things, just how high the 'high' unemployment will really be; and this is not a point on which our diagrams have anything useful to say.

7.4 Some Empirical Trade-Offs: Perry

The preceding analysis depends heavily on the *general properties* of the long-run inflation—unemployment curve but it does not depend in any way on the precise position of the curve or on its precise curvature at any point. In other words, for the purposes of the analysis it is not necessary to draw the *actual* curve; a hypothetical curve with the same general properties as the *actual* curve is quite sufficient. The position would be very different, however, if we wished to apply the analysis to some actual situation. Then we would require the actual empirical curve, not merely a hypothetical curve, because the various unemployment rates shown in Figures 7.6 and 7.7 would need to be known as actual figures.

In the remaining sections of this chapter we shall consider several recent attempts to supply the empirical, long-run curve for some particular economy, beginning with one of the earliest and most notable, namely that made by Perry for the U.S. economy in the mid-1960s.[1]

The basis of Perry's trade-off calculations was a numerical long-run inflation—unemployment relationship for the U.S. economy, and we shall begin by explaining how this was obtained. Perry's starting-point was the numerical version of his 'preferred' wage equation (see Section 5.2) which is set out below:

$$\tilde{w}_t = -4.313 + 0.367p_{t-1} + 14.711u_t^{-1} + 0.424R_{t-1} + 0.792(R_t - R_{t-1}).$$

$$(7.14)$$

We remind the reader that $\tilde{w}_t$ is the percentage change in the index of negotiated wage rates between quarter t and the corresponding quarter one year earlier, u is the unemployment rate (average over four quarters up to and including the quarter in question), R is the annual profit rate (average over four quarters) and p is the percentage change from the preceding quarter in the price index (sum over four quarters).†

His first step was to replace the wage variable on the left-hand side of this equation by $p_t + o_t$, where o is the percentage change in output per man between quarter t and the corresponding quarter one year earlier. This substitution is based on the simplified price equation: ‡

$$
\begin{aligned}
\text{Rate of price increase} = {}&\text{Rate of increase of wage-earnings} \\
&\text{per man } \textit{less} \text{ rate of increase of} \qquad (7.15) \\
&\text{output per man.}
\end{aligned}
$$

However, it is not fully justified even if this equation be accepted. In the first

---

†Note a slight change in the notation as compared with Section 5.2. There we used a 'bar' over the independent variables to indicate that they were averages or sums of the preceding four quarters. We have dropped the bar in writing (7.14) because in the present chapter we are using this symbol to denote 'steady state'.

‡See Section 2.4 for the logic of this equation.

place the p in (7.14) does not correspond with the $\tilde{w}$ that is, it is not a percentage rate of increase over the corresponding quarter one year earlier) and it *should* do if (7.15) is to be applied. Second, $\tilde{w}$ is not the rate of increase of average earnings, as it should be, but the rate of increase of negotiated wage rates (see above, p. 95, footnote). Perry's first move, therefore, was fairly rough and ready.

After the substitution in question had been made, (7.14) took the form:

$$p_t = -4.313 + 0.367p_{t-1} + 14.711u_t^{-1} + 0.424R_{t-1}\ 0.792(R_t - R_{t-1}) - o_t.$$

$$(7.16)$$

The final step was to derive the steady-state version of (7.16) by suppressing the time subscripts. The result was:

$$\bar{p} = -4.313 + 0.367\bar{p} + 14.711\bar{u}^{-1} + 0.424\bar{R} + 0.792(\bar{R} - \bar{R}) - \bar{o}.$$

This reduces, of course, to:

$$\bar{p} = -4.313 + 0.367\bar{p} + 14.711\bar{u}^{-1} + 0.424\bar{R} - \bar{o}.$$

Collecting the terms in $\bar{p}$ we obtain:

$$\bar{p}(1 - 0.367) = -4.313 + 14.711\bar{u}^{-1} + 0.424\bar{R} - \bar{o}.$$

This gives:

$$\bar{p} = -\frac{4.313}{0.633} + \frac{14.711}{0.633}\bar{u}^{-1} + \frac{0.424}{0.633}\bar{R} - \frac{1}{0.633}\bar{o},$$

or

$$\bar{p} = -6.814 + 23.24\bar{u}^{-1} + 0.67\bar{R} - 1.58\bar{o}.\qquad(7.17)$$

Relationship (7.17) is the numerical long-run inflation—unemployment relationship which Perry finally derived. It is not identical with our (7.10) because Perry's model differs from the model underlying (7.10), namely (7.1), (7.2) and (7.3). However, it possesses the essential characteristics of (7.10) in that it is a relationship showing the dependence of the steady inflation rate on the steady unemployment rate and on steady levels of certain other variables. Moreover, for specified values of $\bar{R}$ and $\bar{o}$ the 'other' steady levels in question, Perry's (7.17) gives a long-run curve of $\bar{p}$ against $\bar{u}$ with the same properties as the curve shown in Figure 7.3 (see p. 144).

Having explained the derivation of (7.17), we now consider the way in which Perry used it to provide quantitative trade-off information for the U.S. economy. Clearly, with the help of (7.17) we can calculate the (annual) steady inflation rate that will be associated with any specified steady unemployment rate, for given steady values of the profit rate and the (annual) percentage rate of increase of output per man. Suppose, for example, that the steady profit rate is put at 10.8 per cent, which was the U.S. average for the period 1953—60, and that the steady productivity figure is put at 2.7 per cent per annum. Then according to (7.17) a steady unemployment rate of 4 per cent will mean a steady inflation rate of 2 per cent per annum. The calculation is as follows:

$$\bar{p} = -6.814 + \frac{23.240}{4} + (0.670 \times 10.8) - (1.580 \times 2.7)$$

$$= -6.814 + 5.810 + 7.236 - 4.266 = 1.966.$$

Equally clearly, if we make several such calculations, each time with a different steady unemployment rate but with the same value for $\bar{R}$ and $\bar{o}$, we will be in a position to sketch the entire long-run inflation–unemployment curve corresponding to the values of $\bar{R}$ and $\bar{o}$ in question.

This, in fact, is the method of presenting his trade-off information which Perry chose to adopt. Altogether he provides twelve long-run inflation–unemployment curves for the United States.[2] Four of these correspond to $\bar{o} = 2.7$ per cent per annum, four to $\bar{o} = 3$ per cent per annum and four to $\bar{o} = 3.3$ per cent per annum. In the case of each group one curve corresponds to $\bar{R} = 10$ per cent, one to $\bar{R} = 10.8$ per cent, one to $\bar{R} = 11.8$ per cent and one to $\bar{R} = 12.5$ per cent.

Table 7.1

(1) Unemployment rate (%) $(\bar{u})$	(2) $\dfrac{23.240}{\bar{u}}$	(3) (0.670×10.8) $- (1.580 \times 3)$ $- 6.814$	(4) Inflation rate (% per annum) $(\bar{p})$ (2) + (3)
2	11.620	−4.318	7.302
3	7.747	−4.318	3.429
4	5.810	−4.318	1.492
5	4.648	−4.318	0.330
6	3.873	−4.318	−0.445
7	3.320	−4.318	−0.998

In Table 7.1 we present the basic calculations for one of Perry's curves – the curve for $\bar{R} = 10.8$ per cent and $\bar{o} = 3$ per cent per annum. These calculations show that for the specified values or $\bar{R}$ and $\bar{o}$, a steady unemployment rate of 4 per cent, which appears to have been generally regarded as 'full employment' in the United States throughout the 1960s, would result in a steady annual inflation rate of about 1.5 per cent. A zero inflation rate could be achieved only with an unacceptably high unemployment rate of between 5 per cent and 6 per cent.

7.5 Some Empirical Trade-Offs: Vanderkamp

In this section we shall consider a study by Vanderkamp which provides quantitative information about the long-run trade-off between inflation and unemployment for the Canadian economy.[3]

Vanderkamp's approach to the trade-off question resembles the approach of Perry in that his trade-off calculations are based on a numerical long-run inflation–unemployment relationship. However, the procedure which Vanderkamp uses to derive his relationship is a little more elaborate than the procedure employed by Perry. As we have seen, Perry's procedure is to start with a numerical wage equation, and then to convert this equation into a numerical price–unemployment relationship by means of (7.15) and finally to derive the steady-state version of the numerical price–unemployment equation so obtained by suppressing time subscripts. Vanderkamp's procedure, on the other hand, is to start with a numerical price equation and *two* numerical wage equations – one for the 'organised' sector of the labour market and one for the 'unorganised' sector – then to derive a numerical price–unemployment relationship by substituting the two wage equations into the price equation and finally to derive the steady-state version of the price–unemployment relationship by suppressing time subscripts.

Turning now to the details of Vanderkamp's procedure, we begin by setting out his numerical price and wage equations. These equations, which were derived by application of standard econometric techniques to quarterly Canadian time-series data for the post-war period, are as follows:

$$p_t = -0.018 + 0.139w^a_{1t} + 0.015w^a_{2t} + 0.150m_t + 0.594p_{t-1} \qquad (7.18)$$

$$w^a_{1t} = -0.745 + 0.679p_t + 7.096u^{-1}_{1t} + 0.466o_t \qquad (7.19)$$

$$w^a_{2t} = 0.703 + 0.363p_t + 1.982u^{-1}_{2t} + 7.299[u^{-1}_{2(t-1)} - u^{-1}_{2(t-2)}] \qquad (7.20)$$

In these expressions, p, w^a, o and m denote, respectively, the percentage change from the previous quarter in the price index, the index of average wage and salary earnings, the index of output per man and the index of import prices, and u is the unemployment rate. The subscript '1' attached to w and u denotes 'organized' while the subscript '2' denotes 'unorganised'. When (7.19) and (7.20) are substituted into (7.18) the following price–unemployment relationship results:

$$p_t = -[0.018 + (0.745 \times 0.139) - (0.703 \times 0.015)] + [(0.139 \times 0.679)$$
$$+ (0.015 \times 0.363)]p_t$$
$$+ (0.139 \times 7.096)u^{-1}_{1t} + (0.015 \times 1.982)u^{-1}_{2t} + (0.139 \times 0.466)o_t$$
$$+ (0.015 \times 7.299)[u^{-1}_{2(t-1)} - u^{-1}_{2(t-2)}] + 0.150m_t + 0.594p_{t-1}.$$

This reduces to:

$$p_t(1 - 0.099) = -0.111 + 0.986u^{-1}_{1t} + 0.030u^{-1}_{2t} + 0.065o_t$$
$$+ 0.109[u^{-1}_{2(t-1)} - u^{-1}_{2(t-2)}] + 0.15m_t + 0.594p_{t-1}.$$

Dividing through by $1 - 0.099$ we obtain:

$$p_t = -0.123 + 1.094u_{1t}^{-1} + 0.033u_{2t}^{-1} + 0.072o_t$$

$$+ 0.121\,[u_{2(t-1)}^{-1} - u_{2(t-2)}^{-1}] + 0.166m_t + 0.659p_{t-1}. \tag{7.21}$$

The steady-state version of (7.21), found by suppressing time subscripts, is:

$$\bar{p}(1 - 0.659) = -0.123 + 1.094\bar{u}_1^{-1} + 0.033\bar{u}_2^{-1} + 0.072\bar{o} + 0.166\bar{m}. \tag{7.22}$$

Vanderkamp next transforms (7.22) into a relationship between $\bar{p}$ and $\bar{u}$ by replacing $\bar{u}_1$ by $1.64\bar{u}$ and $\bar{u}_2$ by $0.73\bar{u}$, these being respectively, the average post-war relationship between the 'organised' unemployment rate and the over-all unemployment rate and between the 'unorganised' unemployment rate and the over-all unemployment rate. The result is:

$$\bar{p}(1 - 0.659) = -0.123 + (0.667 + 0.045)\bar{u}^{-1} + 0.072\bar{o} + 0.166\bar{m}.$$

Dividing through by $1 - 0.659$ we obtain:

$$\bar{p} = -0.350 + 2.088\bar{u}^{-1} + 0.211\bar{o} + 0.487\bar{m}. \tag{7.23}$$

. Relationship (7.23) is Vanderkamp's numerical long-run inflation–unemployment relationship.† He uses it to make trade-off calculations for four pairs of values of $\bar{o}$ and $\bar{m}$, namely $\bar{o} = 0.5$, $\bar{m} = 0$; $\bar{o} = 0.5$, $\bar{m} = 0.5$; $\bar{o} = 0.5$, $\bar{m} = 1.25$; and $\bar{o} = 0.5$, $\bar{m} = 2.25$. These figures are of course quarterly rates of change. The calculations for one of the four pairs ($\bar{o} = 0.5$, $\bar{m} = 1.25$) are shown in Table 7.2.‡

Table 7.2

(1) Unemployment rate (%) $(\bar{u})$	(2) $\dfrac{2.088}{\bar{u}}$	(3) (0.211×0.5) $+ (0.487 \times 1.25)$ $- 0.350$	(4) Inflation rate (% per quarter) $(\bar{p})$ (2) + (3)	(5) Inflation rate (% per annum) (4) × 4
2	1.044	0.364	1.408	5.632
3	0.696	0.364	1.060	4.240
4	0.522	0.364	0.886	3.544
5	0.418	0.364	0.782	3.128
6	0.348	0.364	0.712	2.848
7	0.298	0.364	0.662	2.648
8	0.261	0.364	0.625	2.500

† The expression which Vanderkamp actually gives (p. 207 of his study) is:

$$\bar{p} = -0.255 + 2.088\bar{u}^{-1} + 0.487\bar{m},$$

which is (7.23) with $\bar{o}$ put at 0.5 per cent per quarter.

‡ Following Vanderkamp, the calculated $\bar{p}$ values, shown in column 4, which are quarterly rates of change, are roughly converted to annual rates of change by multiplication by 4. Notice that three of the $\bar{p}$ figures, which Vanderkamp shows for the present case (row 3 of his table 1) are not quite correct.

7.6   Some Empirical Trade-Offs: Bodkin et al.

We turn now to an important international study of the long-run trade-off between inflation and unemployment which was undertaken in the mid-1060s by R. G. Bodkin and three associates.[4]

The study in question covered five countries, namely Canada, the United States, the United Kingdom, France and West Germany. For each of these five countries Bodkin *et al.* derived a numerical long-run inflation—unemployment relationship, that is a numerical relationship showing $\bar{p}$ in terms of $\bar{u}$ and certain other steady-state variables. The procedure used for this purpose was the one used by Vanderkamp. Thus, for each of the five countries, numerical wage and price equations were first obtained by applying standard econometric techniques to quarterly post-war data,[†] then the steady-state versions of these two equations were found, and finally the steady-state version of the wage equation was substituted into the steady-state version of the price equation to obtain the desired numerical long-run inflation—unemployment relationship.

The individual long-run relationships which Bodkin *et al.* derived in this way are rather cumbersome and will not be given.[‡] However, we shall make a few general observations on the relationships before considering their use by the authors to make certain international trade-off calculations of great interest.

First of all, at the risk of being repetitive, we note that all of the relationships show the steady inflation rate in terms of the steady unemployment rate and certain other steady-state variables. Hence they enable us to calculate what steady inflation rate will be associated with any given steady unemployment rate, for given levels of the 'other' variables.

Second, in all cases the relationship is linear either in the reciprocal of the unemployment rate or in the square of the reciprocal, that is the unemployment variable has either -1 or -2 as exponent.

Third, in all cases the coefficient of the unemployment variable is positive, thus ensuring that the long-run inflation—unemployment curve has a negative, but decreasingly negative, slope at all points (see above, p. 141).

A fourth point of interest is that in the relationships for Canada and the United States, one of the 'other' variables is a steady profit variable, as in the Perry relationship, (7.17). However, whereas in Perry's relationship the profit variable is a profit-rate variable, in the Canadian and U.S. relationships derived by Bodkin *et al.* the profit variable is a profit mark-up variable.

Finally, it is worth noting that all relationships except that for the United

---

[†] As far as possible non-comparabilities in the data were removed before estimation began.

[‡] To assist the reader who wishes to trace the actual relationships in the original study, we note that they are numbered as follows: (6.7) (Canada), (8.48) (Canada), (8.11) (the United States), (8.24) (the United Kingdom), (8.31) (France) and (8.40) (West Germany).

States incorporates external influences through the inclusion of the (steady) percentage rate of increase of import prices among the 'other' variables.

We turn now to the trade-off calculations which Bodkin *et al.* made from their long-run inflation–unemployment relationships for each of the five countries covered in their study. In fact, two distinct calculations were made for each country. In the first calculation the steady inflation rate corresponding to each of four steady unemployment rates was calculated for the country concerned on the assumption of 'non-inflationary' steady values for the other variables appearing in its long-run relationship. In the second calculation the steady inflation rate was calculated for the same four steady unemployment rates but now on the assumption of 'moderately inflationary' steady values for the other variables.

The four steady unemployment rates involved in both calculations were: (i) the minimum rate experienced by the country in question since 1953 or 1954 (depending on the country); (ii) the maximum rate experienced over the same period; (iii) the average rate experienced over the period since 1953 or 1954, as the case may be; and (iv) the rate of 3 per cent.

To explain the distinction between the 'non-inflationary' and 'moderately inflationary' calculations, take the Canadian case as an example. In the long-run inflation–unemployment relationship which Bodkin *et al.* derived for Canada, the 'other' steady-state variables were a profit variable and a U.S. wage variable. Earlier we defined the profit variable somewhat loosely as 'a profit mark-up' variable. A more precise (and more difficult) definition is: 'a four-quarter moving average of the index of corporate profits before tax in manufacturing, expressed as a percentage of the index of manufacturing production'. Thus the observations on the profit variable were figures round about 100. The U.S. wage variable was a four-quarter moving average of the percentage rate of change from the corresponding quarter a year earlier in average wage-earnings in U.S. manufacturing. Observations on this variable, therefore, were smallish figures in the range, say, from −10 to +10. As the 'non-inflationary' steady values for the profit and U.S. wage variables, Bodkin *et al.* chose 97.75 and 3.2, respectively, while for the 'moderately inflationary' steady values they chose 107.75 and 6, respectively.[5] As both variables appear with positive coefficients in the Canadian long-run relationship, a trade-off calculation in which the former two values are used gives a lower steady inflation rate at any steady unemployment rate (better trade-off) than does a calculation in which the latter two are used. Hence the former set of values is appropriately described as 'non-inflationary' and the latter set as 'moderately inflationary'.

For each country, then, Bodkin *et al.* calculated the steady inflation rate corresponding to the four steady unemployment rates specified above: (*a*) using 'non-inflationary' assumptions about the 'other' steady-state variables; and (*b*) using 'moderately inflationary' assumptions. The four pairs of inflation–unemployment figures calculated for, say, Canada, on the non-inflationary assumptions Bodkin *et al.* treated as four points on the non-inflationary long-run inflation–unemployment curve for Canada and proceeded to use these four points to sketch in the entire Canadian curve. On the same diagram, they then drew the non-inflationary long-run inflation—unemployment curves for each of the other four countries, in each case using the four pairs of inflation— unemployment figures calculated for the country concerned on the non-inflationary assumptions. Finally, on a second diagram they showed the 'moderately inflationary' long-run inflation—unemployment curves for the five countries, these being drawn in each case from the four pairs of inflation— unemployment figures calculated for the country concerned on the 'moderately inflationary' assumptions.

Two important features of these two diagrams are worth noting. The first is that there are wide differences between the long-run inflation—unemployment curves of the five countries covered by the study — both as regards slope and as regards position. This suggests that trade-off information obtained for one country cannot be safely applied to another without further investigation. The second noteworthy feature is that none of the non-inflationary curves crosses the horizontal axis to the left of 4 per cent and none of the moderately inflationary curves to the left of 5 per cent. This suggests that in none of the five countries concerned is there much prospect of combining a steady inflation rate of zero (continuous price stability) with a steady unemployment rate of less than 4 per cent (continuous full employment). In other words, in these countries, at least, the twin objectives of price stability and full employment may well be incompatible, given the existing economic structure. On this point the international study of Bodkin *et al.* appears to be in substantial agreement with the U.S. study of Perry discussed in Section 7.4 and the Canadian study of Vanderkamp considered in Section 7.5.

7.7   Empirical Trade-Offs From Econometric Models

Perhaps the most important and dramatic development in economics since the end of the Second World War has been the emergence of large-scale macro-dynamic econometric models as policy-making tools. Models of this type now exist for all advanced industrial countries (the United States has dozens) and are being widely used to provide the quantitative information which intelligent policy-making demands. A natural question, therefore, is whether these models can be used to provide the quantitative information about the long-run trade-off between inflation and unemployment which is needed by the policy-maker who aims to control inflation *via* demand management.

Before considering this question it may be desirable to explain what we mean by the term 'large-scale macro-dynamic econometric model'. This can be done most conveniently by first explaining the term 'macro-dynamic econometric model' and then the term 'large scale'.

A macro-dynamic econometric model may be described as a set of relationships which links one group of macro variables known as jointly determined or endogenous variables with another group known as predetermined variables and which contains enough information to determine the values of all members of the first group once the values of all members of the second group are given. The requirement that the relationships 'contain enough information etc.' means, first, that they must be numerical relationships (all coefficients, intercepts, etc. must be actual numbers) and, second, that there must be the same number of relationships as there are jointly determined variables. A macro-dynamic econometric model may thus be regarded as a device which generates a time path for each of the jointly determined variables once a set of time paths for the predetermined variables has been 'fed in'.

The three relationships used by Vanderkamp to obtain his numerical long-run inflation–unemployment relationship for Canada, that is (7.18), (7.19) and (7.20), constitute a simple macro-dynamic econometric model in which p_t, w^a_{1t} and w^a_{2t} are the jointly determined variables and m_t, p_{t-1}, u_{1t}, o_t and u_{2t} are the predetermined variables. If a set of time paths for the five predetermined variables were to be fed into the system of three relationships, it would suffice to generate a time path for each of the three jointly determined variables, p_t, w^a_{1t} and w^a_{2t}.

The two relationships which form the foundation of Perry's trade-off calculations, namely (7.14) and (7.15), can also be thought of as a primitive macro-dynamic econometric model in which the rate of increase of the price index and the rate of increase of money wage rates are the jointly determined variables, and in which u_t, R_t, R_{t-1}, p_{t-1} and the rate of increase of output per man are the predetermined variables.

So much for 'macro-dynamic econometric model'. What of 'large scale'? When we refer to a 'large-scale' macro-dynamic econometric model we have in mind a model which consists, not of two or three relationships, but of, say, 100 relationships, or even more, and which, therefore, gives an extremely detailed picture of the complex interrelationships which exist between the various key macro variables.

We turn now to the question of whether an enormous statistical structure of the type just described can be made to yield quantitative information about the long-run trade-off between inflation and unemployment. We shall approach this question in the obvious way – by first asking whether the procedure which has been applied by Perry and Vanderkamp to their *small*-scale macro-dynamic econometric models is applicable also to the large-scale models which are now in use – models which consist of 100, 150, or perhaps 200 relationships.

The answer, it seems, is 'no'. To see why, let us recall the steps in the Perry–Vanderkamp procedure. The first step is to solve the macro-dynamic econometric model for one of the jointly determined variables, namely the inflation rate, in terms of the predetermined variables – in the jargon, the first step is to derive the reduced-form equation for p_t. In the case of Perry's study this reduced-form equation is (7.16) and in the case of Vanderkamp's it is (7.21). The second step is to derive the steady-state version of the reduced-form equation for p_t by suppressing time subscripts. The resulting relationship ((7.17) in the case of Perry's study and (7.23) in the case of Vanderkamp's) gives the steady inflation rate in terms of the steady unemployment rate and steady values of the remaining predetermined variables. The final step is to use the steady-state equation to calculate the steady inflation rates that will be associated with specified steady unemployment rates, using fixed steady levels for the other predetermined variables.

There are two reasons why the above procedure is unlikely to work when the basic macro-dynamic econometric model is large scale. In the first place, in the typical large-scale model the unemployment rate is a jointly determined variable, not a predetermined variable. Consequently, the unemployment rate will not appear on the right-hand side of the reduced-form equation for p_t, nor will it appear on the right-hand side of the steady-state version of this equation. And this means, of course, that the final step in the Perry–Vanderkamp procedure will no longer be possible.

The second difficulty is that the non-linearities in the typical large-scale macro-dynamic econometric model are such that there is no possibility of deriving the reduced-form equation for p_t in the first place. The mere presence of non-linearities is not enough to make it impossible to derive the reduced-form equation, as is clear from the fact that we can derive the reduced-form equation for Vanderkamp's model despite the fact that the unemployment rate appears as a reciprocal in the wage equations. However, when the non-linearities are both complex and numerous, as they are in the typical large-scale model, the reduced form will not exist, in general, and hence the Perry–Vanderkamp procedure will break down at the first step.

In general, therefore, the straightforward procedure which is used to derive long-run trade-off information in the studies examined in Sections 7.4–7.6 will not work within the framework of the typical large-scale macro-dynamic econometric model. What is the alternative? Perhaps the most promising alternative is to employ a computer routine which simulates the behaviour of the economy under conditions of steady unemployment. A few such simulation studies have been performed for the U.S. economy in recent years. All are exceedingly complex and no attempt will be made to describe them in detail.[6] However, broadly speaking, the procedure adopted in these studies is as follows. The computer is given a realistic time path for all but one of the predetermined variables of the model covering a period of, say, twenty years and is instructed to compute the inflation rate which is implied by the model for this particular set of time paths of the predetermined variables, on the assumption that the 'residual' predetermined variable adjusts, period by period throughout the twenty years, so as to keep the (jointly determined) unemployment rate constant at some specified figure. The time path computed for the inflation rate in this way is then examined for evidence of convergence. Assuming that the computed inflation rate shows unmistakable signs of settling down at a particular figure, this figure is taken to be the steady inflation rate which, according to the model, will be associated with the steady unemployment rate underlying the whole exercise; that is, it will be one point on the long-run inflation–unemployment curve which is embedded in the model. Other points on the curve are obtained by repeating the entire computation several times, each time with a different steady unemployment rate, and the general appearance of the curve is revealed by interpolation between these points.

It is of interest to note that the simulation studies just described suggest a somewhat higher steady inflation rate for the U.S. economy, at a steady unemployment rate of 4 per cent, than does Perry's 'small-model' study. Whereas Perry's study suggests that a steady unemployment rate of 4 per cent will be associated with a steady inflation rate of 1.5 per cent to 2 per cent, depending on the profit rate and the rate of increase of productivity (see above, p. 155) the simulation studies suggest that the figure will be of the order of 3 per cent to 3.5 per cent, which is more in line with the figure thrown up for the Canadian economy by Vanderkamp's study (see above, p. 157).

Appendix 7.1

To show that the proposition stated in the text (see p. 146) is indeed an implication of our model, we make use of (7.4), which defines the family of short-run curves, and (7.10), which defines the long-run curve in the case of $\beta_1 \alpha_2$ being less than unity. We first use (7.4) to derive an expression for the absolute change in the inflation rate between successive periods, that is for $p_t - p_{t-1}$. To obtain this expression we lag (7.4) one period to obtain an expression for p_{t-1} and we then subtract this expression from (7.4). The result is:

$$p_t - p_{t-1} = \beta_1 \alpha_1 (u_t^{-1} - u_{t-1}^{-1}) + \beta_1 \alpha_2 (p_t^e - p_{t-1}^e)$$

$$+ \beta_1 (X_t - X_{t-1}) + \beta_2 (s_t - s_{t-1}) - \beta_1 (o_t - o_{t-1}).$$

$$(7.24)$$

By assumption the unemployment rate is kept steady by policy action and the other data are at fixed levels. Using this assumption we see that (7.24) reduces to:

$$p_t - p_{t-1} = \beta_1 \alpha_2 (p_t^e - p_{t-1}^e).$$

Now using (7.3) we can rewrite this expression as

$$p_t - p_{t-1} = \beta_1 \alpha_2 \delta (p_{t-1} - p_{t-1}^e) = \beta_1 \alpha_2 \delta p_{t-1} - \beta_1 \alpha_2 \delta p_{t-1}^e. \quad (7.25)$$

Next we substitute the expression for p_{t-1} given by (7.4) in the right-hand side of this expression, using once again the assumption that the unemployment rate and all other data are fixed, and denoting the fixed levels by means of an overhead bar. Proceeding in this way we obtain:

$$p_t - p_{t-1} = \beta_1 \alpha_2 \delta [\beta_1 \alpha_1 \bar{u}^{-1} + \beta_1 \alpha_0 + \beta_1 \bar{X} + \beta_2 \bar{s} + \beta_1 \bar{o}]$$

$$+ \beta_1 \alpha_2 \delta \beta_1 \alpha_2 p_{t-1}^e - \beta_1 \alpha_2 \delta p_{t-1}^e.$$

Collecting together the two final terms in p_{t-1}^e we obtain:

$$p_t - p_{t-1} = \beta_1 \alpha_2 \delta [\beta_1 \alpha_1 \bar{u}^{-1} + \beta_1 \alpha_0 + \beta_1 \bar{X} + \beta_2 \bar{s} - \beta_1 \bar{o}]$$
$$- \beta_1 \alpha_2 \delta (1 - \beta_1 \alpha_2) p_{t-1}^e$$
$$= \beta_1 \alpha_2 \, \delta N - \beta_1 \alpha_2 \delta (1 - \beta_1 \alpha_2) p_{t-1}^e. \qquad (7.26)$$

where N denotes the square-bracketed term on the right-hand side.

Let us now consider the situation where the inflation rate in period $t - 1$ is above the long-run level as defined by (7.10). Thus we have $p_{t-1} > \bar{p}$. Now, $p_{t-1} > \bar{p}$ implies $p_{t-1} - N > \bar{p} - N$. Also from (7.4) we have:

$$p_{t-1} - N = \beta_1 \alpha_2 p_{t-1}^e. \qquad (7.27)$$

Hence $p_{t-1} > \bar{p}$ implies $\beta_1 \alpha_2 p_{t-1}^e > \bar{p} - N$. Hence from (7.26) we have the result that when $p_{t-1} > \bar{p}$, $p_t - p_{t-1} < \beta_1 \alpha_2 \delta N - \delta (1 - \beta_1 \alpha_2)(\bar{p} - N)$.

Finally from (7.10) we have:

$$\bar{p} - N = \frac{N}{1 - \beta_1 \alpha_2} - N = \frac{N - N + \beta_1 \alpha_2 N}{1 - \beta_1 \alpha_2} = \frac{\beta_1 \alpha_2 N}{1 - \beta_1 \alpha_2}.$$

Therefore

$$(1 - \beta_1 \alpha_2)(\bar{p} - N) = \beta_1 \alpha_2 N.$$

Thus, when $p_{t-1} > \bar{p}$, we have $p_t - p_{t-1} < \beta_1 \alpha_2$ and $N - \delta \beta_1 \alpha_2 N$, that is $p_t - p_{t-1} < 0$. In other words, whenever the inflation rate is *above* the long-run level in any period, period $t - 1$, it will *decrease*.

This argument establishes our proposition for the situation where the economy is *above* the long-run inflation–unemployment curve. To establish it for the situation where the economy is below the curve we use (7.26) in exactly the same way as before except that we start with $p_{t-1} < \bar{p}$ instead of $p_{t-1} > \bar{p}$. With this reversal of the initial inequality we finish up, of course, with the result that when $p_{t-1} < \bar{p}$, $p_t - p_{t-1} > 0$, that is to say, that when the inflation rate is *below* the long-run level in any period, it will *increase*. Finally, to establish that if the economy is on the long-run curve it will stay there, it is simply a matter of using the equality, $p_{t-1} = \bar{p}$, in conjunction with (7.26). This gives the result that if the inflation rate is at the long-run level in any period, $p_t - p_{t-1} = 0$, that is the inflation rate will not change.

Appendix 7.2

In this appendix we show that if the actual inflation rate falls from p_0 in period 0 to $\tilde{p}$ in period 1, and stays thereafter at this level, the expected inflation rate will fall monotonically from p_0^e, beginning with period 2, and will converge on $\tilde{p}$.

The argument is based on (7.3) which can be written as:

$$p_t^e = \delta p_{t-1} + (1 - \delta)p_{t-1}^e. \tag{7.28}$$

This gives:

$$p_1^e = \delta p_0 + (1 - \delta)p_0^e.$$

Since period 0 is a stationary equilibrium situation we have $p_0 = p_0^e$. Hence from the above expression for p_1^e we have $p_1^e = p_0^e$.

Applying (7.28) again we obtain:

$$p_2^e = \delta p_1 + (1 - \delta)p_1^e = \delta \bar{p} + (1 - \delta)p_1^e.$$

Since $\bar{p} < p_0$ and $p_0 = p_0^e = p_1^e$ we have:

$$p_2^e < \delta p_1^e + (1 - \delta)p_1^e,$$

that is

$$p_2^e < p_1^e.$$

Continuing we have:

$$p_3^e = \delta \bar{p} + (1 - \delta)p_2^e.$$

Since $p_2^e < p_1^e$ this gives:

$$p_3^e < \delta \bar{p} + (1 - \delta)p_1^e,$$

that is

$$p_3^e < p_2^e.$$

Again

$$p_4^e = \delta \bar{p} + (1 - \delta)p_3^e.$$

Since $p_3^e < p_2^e$ this gives:

$$p_4^e < \delta p + (1 - \delta)p_2^e,$$

that is

$$p_4^e < p_3^e.$$

Obviously we can continue indefinitely along these lines, which establishes that, if the actual inflation rate falls from p_0^e to $\bar{p}$ in period 1, and stays there forever after, the expected rate will decline monotonically from period 2 onwards.

To show that the expected inflation rate converges on $\bar{p}$, we proceed as follows. From (7.28) we have:

$$p_1^e = \delta p_0 + (1 - \delta)p_0^e$$

$$p_2^e = \delta p_1 + (1 - \delta)p_1^e = \delta p_1 + \delta(1 - \delta)p_0 + (1 - \delta)^2 p_0^e$$

$$= \delta \tilde{p} + \delta(1 - \delta)p_0 + (1 - \delta)^2 p_0^e$$

$$p_3^e = \delta p_2 + (1 - \delta)p_2^e = \delta p_2 + \delta(1 - \delta)\tilde{p} + \delta(1 - \delta)^2 p_0 + (1 - \delta)^3 p_0^e$$

$$= \delta \tilde{p}[1 + (1 - \delta)] - \delta(1 - \delta)^2 p_0 + (1 - \delta)^3 p_0^e$$

$$p_4^e = \delta p_3 + (1 - \delta)p_3^e = \delta \tilde{p} + \delta \tilde{p}[(1 + \delta) + (1 - \delta)^2] + \delta(1 - \delta)^3 p_0$$

$$+ (1 - \delta)^4 p_0^3$$

$$= \delta \tilde{p}[1 + (1 - \delta) + (1 - \delta)^2] + \delta(1 - \delta)^3 p_0 + (1 - \delta)^4 p_0^e$$

$$\vdots \qquad\qquad\qquad \vdots$$

$$p_t^e = \delta \tilde{p}[1 + (1 - \delta) + (1 - \delta)^2 + \ldots + (1 - \delta)^{t-2}] + \delta(1 - \delta)^{t-1} p_0$$

$$+ (1 - \delta)^t p_0^e$$

As $t \to \infty$ the last two terms tend to zero since $0 < \delta < 1$, while the rest of the expression tends to:

$$\delta \tilde{p} \left\{ \frac{1}{1 - (1 - \delta)} \right\} = \tilde{p}.$$

Hence the expected inflation rate converges on $\tilde{p}$.

8

POLICY AGAINST INFLATION:
PRICES AND INCOMES POLICY

8.1   Definition of Prices and Incomes Policy

As pointed out in the opening section of Chapter 7, the economist typically approaches the problem of designing anti-inflationary policy with a particular model of the inflationary process in mind and begins by noting that two types of action are possible within the framework of his chosen model. One possibility is to modify the time paths of the data of the model in a favourable way; the other is to modify the structure of the model in a favourable way. In Chapter 7 we were concerned with the first of these two possibilities, and in this chapter and the next we shall be concerned with the second. The second possibility – favourable modification of the structure of the model – itself embraces two sub-possibilities, which go by the names 'prices and incomes policy' and 'manpower policy'. We shall devote this chapter to the former and Chapter 9 to the latter.

We begin our discussion of prices and incomes policy by giving a broad definition. We say that prices and incomes policy is in force if: (i) the policy-making authorities have formulated a code of behaviour for price-setters which is designed mainly to reduce the rate of price increase associated with given levels of the variables which determine the rate of price increase and/or a code of behaviour for the parties to wage negotiations the main objective of which is to reduce the rate of wage increase associated with given values of the variables which determine the rate of wage increase,† and if (ii) these codes of behaviour have been publicly announced and been backed either by legislation requiring that they be observed, or by pressure on the parties concerned to observe them voluntarily in the national interest, or both.

Looking at this definition in terms of the policy model presented in the last chapter (relationships (7.1), (7.2) and (7.3)) we can say that, under a prices and incomes policy, the policy-making authorities impose a code of behaviour on

---

†The significance of 'mainly' and 'main objective' in the above is that the framers of prices and incomes policies usually intend them not only to moderate the rate of inflation but to promote other objectives as well. Some of these other objectives are a more equitable distribution of income, faster economic growth and an improvement in the working of the labour market.

price-setters with the objective of so changing the values of β_1 and β_2 that p_t is less, for given values of w_t, o_t and s_t, than would have been the case otherwise and/or a code of behaviour on wage-setters with the objective of so changing α_0, α_1, α_2 and the parameters involved in X_t that the value of w_t is less, for given values of u_t, p_t^e and the variables involved in X_t, than it would have been otherwise. To the extent that these codes of behaviour achieve their purpose, the rate of inflation will be less in any period than it would have been in the absence of the prices and incomes policy. For if the policy achieves its aim, p_t will be less than it would have been for the same w_t, and w_t will actually be less than it would have been.†

In the next section we shall try to amplify this definition of prices and incomes policy by giving a brief description of the various ways in which it has operated over the years in the United Kingdom and the United States. While these are by no means the only countries which have attempted to control inflation by employing prices and incomes policy,[1] a description of the arrangements which they have adopted over the years in its name should suffice to add meaning to the formal definition given above.

8.2   Prices and Incomes Policy in the United Kingdom and the United States

A.   The United Kingdom

As far as the United Kingdom is concerned it is possible to identify seven distinct applications of prices and incomes policy in the period between the end of the Second World War and the end of the 1960s. It will be convenient to refer to these as 'episodes'.[2]

1.   Episode 1: 1948–50

The first application of prices and incomes policy in the United Kingdom was the 'wage freeze' of 1948–50. In this episode the emphasis was exclusively on wage

---

† A successful prices and incomes policy may cause w_t to be less than it would have been, not only by producing favourable changes in α_0, α_1 and α_2, but also by strengthening confidence in the ability of the authorities to bring inflation under control. Such a strengthening of confidence would be reflected, presumably, in a reduction in δ and hence in a smaller value of p_t^e, and, in turn, of w_t, than would otherwise have been observed. It should be noted, however, that *any* successful anti-inflation action (for example successful demand management) would have an identical confidence-boosting effect, as indeed might events, such as a change of government, which are not acts of economic policy in any sense. Thus, the effect under discussion cannot be regarded as a specific contribution of prices and incomes policy to the control of inflation, whereas the effect *via* the αs can be so regarded.

restraint — the question of price restraint did not arise because the price controls which had been introduced during the war were still in force — and the objective of the policy was a zero rate of increase of money wages. To achieve this objective the authorities relied mainly on persuading the parties to wages' negotiations in the private sector that any general increase of money wages was undesirable in the national interest and on setting a good example in any wage negotiations in which the government was itself involved. Employers were warned that if they granted money wage increases in defiance of the authorities' wishes, they might find that the resulting cost increases would not be taken into account in settling controlled prices. But apart from this, there was no attempt to bolster the voluntary approach with sanctions of any type, and, in particular, no suggestion of any form of statutory control over wage decisions.

2.   Episode 2: 1956

In the second application of prices and incomes policy, which occurred in 1956, the authorities stressed the need for both price restraint and wage restraint, though they made no attempt to spell out the meaning of these terms in precise codes of behaviour. As in the first episode the authorities avoided legislation and relied on informal discussions with the leaders of labour and management, coupled with public appeals for restraint of a very general kind, to achieve the desired results. While these efforts may have contributed something to price restraint, they appear to have made little impression on the leaders of the trade unions.

3.   Episode 3: 1961–2

The third application of prices and incomes policy in the United Kingdom in the post-war period was the 'pay pause' of 1961–2. The names 'pay pause' and 'wage freeze' suggest that this particular episode had much in common with the first. This, indeed, was the case. In the third episode, as in the first, the authorities stressed wage restraint and aimed to reduce the rate of increase of money wages per man to zero. Also, the means of achieving this aim was exhortation of the private sector backed by the promise of correct behaviour in the public sector — once again there was no question of any form of statutory control over wage decisions. The promise of correct behaviour in the public sector was certainly fulfilled. For example, wage and salary increases which were granted to civil servants and workers in the National Health Service after the beginning of the pause in July 1961 were not implemented until after it ended in March 1962. Again, certain awards of the Civil Service Arbitration Tribunal and the Industrial Court were held in abeyance following government intervention. Whether this good example was followed to any appreciable extent in the private sector, and in those parts of the public sector outside the immediate control of the policy authorities, is, however, open to considerable doubt.

4. Episode 4: 1962–4

In the fourth application of prices and incomes policy, occupying the years 1962–4, the authorities again concentrated on wage restraint, as they had done in the 'wage-freeze' and 'pay-pause' episodes. However, whereas on the two earlier occasions wage-negotiators had been asked to behave in such a way that the rate of increase of money wages per man in the economy as a whole would be zero, in the fourth episode they were asked to work to a target rate of increase ('guiding light' as it was called) of 2 to 2½ per cent per annum. In support of this particular figure the authorities argued that reasonable price stability required that the rate of increase of wage-earnings per man should be equal to the rate of increase in output per man and that a rate of increase of output per man of 2 to 2½ per cent per annum could reasonably be expected in the light of recent U.K. experience.

As on all previous occasions the authorities relied entirely on appeals in the national interest to achieve the desired results; the parties to wage and salary negotiations were exhorted to keep the 2 to 2½ per cent behaviour code in mind and then left to themselves to work out its application to individual cases.

5. Episode 5: 1965–6

The fifth application of prices and incomes policy in the United Kingdom in the post-war period was marked by several interesting developments, of which four will be mentioned.

In the first place, the need for price restraint as well as wage restraint was emphasised, as it had been in episode 2.

Second, a new organisation, known as the National Board for Prices and Incomes (N.B.P.I.), was set up to implement the policy. The intention was that, on a reference from the government, the Board would investigate a particular price increase or wage increase in the light of the codes of behaviour laid down for price- and wage-setters (see next paragraph) and make its recommendations known to the parties concerned. While the parties were to be free to reject these recommendations if they chose, it was hoped and expected that government persuasion and the pressure of public opinion would suffice to guarantee that most of them would be carried out.

Third, in episode 5 the codes of behaviour which the authorities laid down for price-setters and for the parties to wage negotiations were much more detailed and specific than on any previous occasion.

The code of behaviour for *price-setters* stated that prices should not be raised except in certain specified circumstances and that they should actually be reduced in certain other specified circumstances.

The circumstances in which a price rise would be justified were: (i) if an increase in wages consistent with the wages code (see below) had caused wage-earnings per man to rise more rapidly than output per man and hence resulted in an increase in unit labour cost which could not be offset, either by a reduction in unit non-labour cost or in the return sought on investment; (ii) if there had been an unavoidable increase in unit non-labour cost, for example because of an increase in the prices of materials and fuel, which could not be offset by a reduction in unit labour cost or in the desired return on investment; (iii) if there had been an unavoidable increase in unit capital cost which could not be offset either by a reduction in unit non-capital cost or in the desired return on investment; and (iv) if the enterprise was unable to secure the capital required to meet home and overseas demand after making every effort to reduce costs.

The circumstances in which a *reduction* in price would be expected were: (i) if wage increases in line with the wages code had resulted in a decrease in unit labour cost without any offsetting and unavoidable increase in unit non-labour cost; (ii) if there had been a fall in unit non-labour cost and no offsetting and unavoidable increase in unit labour cost or unit capital cost; (iii) if there had been a fall in unit capital cost and no offsetting and unavoidable increase in unit non-capital cost; and (iv) if the enterprise was exercising excessive market power.

The code of behaviour for the *parties to wage and salary negotiations* consisted of a 'norm' for wage and salary increases and a list of circumstances in which pay increases in excess of the norm would be justified. As in episode 4, the norm was fixed with reference to the expected increase in output per man in the economy as a whole, the figure actually prescribed being 3 to 3½ per cent per annum. Those engaged in wage and salary negotiations were expected to work to this figure, except in the following circumstances: (i) where the workers whose wages were being negotiated had contributed to productivity increase in a significant way; (ii) where it was necessary to secure a change in the distribution of manpower; (iii) where the wages of the workers concerned were too low to afford them a reasonable standard of living; (iv) where the wages of the workers concerned had fallen seriously out of line with the wages of those engaged in comparable work.

The fourth important development in episode 5 was the emergence of a strong emphasis on the need for productivity increase. This was largely attributable to the N.B.P.I., which, from the outset, adopted the practice of making two types of recommendation in relation to any case referred to it by the authorities, regardless of whether the case concerned a price rise or a wage rise. The first type were recommendations concerned with the justification or otherwise for the increase in terms of the codes of behaviour which had been laid down; the second were recommendations concerned with ways of increasing productivity in the industry in question.

6. *Episode 6: 1966—7*

The sixth application of prices and incomes policy occupied the twelve-month period, July 1966 to June 1967. The first six months was yet another period of 'freeze'; there were to be no increases in prices or money wages and wage increases which had been granted, but not paid, prior to the beginning of the freeze were to be held in abeyance for a period of six months. There were two important differences between the 'prices and incomes standstill', as this particular freeze was called, and the two earlier freezes — the 'wage freeze' and the 'pay pause'. The first is evident from the name — the 1966–7 freeze applied to *both* prices and money wages whereas the two earlier freezes had applied to money wages only. Second, the 1966–7 freeze differed from those of 1948–50 and 1961–2 in that it was backed by legislation, namely the *Prices and Incomes Act* of 1966. This Act empowered the authorities to order that a specified price or rate of remuneration should not be increased from the date of the order without Ministerial consent. In the event the freeze was widely observed on a voluntary basis and it was not necessary to use the power conferred by the *Prices and Incomes Act* to any appreciable extent.

In the second six months the freeze gave way to a period of severe restraint. Price increases were to be restricted to certain specified exceptional circumstances. The 'norm' for money wage increases was to be zero but, as in the case of prices, exceptional circumstances justifying wage increases were specified. In addition, the wage increases which had been held over for the duration of the freeze could now be paid without violating the zero norm.

7. *Episode 7: 1968–9*

Episode 7 was marked by a return to the codes of behaviour for price-setters and wage-negotiators which had been formulated in episode 5, (see above, p. 170) but which had been suspended in the year of 'prices and incomes standstill'. Now, however, the codes were rather more strongly supported — first by the 'early-warning system' and second by legislation.

The early-warning systems was a set of voluntary arrangements under which the government was to be notified of proposed price and pay increases. Under the early-warning system for *prices*, price increases were to be notified to the appropriate government department not less than four weeks before the date from which the increase was to take effect. The notification was to be accompanied by certain information. This varied in detail from case to case but in general consisted of: (i) a description of the good or service whose price was to be increased; (ii) the present price, the proposed price and the movement in price over the past three years; (iii) the annual sales value of the good or service in question; (iv) the reason for the increase; and (v) the justification for the increase in terms of the code of behaviour prescribed for price-setters.

Under the early-warning system for *pay increases*, details of impending pay claims by organisations affiliated to the Trades Union Congress were to be supplied to the Department of Employment and Productivity by the General Council of the Congress while impending claims by unaffiliated organisations were to be notified by the organisations concerned. In addition, the Confederation of British Industry was to supply the Department with information relating to national pay negotiations and settlements in which member organisations were involved, while details of local and company negotiations were to be supplied by the member organisations and firms concerned.

The specific information to be furnished to the Department of Employment and Productivity under the early-warning system for pay increases was information relating to: (i) the nature of the claim or settlement; (ii) the proposed date of implementation; (iii) the number and types of workers involved; (iv) the date and terms of the previous settlement; and (v) the justification for the claim or settlement in terms of the code of behaviour laid down for wage-negotiators.

The early-warning system supported the codes of behaviour in two main ways. In the first place, the mere fact that the notification of the proposed price increase or pay settlement was to be accompanied, in each case, by a justification in terms of the prescribed behavioural code, meant that price-setters and wage-negotiators were constrained by the codes to a far greater extent than they would have been in the absence of the system. Second, by giving the authorities the opportunity to intervene *before* the event, the system almost certainly meant that official pressure on price-setters and wage-negotiators to conform with the codes was more successful than it would otherwise have been; for, as a general rule, it is easier to persuade people not to take a proposed course of action than it is to persuade them to reverse a course of action once it has been taken.

The early-warning system was one form of support provided for the codes of behaviour in episode 7. The other was legislation – specifically the *Prices and Incomes Act*, 1966, as extended by the *Prices and Incomes Acts* of 1967 and 1968. One of the powers conferred by this legislation was the power to enforce the early-warning system. This was regarded as a reserve power to be used only if it proved impossible to operate the system on a voluntary basis. In the event the voluntary system worked well and the power of enforcement remained unused. Another important power conferred by the various *Prices and Incomes Acts* was a power of delay. The 1967 Act empowered the authorities to delay proposed price and pay increases for a maximum of seven months pending an enquiry and report by the N.B.P.I. This power was extended in the 1968 Act which made possible a delay of up to twelve months, subject to a reference to the N.B.P.I.

B.   The United States

We turn now from the United Kingdom to the United States. In the case of the latter, prices and incomes policy has been tried on two separate occasions in the post-war period, first in the years 1962–6 and again in the years following 1971. We shall refer to these two distinct applications of prices and incomes policy as 'episode 1' and 'episode 2' respectively.[3]

1.   Episode 1: 1962–6

In episode 1, prices and incomes policy took much the same form as in U.K. episode 5, that is the policy consisted essentially of the formulation by the authorities of a code for non-inflationary wage behaviour and a code for non-inflationary price behaviour and of attempts on their part to persuade wage-negotiators and price-setters to take these codes of behaviour into account in arriving at their decisions.

The codes of behaviour in question, which came to be known as 'the guidelines', were first laid down by the Council of Economic Advisors in their 1962 Report. They consisted, in each case, of a 'general guide' and 'specific modifications to the general guide' designed to adapt them to the circumstances of particular industries. The general guide for wage-negotiators was that the rate of increase in wage rates be equal to the trend rate of increase in productivity in the economy as a whole. For price-makers, the general guide was that price should fall, stay the same or rise in an industry according to whether the rate of increase of productivity in the industry exceeded, equalled or fell short of the trend rate of increase of productivity in the economy as a whole.

The specific modifications to the general guide for wages were: (i) that the rate of wage increase should exceed the rate indicated by the general guide in an industry which would otherwise be unable to attract sufficient labour or in which wage rates for particular types of labour were exceptionally low compared with those applying in other industries for similar types of labour; and (ii) that the rate of wage increase should be below the rate indicated by the general guide in an industry which could not provide jobs for its entire labour force even in conditions of full employment or in which wage rates for particular types of labour were exceptionally high compared with those applying in other industries for similar types of labour. For prices, the specific modifications were: (i) that price should rise more rapidly, or fall more slowly, than indicated by the general guide in an industry in which the profit level was too low to attract the necessary capital or in which unit non-labour costs had risen; and (ii) that price should rise more slowly, or fall more rapidly, than indicated by the general guide in an industry in which an outflow of capital was desirable or in which unit non-labour cost has fallen.

To implement the guidelines the authorities relied entirely on public and private exhortation, both general and related to specific situations; no back-up legislation was introduced and no investigatory body like the U.K. N.B.P.I. was established to lend expert support.

2. Episode 2: The Years following 1971

Episode 2 consisted of four sub-episodes which came to be known, respectively, as Phase I, Phase II, Phase III and Phase IV. Each of these will now be described in turn.

Phase I was a ninety-day freeze on prices, rents, wages and salaries which was imposed on 15 August 1971. Like the U.K. 'prices and incomes standstill' and unlike the two earlier U.K. freezes, the 1971 U.S. freeze was legally enforceable, the source of the supporting legal power being the *Economic Stabilization Act* of 1970. To administer the freeze, a Cost of Living Council was created. This body, which consisted of a small group of high government officials, issued the orders which put the freeze into operation and made the main policy decisions during the freeze but delegated the task of enforcement to the Office of Emergency Preparedness. In the event the freeze was widely complied with on a voluntary basis, and legal action to enforce it was taken in no more than some thirty cases during the ninety-day period.

Phase II operated for a little over twelve months – from the end of the freeze on 14 November 1971 to 11 January 1973 – and was characterised by a set of notification arrangements not unlike the U.K. early-warning system of 1968–9. Before describing these arrangements it will be convenient to give a brief account of the administrative organisation which was responsible for devising them and for seeing that they were carried out.

The Phase II administrative machinery was fairly complex but there were three key administrative units. The first was the Cost of Living Council, which had been created to implement the ninety-day freeze, and which was continued in existence throughout the later phases of episode 2. The second basic unit was the Price Commission while the third was the Pay Board. Both were small policy-making bodies. In the case of the Price Commission, there were seven members, all of whom were representatives of the general public; in the case of the Pay Board there were fifteen members divided equally between public representatives, business representatives and representatives of labour.

Briefly, the notification arrangements which these three policy-making bodies created for Phase II were as follows. First, all firms with annual sales of $100 million and over were legally bound to give the Price Commission thirty days' notice of any proposed price increase and to obtain the approval of the Price Commission before putting the increase into effect. Second, all wage increases affecting 5000 workers or more and all increases above the standard set by the Pay Board (to be discussed below), regardless of the number of workers involved, were to be notified in advance to the Board, whose approval was to be obtained before the increase took effect. This, too, was a legal requirement. Third, all firms whose annual sales were between $50 million and $100 million were legally bound to notify the Price Commission of any price increase which had been made in accordance with the standard set by the Price Commission (also to be discussed below). Fourth, any wage increase affecting between 1000 and 5000 workers, made in accordance with the standard set by the Pay Board, was legally notifiable to the Board. Fifth, price increases by firms with sales of less than $50 million annually (wage increases affecting less than 1000 workers) were not notifiable but could legally be made only in accordance with the Price Commission's (Pay Board's) standard. Finally, all firms with annual sales of $50 million or more were required to submit quarterly price–cost–profit reports to the Price Commission.

We turn now to the standards set by the Price Commission and the Pay Board. The Pay Board's standard consisted of a 'norm' for pay increases of 5½ per cent per annum, together with certain allowable exceptions to the norm to correct gross inequities, to enable firms to attract or retain essential labour and to deal with workers whose past wage increases had been exceptionally low. The standard set by the Price Commission ran in terms of increases in unit cost. Briefly, an increase in price was allowable if an increase in unit cost had occurred since the last price increase (though not before 1971). However, there was no presumption that the allowable price increase would reflect the whole of the increase in unit cost; in particular it would not reflect any cost increase which was attributable to wage increases in excess of the standard set by the Pay Board. Moreover, a price increase was not allowable if the effect of the increase would be to increase the firm's profit margin above the level prevailing in a specified base period.

Phase III divides into two sub-phases, the first of which ran from the end of Phase II until 13 June 1973, and the second of which ran from then until 12 August 1973. In the first sub-phase the Phase II arrangements continued to operate but with certain modifications designed to make them somewhat less burdensome. For example, the pre-notification and report-filing requirements were largely dispensed with and the profit-margin limitations were relaxed. The general effect of the modification can be described by saying that the arrangements developed in Phase II were to be self-adminstered in Phase III. The second sub-phase was a sixty-day price freeze. This was instituted because of the speed with which prices rose when the Phase II arrangements were relaxed, and was designed to provide a breathing space for the development of a set of arrangements that would be more flexible than those of Phase II, while being somewhat tighter than those of the first sub-phase of Phase III. Such a set of arrangements was announced early in August 1973 and became the arrangements of Phase IV.

Two features of the Phase IV arrangements deserve a mention. The first is that they restored the pre-notification and reporting-filing arrangements of Phase II for prices, though not for wages. The second is that, in one important respect, they involved a stiffer standard for allowable prices increases than did the arrangements of Phase II. Specifically, in Phase IV the allowable price increase was limited to the allowable increase in unit cost itself, no addition in the cost increase being permitted to keep the profit margin intact.

8.3   Types of Prices and Incomes Policy

A brief glance at the history of prices and incomes policy in the United Kingdom, the United States, and other European and North American countries shows that policy interventions which satisfy the definition of prices and incomes policy given in Section 8.1 are of four types, namely: (i) 'tough' direct controls over prices and wages; (ii) temporary freeze of prices and wages; (iii) 'mild' direct controls over prices and wages; and (iv) 'guidelines' for prices and wages.

By 'direct controls over prices and wages' we mean a set of arrangements under which certain specified prices and money wages cannot be raised without prior approval of the appropriate government authority, and by 'tough' direct controls over prices and wages we mean to convey that virtually all prices and money wages are covered by the controls and that no time limit is set on their operation, so that they are widely regarded as a 'fact of life'. Thus the first of the four types of prices and incomes policy distinguished above is a price and wage control system such as operated in most of the belligerant countries during the Second World War.

A prices and incomes policy of this type has many serious disadvantages. In the first place, since it is enormously difficult to administer, it calls for a large, expert and expensive administrative machine. One or two illustrations will suffice to reveal something of the administrative complexity involved in the operation of tough direct price and wage controls. Take the case of a firm which wishes to increase the pay of one of its employees to stop him moving to another job. Suppose the wage-control regulations prevent this. An obvious way for the firm to get round the regulations would be to create a new, more highly paid position or one carrying superior fringe benefits, and then to 'promote' the employee in question to the new position. To prevent this type of evasion, the administrators of the wage controls will have to be able to distinguish between new positions which are genuine and those which are not. This will be almost impossible to do because a firm will usually have little difficulty in justifying the creation of a new position, whether genuine or not. As a second illustration, take the case of a firm which wishes to increase the price of one of its products on the ground of an unavoidable increase in unit cost. Suppose that this is permitted under the price-control regulations. Then the administrators of these regulations will be obliged to determine whether the firm has indeed suffered an unavoidable increase in unit cost as claimed. This will not be simply a matter of checking the arithmetical accuracy of the calculations which the firm has supplied. It will also involve a check on the validity of the various judgements which must enter into any cost-accounting exercise of this type, usually in a crucial way. For example, it will require some attempt to assess the validity of the assumptions about volume underlying the calculation of unit overhead cost and the assumptions about productivity made in the calculation of unit labour cost. Now this checking of critical judgements may be feasible if the administrators happen, by accident, to have a good background knowledge of the firm's operations. Otherwise the task will be a near-impossible one because the firm's negotiators will be vastly better equipped, in terms of basic factual knowledge, to defend the assumptions on which the calculations rely than the administrators will be to attack them.

A second disadvantage of tough direct controls over prices and wages is that they are likely to lead to a substantial loss of individual freedom. There is of course the obvious loss of freedom to fix prices and to negotiate about money wages. But individual freedom may well be lost in other, less obvious ways. As an example, consider again the point about the likelihood that firms will create phoney new positions as a means of defeating the wage controls. Given the difficulty of distinguishing between genuine and non-genuine new positions, it may be that the only way to stop this type of evasion is to disallow the creation of new positions altogether, thereby curtailing the freedom of management still further. Again, if the wage controls are effective, and firms are unable to keep workers by offering them higher pay, there will be a significant increase in labour turnover. This may become such a serious problem that restrictions have to be placed on the freedom of workers to move between jobs. As a third example, take the case of a firm which is faced with an unavoidable increase in unit cost and which is denied a price rise to cover this cost increase. The firm may well react by ceasing to produce the now unprofitable product. But if the product is, say, a basic raw material on which many other firms are dependent, it may be necessary to require the firm to continue its production, thus curtailing management freedom once again.

A third serious disadvantage of a type (i) prices and incomes policy is that under such a policy prices can no longer perform their proper allocative function. In the absence of controls over prices, the price of a product which is in short supply will increase, and the resulting increase in profits will tend to stimulate the addition of new capacity. This will enable the output of the product to be expanded and the shortage to be eliminated. This mechanism for channelling resources into the production of commodities which are in short supply disappears under direct price controls since prices are no longer free to respond to market pressures. As a result, shortages tend to persist under such a regime and are reflected in queues and black-market operations of various types.

Finally, tough direct controls over prices and wages share the disadvantage of all tough direct controls, that since they offer almost unlimited scope for the corruption of public officials, they are likely to lead to such corruption unless determined efforts, possibly requiring the addition of special anti-corruption officials to the administrative machine, are made to prevent it.

Because of these difficulties prices and incomes policies of the first of the four types distinguished at the outset of this discussion find little favour with economists, and for all practical purposes their use has been restricted to periods of war and recovery from war. On the other hand, policies of the second type — the temporary price and wage freeze — are generally regarded as having a useful contribution to make to the control of inflation under normal peacetime conditions.

The nature of this contribution can be seen by returning to the model which was chosen in Section 7.1 as a framework for discussing anti-inflation policy, namely relationships (7.1), (7.2) and (7.3). Let us suppose that the economy is operating with a very high expected rate of inflation. To make the discussion specific, suppose that p^e is 4 per cent per period where the period in question is a quarter. Let a price–wage freeze be imposed in such a situation and assume that the freeze is effective. Then p_{t-1} in relationship (7.3) will be zero, while p^e_{t-1} will be 4. If δ is, say 0.5 then $p^e_t - p^e_{t-1}$ will be $-(0.5 \times 4)$, or -2, that is the expected rate of inflation will fall in period t, the period following the imposition of the freeze from 4 per cent per quarter to 2 per cent per quarter. If the freeze can be maintained for two successive quarters, then p_t will be zero, while p^e_t will

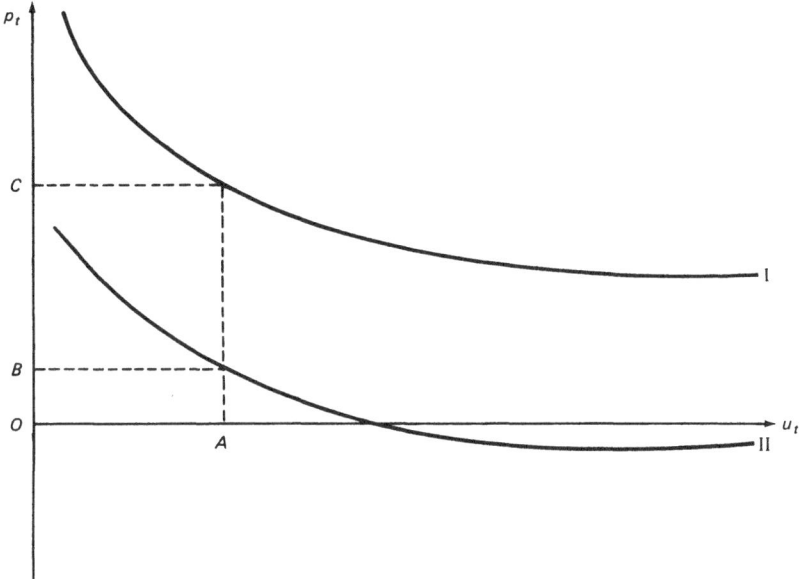

Fig. 8.1

be 2. With δ equal to 0.5, $p_t^e - p_{t-1}^e$ will be $-(0.5 \times 2)$, or -1, that is the expected rate of inflation will fall in period $t + 1$ from 2 per cent per quarter to 1 per cent per quarter. If the freeze can be maintained for three successive quarters, the expected rate of inflation will fall in period $t + 2$ from 1 per cent per quarter to 0.5 per cent per quarter; and so on. Thus at the end of the freeze the expected rate of inflation will be lower than it was at the beginning. From (7.2) it follows that the level of w corresponding to any given unemployment rate will be lower than before, and hence, from (7.3), that the rate of inflation at any given employment rate will be lower than before.†

Figure 8.1 shows the contribution of the freeze in diagrammatic terms. The contribution of the freeze will be to shift the economy from a short-run inflation–unemployment curve (see above, p. 141) such as I to one such as II and to enable the existing unemployment rate (OA let us say) to be maintained with an inflation rate of OB instead of OC.

The limitations of the temporary price–wage freeze must also be noted, however. In the first place, because the freeze is, by definition, temporary, it will not be practicable to set up an administrative body charged with the responsibility of seeing that the freeze is observed. Consequently the authorities must

---

†Note that the development just described requires only that *prices* be frozen. However, it is inconceivable that prices could be frozen unless wages were also frozen.

necessarily rely, to a large extent, on voluntary observance. This means, however, that the temporary freeze is a form of prices and incomes policy which can be effectively applied only when the country concerned is facing a national crisis or a set of circumstances which can be represented as such, because only in such an atmosphere is there any real likelihood of widespread voluntary observance of anything as drastic as a total ban on any price or wage increase. In this connection it is significant that the only occasions on which a temporary price—wage freeze has been instituted in the United Kingdom and the United States since 1945 have been periods of acute balance-of-payments difficulty in which it has been easy for the authorities to represent the freeze as essential for the avoidance of national bankruptcy.

Second, a price—wage freeze will usually be a fairly shortlived affair because it will inevitably give rise to serious anomalies (for example between the situations of those who obtain a wage increase the day before the freeze and those who would normally have obtained a 'flow-on' from this increase within a matter of days or weeks), and it will not be possible to contain the pressure for correcting these anomalies for more than a short period unless the country is facing a 'crisis' of unusual intensity. Some idea of the feasible time limit can be gained by recalling that the U.S. freeze of 1971 was imposed for ninety days and the U.K. freeze of 1966 for six months. But if the freeze is really shortlived and if the revision of expectations is a slow process, for example if δ is, say, only 0.1, the contribution of the freeze to a lowering of the expected inflation rate may be quite insignificant, as will be clear from the analysis presented a moment ago.

Third, there is a danger that this contribution, whatever it proves to be, will be nullified by unfavourable shifts in the price and wage equations when the freeze is terminated. In terms of Figure 8.1, the danger is that the movement to a lower short-run curve resulting from the freeze may be offset by an upward shift of the entire family of short-run curves. Such an upward shift will occur if, when the freeze is removed, workers press for wage increases which are above normal in relation to existing levels of the independent variables in (7.2), in an attempt to compensate for the absence of wage increases during the freeze, and employers for price increases which are above normal in relation to existing levels of the independent variables in (7.1). To minimise this particular difficulty it will be necessary for the authorities to be ready to institute a prices and incomes policy of either the third or the fourth type distinguished at the outset, immediately the freeze is removed.

Finally, a temporary freeze of prices and wages is likely to be beneficial only if it can be instituted without warning so that price-makers and wage-negotiators are taken by surprise. Should there be extensive public discussion about the need for a freeze, employers and workers will be encouraged to 'beat the freeze' by rushing through abnormally large price and wage increases before it comes into effect. In this event talk of the freeze may well do more to increase the expected rate of inflation than the freeze itself does to reduce it, so that the net effect of the freeze is actually perverse.

We turn now to the third of the four types of prices and incomes policy listed at the beginning of this section, the type labelled 'mild direct controls over prices and wages'. The difference between this type of prices and incomes policy and the first type is that in this case the controls over prices and wages are selective, only a few key prices and wage bargains being covered, and are intended to last for no more than, say, two to three years instead of being a more or less permanent feature of economic life. Mild direct controls suffer from the same disadvantages as tough direct controls (see above, p. 177). However, since the seriousness of these disadvantages increases with the comprehensiveness and duration of the controls, they are rather less serious in the mild case than in the tough case. A further difficulty of mild direct controls is that, because of their selective nature, they encourage a shift of resources from the sector in which prices are controlled to the sector in which they are uncontrolled, and since the first sector usually consists of essential, and the second sector of inessential, industries this movement is likely to be harmful from the point of view of economic growth, as well as from other points of view. Once again, however, the seriousness of the difficulty is an increasing function of the duration of the controls, and it is likely to be of minor importance if they last for no more than two or three years. In sum, the disadvantages of mild direct price and wage controls are not especially serious and most economists are prepared to contemplate this form of prices and incomes policy as an adjunct of a temporary price and wage freeze.

This brings us to the last of the four types of prices and incomes policy listed at the beginning of this section. Since there is a great deal more to be said about this type of policy than about the other three, we shall give it a section of its own.

8.4 Guidelines for Prices and Wages

The common characteristic of prices and incomes policies of the types discussed in the previous section is that they allow the policy-making authorities to interfere in decisions about prices and wages and so restrict the freedom of action of decision-makers in this area. By contrast, under the fourth type of policy, price-setters and wage-negotiators remain entirely free to make their decisions in the usual way, but are under pressure of one sort or another to follow certain principles or guidelines drawn up by the authorities with a view to achieving a lower inflation rate and perhaps other objectives as well. Something of this type was attempted in the United States in episode 1 and in the United Kingdom in episodes 2, 4, 5 and 7.

It goes without saying that a prices and incomes policy of the guidelines type will have no real impact on the rate of inflation unless it has widespread support. To begin with, the policy must have the active support of the leaders of the central trade-union organisations and the central associations of employers. There must also be support from the lower levels of organised labour and organised management. This is particularly necessary where, as in the United Kingdom, the process of price and wage determination is highly decentralised, and important decisions about prices and wages are made at the industry level and even at the level of the individual plant. Finally, the policy must have the support of the community at large if it is to have any significant influence on the rate of inflation.

The crucial problem associated with the fourth type of prices and incomes policy, then, is the problem of obtaining, and keeping, the widespread support without which the policy has little chance of success. There are three main ways of approaching this problem. The first is to try to get the policy supported on its merits; the second is to offer 'bribes' of various sorts to the groups whose support is most needed; and the third is to threaten to impose, and if necessary actually impose, penalties of various sorts on those who oppose the policy. Clearly, no one of these approaches excludes either of the other two, and there is no reason why all three should not be followed simultaneously. We shall now consider each of these three approaches in turn.

A. Getting the Policy Supported on its Merits

There are various ways in which the authorities can help to ensure that the policy gets wide support strictly on its merits — without the help either of bribes or of penalties.

In the first place, it seems clear that organised labour and management, and the community generally, will be more ready to support the policy if they feel that they have played some part, direct or indirect, in formulating the guidelines, or at least that they have had the opportunity to do so. One way in which the authorities can help to get the policy supported on its merits, therefore, is to see that the national leaders of organised labour and management are directly involved in all discussions concerned with the drawing up and revision of the guidelines. Another is to arrange public hearings of various types aimed at explaining the guidelines — why they are necessary and how they can be expected to help, at listening to suggestions for improvement and at answering questions and complaints.

Second, there is little chance that the policy will be widely supported on its merits unless it is well understood by the community in general and by organised labour and management in particular. The public consultation referred to in the previous paragraph will make an important contribution to the development of this understanding. But however much effort is expended in this direction, a high level of community understanding is unlikely to be achieved unless the guidelines are *easy* to understand. A further way in which the authorities can help to ensure that the policy is widely supported on its merits, therefore, is to eschew any but the simplest of guidelines. Since the key element of any set of guidelines must be a rule for determining the average rate of increase of money wage-earnings per man in the economy as a whole, or the wage norm, as it is usually called, the requirement that the guidelines be extremely simple implies a requirement that the rule for determining the wage norm must be so simple that the ordinary man can understand it and appreciate its relevance to the problem of containing the rate of inflation. This explains the popularity among policy-makers of the 'average productivity rule' – the rule which was used to determine the wage norm in the United Kingdom in episodes 4, 5 and 7. According to this rule the rate of increase of wage-earnings per man in the economy as a whole should be equal to the rate of increase of output per man in the economy as a whole. It is hard to imagine a simpler rule than this. Moreover, it is reasonably easy to get across the idea that observance of this rule will ensure that one important source of upward pressure on the price level – namely rising unit labour cost – will be eliminated, and hence comparatively easy to demonstrate its relevance to the problem of inflation. Many variations and refinements of the average productivity rule have been proposed in recent years. It seems, however, that all of these rules are too sophisticated to be generally understood and that a policy whose guidelines go beyond the average productivity rule, as regards the prescription of the norm, is unlikely to win widespread support on its merits alone.

Third, it seems likely that, if the policy is to command wide support without the help of bribes or penalties, the guidelines must not only be simple but also obviously fair. It would help enormously to give this appearance of fairness if the guidelines, in addition to specifying the wage norm, were to give a precise indication of which groups were to be allowed a rate of increase of earnings in excess of the norm and which groups were to be held back, together with a definite figure for the amount of the excess or the deficiency in each case. A further way, then, in which the authorities could help to ensure that the policy was supported on its merits would be to work for a consensus on these controversial questions both within the trade-union movement, and also within the community at large, so that guidelines containing rules for exceptional treatment of the type envisaged would become a practical possibility.

A fourth point is that the policy is unlikely to be supported on its merits if the guidelines are such as to lead to a change in factor shares, if observed. In particular, the policy will not be widely supported if it allows wage- and salary-earners, by observing the guidelines, to suffer a decline in their share of total factor income. Thus another way in which the authorities can help to build up support for the policy on its merits is by framing the guidelines so that there is no possibility that wage- and salary-earners as a group will find themselves rewarded for loyal observance of the guidelines with a fall in their share of total income.

From this point of view, it would appear that the average productivity rule for determining the wage norm is deficient and that it should not form part of the guidelines without amendment. To develop this point let us note that the wage share in period t is given by:

$$(WS)_t = \frac{W_t N_t}{O_t P_t},$$

$$(8.1)$$

where WS denotes wage share, W denotes wage-earnings per man, N the number of wage-earners, O total real factor income and P the price index used in the deflation of O. This expression can also be written as:

$$(WS)_t = \left[\frac{W_t}{(O_t/N_t)}\right]\frac{1}{P_t}. \tag{8.2}$$

From this it follows that:

$$\frac{(WS)_t}{(WS)_{t-1}} = \left(\frac{W_t}{W_{t-1}}\right)\left(\frac{O_{t-1}}{N_{t-1}}\bigg/\frac{O_t}{N_t}\right)\left(\frac{P_{t-1}}{P_t}\right). \tag{8.3}$$

Now if the average productivity rule is observed we shall have:

$$\frac{W_t}{W_{t-1}} = \frac{O_t}{N_t}\bigg/\frac{O_{t-1}}{N_{t-1}}.$$

Hence if the average productivity rule is observed it will be the case that:

$$\frac{(WS)_t}{(WS)_{t-1}} = \frac{P_{t-1}}{P_t}. \tag{8.4}$$

From this expression it is clear that $(WS)_t/(WS)_{t-1} < 1$ if $P_{t-1}/P_t < 1$, that is to say, that observance of the average productivity rule will cause the wage share to fall if the price index increases nevertheless. This would happen if there were some source of inflation other than rising unit labour cost, for example rising unit cost of imported materials or rising profit margins.

It is clear, then, that observance of the average productivity rule could result in a fall in the share of wage- and salary-earners in total factor incomes. It is also clear that a rule which prescribed that the rate of increase of wage-earnings per man should be equal to the rate of increase of output per man multiplied by the rate of increase of prices would eliminate this possibility. For if W_t/W_{t-1} is replaced in (8.3) by:

$$\left(\frac{O_t}{N_t}\bigg/\frac{O_{t-1}}{N_{t-1}}\right)\left(\frac{P_t}{P_{t-1}}\right)$$

the right-hand side reduces to unity.

To sum up, we can say that from the standpoint of generating support for the policy simply on its merits, the authorities should try to frame the guidelines in such a way that there is no possibility that observance of the guidelines will lead to a fall in the wage share. This means that the average productivity rule should not form part of the guidelines unless amended to read that the rate of increase of wage-earnings per man should be equal to the rate of increase of output per man multiplied by the rate of increase of prices. If this amended rule threatened to be insufficiently simple (see above, p. 182), the same result could be achieved by allowing the average productivity rule to stay and making separate provision in the guidelines for the indexation of all wages and salaries, that is for the automatic adjustment of all wages and salaries for changes in prices. Either way, both productivity increase and price increase would be allowed for in the determination of the wage norm, and this is the essential requirement from the present point of view.

Finally, it seems safe to say that the policy will get no support from any group of wage- or salary-earners who stand a chance of being actually worse off in real terms if they observe the guidelines. Such a situation could arise, for example, if the guidelines were to prescribe a zero rate of increase of earnings for some group of highly paid salary-earners such as salaried doctors, university professors, airline pilots, and the like (cf. above, p. 183). If the group in question were to observe the guidelines, and prices were to continue rising nevertheless, they would find that their reward for responsible behaviour was a fall in their real income. If this point is accepted it would appear that yet another way in which the authorities can help to generate maximum support for the policy strictly on its merits is by so framing the guidelines that no group can find themselves worse off in real terms by observing them. A simple way of achieving this objective would be for the guidelines to allow full indexation, in addition to the increase prescribed by the norm or the list of exceptions to the norm, for all wages and salaries. The case already presented for indexation is thus strengthened when the need to remove the possibility of any group being actually worse off in real terms through observance of the guidelines is taken into account.

B. Getting the Policy Supported By Offering 'Bribes'

In the preceding sub-section we suggested that one obvious way of securing widespread support for a prices and incomes policy of the 'guidelines' type is by ensuring that it is generally regarded as *worthy* of support – in particular, that it meets with the approval of organised labour and management. A second possible approach is to offer advantages of one sort or another ('bribes' we shall call them) to various key groups on condition that they support the policy. By making these bribes sufficiently attractive the authorities may induce the groups in question to support the policy even though they disapprove of it and would not be prepared to support it strictly on its merits. We shall explore this alternative approach in the present sub-section.

One way of bribing wage- and salary-earners into supporting a policy whose main aim is to restrict the rate of growth of their incomes is to guarantee that comparable restrictions will be imposed on the growth of non-wage incomes – in particular, dividend incomes and capital gains – even though these additional restrictions may be largely irrelevant from the point of view of lowering the inflation rate.

The main difficulty with such a guarantee is that of determining precisely what form the restriction should take. In the case of dividend income the obvious approach would be to promise legislation prohibiting a company from raising its dividend rate by more than x per cent per annum, where x per cent per annum is the norm laid down by the guidelines for wages and salaries. However, this restriction would almost certainly mean a heavier burden on dividend-receivers than on wage- and salary-earners, despite the appearance of comparability. In the first place, whereas *x* per cent per annum would be a *certain* maximum as far as the average rate of growth of dividend income was concerned, it would be no more than a *hoped-for* maximum as far as the average rate of growth of wage income was concerned. Second, all dividend-earners would be treated alike, regardless of their financial position, whereas, presumably, the guidelines would provide for better-than-average treatment for some wage-earners and worse-than-average treatment for others (see above, p. 183). Third, dividend-earners would be offered no protection against the possible ineffectiveness of the guidelines in preventing inflation. On the other hand, wage- and salary-earners would be likely to receive such protection through indexation (see above, p. 184). Thus while a restriction of the suggested type would probably be quite satisfactory, regarded simply as a bribe, it would be open to question from the point of view of equity. In the case of dividend income, therefore, the most obvious and straightforward form of restriction might not be acceptable, and no clear alternative presents itself.

In the case of capital gains the difficulty of devising an appropriate form of restriction arises from the fact that there is no way of restricting capital gains other than by taxation, so that the only bribe which can be offered is legislation imposing a tax on capital gains or increasing the severity of an existing tax. But how does one find a tax rate such that the rate of increase of capital gains per £1 of outlay will be, on average, *x* per cent per annum? And supposing that this special rate could somehow be determined, what chance would there be of convincing wage- and salary-earners that it did, in fact, have the property that it was supposed to have? If there were no chance of doing so, the tax would not be a very effective bribe because wage- and salary-earners would be uncertain about what they were getting in exchange for their support of the policy. Finally, imposition of the special tax rate, supposing that it could be found, would not really put the receivers of capital gains on the same footing as wage- and salary-earners because, while the former would be enjoying an average rate of growth of *x* per cent per annum *after* tax, the latter would be enjoying an average rate of growth of *x* per cent per annum *before* tax.

Another bribe which could well be attractive is an undertaking to establish a prices-investigation body or to strengthen an existing body. The function of this body ('Prices Justification Tribunal' might be an appropriate name) would be to conduct a public investigation into any specified price increase and to make public its findings as to whether this increase was justified or not in terms of the criteria for price increases which have been laid down in the guidelines. The Tribunal's investigations could be initiated either by its own action or by a reference from the authorities in the case of an increase that had already occurred. In the case of a proposed increase the firm itself could take the initiative.

The promise of a new or strengthened Prices Justification Tribunal would hold attractions both for wage- and salary-earners and for firms, particularly large firms. Wage-earners would be attracted because the Tribunal would be a source of pressure on profit margins; and this pressure would be desirable from their point of view, either on ideological grounds (because they disapproved of profits) or because it would offer some assurance that prices would not continue to rise as a result of a lengthening of profit margins once they had agreed to observe the guidelines for wages and salaries. On the other hand, large firms would see the Tribunal as a means of obtaining prestigious support (hopefully) for proposed price increases, and hence as helping them in their efforts to preserve a good public image.

Both labour and management, therefore, might well find the promise of a new or strengthened Prices Justification Tribunal an attractive bribe. Just how attractive would depend on whether the Tribunal appeared likely to acquire great authority and prestige and to be able to mobilise a considerable pressure of public opinion behind its findings or whether it appeared destined to become something of a joke, either because of the poor quality of its permanent staff, or because of inadequate finance, or for some other reason. Also, since part of the Tribunal's attractiveness to wage-earners would lie in its assurance that prices would not continue to rise from the side of profit margins once they had committed themselves to the wage guidelines, wage-earners would not be likely to regard the promise of a Tribunal as an irresistible bribe if the guidelines allow for the indexation of all wages and salaries (see above, p. 184).

A third, possibly very effective bribe which has been proposed recently is the real after-tax income guarantee.[4] The essence of this proposal is that, following specific undertakings from organised labour that the guidelines for wages and salaries will be observed, the authorities would guarantee a specified increase in real wage- and salary-earnings per man *after tax* (say 4 per cent per annum) for a specified number of years ahead (say for the next two or three years).

A guarantee of this type could be an extremely effective means of winning the support of wage-earners for a prices and incomes policy. In most advanced industrial countries the income-tax structure is steeply progressive, and as a result the rate of increase in average *real* earnings *after* tax tends to be extremely small even when the rate of increase in average *money* earnings *before* tax is quite high. To illustrate the point take the case of a wage-earner whose money earnings before tax increase by 20 per cent from $5000 per annum to $6000 per annum. Suppose that the tax rate is 20 per cent for an income of $5000 and 25 per cent for an income of $6000. Then the wage-earner's tax bill rises from $1000 to $1500. Consequently, his income after tax rises from $4000 to $4500, that is by only 12½ per cent. Moreover, if the inflation rate is, say, 10 per cent per annum, this 12½ per cent increase in *money* income after tax represents an increase of only a little over 2 per cent in his *real* income after tax.

In most advanced industrial countries, then, a rate of increase in average real wage-earnings after tax of even a few per cent per annum would constitute a substantial improvement over historical rates, and it should not be difficult for the authorities to convince wage- and salary-earners that the guarantee of such a rate would be well worth having even if this meant supporting a prices and incomes policy of which they disapproved.

Since the guarantee relates to real earnings *after tax*, the authorities will presumably have to reduce tax rates on wage and salary income from time to time if the guarantee is to be met. These tax cuts will add to the real disposable income of wage- and salary-earners, and hence will stimulate their real consumption spending. Should the unemployment rate be higher than the desired level, this stimulus to aggregate demand, *via* wage-earners' real consumption spending, will be just the sort of action that is required from the standpoint of the employment objective, and hence will raise no real problems. On the other hand, if the unemployment rate is already at, or below, the desired level, the effects of the tax cuts will be unwanted, and it will be necessary for the authorities to take some type of offsetting action. One way of offsetting the unwanted stimulus to aggregate demand would be by taking steps to stimulate the flow of imports, thereby adding to available supplies. If the external situation did not permit this, the only alternative would be to take steps to cut back some component of aggregate demand other than the real consumption spending of wage- and salary-earners, for example real government spending, real spending on housing, real spending on business plant and equipment.

To minimise problems of this sort the guarantee-honouring tax cuts should clearly be as small as possible. This implies that the tax cuts should not have to compensate, to any appreciable extent, for a small rate of increase in real wage- and salary-earnings per man *before* tax. In turn, this implies that the rate of increase of *money* wage- and salary-earnings per man before tax which the guidelines permit should, as far as possible, represent an equivalent rate of increase in real wage- and salary-earnings per man before tax; and this means either that indexation of wages and salaries should be associated with the scheme or that special efforts should be made to see that the inflation which still occurs once the wage and salary guidelines have been observed, for example because of rising profit margins, is of no more than minor proportions. This brings us back to the Prices Justification Tribunal – a body charged with the responsibility of seeing that the guidelines for prices are observed. We have suggested that such a Tribunal might itself be a useful bribe. It now appears that it could also be a useful adjunct to the real-income guarantee in that it would help to lessen the difficulties associated with this particular bribe.

Finally, our discussion of possible bribes should contain some reference to what is sometimes called a 'social contract'. By this is meant a deal between the authorities and organised labour under which the authorities promise to institute various social reforms that appear highly desirable to most people, and to wage-earners in particular, and the union movement undertakes, in return, to give its backing to a prices and incomes policy. The social reforms covered by the social contract might include such things as larger social-security payments, indexation of pensions, the introduction of a national health scheme or the improvement of an existing scheme, reduction in income and wealth inequalities, continuous research into poverty and its origins, and action to eliminate poverty based on this research.

· A social contract is likely to be a highly effective way of persuading the unions to back a prices and incomes policy which is about to be introduced. On the other hand, it will probably not help greatly to ensure their continued support for the policy once it is a going concern. The reason for this is that, once introduced, the various social reforms which are covered by the social contract can hardly be undone; indeed, since they are desirable in themselves, it would be wrong to undo them even if this were possible. Consequently, if the unions threaten to withdraw their support for the policy at any stage of its operation, no counter-threat to withdraw the social reforms already granted is likely to be made, and it would not carry much weight in any case. By contrast, restrictions on non-wage income, prices justification and a real-income guarantee are all arrangements which can be unmade without difficulty and which have no particular virtue as such.† The threat to withdraw them is, therefore, likely to carry conviction and so help to bring the unions 'into line' should they fail to honour their part of the bargain.

C. *Getting the Policy Supported By Imposing Penalties*

At the beginning of the present section it was pointed out that the central problem of a prices and incomes policy which consists solely of the promulgation of guidelines for prices and wages is to secure, and keep, the widespread support which is the key to success. It was also mentioned that there are three distinct, though by no means mutually exclusive, ways in which the authorities can approach this problem – by striving to make the guidelines attractive so that the policy will be supported on its merits; by offering bribes to the groups whose support is most needed; and by threatening to impose penalties on those who are not prepared to co-operate in making the policy work. Having now considered the first two of these three approaches, we turn to the third.

One penalty which the authorities can threaten to impose, and actually impose, on opponents of the policy is the penalty of adverse publicity. What we have in mind here is that there should be an investigating body along the lines of the U.K. National Board for Prices and Incomes, and that this body should be equipped to give wide and damaging publicity to gross breaches of the guidelines for wages by particular groups of workers and to gross breaches of the guidelines for prices by particular firms, and that there should be no doubt of the willingness of the body in question to bring the pressure of public opinion to bear on workers or firms who are attempting to gain an advantage by disregarding the guidelines.

---

†This statement must be qualified as far as prices-justification machinery is concerned. This *does* have virtue as such, that is quite apart from its usefulness as a means of bribing wage-earners into accepting the wage guidelines, since it makes a *direct* contribution to the control of inflation by helping to ensure observance of the guidelines for prices and thus limiting the rate of increase of profit margins.

Effective adverse publicity of the type envisaged would probably be regarded as quite a serious penalty, both by unions and by firms, and the mere threat of such publicity should therefore help significantly to discourage breaches of the guidelines. This is especially true of large firms, most of which are anxious to have a good public image and are prepared to devote a great deal of expense and effort to achieving healthy public relations.

Perhaps the most effective way in which the authorities can strengthen the position of the National Board-type investigating body in its role as a mobiliser of public opinion is by ensuring that the quality of its members and staff and the extent of its financial support are such that its findings and recommendations inevitably carry great prestige and authority. There is, however, another, less obvious, way in which the authorities can help. This is by seeing that the guidelines are as tightly formulated as possible. If the guidelines are loosely worded and full of loopholes, the possibility of bringing a strong pressure of public opinion to bear on offenders is likely to be very limited indeed. For example, if the guidelines for wages provide for wage increases in excess of the norm in exceptional cases which are so vaguely specified that almost any case can be represented with some justification as 'exceptional', it will be very difficult indeed for the investigating body to convince the public that the guidelines have in fact been breached in particular cases, and hence very difficult for it to arouse public opinion against those who are failing to observe the spirit, if not the letter, of the guidelines.

Legal penalties are another possibility. That is, the prices and incomes policy can be given some form of legislative support, and breaches of the relevant legislation can be made punishable by fines or other more drastic legal penalties. An example of legislative support for a prices and incomes policy are the U.K. *Prices and Incomes Acts* of 1967 and 1968 which empowered the authorities to require that particular price and wage increases be delayed pending a report by the National Board for Prices and Incomes, and for a further period in the event of an adverse finding by the Board. Failure to observe an order for delay was punishable under the Acts by a fine.

It is generally agreed that legal penalties are subject to definite limitations as a means of securing support for a prices and incomes policy. The reasons for this are well put by Clegg in the following way:[5]

> a law enforcing an incomes policy has to create some novel offences which upset cherished principles of democratic thought. We can perhaps stomach penalties against unconstitutional strikers because they have broken their undertaking to use the agreed procedure first. We may even allow that sympathetic strikers should be subject to penalties for interfering in someone else's quarrel. But what offence are workers committing if, having given notice and observed the procedure, they come out in support of a claim for an increase in their own pay? ... Then there is still the employer. The workers may not need to strike because he agrees to give them the money. The breach

of the law will then be his. But what kind of crime is it for a man to agree to pay his employees higher wages?

Legal regulation has yet another shortcoming. There has to be a reasonable chance of detecting offenders . . . . Pay increases can easily be detected if they are granted by industry agreements, or throughout a great company such as I.C.I. or Ford. But the thousands of workshop decisions about price-rates, allowances, overtime and plus rates are quite another matter.

On the other hand, it should not be concluded that legal penalties have *nothing* to offer by way of support for a prices and incomes policy. By providing for such penalties and invoking them in a few well-chosen cases the authorities can at least create the definite impression that they are determined to make the policy work; and this show of determination will help to reassure those who favour the policy that they will not suffer if they support it. Again, we may quote Clegg's summing-up on the matter:

> the function of the law in an incomes policy is not to force the country to conform to a policy that would otherwise be unacceptable. It can do little for an unpopular policy. Where a policy has widespread support, however, the government can take powers in order to reassure the country that the policy will not be undermined by self-seekers trying to turn the sacrifice of others to their own advantage.

A third type of penalty which has been widely canvassed in recent years, and which is usally associated with Weintraub and Wallich,[6] is a tax penalty. The Weintraub—Wallich proposal assumes that the guidelines for wages lay down a wage norm — a rate of increase of average wage-earnings which should apply over the economy as a whole, though not necessarily to any particular worker or group of workers. The proposal, then, is that any firm whose rate of increase of average wage-earnings exceeds the norm in any year should be subject to a tax surcharge, that is the firm should pay profits tax for that year at a higher rate than the basic rate specified in the tax legislation, the tax surcharge being some multiple of the number of percentage points by which the rate of increase of wage-earnings actually incurred by the firm exceeds the norm. To take some hypothetical figures, suppose that the norm for some given year is 5.5 per cent per annum and that a firm is found by the tax authorities to have granted a rate of increase of average earnings of 7 per cent in that year. Then the number of percentage points by which the rate of increase of average earnings actually incurred by the firm exceeds the norm is 1.5. If the multiple referred to above had been fixed at, say, 3, and the basic tax rate on profits was, say, 40 per cent, then the tax paid by the firm in question on its profits would be at the rate of $[40 + (3 \times 1.5)]$ per cent or 44.5 per cent, instead of the 40 per cent it would have incurred had its rate of increase of average earnings not exceeded the norm.

The idea behind this proposal is that fear of incurring the tax surcharge will cause firms to adopt a tougher bargaining stance in wage negotiations than they would otherwise have done, and that, as a result, the rate of increase of average wage-earnings in the economy as a whole will be closer to the norm than would have been the case in the absence of the surcharge.

It is clear that the efficacy of the Weintraub—Wallich proposal depends on whether or not the firms which incur the tax surcharge can recover the extra tax to which they are liable by charging a higher price. If they can do so, they will have nothing to fear from the surcharge and hence will be no more inclined to resist wage demands than in the absence of the scheme.

According to Weintraub and Wallich, however, the extent to which the extra tax could be passed on by means of price increases is strictly limited. Their argument is that if the extra tax resulting from a given surcharge were regarded simply as a cost to be passed on, some firms in an industry would find that their unit cost had risen by a much greater percentage than others. Hence some firms would find it necessary to raise prices by a much greater percentage than others; and some of these, at least, would not be able to withstand the loss of competitiveness which this would entail.

The reason why different firms would be faced with different percentage increases in unit cost if the extra tax were to be regarded as a cost increase is, basically, that profits per unit of sales vary widely between different firms in the one industry, for example because of differences in the proportion of debt in the capital structure. If there are wide differences in profits per unit of sales, there will also be wide differences in extra tax per unit of sales, as a result of a given surcharge, and hence wide differences in extra tax per unit of cost, that is in the percentage increase in unit cost.†

---

†If all firms pay the same surcharge, k, the extra tax for firm i will be given by:

$$(\text{Extra tax})_i = k(\text{Profits})_i.$$

Therefore
$$\frac{(\text{Extra tax})_i}{(\text{Sales})_i} = k\frac{(\text{Profits})_i}{(\text{Sales})_i} \ .$$

Hence variability in profits per unit of sales implies variability in extra tax per unit of sales. Now extra tax per unit of sales can be written as:

$$\frac{(\text{Extra tax})_i}{(\text{Sales})_i} = \frac{(\text{Extra tax})_i}{(\text{Profits})_i + (\text{Cost})_i} = \frac{(\text{Extra tax})_i}{(\text{Cost})_i} \Bigg/ 1 + \frac{(\text{Profits})_i}{(\text{Cost})_i}$$

$$= \frac{(\text{Extra tax})_i}{(\text{Cost})_i} \Bigg/ 1 + (\text{Profit margin})_i.$$

Therefore
$$\frac{(\text{Extra tax})_i}{(\text{Cost})_i} = (\text{Proportional increase in total cost})_i$$

$$= \left[\frac{(\text{Extra tax})_i}{(\text{Sales})_i} \right] [1 + (\text{Profit margin})_i].$$

While this argument is convincing the question of shiftability of the surcharge under a Weintraub–Wallich regime is basically an empirical question which can be decisively answered only by observing what firms actually do after the proposal has been put into effect.

Let us assume for the purposes of further discussion that some firms will find it impossible to pass on the whole of the extra tax so that the Weintraub–Wallich surcharge will, in fact, constitute a real deterrent to the granting of excessive wage demands. Certain questions then arise on the purely technical side. One such question of obvious importance is the question of the precise way in which the rate of increase of average wage-earnings is to be determined for tax purposes. Weintraub–Wallich mention four possibilities in this connection.[7] They are the rate of increase from the previous year in: (i) total wages and related payments for the year divided by the number of employees on a particular date, for example the end of the year; (ii) total wages and related payments for the year divided by the average daily number of employees over the year; (iii) total wages and related payments for the year divided by the total man-hours worked in the year; and (iv) a wage index computed by determining the total wages and related payments per man-hour worked for each job classification and applying a fixed weight, for example the average daily number of employees in the classification in some past year, to each.

Each of these four methods of computing the firm's rate of increase of wage-earnings for tax purposes has definite, or possible, disadvantages. The first is open to abuse in that it enables the firm to reduce its average wage figure to any prescribed level simply by inflating the number of 'employees' on its books on the critical date. The second and third encourage the firm to substitute unskilled for skilled labour wherever possible because in this way it may be able to keep the average wage figure down while still conceding excessive wage demands. This downgrading of the skill mix, should it occur, may in turn discourage the adoption of advanced technology since it is more difficult to combine advanced

---

But the proportional increase in unit cost is approximately equal to the proportional increase in total cost *minus* the proportional increase in output. Therefore:

$$(\text{Proportional increase in unit cost})_i \simeq \left\{ \frac{(\text{Extra tax})_i}{(\text{Sales})_i} \right\} \{ 1 + (\text{Profit margin})_i + (\text{Proportional increase in output})_i \}.$$

If we suppose that profit margins and percentage output charges are roughly the same for all firms in an industry, we see from this expression that variability in extra tax per unit of sales will mean variability in the percentage increase in unit cost. Our final conclusion, therefore, is that given wide variability between firms in the same industry in profits per unit of sales, there will be wide variability in extra tax per unit of sales and, in turn, in the percentage increase in unit cost.

technology with an unskilled, than with a skilled, labour force. On the other hand, it may have offsetting social advantages, particularly in a situation where a shortage of employment opportunities for unskilled labour is contributing to an intractable structural unemployment problem. The main disadvantage of the fourth method is the computation difficulty which it would involve, particularly for a large firm with numerous plants.

Various tax penalties have been suggested as alternatives to the Weintraub–Wallich surcharge, and before leaving this particular proposal we shall briefly consider them. Three, in particular, are of interest. The most obvious alternative is a straight payroll tax – say 2.5 per cent of the firm's total payroll. Under such a tax the less resistant a firm to excessive wage demands, the greater its payroll and the greater, therefore, the payroll tax which it would pay. A second suggested alternative is to make the wage bill in excess of last year's *plus x* per cent, where *x* is the norm, non-deductible for tax purposes. Under this arrangement a firm which had given in to excessive wage demands would find its taxable profit higher, and hence its profits tax higher, than would have been the case had it been less easy-going in its wage negotiations. Finally, it has been suggested that instead of penalising the firm which gives in too easily, one might penalise the workers who press too hard, by placing a tax surcharge on excessive labour income. The idea here is that the income tax of a particular wage- or salary-earner would be determined in the usual way. Then if his income before tax had risen by more than *x* per cent since the previous year, a surcharge of anything up to 100 per cent of the excess would be added to his tax bill. If the surcharge were made high enough, it is argued, wage-earners would have very little to gain from pressing for wage increases in excess of the norm, and hence would be unlikely to do so.

Each of these alternatives has superficial attractions but is found to be defective on closer examination.

The difficulty with the payroll-tax alternative is that firms will find it relatively easy to pass on the tax by means of a price increase, and hence will not be deterred from granting wage increases in excess of the norm by the fact that this will add to their payroll tax liability. The reason why it will be easy to shift the tax is that the required price increase will be much the same, in percentage terms, for all firms; and this will be the case because the absorption of the tax into cost will raise the unit cost of all firms by roughly the same percentage.†

†We have:

$$(\text{Extra tax})_i = g(\text{Wage bill})_i,$$

where g is the rate of payroll tax. Hence:

$$\frac{(\text{Extra tax})_i}{(\text{Cost})_i} = g \times \frac{(\text{Wage bill})_i}{(\text{Cost})_i} = g \times \frac{(\text{Wage bill})_i}{(\text{Wage bill})_i + (\text{Non-wage cost})_i}$$

$$= \frac{g}{1 + [(\text{Non-wage cost})_i/(\text{Wage bill})_i]}.$$

The proposal to make excess wage payments non-deductible is subject to the same difficulty. Once again it will be easy for firms to shift the additional tax to which they will be liable because the required price increase will be much the same, percentage-wise, for all firms.†

Finally, the proposal to levy a surcharge on excess labour income suffers from the weakness that the wage-earner's reaction may well be the opposite to that intended. That is, instead of reacting by keeping their wage demands within the limit imposed by the norm, wage-earners may make demands, in an attempt to recoup the tax loss, which are even more excessive than they would have been in the absence of the tax.

To conclude this discussion of the use of penalties as a means of securing, and maintaining, support for a prices and incomes policy of the 'guidelines' type, we shall consider a penalty (more precisely a system of penalties) proposed recently by Meade.[8] Like the Weintraub—Wallich proposal, the proposal advanced by Meade is designed to check the rate of increase of average wage- and salary-earnings by altering the relative bargaining power of the parties to wage negotiations. But while the former proposal attempts to achieve this result by strengthening the bargaining stance of the employers, the latter attempts to do so by weakening the bargaining stance of the trade unions. In approach, therefore, it resembles the third of the alternatives to the Weintraub—Wallich surcharge which we discussed a moment ago.

In outline the Meade proposal is as follows. The authorities would fix a wage norm – say x per cent per annum. Wage bargaining would remain free as at present. However, in the event of a dispute about wages or salaries a wage tribunal would be asked to determine whether the granting of the wage claim in question would have the effect of making the average earnings of the workers concerned more than x per cent higher than they were one year earlier, that is whether it would constitute a violation of the norm. If the tribunal were to rule that the norm would indeed be violated by the granting of the claim, regulations designed to curb the bargaining power of the workers concerned would be invoked.

Therefore

$$\text{(Proportional increase in unit cost)}_i \simeq \frac{g}{1 + [(\text{Non-wage cost})_i/(\text{Wage bill})_i]}$$
$$+ \text{(Proportional increase in output)}_i.$$

If we assume that neither the ratio of wage cost to non-wage cost nor proportional output changes vary significantly between firms in an industry, we can say from this expression that absorption of the payroll tax into cost will raise the unit cost of all firms by roughly the same proportion.

†The reason for this, once again, is that absorption of the additional tax into cost will raise the unit cost of all firms by roughly the same percentage, as can be shown by an argument similar to the one used in the preceding footnote.

Examples of the type of regulation envisaged are: (i) regulations under which workers who went on strike in support of the claim would lose accumulated rights to redundancy payments in their present jobs; and (ii) regulations providing that the trade union to which the workers in question belonged would be liable to a tax on any strike benefits which it paid to them.

Some doubts exist as to the efficacy of the Meade proposal. In the first place, it seems unlikely that wage disputes at the plant level could be covered — referral of all disputes to a wage tribunal would be quite impracticable because they are so numerous. Second, it would have no relevance to cases, such as top-level managerial salaries and academic salaries, in which, for all practical purposes, the type of wage dispute envisaged by the Meade proposal never arises.

A further objection to the proposal (and this applies equally to the Weintraub–Wallich tax surcharge) is that, in effect, it makes it possible for individuals to be legally punished without their having had the benefit of proper legal procedures and safeguards and without adequate rights of appeal.

8.5   The Effectiveness of Prices and Incomes Policy

In the opening section of this chapter we presented a definition of prices and incomes policy running in terms of the price equation and the wage equation. One of the virtues of this particular definition is that it provides a convenient framework for assessing the effectiveness of prices and incomes policy, and many studies of effectiveness which take it as a starting-point have been undertaken in recent years. The main purpose of the present section will be to give a general account of the methods used in these studies and some idea of the conclusions which have been reached.

According to the definition under discussion, the immediate aims of prices and incomes policy, in so far as it relates to the control of inflation, are: (i) to so change the parameters of the wage equation that the rate of wage increase is less than it would have been at given levels of the determining variables of the wage equation: and (ii) to so change the parameters of the price equation that the rate of price increase is less than it would have been at given levels of the determining variables, including the rate of wage increase, of the price equation. Once the definition is accepted, therefore, the task of any investigator who attempts to assess the effectiveness of prices and incomes policy is clear. What he must do is to determine whether the wage and price equations have indeed shifted in the appropriate way, and to a significant extent, in the period in which the policy has been in force. He may find that neither the wage equation nor the price equation has shifted. In that case he can conclude that prices and incomes policy has failed to achieve its two immediate aims, and hence that it has been ineffective as a means of dealing with the problem of inflation. On the other hand, he may find clear evidence of an appropriate shift in one or both of the wage and price equations. If so he will be justified in maintaining that the prices and incomes policy has been effective — at least until someone else shows that the shifts which he has detected could have been produced by events other than the prices and incomes policy.

In all of the studies to be reviewed in this section the task which the author has set himself is precisely the one described in the preceding paragraph. The method used to perform the task is invariably econometric in character but the precise nature of the econometric method employed differs from study to study. There are, in fact, three main types of method to be found. We shall refer to these three types as: (1) E.R. (examination of residuals) methods; (2) D.V. (dummy variable) methods; and (3) S.E. (separate equation) methods; and we shall proceed to discuss them in turn, ending with a conclusion on the effectiveness of prices and incomes policy.

(1) E.R. Methods

In the case of E.R. methods the first step is to derive a numerical wage equation and/or price equation using data relating to a period of time in which no prices and incomes policy was in force. The wage equation (price equation) is then used to calculate the rate of increase of money wages (rate of increase of prices) quarter-by-quarter throughout the policy period under review. Next, the calculated figure for the rate of increase of money wages (rate of increase of prices) is subtraced from the actual figure quarter-by-quarter to obtain the so-called residual series for the policy period under review. Now if the prices and incomes policy has produced the right sort of shift in the wage equation (price equation), the calculated rates of increase will tend to exceed the actual rates of increase, that is the residual series for the policy period in question will tend to be predominantly negative in sign. This is because the calculated rates of increase have been generated, effectively, by the pre-policy equation† whereas the actual rates of increase have been generated, in effect, by the post-policy equation; and if the policy has been effective, the pre-policy equation should tend to throw up higher values for the rate of wage increase (rate of price increase) than the post-policy equation. The final step in an E.R. method, then, is to examine the signs of the residual series. If the signs are predominantly negative, it is concluded that the policy has succeeded in shifting the wage equation (price equation) in the desired manner — subject to the proviso that the negativeness of the residuals cannot be reasonably accounted for by some change other than the introduction of the prices and incomes policy. On the other hand, if there is a roughly equal balance between positive and negative residuals, with neither sign tending to predominate, the conclusion drawn is that the policy has failed to produce the desired shift in the wage equation (price equation).

†Recall that the numerical wage equation (price equation) is assumed to have been estimated from data relating to a time period in which no prices and incomes policy was in force.

Having established that a prices and incomes policy has been effective, one would normally wish to provide some measure of the degree of effectiveness. In the case of E.R. methods, this can be done by calculating the average value of the residuals over the policy period in question. Then, if the average residual from the wage equation (price equation) is, say, -1.39, it is argued that, in the policy period, the rate of increase of money wages was less, on average, than it would have been by 1.39 percentage points. This reduction is taken as a measure of the extent of the favourable shift in the wage equation (price equation) in the policy period and, in the absence of any other convincing explanation, the policy is given the credit. The logic of this approach is quite simple. The numerical wage equation (price equation), having been estimated from data relating to a policy-off period, can be regarded as the equation that would have applied if the policy had not been introduced. Hence the rates of wage increase (rates of price increase) calculated from the equation for the policy period can be interpreted as the rates of increase that would have been observed if the policy had not been introduced. Therefore, by subtracting the calculated rate of increase for any quarter in the policy period from the rate of increase actually observed, one obtains a figure for the extent to which the actual rate of increase falls below what it would have been in the absence of the policy; and by taking the average of these figures (by averaging the residual series) one obtains a figure for the extent to which the actual rate of increase was below what it would have been, on average.

One study in which use is made of an E.R. method is Perry's study of the effectiveness of the U.S. guidelines of the 1960s.[9]

Perry confined his attention to the wage equation and took the numerical version of his 'preferred' wage equation as a starting-point. This equation has been presented already in Chapter 7 (equation (7.14)) but is set out again for the reader's convenience:

$$\tilde{w}_t = -4.313 + 0.367 p_{t-1} + 14.711 u_t^{-1} + 0.424 R_{t-1} + 0.792(R_t - R_{t-1}).$$
$$(8.5)$$

The data used in the estimation of (8.5) was for the years 1947–60, during which no prices and incomes policy operated. Hence it can be regarded as the wage equation which applied prior to the introduction of the guidelines.

Perry used (8.5) to calculate $\tilde{w}$ quarter-by-quarter from first quarter 1962 to first quarter 1966 – the years in which the guidelines were operative. To make the calculation for first quarter 1962, for example, the value of p and R observed for the fourth quarter 1961, the value of u observed for the first quarter 1962 and the observed change in R between the fourth quarter 1961 and the first quarter 1962 would have been substituted in the right-hand side of (8.5) for p_{t-1}, R_{t-1}, u_t and $R_t - R_{t-1}$, respectively.

When the calculated rates of increase were compared with the actual rates of increase, it was found that the calculated figure exceeded the actual figure in every quarter except the first two, that is there was a definite preponderance of negative residuals. On this basis Perry was prepared to claim that the guidelines had been effective — at least until some other convincing reason for the predomin antly negative residuals could be advanced.

(2) D. V. Methods

At the outset of the present section we said that the methods which econometricians have devised for determining whether a particular prices and incomes policy has shifted the wage and/or price equations in the appropriate manner and to a significant extent are of three main types: E.R. methods, D.V. methods and S.E. methods. We have now dealt with the first of these three types of methods and we turn our attention to the second.

To explain the D.V. (dummy variable) methods we shall concentrate on the wage equation and suppose that it takes the form:

$$w_t = \alpha_0 + \alpha_1 X_{1t} + \alpha_2 X_{2t}, \tag{8.6}$$

where w denotes the rate of increase of money wages, X_1 and X_2 the independent variables in the wage equation (they can be any variables at all) and α_0, α_1 and α_2 three constants. Once this case has been treated the reader will have no difficulty in seeing how the methods would work for a linear wage equation with any number of independent variables or for a linear price equation with any number of independent variables.

The simplest type of D.V. method is one which employs a single intercept dummy. In this case, the first step is to extend the wage equation in the following way:

$$w_t = \alpha_0 + \alpha_1 X_{1t} + \alpha_2 X_{2t} + \alpha_3 D_t. \tag{8.7}$$

The variables X_1 and X_2 in (8.7) are genuine independent variables; they might be, for example, the unemployment rate and the expected rate of increase of prices. On the other hand, the variable D is one which assumes the value unity when a prices and incomes policy is in operation and a value zero otherwise. Thus it is an artificial, non-genuine independent variable, and to convey this idea it is called a 'dummy variable'.

The next step is to estimate (8.7) using the actual time series for the dependent variable, w, and the two genuine independent variables, X_1 and X_2, and an appropriately constructed zero-unity series for D. For example, if the estimation period comprised the sixty quarters, first quarter 1956 to fourth quarter 1970, and a prices and incomes policy was in force from the first quarter 1956 to fourth quarter 1956, and again from first quarter 1970 to fourth quarter 1970, the time series used for D in the estimation of (8.7) would be of the form: 1, 1, 1, 1, 0, 0, . . . , 0, 1, 1, 1, 1.

Finally, the numerical coefficient of D in the estimated version of (8.7) is examined. A negative coefficient is taken as indicating that a prices and incomes policy does indeed shift the wage equation in the appropriate way.†

The reasoning behind the final step is as follows. In the absence of a prices and incomes policy, that is if $D_t = 0$, the wage equation takes the form:

$$w_t = \alpha_0 + \alpha_1 X_{1t} + \alpha_2 X_{2t}. \qquad (8.8)$$

On the other hand, in the presence of a policy (if $D_t = 1$), the wage equation is:

$$w_t = (\alpha_0 + \alpha_3) + \alpha_1 X_{1t} + \alpha_2 X_{2t}. \qquad (8.9)$$

Now if α_3 is negative the intercept in (8.9) will be smaller (less positive or more negative) than the intercept in (8.8), that is the w_t figure given by the 'policy-on' equation will be smaller for any given levels of X_{1t} and X_{2t} than the w_t figure given by the 'policy-off' equation. Hence anything which suggests that α_3 is negative constitutes evidence that a prices and incomes policy produces the right sort of shift in the wage equation. But a negative coefficient for D_t in the estimated version of (8.7) suggests that α_3 is negative. Consequently a negative coefficient for D_t in the estimated version of (8.7) constitutes evidence that a prices and incomes policy is effective in shifting the wage equation.

We have seen that D is called a dummy variable. A fuller title is 'intercept dummy variable'. The point of this fuller title is apparent from (8.9), which shows than when D is operative the intercept of the wage equation is raised or lowered according to the sign of α_3, while the slope coefficients, α_1 and α_2, are unaffected.

From the sign of the estimated coefficient of D, then, we can get some idea as to whether a prices and incomes policy shifts the wage equation in the appropriate way. From the *size* of the coefficient we can learn something about the extent of the shift, that is we can perform the second of the two tasks involved in assessing the effectiveness of prices and incomes policy (cf. above, p. 198). Suppose that our estimate of α_3 turns out to be -1.76. Then by comparing (8.8) and (8.9) we can estimate that if a prices and incomes policy is in operation (if (8.9) is the relevant wage equation), the rate of increase of money wages will be 1.76 points less, on average, then it would have been otherwise (if (8.8) had been operative). Thus the estimated coefficient of D provides a direct estimate of the extent of the shift in the wage equation which can be attributed to a prices and incomes policy.

The view underlying (8.7) is that the reduction in the intercept occurs in its entirety immediately the policy is introduced. An alternative, and perhaps more plausible, view is that the reduction of the intercept occurs *progressively*, implying

---

†To be strictly accurate we should add 'provided the t ratio associated with the coefficient is acceptable — say two or more in absolute value'. This proviso needs to be added because the estimated coefficient must be significantly different from zero before its negativeness is taken as evidence of the effectiveness of a prices and incomes policy: cf. p. 73 above.

that the effectiveness of prices and incomes policy increases with the length of time it remains in force. If this view is taken it becomes necessary to redefine the dummy variable. As before, D is given the value zero when there is no policy in force. However, instead of assuming the value unity wherever a policy is operative, D takes the value unity in the first quarter and rises progressively quarter-by-quarter while the policy is in force, up to some limit. For example, D might start at unity, rise by unity each quarter up to ten and stay at ten thereafter until the policy ceases to operate.

With D thus redefined the procedure is as before. That is, (8.7) is estimated from time-series data, using an appropriately constructed series for D. Given D defined as in the example of the previous paragraph, and an estimation period of the type used in the earlier example, the D series used in estimation would be: 1, 2, 3, 4, 0, 0, . . . , 0, 1, 2, 3, 4. Having estimated (8.7), the sign of the estimate of α_3 is examined. As before, a negative sign for the estimate of α_3 is taken as evidence that prices and incomes policy is effective in shifting the wage equation in the appropriate way. In this type of D.V. method, however, the estimated value of α_3 measures the extent of the *initial* shift only. Denoting the estimate of α_3 by $\hat{\alpha}_3$, we can say that, after two quarters of a prices and incomes policy, the rate of increase of money wages will be an estimated $2\hat{\alpha}_3$ percentage points less, on average, than it would have been in the absence of a policy, that it will be an estimated $3\hat{\alpha}_3$ percentage points less after three quarters, and so on.†

Neither of the D.V. methods considered so far distinguishes between the four types of prices and incomes policy discussed in Section 8.3. This is clear from the fact that, in both methods, the value assumed by the dummy variable in a particular policy-on quarter is the same regardless of whether the policy takes the form of, say, 'tough' direct controls or guidelines. One may wish to make this distinction, however, to allow for the possibility that some forms of prices and incomes policy are more effective than others. In this case a third type of D.V. method is available, namely one which employs *multiple* intercept dummies. For this method, (8.7) is replaced by:

$$w_t = \alpha_0 + \alpha_1 X_{1t} + \alpha_2 X_{2t} + \alpha_3 D_{1t} + \alpha_4 D_{2t} + \alpha_5 D_{3t} + \alpha_6 D_{4t}, \quad (8.10)$$

where D_1, D_2, D_3 and D_4 are four dummy variables. The dummy variable D_1 has the value unity when a policy of the first type is in force (or, if preferred, a value rising progressively from unity) and the value zero otherwise, and similarly for the other three dummies. In the absence of a policy of any type the wage equation takes the form (8.8). On the other hand, in the presence of a policy of the first,

---

†This does not mean, of course, that the estimate of the downward shift given by the second D.V. method for two periods of operation, say, will be twice as large as the estimate of the entire downward shift given by the first method, because the two methods will give different values for α_3 due to the fact that different series are used for the dummy variable in the estimation of (8.7).

second, third and fourth types, respectively, the wage equation takes the form:†

$$w_t = (\alpha_0 + \alpha_3) + \alpha_1 X_{1t} + \alpha_2 X_{2t}$$

$$w_t = (\alpha_0 + \alpha_4) + \alpha_1 X_{1t} + \alpha_2 X_{2t}$$

$$w_t = (\alpha_0 + \alpha_5) + \alpha_1 X_{1t} + \alpha_2 X_{2t}$$

$$w_t = (\alpha_0 + \alpha_6) + \alpha_1 X_{1t} + \alpha_2 X_{2t}$$

Thus, if α_3 is negative the intercept in the first of the above four equations is smaller than the intercept in (8.8), that is a prices and income policy of the first type produces the right sort of shift in the wage equation. Similarly, if α_4 is negative the intercept in the second of the four equations is smaller than the intercept in (8.8). It follows that a prices and incomes policy of the second type is effective; and similarly with α_5 and α_6.

These propositions form the basis of the assessment procedure, as when a single intercept dummy is employed. If the coefficient of D_1 is found to be negative when (8.10) is estimated from actual time series for X_1 and X_2, and from appropriately constructed time series for the four dummy variables, it is concluded that the first type of prices and incomes policy is effective and the degree of effectiveness is measured by the estimated coefficient. The same applies, *mutatis mutandis*, to the estimated coefficients of D_2, D_3 and D_4.

An estimation of (8.10) may well throw up negative values for some estimated dummy coefficients and non-negative values for others. Thus, when multiple intercept dummies are employed, the conclusion that some forms of prices and incomes policy are effective while others are ineffective becomes possible. Also, even when they are all negative the estimated dummy coefficients may vary considerably in magnitude. Hence the conclusion that all forms of prices and incomes policy are effective but that some forms are much more effective than others also becomes possible.

The view underlying all three of the D.V. methods discussed so far is that a prices and incomes policy works by reducing the intercept of the wage equation – either in a single step or in a series of steps – leaving the slope coefficients, α_1 and α_2, unaffected. Thus the downward shift is a parallel shift, that is one which reduces w by the *same* amount at all combinations of X_1 and X_2.

A less restrictive view is that the downward shift may be either parallel or non-parallel, that is to say, that a prices and incomes policy may work through the

---

†We are assuming here, of course, that D_1 has the value unity whenever a policy of the first type is operative, and similarly for the rest, that is to say, that no allowance is being made for the possibility that effectiveness may increase with length of operation. The reader will be left to adapt the argument to cover this more complicated case.

intercept alone, through the slope coefficients alone, or in both ways. If this view is taken a D.V. method employing both intercept and slope dummies is available. To explain this method we shall take the simplest case of a single intercept dummy, leaving it to the reader to work through the case of multiple intercept dummies for himself.

Corresponding to (8.7) we now have:

$$w_t = \alpha_0 + \alpha_1 X_{1t} + \alpha_2 X_{2t} + \alpha_3 D_{1t} + \alpha_4 (D_{2t} X_{1t}) + \alpha_5 (D_{3t} X_{2t}), \qquad (8.11)$$

where the Ds are dummy variables having a value of unity (or a value rising progressively from unity) when a policy is operative and a value of zero otherwise. In the absence of a policy, (8.8) is the wage equation. In the presence of a policy the wage equation is:

$$w_t = (\alpha_0 + \alpha_3) + (\alpha_1 + \alpha_4) X_{1t} + (\alpha_2 + \alpha_5) X_2 t. \qquad (8.12)$$

If α_3, α_4 and α_5 are all negative, the intercept and both slope coefficients are smaller in (8.12) than in (8.8). Consequently, w will be less, for given values of X_1 and X_2, with prices and incomes policy than without it, that is to say, that prices and incomes policy is effective. The same is true if any one of α_3, α_4 and α_5 is negative and the other two are zero and also if any two of α_3, α_4 and α_5 are negative and the other one is zero. If any one of α_3, α_4 and α_5 is positive, however, there is doubt as to whether a prices and incomes policy is effective, even if all the rest are negative.

The procedure, then, is to estimate (8.12) and examine the signs of the coefficients of the dummy variable D_1 and the composite variables $D_2 X_1$ and $D_3 X_2$ in the estimated equation. If at least one of these coefficients is negative and none is positive and significantly different from zero (on the t-ratio criterion) it is concluded that prices and incomes policy is effective. Once effectiveness has been established the magnitude of the estimated coefficients of D_1, $D_2 X_1$ and $D_3 X_2$ is then used to measure the degree of effectiveness.

D.V. methods have been widely used to assess the effectiveness of prices and incomes policy, both in the United States and the United Kingdom. One of the earliest studies to employ D.V. methods was a study of the effectiveness of both U.K. and U.S. prices and incomes policy undertaken in the mid-1960s by Brechling.[10]

Brechling confined himself to intercept dummies but experimented with the multiple, as well as the single, form. His study also provides an example of the use of a single intercept dummy with policy-on values rising progressively from, rather than being fixed at, unity.

Two early U.K. studies in which D.V. methods were used were those undertaken by the National Board for Prices and Incomes[11] and D. C. Smith,[12] respectively. Like Brechling's study, both of these studies employed intercept dummies only. In both cases, however, the more complex multiple intercept dummies were used in preference to the single form. In the National Board study two dummies were used to introduce the broad distinction between 'loose' forms of policy and 'fairly tight' forms. In the Smith study, on the other hand, six dummies were used — one for each of the first six episodes of U.K. prices and incomes policy dealt with in Section 8.2. Also, Smith's study provides yet another example of the use of intercept dummies with values rising progressively from unity to allow for the possibility that the effectiveness of a prices and incomes policy may increase with the length of time it has been in force.

Three recent studies — one concerned with the effectiveness of U.S. prices and incomes policy and the other two with the effectiveness of U.K. policy — also deserve a mention. The U.S. study, undertaken by Wallack in the late 1960s,[13] employs only the most rudimentary form of the D.V. method (a single intercept dummy with no allowance for the possibility that effectiveness may increase with length of operation) but is notable for the fact that it attempts to study the effectiveness of prices and incomes policy at the level of the individual industry. The two U.K. studies, undertaken by Burrows and Hitiris and by Godfrey respectively,[14] are of interest mainly because they use the most complex of the D.V. methods in which both slope and intercept dummies are combined.

(3)　S.E. Methods

We turn now to S.E. (separate equations) methods — the last of the three approaches to the problem of assessing the effectiveness of prices and incomes policy which we distinguished at the outset of this section.

S.E. methods differ from E.R. and D.V. methods in that they involve a preliminary investigation to determine whether prices and incomes policy produces a shift *of some sort* in the wage and price equations. If this preliminary investigation shows that no shift is produced, it is immediately concluded that prices and incomes policy is ineffective because if there is no shift of *any* sort then *a fortiori* there is no shift of the *right* sort. If, however, it is clear from the preliminary investigation that prices and incomes policy shifts the wage and/or price equations in some way, further steps are taken to determine whether the shift is of the appropriate type and significant in extent. Let us now consider this procedure in a little more detail.

To determine whether prices and incomes policy produces a shift of some sort in the wage and price equations, the following procedure is adopted. First, time-series data covering all the variables in the wage equation (price equation) are assembled for a succession of, say, sixty consecutive quarters comprising some quarters in which prices and incomes policy operated and some in which no policy was in force. This body of time-series data is then divided into two parts, the observations for 'policy-on' quarters forming the first part and the observations for 'policy-off' quarters forming the second part. Standard econometric methods are then applied to the 'policy-on' section of the data and a 'policy-on' wage equation (price equation) is estimated. Likewise, a 'policy-off' wage equation (price equation) is estimated from the 'policy-off' observations. Finally, a statistical test based on the F distribution is performed on the estimated policy-on and policy-off equations. The purpose of this test is to determine whether the differences between the intercepts and the respective slope coefficients in these two estimated equations are such that the null hypothesis can be accepted at some predetermined level of significance, the null hypothesis being that the 'true' policy-on and policy-off equations have identical intercepts and an identical set of slope coefficients. If so, it is concluded that the wage equation (price equation) remains unchanged in the face of prices and incomes policy and the assessment is complete. If, however, the hypothesis of identical true policy-on and policy-off equations must be rejected on the basis of the F test, the conclusion is that prices and incomes policy produces some sort of shift in the wage equation (price equation), and it then becomes necessary to consider whether this shift is of the right sort and whether it is significant in quantitative terms. To this end the estimated 'policy-off' equation is used to calculate the rate of increase of money wages (rate of increase of prices) for each policy-on quarter in the estimation period. Each of these calculated rates of increase is then subtracted from the corresponding observed rate of increase. Finally, the resulting residuals are averaged. If the average is negative in sign and numerically well in excess of zero, it is concluded that prices and incomes policy shifts the wage equation (price equation) in an appropriate way and to a significant extent.

The idea behind this procedure is quite straightforward. If prices and incomes policy produces the right sort of shift in the wage equation (price equation) the rate of wage increase (price increase) will be less, for any quarter in which policy is in force, than it would have been otherwise. Now for any policy-on quarter an estimate of the 'otherwise' rate of wage increase (price increase) can be found by using the policy-off equation to calculate the rate of increase for the quarter. Thus, if prices and incomes policy shifts the wage equation (price equation) in the right way and to a significant extent, the actual rates of wage increase (price increase) in the policy-on quarters should tend to be less than those calculated from the policy-off equation, and less, moreover, by a significant amount. A substantially negative average for the policy-on residuals constitutes evidence, therefore, that prices and incomes policy achieves what it is meant to achieve.

The use of S.T. methods to assess the effectiveness of prices and incomes policy originated in a well-known study of U.K. policy by Lipsey and Parkin.[15] Since then the S.E. approach has been followed in several other U.K. studies, notably those of Hines, Taylor and Thomas and Stoney.[16]

(4) Conclusions on Effectiveness

Having explained the various methods developed by econometricians to assess the effectiveness of prices and incomes policy, we turn to the second main task of the present section. This is to review the conslusions on effectiveness which have been reached with the help of these methods in the last ten or so years.

We shall begin by giving a brief summary of the conclusions which have emerged in relation to the U.K. economy.

The conclusions of the early U.K. studies of Brechling, the National Board for Prices and Incomes and Smith show a large measure of consistency; all three studies suggest that prices and incomes policy may be effective as far as shifting the wage equation is concerned but is likely to be ineffective as far as shifting the price equation is concerned.

A summing-up of the Brechling study by Brechling himself is as follows: 'the three post-war price and incomes policies appear to have reduced the rate of increase of weekly wage rates quite markedly. By contrast the evidence of the effects of price and incomes policies upon the G.N.P. deflator and manufacturing wholesale prices is very weak. If there are any effects at all, they appear only after a lag of three to four quarters.'[17]

The National Board study has been summed-up by Dasgupta and the present author in the following way:

In the re-estimated wage equation both [dummy] variables appeared with coefficients of round about −1, suggesting that in years in which [prices and incomes policy] was being tried, whether on a voluntary or a non-voluntary basis, the rate of increase of money wages was about 1 percentage point less, at a given level of excess demand and a given rate of past inflation, than it was in years in which the approach was not being followed in either form. On the other hand, in the re-estimated price equation, both of the dummy variables appeared with positive coefficients, suggesting that as far as prices are concerned, the direct effect of employing the [prices and incomes policy] approach was perverse. The results have to be treated with considerable caution, however, because in all four cases the estimated coefficient of the dummy variable was less than twice its standard error.[18]

The following summing-up of Smith's study, based on a detailed examination of his work, is also to be found in Dasgupta and Hagger:

There is little in [Smith's study] to suggest that the [prices and incomes policy] approach can help to reduce the rate of increase of prices directly. On the other hand, the study suggests that it can help indirectly, by reducing the rate of increase of money wages .... On the evidence of the ... study, if conditions are right, a reduction in the annual rate of increase of money wages per man of as much as 2 percentage points can be expected from a vigorous application of the [prices and incomes policy] approach.[19]

The early U.K. studies, then, are somewhat favourable to prices and incomes policy. On the other hand, the later studies are decidedly unfavourable. Like the early studies, the studies of the early 1970s suggest that prices and incomes policy is ineffective as a means of shifting the price equation. In addition, however, they cast considerable doubt on its efficacy as a means of shifting the wage equation. This is true both of the S.E. studies and the D.V. studies.

Taking the S.E. studies first, we find that in the original S.E. study of Lipsey and Parkin, the conclusion from the F test (see above, p. 204) is that prices and incomes policy definitely shifts both the wage equation and the price equation. On the question of whether the shifts are of the right sort, however, and of significant extent, Lipsey and Parkin conclude that 'the data are not inconsistent with the view that wage and price restraints have usually been ineffective in restraining inflation, and also that the restraints have sometimes actually had the effect of raising the rate of inflation above what it would otherwise have been'.[20] The follow-up S.E. studies of Taylor and Thomas and Stoney, cited in the previous sub-section, are more negative still in that they fail to support shifts of any kind, helpful or otherwise. Taylor's study, which is confined to the wage equation, concludes that the wage equation is stable in the presence of prices and incomes policy while the study of Thomas and Stoney comes to the same conclusion in relation to both the wage equation and the price equation.

The recent D.V. studies of Godfrey and Burrows and Hitiris (see above, p. 204) are also highly discouraging to the proponents of prices and incomes policy. It will be recalled that intercept and slope coefficient dummies are used in combination in both of these studies. On the price equation Godfrey reports that 'no significant [dummy] variable could be found when the augmented price equation was estimated',[21] while on the wage equation his finding is that 'No significant [dummy] variable could be detected, and most of the relevant t-ratios were below one.'[22] The implication of these conclusions is, of course, that prices and incomes policy fails to shift either the price equation or the wage equation in any way and *a fortiori* that it fails to shift them in the right way. The Burrows–Hitiris study presents no clear conclusion as regards the wage equation, but the finding on the price equation is practically identical with that of Godfrey's study: 'there is no evidence [from the price equation estimates] that there is even a significant *change* in the constant or slopes as a result of incomes policy.'[23]

We turn now to the findings on the effectiveness of prices and incomes policy which have emerged from the U.S. studies. As we have seen (see above, p. 198) Perry's conclusion was that the U.S. guidelines of the early 1960s had definitely been effective in shifting the wage equation.

The conclusions reached in both of the other two studies cited in earlier sections – those of Brechling and Wallack – though somewhat guarded, were also reasonably favourable to prices and incomes policy. Brechling's summing up of his investigation of the 'guidelines' episode was as follows:

We have found that wages, the G.N.P. deflator and manufacturing wholesale prices have all tended to rise at a slower rate after 1961 than in comparable periods before 1961. This evidence is thus consistent with the proposition that the Administration's price and incomes policy has been effective in reducing the rate of wage and price inflation. Unfortunately, however, it is also consistent with other plausible propositions.[24]

Finally, Wallack, who was also concerned with the 1960 guidelines, concluded that his results 'lend support to those arguing that the guidelines worked'.[25]

To sum up this discussion of the findings of the various econometric studies of the effectiveness of prices and incomes policy, we may say that while the U.S. studies give consistent support to the view that prices and incomes policy is effective, the weight of the U.K. studies appears to be fairly heavily in the other direction.

9

POLICY AGAINST INFLATION: MANPOWER POLICY

9.1   Incomes Policy *versus* Manpower Policy

In the previous chapter prices and incomes policy was viewed as an approach to the control of inflation which works, if it works, by so modifying the structure of the model that the rate of inflation is less, for given values of the data, than it would have been otherwise. Regarded in this light, prices and incomes policy has one very special feature. The essence of prices and incomes policy is that price-makers and wage-setters are required, or urged, to conform to a code of behaviour which the authorities have laid down. Presumably the behaviour which is being looked for is not the behaviour which price-makers and wage-setters would adopt if left to their own devices; for if it were, there would be no need to impose, or urge, this behaviour on them, and prices and incomes policy would be an entirely pointless exercise. The special feature of prices and incomes policy, then, is that it attempts to bring about the intended favourable modification of the structure by forcing, or persuading, economic agents to behave in a manner which, as they see it, is opposed to their own best interests. In short, prices and incomes policy is a means of modifying the structure of the model which works against market forces, rather than with them.

There are several other approaches to the control of inflation which resemble prices and incomes policy inasmuch as they purport to work by modifying the structure of the model in a favourable way but which differ sharply from prices and incomes policy in attempting to work with, rather than against, market forces. Three examples of such approaches are: (i) a progressive weakening of tariffs and other protective devices; (ii) a progressive strengthening of anti-monopoly legislation; and (iii) a progressive development of consumer-protection agencies.† All three are meant to make the general climate in which businesses operate more competitive. To the extent that they achieve this objective, profit

---

†The items in this list resemble prices and incomes policy in yet another way. Just as the proponents of prices and incomes policy see it as contributing to objectives other than the control of inflation (see footnote, p. 167), so those who advocate a progressive weakening of tariffs, etc. frequently do so without reference to their possible beneficial effects on the rate of inflation.

margins will be squeezed, that is the rate of price increase associated with a given rate of increase of unit cost will be less than it would otherwise have been – the price equation will be shifted in a favourable manner. The general strategy of the above three approaches is therefore the same as that of prices and incomes policy. By contrast with prices and incomes policy, however, there is no attempt to persuade price-setters to do what they would not do if left to themselves. In the case of tariff revision, for example, the domestic producer is faced with more competitive prices from foreign producers and is then left to make whatever adjustments seem best from his point of view in the light of his changed market situation.

In the following sections of this chapter we shall be discussing in detail another approach to the control of inflation which belongs to the same family as the three mentioned in the previous paragraph, namely manpower policy. Like tariff revision, etc., manpower policy purports to work through a favourable modification of the structure of the model, and, again like them, attempts to work with the market. There is thus a definite family resemblance between manpower policy and tariff revision, etc. On the other hand, manpower policy has a much stronger theoretical basis than the alternatives of tariff revision, etc. and it is largely for this reason that we have decided to give it more detailed attention.

9.2 Theoretical Foundations of Manpower Policy

We began our discussion of prices and incomes policy by defining the term, at least in a general way. We shall begin our discussion of manpower policy in the same fashion, though our preliminary definition will be still more general than the definition of prices and incomes policy given in Section 8.1. In the context of inflation control, manpower policy may be defined as a series of proposals affecting the working of the labour market which are intended to shift the wage equation in a favourable way and so reduce the inflation rate corresponding to given levels of the data of the model. Thus, whereas tariff revision, monopoly control and consumer protection purport to contribute to the control of inflation by producing a favourable shift of the *price* equation, the emphasis of manpower policy is on the *wage* equation.

One of the attractive features of manpower policy is that the proposals which comprise it are derived directly from a tight theoretical argument. We shall expound this argument in the present section. We shall then present the manpower-policy proposals themselves in Section 9.3 and show their precise connection with the underlying theoretical argument.

The theoretical basis of manpower policy consists of two parts. First, a set of simple micro labour-market relationships are developed. Then these relationships are manipulated to give a macro wage equation. It is from the latter that the proposals constituting manpower policy are derived.

We shall begin by discussing the micro relationships which constitute the first part of the theoretical structure. These are referred to by Holt, the main architect of the manpower-policy approach to the control of inflation, as 'the job-search/labour-turnover model of the labour market'. Several slightly different versions of this model have appeared in recent years,[1] and in the statement of the model which follows, these different versions are combined.

As is well known, the labour market is characterised by regional, occupational, industrial and other forms of segmentation. Thus there may be vacant jobs in one region and unemployed workers in another. Again, there may be vacancies for doctors in a particular region and unemployed plumbers in that region or vacancies for males and unemployed females. In reality, this segmentation can be partially overcome if unemployed workers are prepared to incur certain real costs or if society as a whole is prepared to do so on their behalf. Thus the unemployed workers in region *A* can fill the vacant jobs in region *B* if they are willing to meet the costs of moving themselves, their family and their possessions from the one region to the other, or if some government agency or prospective employer is prepared to meet these costs on their behalf. Again, assuming that they have the necessary intellectual equipment, the unemployed plumbers can fill the vacancies for doctors if they are prepared to pay for the necessary training and suffer the loss of income which the training will entail, or if the government is prepared to pay for the training and provide an income while it is being undertaken.

In the present stage of its development the job-search/labour-turnover model of the labour market recognises the phenomenon of segmentation but departs from reality in assuming that the real costs associated with surmounting the regional, occupational and other barriers to movement in the labour market are so high that no movement, in fact, takes place. Thus the labour market is viewed as a set of mutually isolated compartments rather than as a set of mutually interacting segments.

Five relationships are postulated for each of these 'labour-tight' compartments, namely: (i) a change-in-employment identity; (ii) a new-hire-inflow relationship; (iii) a separations-outflow relationship; (iv) an equilibrium condition; and (v) a wage-response relationship. Let us take them in turn.

The *change-in-employment identity* says that the change in employment between any two periods (quarters, say) will be the excess of the inflow *to* employment represented by new hires over the outflow *from* employment represented by quits and lay-offs. Thus if we denote employment at the end of any quarter by N, the number of new hires in the quarter by H and the number of quits and lay-offs in the quarter by Q, we have as our change-in-employment identity:

$$N_t^i - N_{t-1}^i = H_t^i - Q_t^i, \qquad i = 1, \ldots, k, \tag{9.1}$$

where the i superscript indicates that we are referring to a particular compartment, compartment i, and k is the number of compartments.

The *new-hire-inflow relationship* for compartment i is:

$$H_t^i = h^i(U_t^i)^{\alpha^i}(V_t^i)^{\beta^i}, \qquad i = 1, \ldots, k, \tag{9.2}$$

where U^i is the stock of unemployed workers in compartment i, V^i the stock of vacancies and where h^i, α^i and β^i are positive constants. This relationship implies that new hires into employment in compartment i will be greater, *ceteris paribus*, the larger is the stock of unemployed workers in compartment i, and greater, *ceteris paribus*, the larger is the stock of vacancies. It is also implies that the flow of new hires will be greater, for a given stock of unemployed workers and a given stock of vacancies, the larger is h^i. The constant h^i may be interpreted, therefore, as an 'efficiency' parameter, greater speed in matching unemployed workers and unfilled vacancies being reflected in a larger value of h^i.

Turn now to the *separations-outflow relationship*. This is based on the observation that the two components of the separations-outflow (quits and lay-offs) respond in opposite directions to changes in the tightness of the labour market, a tighter labour market inducing more quits and fewer lay-offs, and *vice versa*. In the short run, therefore, the separations outflow of compartment i can be regarded as approximately constant. In the long-run, however, it will rise as the scale of the economy increases. A relationship which implies that the separations outflow of compartment i is constant apart from changes in the scale of the economy is:

$$Q_t^i = f^i L_t^p, \qquad i = 1, \ldots, k, \tag{9.3}$$

where $f^{i\cdot}$ is a constant and L^p is the 'potential' labour force, that is the labour force corresponding to some specified unemployment rate, say 4 per cent.

The variable L^p is a good indicator of scale since it reflects long-run growth influences while being free from short-run cyclical influences because of its definition in terms of a specified unemployment rate.[†] This being so, (9.3) says, in effect, that the separations outflow of compartment i will increase as the scale of the economy increases but will be fixed apart from scale changes.

The fourth of the five relationships which are postulated for compartment i is an equilibrium condition, namely:

$$\frac{N_t^i - N_{t-1}^i}{N_t^i} = g, \qquad i = 1, \ldots, k, \tag{9.4}$$

where g is constant. This says that the percentage rate of change of employment

---

[†] *Actual* labour force would be less satisfactory as a scale indicator because the actual labour force rises as the labour market becomes more tight, and vice versa, so that the actual labour-force variable picks up short-run as well as long-run influences.

in all compartments is constant at g, which condition is a necessary condition for growth equilibrium.†

Before presenting the fifth and final relationship of the job-search/ labour-turnover model, we shall combine the four relationships presented already into a single relationship. First we divide (9.1) through by N_t^i and substitute (9.4) to obtain:

$$\frac{H_t^i}{N_t^i} - \frac{Q_t^i}{N_t^i} = g, \qquad i = 1, \ldots, k \tag{9.5}$$

Next (9.2) and (9.3) are used to obtain the following expression for H_t^i/N_t^i and Q_t^i/N_t^i:

$$\frac{H_t^i}{N_t^i} = h^i \left(\frac{U_t^i}{N_t^i}\right)^{\alpha^i} \left(\frac{V_t^i}{N_t^i}\right)^{\beta^i} (N_t^i)^{\alpha^i + \beta^i - 1} = h^i (u_t^i)^{\alpha^i} (v_t^i)^{\alpha^i} (N_t^i)^{\alpha^i + \beta^i - 1} \tag{9.6}$$

and

$$\frac{Q_t^i}{N_t^i} = f^i \frac{L_t^p}{N_t^i}, \qquad i = 1, \ldots, k, \tag{9.7}$$

where u^i and v^i denote U^i/N^i and V^i/N^i, respectively. These expressions are now substituted in (9.5) to obtain:

$$h^i (u_t^i)^{\alpha^i} (v_t^i)^{\beta^i} (N_t^i)^{\alpha^i + \beta^i - 1} - f^i \frac{L_t^p}{N_t^i} = g, \qquad i = 1, \ldots, k. \tag{9.8}$$

Finally (9.8) is solved for v^i to obtain:

$$v_t^i = \left[\frac{g + f^i \dfrac{L_t^p}{N_t^i}}{h^i}\right]^{1/\beta^i} (N_t^i)^{(1 - \alpha^i - \beta^i)/\beta^i} (u_t^i)^{-\alpha^i/\beta^i}, \qquad i = 1, \ldots, k. \tag{9.9}$$

The final relationship of the model, the wage-response relationship, is:

$$(1 + w_t^i) = A^i \left(\frac{V_t^i}{U_t^i}\right)^{\tau^i} (p_t^e)^{\epsilon^i} = A^i \left(\frac{v_t^i}{u_t^i}\right)^{\tau^i} (p_t^e)^{\epsilon^i}$$

$$= A^i (v_t^i)^{\tau^i} (u_t^i)^{-\tau^i} (p_t^e)^{\epsilon^i}, \qquad i = 1, \ldots, k, \tag{9.10}$$

† It is no criticism of the model to point out that the economy is never in growth equilibrium. That is undeniable. The point is that all the relationships of this and any other model are violations of reality (intentionally so); and the model is to be judged, not by checking the relationships one by one for realism but by deriving the testable predictions of the model as a whole, or of individual relationships, and checking these against the relevant facts when they become available. See Sections 2.1 and 3.1 for further discussion.

where A^i, τ^i and ϵ^i are positive constants and w^i and p^e have their usual meanings – the percentage rate of increase of the index of money wages in compartment i and the expected rate of inflation, respectively. Thus, $1 + w_t^i$, the ratio between successive values of the wage index in compartment i, is made to respond to labour-market tightness as indicated by V^i/U^i (the higher the vacancy–unemployment ratio, the tighter the labour market) and also to price expectations, the relevant elasticities being τ^i and ϵ^i.

We come now to the second part of the theoretical argument which underlies manpower policy. Here relationships (9.9) and (9.10) are used to derive the macro wage equation from which the proposals which constitute manpower policy eventually emerge.

This equation is as follows:

$$w_t = \gamma_0 + \gamma_1 \ln u_t + \gamma_2 \ln p_t^e + \sum_{i=1}^{k} \gamma_{3i} \ln \frac{u_t}{u_t^i} + \sum_{i=1}^{k} \gamma_{4i} \ln Z_t^i + \sum_{i=1}^{k} \gamma_{5i} \ln N_t^i,$$

$$(9.11)$$

where 'ln' denotes 'log to the base e', $Z_t^i = [g + f^i(L_t^p/N_t^i)]/h^i$ and the γs are constants which are functions of the constants in (9.9) and (9.10) and of c_i^i the proportion of total employment in the ith compartment. The details of the derivation of (9.11) are somewhat complicated and will be omitted.

The macro wage equation. (9.11), represents the end point of the theoretical argument which underlies manpower policy. As we shall show in the next section, the list of proposals for shifting the wage equation which constitute manpower policy emerges directly from an examination of this particular wage equation.

Before leaving the basic theory, we ask the reader to note that (9.11) has all the characteristics of the macro wage equation which the empirical studies of Chapter 5 have brought to light. It turns out, therefore, that the theoretical argument presented in this section belongs to the same class as the three presented in Sections 6.2, 6.4 and 6.5 of Chapter 6; like them the present argument is directed towards showing that the extended Phillips-type macro wage equation which emerges from the empirical studies can be derived from certain more basic relationships, that is, it is concerned with the microeconomic foundations of this macro wage equation. Indeed, the discussion of this section could have been included quite appropriately in Chapter 6, and it was for convenience only that we chose to place it here rather than in that chapter.

In the previous paragraph we asserted that (9.11) has all the characteristics of the macro wage equation revealed by the empirical literature of the last two decades. We now support this assertion (cf. above, p. 113).

To begin with we note that the over-all unemployment rate, u_t, is one of the independent variables of the equation, as required. Second, by taking the partial derivative of w_t with respect to u_t, we see that the curve of w_t against u_t, the other independent variables held fixed, possesses the traditional Phillips-curve properties.† Third, we note that the unemployment rate is not the only independent variable; indeed the last three terms on the right-hand side themselves involve $3k$ independent variables. Next, we note that one of the 'extra' independent variables is p^e, the expected inflation rate, and, finally, we note that the $3k$ independent variables first mentioned are all extraneous from the standpoint of the original Phillips–Lipsey studies.

Thus the assertion that (9.11) has all the characteristics of the extended, Phillips-type, macro wage equation revealed by the empirical studies appears to be correct.

Finally, it will be instructive to compare (9.11) with the wage equation of our policy model (equation (7.2)). It will be recalled that the X in (7.2) denotes one or more terms in independent variables outside the original Phillips–Lipsey list (see above, p. 138). Thus it generalises the last three terms on the right-hand side of (9.11). It appears, therefore, that if two small and unimportant adjustments were to be made to (7.2), (9.11) would become a special case of (7.2). The two adjustments in question are: (i) to introduce the desired Phillips curvature by expressing the unemployment rate as a natural logarithm rather than as a reciprocal; and (ii) to introduce non-linearity in the price term by expressing the expected inflation rate as a natural logarithm.

9.3 Manpower-Policy Proposals

Examination of (9.11) reveals a number of obvious ways of shifting the wage equation so that the rate of increase of money wages per man will be less than before, for given levels of the independent variables which determine the rate of increase. For example, if the values of some or all of the A^i are reduced, the intercept of (9.11) will be a smaller positive figure than before ($\gamma_0 = \Sigma_{i=1}^{k} c^i \ln A^i$), and hence the value of w, the dependent variable, will be smaller, at given levels of the independent variables, than previously. Or if some or all of the ϵ^i are reduced, the coefficient of the expected inflation rate will be a smaller

---

†We have:

$$\frac{\partial w_t}{\partial u_t} = \gamma_1 u_t^{-1}.$$

It can be shown that γ_1 is a negative constant. Hence the slope of the curve of w_t against u_t is negative at all points, as required. Also:

$$\frac{\partial^2 w_t}{\partial u_t^2} = -\gamma_1 u_t^{-2},$$

from which it is clear that the second-order partial is positive for all values of u_t, that is to say, that the negativeness of the slope of the curve of w_t against u_t diminishes as u_t increases — again as required.

positive figure than previously ($\gamma_2 = \Sigma_{i=1}^k c^i \epsilon^i$) so that, once again, w will be less, for given levels of the independent variables, than was the case previously.

The difficulty with these, and other equally obvious suggestions, is that they are not easily translated into precise policy proposals. It is obvious that one can shift the wage equation in a favourable way by reducing some or all A^i but what precise steps should the authorities take in order to effect the desired reduction in the A^i? This is not at all obvious. Because of this difficulty, the proponents of manpower policy have directed their attention away from the obvious possibilities to three which are somewhat subtle but which have clear implications for policy. They are: (i) reduce all or some f^i; (ii) increase some or all h^i; and (iii) reduce the spread of the u^i.

As regards (i), if some f^i, say f^1, is reduced the term:

$$\frac{g + f^1 \dfrac{L_t^p}{N_t^1}}{h^1}$$

will be smaller than before for given levels of the independent variable, L_t^p/N_t^1. Hence ln of this term will be smaller, and hence, in turn, γ_{41} times ln will be smaller ($\gamma_{41} = c^1 \tau^1 /\beta^1$, and is therefore positive). Thus if one or more of the f^i are reduced, the sum which forms the second-last term on the right-hand side of (9.11) will be smaller than before, for given levels of the L_t^p/N_t^i, and hence w_t will be smaller — there will have been a favourable shift in the wage equation. A similar argument can be used to show the *modus operandi* of (ii); the reader will be left to supply the details for himself. The third possibility is less straight-forward and requires rather more discussion.

For this purpose attention must be focused on the term:

$$\sum_{i=1}^k \gamma_{3i} \ln \frac{u_t}{u_t^i} \, .$$

The essential point is that this term, though not necessarily positive, is likely to be so provided the u^i differ. The reason has been stated by Holt *et al.* in the following way: 'if the [u^i] differ, the curvilinearity of the log transformation will tend to make [this term] positive. For those market compartments whose unemployment rates are relatively low, [$\ln(u_t/u_t^i)$] will be much more sharply positive than it will be negative for high unemployment compartments.'[2] Furthermore, the greater the differences among the u^i, the more positive is the term in question likely to be. Hence the likelihood is that, by reducing the differences among the u_t^i one can reduce the positive contribution which the term involving the u_t/u_t^i makes to w_t, that is one can make w_t less than it would have been otherwise. Certainly, if the differences can be eliminated altogether, the term in question will make a zero contribution since then all u^i will be identical with u and $\ln(u_t/u_t^i)$ will be ln 1 or zero, for all compartments.

It should be noted, in passing, that while we have followed the architects of manpower policy in grouping the operation of reducing the spread of the u^i together with the operations of reducing the f^i and increasing the h^i, only the last two can be properly regarded as ways of shifting the wage equation, that is only the last two ought, strictly speaking, to be under discussion in the present chapter. The first is an operation on one of the independent variables of the wage equation, that is, it is an operation which produces a movement along, rather than a shift of, the wage equation. In fact, reducing the spread of the u^i is on all fours with reducing the over-all unemployment rate, u, and it would have been more appropriate, though much less convenient, to have discussed it in association with the latter in Chapter 7. Had we chosen this course, the natural approach would have been to interpret the manipulation in question as a manipulation of one of the unspecified data of the model which are lumped together in the global term X_t in equation (7.2).

Having clarified the *modus operandi* of the proposals which constitute, manpower policy, we now turn to the proposals themselves. We shall deal with them under three heads, namely: (1) proposals which work *via* the f^i; (2) proposals which work *via* the h^i; and (3) proposals which work *via* the spread of the u^i.

(1) Proposals for Reducing the f^i

We begin by considering several proposals which are directed towards reducing some or all of the f^i.

Looking back to (9.3) we see that f^i is the ratio between the number of separations per period in compartment i and the potential labour force. Since the denominator of the ratio is effectively given, reducing f^i means making the flow of separations in compartment i smaller period by period, than was previously the case. Manpower-policy proposals for bringing this result about fall into three groups: (*a*) proposals for improving the matching between jobs and workers 'so that a strong mutually rewarding relationship is built that will not be casually dissolved',[3] (*b*) proposals for reducing the flow of separations in the form of lay-offs; and (*c*) proposals for reducing the flow of separations in the form of quits. We shall consider each group in turn.

The first group of proposals are directed towards improving the functioning of the public 'employment service', assuming that one exists. One proposal is that the employment service should be structured so that in each office some officers are specially trained for, and concentrate on, meeting the needs of the workers who are looking for jobs, while others are specialised to meeting the needs of the employers who are trying to fill jobs. A second proposal is that incentive schemes with a stress on *quality* of placement, measured in terms of length of job tenure, be introduced to provide officers of the service with the right motivation. Third, it is suggested that the service should establish salary levels that will attract well-qualified professionals to its interviewing, counselling and placement positions.

Finally, it is proposed that a powerful, nation-wide, computerised system be introduced to improve the communication between workers who are looking for jobs and employers who are trying to fill vacancies. This proposal, which is the major proposal in group (*a*), is spelt out by Holt in the following way:

> Only a very small fraction of the huge combinatoric number of potential matches [between workers and employers] and the attendant information would be of interest to *both* parties. To be genuinely useful, the information needs to be classified, screened, selectively disseminated, and wisely used in seeking out prospective matches that are sufficiently promising mutually to justify the costs of interviews to explore in depth the prospects of placing particular workers in particular jobs.... This process involves not only information on qualifications and desires, job requirements, and inducements, but also its analysis in making decisions on the most promising directions of search and ultimately on offers and acceptances. The importance of such information ... spotlights the critical role of organized employment services and their needs for powerful computerized processing.[4]

Further elaboration of the proposal for the establishment of a nation-wide computerised system for matching workers and jobs appears in another publication: 'The computer-matching system would incorporate behavioural relationships to help predict for human follow-up which of the astronomic number of possible matches hold the greatest promise of being both satisfying for the worker and productive for the employer.'[5]

Turn now to the second group of proposals – those concerned with reducing the flow of separations from lay-offs. The main suggestion in this area is that businesses be encouraged to reduce avoidable work-force fluctuations, for example by '(a) forecasting their sales more accurately to avoid having to make short-term responses to unanticipated sales fluctuations, (b) using inventory and back-order buffers to smooth production fluctuations, and (c) using overtime and idle time to accommodate production fluctuations rather than alternatively hiring and laying off workers.'[6] A second proposal is that lay-offs be discouraged by means of an education programme which would aim to increase management awareness of the significance of training costs. Holt argues that there is considerable scope for such a programme since 'The cost of training often escapes management's attention because of its "invisible" character, which frequently escapes routine accounting reports even though these costs may be quite large.'[7] Third, it is suggested that programmes which aim to encourage investment in training should be introduced on the grounds that a firm which has invested heavily in the training of its work force will have a stronger incentive to keep its work force together than one which has neglected training, and hence a stronger incentive to avoid lay-offs.

The third group of proposals – those directed towards reducing the flow of quit-separations – contains several which are novel. Perhaps the most interesting is a proposal for reducing the asymmetry in the information conveyed in the placement process. The nature of the asymmetry in question, and its significance in the context of reducing the flow of quit-separations, is well conveyed in the following passage from Holt:

> The employer characteristically collects considerable information on the worker in writing while usually the worker must be content with verbal descriptions of the job being offered that omit most of the information that is really important to him. This hardly is conductive to achieving a *mutually* satisfying job—worker match. In this situation the worker has little choice but to lightly accept the job and lightly drop it if it does not work out.[8]

The second main proposal takes as its starting-point the fact that quits are heavily concentrated in the young-worker group. This can be attributed, so it is argued, to inadequate preparation of young people for employment:

> it is clear that for many young workers a series of short-term jobs constitutes an extended placement process. Lacking really adequate information about career opportunities in general, or about the particular job being offered, the worker accepts it together with the company's training only to discover later that the job does not fit. Our educational system often teaches almost nothing about the world of work to help prepare young people for their important career choices ahead.[9]

To meet this problem it is proposed, first, that vocational counselling in schools be strengthened, both in terms of the number of counsellors engaged and also in terms of the extent and quality of their training, and that attempts be made to achieve closer co-operation between school counsellors and the public employment service. A second suggestion is that employers be subsidised so that they can offer students short periods of realistic work experience while they are still at school.

(2) Proposals for Increasing the h^i

So far in this section we have been discussing certain manpower-policy proposals which aim to bring about a reduction in some or all of the f^i parameters of the wage equation (9.11). We now switch our attention to the h^i parameters.

We saw earlier (see p. 212) that the constant h^i can be interpreted as a placement-efficiency parameter — the larger is h^i, the greater is the average speed with which unemployed workers are matched with unfilled vacancies in compartment i. Proposals for increasing the h^i, therefore, are effectively proposals for increasing the speed with which unemployed workers are placed in vacant jobs.

The proposal for a nation-wide, computerised system for matching unemployed workers and vacant jobs, which was discussed earlier in another connection, is obviously relevant here too. As already explained, the main object of such a data-processing system would be to weed out, from the vast number of possible matches, the comparatively small number that are likely to hold interest for both parties. Thus the system would provide a vast amount of information of the greatest relevance to the individual placement problem with a degree of accuracy and speed that human resources could not possibly attain and would be bound, therefore, to reduce the average time taken to place unemployed workers in vacant jobs as well as improving the average quality of placements.

A second proposal for increasing the h^i, which is specific to this particular objective, is that appropriate steps be taken to shorten the duration of the 'wage gap'. This proposal is best elaborated in terms of the simple diagram shown in Figure 9.1.

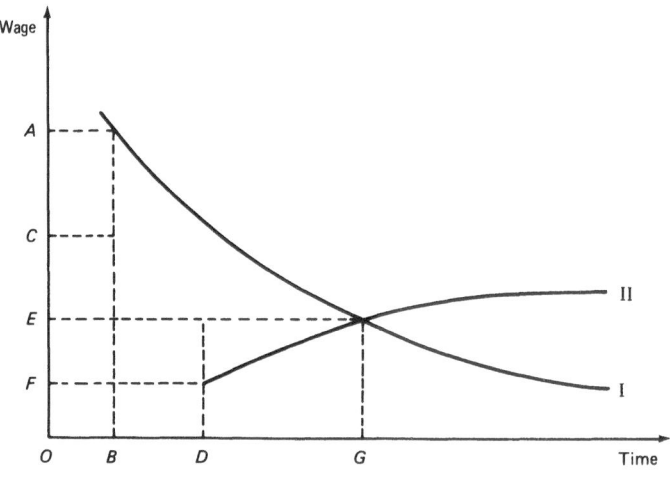

Fig. 9.1

The curve labelled I relates to a particular unemployed worker. We suppose that the worker becomes unemployed at time OB. His wage aspiration as he begins his search for a new job is OA, which exceeds OC, his last wage in his previous job, by CA. Assuming that the general level of money wages remains constant, the worker's wage aspiration will fall along a curve of the form of curve I as time passes (see pp. 129–30 above for further discussion).

The curve labelled II relates to a particular employer who is trying to fill a vacant position. The position becomes vacant, we shall say, at time OD. As the employer begins his search for someone to fill the vacancy, the maximum wage which he is prepared to offer is OF, which falls short of OE, the wage paid to the previous occupant of the position, by FE. We suppose that, as time passes, the employer's maximum wage offer will rise continuously along the curve labelled II.

Prior to time OG there is a 'wage gap', in the sense that the minimum wage which the unemployed worker would be prepared to accept exceeds the maximum wage which the employer would be prepared to offer to the occupant of his vacant position. There is no chance, therefore, that an interview arranged prior to time OG would result in an offer being both made and accepted. From time OG on, however, there is a 'wage overlap', in the sense that the maximum wage being offered exceeds the minimum wage being asked for. There is some chance therefore, that an interview will lead to an acceptable offer. Moreover, since the wage overlap increases continuously from time OG on, the chances that an acceptable offer will emerge from an interview will likewise increase continuously from time OG on.

This analysis makes it clear that, for an individual unemployed worker, placement will be speeded up if the time interval during which a wage gap exists in relation to any vacant position (the time interval typified by DG in Figure 9.1) is reduced. It is also clear that the typical wage-gap interval can be reduced in one or more of the following ways: (i) by reducing the worker's initial wage aspiration (by lowering the point A); (ii) by increasing the speed with which his wage aspiration declines (by making curve I fall more sharply from left to right); (iii) by increasing the initial wage offer for the typical vacancy (by raising the point D); and (iv) by increasing the speed with which the wage offer for the typical vacancy increases (by making curve II rise more sharply from left to right). The conclusion which emerges, therefore, is that placement would be speeded up all round (the h^i will be increased) if steps which tend to reduce initial wage aspirations, and/or increase initial wage offers, and/or make wage aspirations and wage offers adjust more rapidly, were to be taken.

As to what the steps might be, the proponents of manpower policy rely heavily on the provision of better information and better advice, both to unemployed workers and to firms with vacancies to be filled. Holt states the case in the following way:

> The worker optimally should set his aspiration wage high enough to prevent his accepting prematurely a relatively poor opportunity before he has searched enough to get the feel of his likely options. Any reduction in his uncertainty through better information should enable him safely to set a lower initial acceptance wage . . . . By the same reasoning, the employer could safely offer a higher wage to output ratio, if he had better knowledge . . . . Better information and counselling may enable the worker to learn more quickly and help him to make the psychological adjustments involved in accepting lower wage aspirations that are necessitated by the economic opportunities that are available. By the same reasoning, information and consultation may help the employer learn and adjust faster to prevailing market conditions.[10]

(3) *Proposals For Reducing the Spread of u^i*

To conclude this section on manpower-policy proposals, we give some attention to certain proposals for reducing the spread of the u^i. From a purely mathematical point of view the spread of the u^i can be reduced both by *increasing* the unemployment rate in those compartments in which it is relatively low and by reducing the unemployment rate in those compartments in which it is relatively high. From a social standpoint, however, only the latter alternative is acceptable, and the proposals which we are about to consider are all aimed at reducing the unemployment rate in those regional, occupational, age, racial and other compartments in which it happens to be relatively high.

Frequently, unemployed workers who are capable of filling certain vacant positions, and who are anxious to fill them, are prevented from doing so by irrelevant barriers, for example those based on race, sex and age, or by monopolistic barriers of one sort of another, for example unnecessarily rigid training requirements. One of the main proposals for reducing the relatively high u^i is that research directed towards identifying such undesirable barriers to worker mobility be undertaken and that government programmes for eliminating or reducing them be implemented.

A second proposal for reducing the relatively high u^i is that a government training organisation be established. The function of this organisation would be to train or retrain unemployed workers and to support them during training, the object being to enable such workers to fill vacancies which they are incapable of filling at present because they lack the necessary trade or professional skills.

Third, it is suggested that unemployed workers, for whom no suitable vacancies exist in their own locality, should be given financial and other assistance to move themselves and their families to other parts of the country where suitable employment would be available. Action along these lines would help to reduce the unemployment rate in regions with relatively high rates and in this way tend to narrow regional unemployment differences.

Finally, it is suggested that the public employment service should employ industrial engineers, psychologists and members of other relevant professions specifically to advise and assist employers in job restructuring. This proposal is based on the belief that appropriate job restructuring would enable many vacancies to be tailored to fit the existing skills of unemployed workers. To the extent that this can be done, it will be possible to reduce relatively high regional, occupational and other unemployment rates without recourse to retraining or relocation of unemployed workers, both of which are expensive and likely to provoke a certain amount of resistance.

9.4   Consensus on Policy

In the last few years, professional economists have reached a substantial measure of agreement on the central issues of anti-inflation policy, and we shall conclude our policy discussion by attempting to sketch in the boundaries of this agreement. Our method of doing this will be to state a series of broad propositions to which, we believe, the vast majority of economists would, nowadays, give their assent.

Each of these propositions will be set out in italics and will be accompanied by discussion in ordinary type in which the proposition will be elaborated and, if necessary, qualified. The reader will find that this supporting discussion draws heavily on the material presented in this and the two earlier policy chapters, and, hopefully, that it provides an effective way of summarising the entire policy argument.

PROPOSITION 1

A long-run trade-off exists between inflation and unemployment.

By this we mean that the community can enjoy a lower steady inflation rate if it is prepared to tolerate a higher steady unemployment rate and vice versa. In diagrammatic terms proposition 1 implies that the long-run inflation—unemployment curve is a curve which slopes downward from left to right, as in Figure 7.3 (p. 144).

The weight of professional opinion appears to be solidly behind the above proposition. Nevertheless, there is a significant group of economists (led by Friedman and Phelps) who dispute it and holds instead that the long-run inflation—unemployment curve is a vertical line drawn at the 'natural' unemployment rate, as in Figure 7.4 (p. 145).

The dispute between those who hold that a long-run trade-off exists and those who deny its existence can be approached in a number of different ways. One possibility is to set up a simple expectational model such as the policy model, (7.1), (7.2) and (7.3), and then measure the coefficient of p^e (the expected inflation rate) in the wage equation of the model. This helps to resolve the dispute since a vertical long-run inflation—unemployment curve requires that this coefficient be unity, a downward-sloping long-run curve that it be less than unity. A second possible approach is to set up a small-scale macro-dynamic model, then derive a numerical version of this model and finally use this numerical model to derive a numerical relationship between $\bar{p}$, the steady-state inflation rate and $\bar{u}$, the corresponding steady-state unemployment rate. This procedure also contributes to a resolution of the dispute since it provides the means of actually sketching the long-run inflation—unemployment curve and inspecting it for curvature or absence of curvature. Finally, one can conduct a series of computer experiments based on a large-scale, macro-dynamic econometric model. The computer is fed a set of realistic time paths for all but one of the predetermined variables and instructed to track the time path of the inflation rate on the assumption that the time path of the one remaining predetermined variable adjusts so as to keep the unemployment rate constant at some specified figure. The figure on which the inflation rate converges (assuming that convergence takes place) is taken to be the steady inflation rate which is associated with the particular steady unemployment rate involved in the exercise, that is to say, it is taken to be one point on the long-run inflation—unemployment curve. Other points on the curve are then obtained by repeating the entire computation with different steady unemployment rates. Once again the procedure helps to resolve the dispute since, if repeated sufficiently often, it makes possible a rough sketch of the long-run inflation—unemployment curve which can be examined for curvature.

Each of these three approaches has been considered in detail already in Chapters 3 and 7 and the relevant empirical literature surveyed. It would appear from this earlier discussion that, regardless of the approach adopted, the weight of the evidence favours the existence of a long-run trade-off. With few exceptions, the studies reviewed in Chapter 3 point to a value well below unity for the coefficient of p^e, while those reviewed in Section 7.4—7.6 of Chapter 7 point to a steep, but far from vertical, long-run inflation—unemployment curve (see Tables 7.1 and 7.2, pp. 155, 157). The same is true of the computer-based studies reviewed in Section 7.7. Thus proposition 1 has solid empirical support and it is this, one can assume, which accounts for the fact that the proposition is now very widely accepted by professional economists.

PROPOSITION 2

The long-run trade-off between inflation and unemployment may differ widely between countries at any point in time and may change over time in any one country.

In other words, the position and/or curvature of the (downward-sloping) long-run inflation—unemployment curve may differ from country to country at any point in time, and many change for any one country over time.

The possibility of variation over *space* in the long-run inflation—unemployment curve can be accounted for in terms of *differences* in the parameters of the long-run inflation—unemployment relationship. Similarly, the possibility of variation over *time* in the long-run curve can be explained in terms of *changes* in the parameters of the long-run relationship. There is general agreement, largely as a result of the international study of Bodkin and his associates (see Section 7.6 above), that the possibility of inter-country differences has, in fact, been realised — that the long-run trade-off is at present less favourable in some countries than in others. It has also been suggested that in some countries, notably the United States,[11] the long-run trade-off is less favourable now than it was in the 1950s and 1960s, though it is doubtful whether genuine consensus exists on this particular point at the time of writing.

PROPOSITION 3

For any given economy at any given time there may be no point on the long-run inflation—unemployment curve which is acceptable, that is for any given country at any given time there may be a conflict between the unemployment and inflation objectives.

Different countries have different ideas about the maximum inflation rate that is tolerable and different ideas as to what constitutes an acceptable upper limit for the unemployment rate. Also, in any one country ideas on these two matters change over time. It seems clear that most countries have become more tolerant of inflation in the last ten years, possibly because some of the arguments that were advanced to support the ambitious inflation targets of the 1950s and early 1960s (for example price stability or a zero inflation rate) have clearly lost force. Also, some countries appear to be moving towards acceptance of a higher unemployment rate at the present time. This can be accounted for, possibly, by a growing awareness that many people, particularly young people, now find unemployment an attractive state and have no wish to leave the ranks of the unemployed, so that the degree of social evil associated with a given unemployment rate is now significantly less than was once the case. However this may be, one can reckon on there being general agreement, at any time and place, that the inflation rate should not exceed x per cent per annum and that the unemployment rate should not be higher than y per cent. Now it may well be that the long-run inflation–unemployment curve is such that the steady inflation rate associated with a steady unemployment rate of y per cent is greater than the target rate of x per cent per annum. In this case there will be no point on the long-run inflation–unemployment curve which is acceptable to the community at large; all points to the left of the vertical broken line at y (see Figure 9.2) are unacceptable because they involve an inflation rate in excess of x while all points to the right are unacceptable because they involve an unemployment rate in excess of y. Putting the point in another way, in the situation envisaged there will be a conflict between the inflation and unemployment objectives — either one of the two

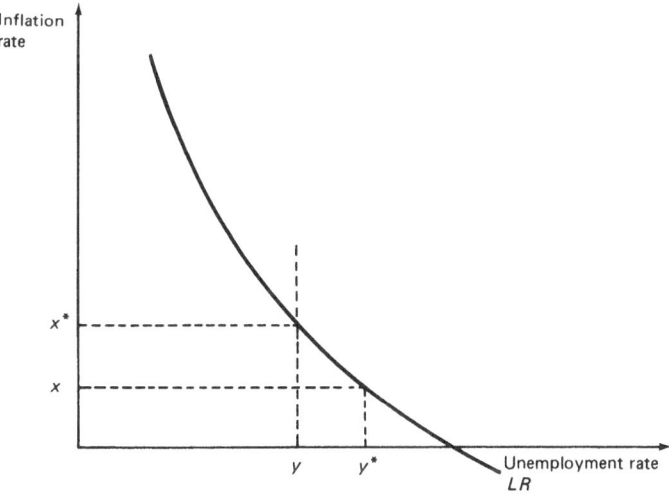

Fig. 9.2

objectives is capable of achievement, given the existing long-run trade-off between inflation and unemployment, but not both. Achievement of the inflation objective implies a steady unemployment rate of y^*, that is sacrifice of the unemployment objective; achievement of the unemployment objective implies a steady inflation rate of x^*, that is sacrifice of the inflation objective. There is no way in which both the inflation target and the unemployment target can be achieved, given the existing long-run trade-off between inflation and unemployment.

PROPOSITION 4

By appropriate manipulation of the unemployment rate the policy-maker may be able to mask a conflict between the inflation and unemployment objectives, but it is undesirable that he should attempt to do so.

For elaboration of this proposition we make use of Figure 9.3, which shows three of the family of short-run inflation—unemployment curves together with the long-run curve. We suppose that y is the acceptable upper limit for the unemployment rate and x the acceptable upper limit for the inflation rate. Thus there is a conflict between the inflation and unemployment objectives.

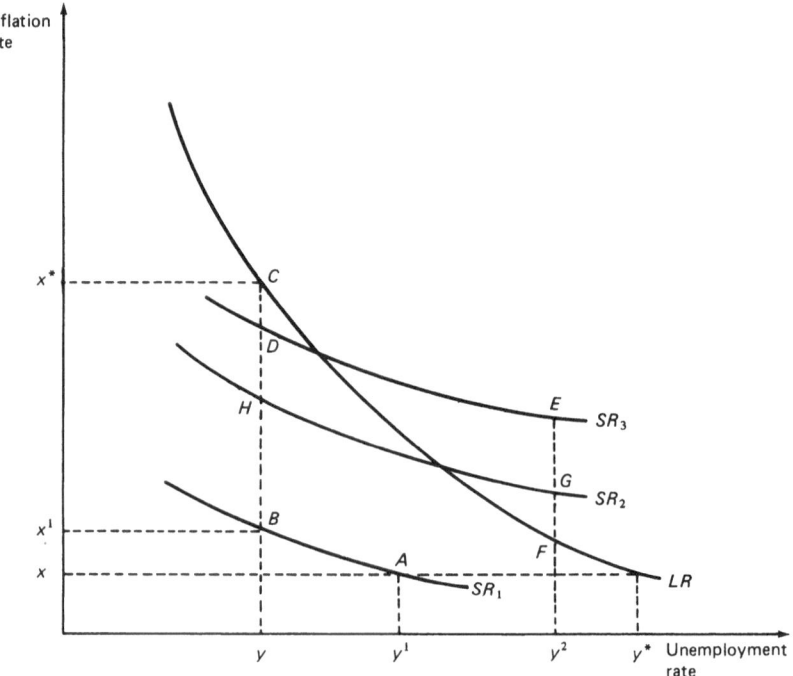

Fig. 9.3

Let the economy be initially at A with an inflation rate at the target level x but with an unacceptably high unemployment rate y^1, and let the policy-maker reduce the unemployment rate to the target level y. The *short*-run consequence of this action is to shift the economy to B, at which point the inflation rate is x^1, somewhat above the target level. The *long*-run consequence is to move the economy to C, at which point the inflation rate is x^*, which is still further above the target level. Suppose, however, that at point D, before the long-run implications of the target unemployment rate become clear, the unemployment rate is raised to, say, y^2. The short-run consequence of this action is to move the economy to E, the long-run consequence to move the economy to F. Suppose that before F is reached, say at G, the unemployment rate is reduced a second time to the target level, y. The short-run consequence of this action is to shift the economy to H. With the move to H the economy will have completed a loop round the long-run curve – from A to B to D to E to G to H. Suppose now that before the long-run implications of the second reduction in the unemployment rate have emerged, the unemployment rate is raised again. Then the economy will begin on a second loop round the long-run curve.

Clearly, then, it will be possible for the policy-maker to keep the economy moving round the long-run curve in a loop-wise fashion simply by manipulating the unemployment rate in an appropriate way. Moreover this 'stop–go' routine is likely to have its attractions for the policy-maker because it will give him some periods of success in relation to the unemployment objective (for example when the economy is moving from point B to point D) and may give him other periods of success in relation to the inflation objective.

While conceding that 'stop–go' may have some merit, most economists would take the view that, on balance, it represents an undesirable approach to anti-inflation policy.† For one thing the fluctuations in the unemployment rate which characterise stop–go will be engineered by fluctuations in the rate of growth of aggregate demand. But fluctuating (and hence uncertain) demand growth is likely to have a depressing effect on the level of business investment, and through this on the rate of economic growth. Thus, a regime of stop–go provides a bad climate for fast growth; from this viewpoint a steady unemployment rate, implying a steady rate of growth of aggregate demand, is much to be preferred.

A second argument in favour of a steady, rather than a fluctuating, unemployment rate is that, with a steady unemployment rate, there is at least the possibility of steady inflation;‡ and, as we saw in Section 1.5, a steady inflation rate is much to be preferred to a variable one.

Finally, it can be argued that stop–go is essentially a means of hiding the fact

---

†The policy approach described here as 'stop–go' is of course the first of the two approaches to demand management discussed in Section 7.3.

‡As well as a steady unemployment rate, steady inflation requires that the long-run levels of the other data should be steady.

that there is a conflict between the inflation and unemployment objectives, because as soon as the full implications of maintaining the unemployment rate, year-in, year-out, at y (that is a steady inflation rate of x^*) begin to be revealed, stop—go orders that the unemployment rate be raised. However, instead of hiding the fact that the unemployment rate which the community desires is incompatible, on a year-in—year-out basis, with the inflation rate which it desires, the policy-maker should be giving it the greatest possible prominence. For unless the community is fully aware that the conflict exists, there will be little chance of effecting the fundamental changes in the economic structure which are required to remove, or at least to mitigate, the conflict.

PROPOSITION 5

If there is one or more acceptable points on the long-run inflation— unemployment curve (no conflict of objectives), the unemployment rate should be kept steady at the level corresponding to the maximum acceptable inflation rate. If there is no acceptable point on the long-run curve the unemployment rate should be kept steady at the maximum acceptable level.

Figures 9.4 and 9.5 help to clarify this proposition. Figure 9.4 shows the first of the two situations covered by the proposition. The maximum acceptable steady inflation rate being x and the maximum acceptable steady unemployment rate being y any point on the long-run curve between A and B is acceptable — there is no conflict of objectives. According to the proposition the point A should be chosen in these circumstances. That is, the unemployment rate should be kept steady at $\hat{y}$ and the inflation rate steady, in consequence, at x, the maximum acceptable figure. The second situation is shown in Figure 9.5. In this case there is

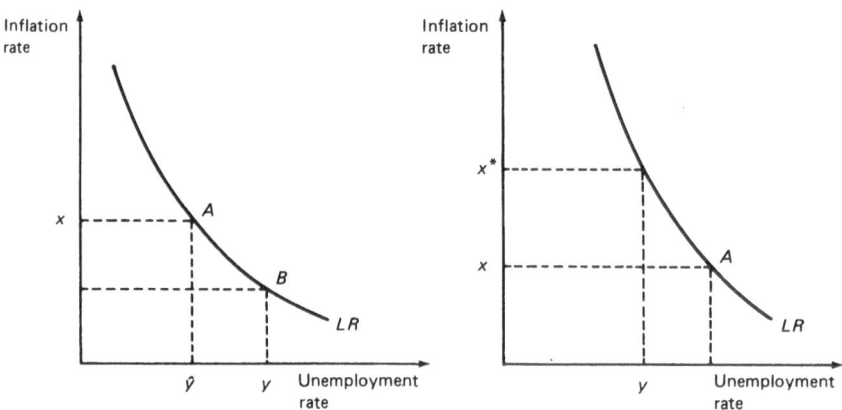

Fig. 9.4   Fig. 9.5

no acceptable point on the long-run curve, all points to the left of A being unacceptable because they imply a steady inflation rate in excess of x and all points to the right of A being unacceptable because they imply a steady unemployment rate in excess of y. This is the case of conflict of objectives. The proposition prescribes that in this situation the unemployment rate should be held steady at y and the inflation rate steady, in consequence, at x^*, which is above the maximum acceptable level.

The consensus of proposition 5 reflects a more basic consensus. As explained earlier, there is general agreement that a steady unemployment rate is to be preferred to a fluctuating unemployment rate. But it is known that if the unemployment rate is kept steady at, say, 3 per cent, the inflation rate will eventually steady at the figure corresponding to 3 per cent on the long-run inflation—unemployment curve (see Appendix 7.1). Thus general agreement on the desirability of a steady unemployment rate is tantamount to general agreement on the proposition that the aim of policy should be to keep the economy at *some* point on the long-run inflation—unemployment curve — that the second of the two forms of demand management discussed in Section 7.3 is to be preferred to the first. This is one element of the more basic consensus referred to above; there could be no consensus on proposition 5 without a consensus that *some* long-run position should be aimed for.

The second element is a value judgement held by most economists, as indeed by most people, that the unemployment objective is more important than the inflation objective — so much so that, in the no-conflict situation, the unemployment rate should be held steady at the lowest figure consistent with the achievement of the inflation objective (not the other way round) and that in the conflict situation the unemployment objective should be given absolute priority.

PROPOSITION 6

Should there be a conflict between the inflation objective and the unemployment objective, steps should be taken to shift the long-run inflation—unemployment curve in such a way that the steady inflation rate associated with the maximum acceptable unemployment rate is lower than before.

Again a diagram is helpful. The unbroken curve in Figure 9.6 is the original long-run inflation—unemployment curve. Given this curve, there is a conflict between objectives. In line with proposition 5 the point A should be chosen, that is the unemployment rate should be kept steady at y. At the same time, however, the inflationary consequences of this choice should be mitigated, if possible, by an appropriate shift of the long-run curve. For example, if the curve were shifted bodily to the left to position I, the steady inflation rate associated with y would be reduced from x^* to x^1. Alternatively, if the curve were shifted to position II by a change of curvature, the steady inflation rate associated with y would be reduced to x^2.

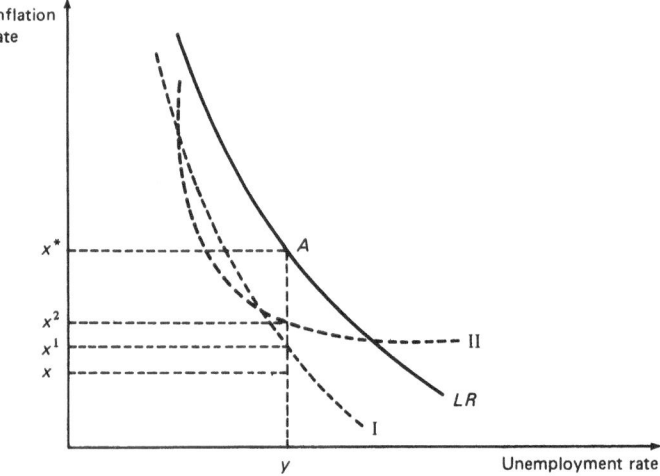

Fig. 9.6

PROPOSITION 7

The possible ways of shifting the long-run inflation–unemployment curve in the manner specified by proposition 6 may be grouped into some form of prices and incomes policy, on the one hand, and fundamental structural changes, such as are embraced by the term 'manpower policy', on the other hand. The former group are of doubtful effectiveness.

In earlier discussion, prices and incomes policy and manpower policy have been represented as possible ways of shifting the *price and wage equations* in a favourable way. In proposition 7 they are represented as possible ways of shifting the *long-run inflation–unemployment curve* in a favourable way. A full understanding of proposition 7 requires a reconciliation of these apparently conflicting approaches.

To facilitate this reconciliation we first remind the reader of the origins of the long-run inflation–unemployment curve. As will be clear from the discussion of Chapter 7, the long-run inflation–unemployment curve associated with any model of the inflationary process (for example the policy model of Section 7.1 or Vanderkamp's model, (7.26), (7.27) and (7.28)) is a curve based on the long-run inflation–unemployment relationship belonging to that model. This, in turn, is based on the price and wage equations of the model. Specifically, the long-run inflation–unemployment curve comes into being in the following way: (1) the steady-state version of the price equation is derived; (2) the steady-state version of the wage equation is derived; (3) the steady-state wage equation is substituted into steady-state price equation to get a relationship showing the dependence of $\bar{p}$ on $\bar{u}$ and certain other steady-state variables; and (4) this relationship is used to draw a curve of $\bar{p}$ against $\bar{u}$ based on specific values of the 'other' steady-state variables.

This brief recapitulation shows what must be done to produce a shift in the long-run inflation—unemployment curve of the type envisaged in proposition 6. In view of steps 1—4 of the previous paragraph, the *slope* of the long-run inflation—unemployment curve will be governed by the coefficient of $\bar{u}$ in the long-run inflation—unemployment relationship while the *position* of the curve will be determined by the intercept of that relationship, the coefficients of the 'other' steady-state variables and the values assumed by those variables (cf. relationship (7.10), p. 143). Hence a curve shift of the appropriate kind requires the right sort of change in the intercept of the long-run inflation—unemployment relationship and/or the right sort of change in the slope coefficients and/or the right sort of change in the steady-state levels of the 'other' variables. But the intercept and slope coefficients of the long-run inflation—unemployment relationship are just mixtures of the intercepts and slope coefficients of the price and wage equations (cf. relationship (7.10) again). In the end, therefore, a shift to the right in the long-run inflation—unemployment curve calls for the right sort of changes in the intercepts of the price and wage equations and/or in their slope coefficients and/or in the steady levels of certain of the independent variables in those equations.†

So it emerges that there is no inconsistency between representing prices and incomes policy and manpower policy as ways of shifting the price and wage equations in a favourable way and as ways of shifting the long-run inflation—unemployment curve in a favourable way. For the latter is not possible without the former.

Proposition 7 asserts that, of the two broad approaches to the problem of producing a favourable shift in the long-run curve which have been advocated in recent years — some form of prices and incomes policy or fundamental structural changes such as those included in the manpower-policy package — the former, at least, is not likely to be effective. The scepticism thus conveyed appears to be very widespread amongst professional economists and can be attributed partly to the fact that, whatever its form, prices and incomes policy constitutes an attempt to resist market forces, and partly to the rather damaging conclusions on the effectiveness of prices and incomes policy which have emerged from the numerous U.K. econometric studies of the last ten to fifteen years.

PROPOSITION 8

Should there be a conflict of objectives and should it become clear that no possible improvement of the long-run trade-off between inflation and

---

†The independent variables in question are the independent variables, other than the wage variable, in the price equation and the independent variables, other than the unemployment rate, in the wage equation.

unemployment will remove this conflict, institutional changes which will help the community to 'live with' the excessive inflation, implied by adherence to proposition 5, should be put in train.

The situation envisaged in this proposition is that illustrated in Figure 9.6 (p. 230). That is, on the basis of the original long-run inflation–unemployment curve, there is a conflict of objectives since the steady inflation rate which is associated with the maximum acceptable steady unemployment rate is x^*, and this exceeds x, the maximum acceptable inflation rate. Also the conflict remains when the long-run curve has been shifted in the most favourable way – say to position I or II. If proposition 5 is adhered to, the community will be faced, year-in, year-out, with an unacceptably high inflation rate – say a rate of x^1 or x^2 rather than x. In this event, according to the present proposition, institutional changes which would help to lessen the difficulties associated with the excessively high inflation rate should be put into effect.

The institutional change which has been most widely discussed, and supported, by economists as a means of offsetting the undesirable effects of an excessive inflation rate is that known variously as 'index-linking', 'indexation', 'value-linking', 'escalation'. Index-linking can be either complete or partial.

Complete index-linking involves the adjustment of all income payments and all debt, including money balances, according to changes in some agreed price index. One strong advocate of this comprehensive institutional change has described it in the following way:

> What is suggested ... is ... that, unless explicitly denied in contracts, all contractual payments should be escalated in relation to a price index agreed upon for the purpose. Thus all receivers of wages, salaries, rents, interest, pensions and other transfer payments ... will be protected from inflation. All that is required is a clause in contracts stating that all money payments explicitly stated relate to a given date, and should be adjusted according to a conversion factor derived from a price index agreed upon .... But it would not be sufficient to protect income payments only; all payments, including capital payments (both interest and principal) should be submitted to the same kind of escalation .... It is important to include money in this arrangement.[12]

Partial index-linking differs from complete index-linking, as just described, in that some income payments and/or some forms of debt are subject to adjustment but not others.

There would be near-universal agreement among economists that *some* degree of index-linking is called for in the circumstances envisaged in proposition 8. Hardly any would deny that the incomes of all pensioners, all recipients of social-security payments and all poorly paid wage- and salary-earners should be escalated in these circumstances. There would be a substantial body of opinion in favour of extending the arrangement to *all* wages and salaries, especially where a 'guidelines' type of prices and incomes policy is being employed to hold the long-run inflation—unemployment curve in its 'new' position (cf. Section 8.4). Extensions beyond this point would be increasingly controversial and complete index-linking would command comparatively little support.

Why is it that proposals for index-linking attract less and less support as they become increasingly comprehensive? Doubtless the answer lies partly in a deep-seated distrust of radical institutional change. However, the major part of the answer is probably to be found in the fear, which may or may not be well-founded, that the greater the degree of protection against the more obvious injustices of inflation, the weaker the pressure on the authorities to act against it, and hence the less the likelihood of their doing so.

The aim of index-linking is of course to eliminate, partly or wholly, the arbitrary redistribution of income and wealth which inflation brings about. Other institutional changes have been proposed for dealing with the hardships, as distinct from the injustices, to which inflation leads. An example of this type of change is the revision of the traditional system of housing finance recently proposed by Black.[13] The present system is that the borrower pays a fixed sum each year, the amount being just sufficient to pay the interest on the loan and to repay the principal over a period of, say, twenty years. The reason why this system imposes hardship under conditions of inflation is well explained by Black in the following passage:

> The consequence of inflation is that the present type of mortgage . . . actually implies a rapidly decreasing real payment each year. Taken by itself, such a decrease in real payments would appear to be beneficial to borrowers. A concomitant to inflation, however, has been a rise in interest rates, with the rate on mortgages now 11 per cent . . . . The effect of fixed-money payments and a high rate of interest is that the stream of payments by the borrower, though it is due to fall rapidly in real terms, has to start off so high that for many borrowers the problem of financing the payments in the early years has become very serious.[14]

The change in the present system which Black suggests to deal with this problem is a very simple one. Instead of the borrower's payments being constant over time, the proposal is that they should *rise* gradually over time. The following arithmetic example, which relates to a loan of £10,000 repayable over twenty years at an interest rate of 11 per cent, is given by Black to illustrate the proposal:

> Under the present fixed-payments system, the borrower must pay £1256 per annum . . . . The borrower's main problem is how to find the £1256 per annum at the start of the loan. Suppose, however, that payments were to rise in money terms by 3 per cent each year. Repayment in 20 years would require a payment at the end of the first year of £1031. Payments rise each year, but only in the eighth year do they exceed £1256 . . . . It looks a safe bet at present that we shall not see inflation controlled sufficiently to make incomes rise at less than 3 per cent a year. Thus, a system of payments rising at 3 per

cent means that a borrower can start off paying 18 per cent less than under the fixed-payments system in the first year and still find that his payments fall relative to his income over time. If we are prepared to bet on a higher rate of inflation, a faster growth of payments would be safe. If payments grow at 5 per cent, the first year payment needs to be only £894 .... Initial payments are 29 per cent lower than with the fixed-payments system. [15]

Under inflationary conditions the traditional system has the advantage from the borrower's point of view that it implies a continuous reduction in the burden of the annual payment over the term of the loan. As Black's arithmetical example shows, the new system retains this advantage to some extent while at the same time eliminating the hardship which the present system imposes on the borrower in the early years of the loan.

In the preceding pages we have listed, and expounded, a set of eight coherent propositions relating to anti-inflation policy to which, we believe, the great majority of economists would nowadays subscribe. These propositions represent, in our view, the current consensus on policy against inflation. It seems possible, without being misleadingly brief, to summarise these eight propositions in a single statement and it may be helpful to close the chapter by doing so as follows: *Assuming, as is likely, that there is no point on the long-run inflation–unemployment curve which is acceptable, the authorities should hold the unemployment rate steady at the maximum acceptable level and allow the inflation rate to settle at the figure corresponding to that steady unemployment rate. At the same time they should take whatever steps are open to them to shift the long-run curve in such a way that the steady inflation rate associated with the maximum acceptable unemployment rate is reduced. Should the community still be faced with a continuing inflation rate which is unacceptably high, the possibility of making institutional changes which will allow it to live more easily with this excessive inflation rate should be actively pursued.*

10

INFLATION IN DEVELOPING COUNTRIES

10.1 Relevance of Preceding Discussion to Developing Economies

Up to this point we have been concerned exclusively with inflation in *developed* economies (see above, p. 23). In Chapters 2–6 we examined various aspects of the question, 'What causes inflation in developed economies?' and emerged with a concise and fairly straightforward working answer – the three-equation expectational model of the inflationary process presented in Section 7.1. In Chapters 7–9 we put this model to work, its role being to provide a theoretical framework for discussing policy against inflation in developed economies.

It is possible, of course, that the answer that we have given to the question, 'What causes inflation in developed economies?', that is our three-equation expectational model, is valid for developing economies as well, and hence possible that the policy discussion of the last three chapters, which was based on this model, is as relevant to these economies as to the developed economies. Possible, but hardly likely. For the presumption must be that the inflationary process in advanced, urbanised, industrial economies, such as those of North America and Western Europe, is very different from the inflationary process in such primitive, basically agricultural and semi-traditional economies as those of, say, Thailand, Zambia, Nigeria and Paraguay. This being so, it is not to be expected that a simple three-equation model which (hopefully) captures the essence of the former should succeed in capturing the essence of the latter at the same time. In other words, it is too much to expect that an answer to the question, 'What causes inflation?', which works for developed economies, in the sense of providing a helpful framework for policy discussion in relation to such economies, should work for the developing economies as well.

The point of view expressed in the preceding paragraph is plausible and appears to have found ready acceptance in most parts of the developing world. Since the early 1950s it has become especially influential in the Latin American countries[1] where it has led to the development of a much discussed Latin American model of the inflationary process, known as the *structural* model. The framers of this model hold that the key feature of Latin American inflation is its inseparability from growth; and they would regard this as the essence which must be captured by a model of the inflationary process if it is to succeed (in the sense of predicting well) in the Latin American context. This view is clearly reflected in the structural model, as we shall see in the next section where the model is discussed in detail.

10.2   The Structural Model

All existing accounts of the structural model are in literary form.[2] In this section we shall give a symbolic statement of the model which, because of its compactness, may be easier to understand than the somewhat diffuse literary statements that have appeared. Another reason for attempting a symbolic statement is that it will facilitate the treatment of such points as the distinction between the data and the unknowns of the model, the structure which transmits changes in the data through to the price index used to measure inflation and the testable implications of the model. These are vital points which, nevertheless, tend to be given very sketchy, imprecise and incomplete treatment in the existing literary accounts.

We begin by explaining the notation to be used. The structural model is a three-sector model, the three sectors being agriculture, other domestic industry and foreign trade. Symbols relating to the agricultural sector will have the superscript 1 attached, those relating to the other-domestic-industry sector (to be referred to henceforth simply as the 'industrial sector') the superscript 2, and those relating to the foreign trade sector the superscript 3. The symbols to be used are as follows:

p^1 — percentage rate of increase of index of prices in agricultural sector

p^2 — percentage rate of increase of index of prices in industrial sector

p^3 — percentage rate of increase of index of prices of imports in domestic currency

S^1 — variable measuring structural element in agricultural sector

S^2 — variable measuring structural element in industrial sector

S^3 — variable measuring structural element in foreign-trade sector

w^1 — percentage rate of increase of index of wage-earnings per man in industrial sector

o^1 — percentage rate of increase of index of real output per man in industrial sector

p — percentage rate of increase of price index used to measure inflation (rate of inflation)

y — percentage rate of increase in real G.N.P.

u — unemployment rate

a — actual percentage rate of increase of output in agricultural sector

We shall now set out the relationships of the model one by one and briefly discuss each relationship as it is introduced.

The first relationship is:

$$p^2 = \beta_1(w^2 - o^2) + \beta_2 p^3, \tag{10.1}$$

where β_1 and β_2 are constants.† This relationship requires little comment since it is a simple variant of the 'mark-up' price equation (2.5), a relationship which was fully discussed in Chapter 2 (see Section 2.3). Specifically, (10.1) is a variant of (2.5) in which profit margins in the industrial sector are taken to be constant $(m = 0)$ and in which p^3, the rate of increase of the index of import prices, is used as a proxy for the rate of increase of the index of unit non-labour cost in the industrial sector.

The second simplification is the more controversial of the two. For p^3 to be an effective proxy for s, the following must apply: (i) the index of the prices of imported materials must move in line with the index of prices of imports as a whole, that is p^3 must be an effective proxy for the rate of increase of the index of the prices of imported materials; (ii) the usage of imported materials per unit of output in the industrial sector must remain roughly constant, that is the rate of increase of the index of the prices of imported materials must be an effective proxy for the rate of increase of the index of the unit cost of imported materials to the industrial sector (see above, p. 89); (iii) the quantity of output absorbed by the industrial sector from the agricultural sector as raw materials must be negligible, that is the rate of increase of the index of the unit cost of imported raw materials to the industrial sector must be an effective proxy for the rate of increase of the index of unit non-labour cost in the industrial sector.

There is of course nothing characteristically Latin American about relationship (10.1); it could easily fit into a developed-economy model of the sectoral variety. By contrast, the relationships to be introduced next all have marked developing-economy flavour and would be quite out of place in a developed-economy model. The relationships concerned explain, respectively, p^1, p^3 and w^2.

The relationships explaining p^1 are:

$$p^1 = f(S^1) \tag{10.2}$$

and

$$S^1 = \phi(y, a), \tag{10.3}$$

where f and ϕ denote 'function of' and where the function ϕ is such that S^1 is an increasing function of y for fixed a.

Briefly, the idea behind these relationships is that, in the Latin American economies, the agricultural sector finds it impossible to meet the demands for extra output which are imposed by population growth and rising real income, and

---

† Following the practice of Chapter 2 we shall omit period subscripts and attach a star superscript to any variable which belongs to a period prior to the current period, period t.

that, consequently, economic growth is bound to be accompanied by rising agricultural prices.

To develop this idea and to show its connection with (10.2) and (10.3) consider the following figures which are hypothetical, but not implausible in the Latin American context: (i) a constant rate of increase of population of 3 per cent per annum; (ii) a constant rate of increase of real G.N.P. *per capita* of 2 per cent per annum; (iii) each 1 per cent increase in real income *per capita* means an 0.6 per cent increase in the quantity of food demanded *per capita*, other things being equal, that is an income elasticity of demand for food of 0.6 on a *per capita* basis. Together (ii) and (iii) imply a constant rate of increase of 1.2 per cent per annum in the quantity of food demanded *per capita*. Since

Total quantity demanded = (Quantity *per capita* demanded) x (Population),

the rate of increase of the total quantity of food demanded will be constant at 4.2 per cent per annum.† Hence on these figures a constant rate of increase of the order of 4.2 per cent per annum in agricultural output will be required if the increased demand for agricultural output generated by rising population and rising real incomes is to be met. However, the structuralists argue that the agricultural sector is incapable of a growth rate of this order given the prevailing outmoded system of land tenure. As Mueller puts it:

Land ownership is ... predominantly characterized by *latifundio* and *multifundio*. This is a system of tenure usually inherited from the days of the Spanish Conquest in which most of the land is in large farms run by hired managers for the absentee owners who, the structuralists claim, value the land primarily for the social prestige its ownership confers and are content with the low yield it brings them. The remainder of the land is in extremely small farms which are cultivated by owner-managers who have neither the capital nor the education for efficiency.[3]

According to the framers of the structural model, then, economic growth in Latin America implies a positive gap between the rate of growth of output required in the agricultural sector, if the rising demand for agricultural output is to be met, and the rate of growth actually achieved. Hence it implies a chronic upward pressure on agricultural prices varying in intensity with the size of the gap.

It remains to link this discussion with relationships (10.2) and (10.3). The sole independent variable in (10.2) is S^1, a variable which measures an unspecified 'structural element' in the agricultural sector. This structural element can now be identified as the 'agricultural bottleneck' (chronic excess demand for agricultural output) described in the preceding paragraph. Thus S^1 is to be thought of as any variable which constitutes a suitable indicator of the size of the persistent gap

---

† This uses the rule that the percentage rate of increase of a product of two variables is approximately equal to the sum of the percentage rates of increase of the two variables forming the product when the latter are small.

between the rate of growth of agricultural output which is required if the rising demand for food is to be met and the actual rate of growth. Since the rate of increase of agricultural prices is an increasing function of the gap, and since S^1 is an indicator of the gap, the rate of increase of agricultural prices can be made an increasing function of S^1. This is the justification for (10.2).

As our arithmetical example shows, the required rate of growth of agricultural output will be higher, the higher are the rates of increase of population and real G.N.P. *per capita*. Hence for a given actual rate of growth, the output gap indicated by S^1 will be an increasing function of: (i) the rate of increase of population; and (ii) the rate of increase of real G.N.P. *per capita*. To economise on the number of variables in the model, (10.3) makes S^1 an increasing function not of (i) and (ii) separately but of their *sum*, that is the rate of increase of real G.N.P.† for a given value of the actual rate of growth of agricultural output.

We turn now to the relationships explaining p^3, the rate of increase of the index of import prices in domestic currency which, like (10.2) and (10.3), have features which make them particularly appropriate for a developing-economy model. The relationships in question are:

$$p^3 = g(S^3)$$ (10.4)

and

$$S^3 = \psi(y),$$ (10.5)

where g and ψ denote 'increasing function of'.

As we have seen, the idea embodied in (10.2) and (10.3) is that, in Latin American economies, there is a basic structural weakness in the *agricultural* sector because of which economic growth is almost certain to impose chronic upward pressure on *agricultural* prices. The idea underlying (10.4) and (10.5) is of the same general type. In framing these relationships, the structuralists have in mind a basic structural weakness in the *external* sector of Latin American economies because of which economic growth is most likely to produce rising *import* prices in terms of domestic currency.

More specifically, the structuralists maintain that growth in real G.N.P. as such will mean persistent balance-of-payments difficulties for the developing countries in general and for the Latin American countries in particular. The reason for this is that the developed countries have a much lower income elasticity of demand for imports than do the developing countries, so that with the same rate of growth of real G.N.P. in both, the developing countries will be faced with a larger rate of increase of import payments than of export earnings,‡ that is they will be faced

---

†Once again we use the rule that the rate of increase of a product is approximately equal to the sum of the rates of increase.

‡The same will be true, of course, if the growth rate is less in the developed countries than in the developing countries and also if it is greater so long as the higher growth rate does no more than offset the lower income elasticity.

with chronic balance-of-payments difficulties, and the faster the rate of growth of real G.N.P. in the developing countries the more acute will be their balance-of-payments difficulties.

Now the more acute their balance-of-payments difficulties, the greater the pressure on the developing countries to take remedial action. This could take the form of a reduction of the growth rate, but in view of the vital importance of growth to the developing countries, action along these lines is not to be expected. It is much more likely that the remedy will be sought in devaluation, tariff increases or the imposition of import quotas. Devaluation and tariff increases will cause import prices to rise in terms of domestic currency in an obvious way. Import quotas are likely to have the same result because importers will almost certainly use the monopoly position which the quotas give them to raise their profit margins.

To sum up, the structuralist argument is that the faster the rate of growth of real G.N.P. in the developing countries, the greater the pressure on their balance of payments, and the greater the pressure on their balance of payments, the greater the likelihood that they will take remedial action of a type that will stimulate the rate of increase of import prices in domestic currency − action such as devaluation, tariff increases or the imposition of import quotas.

To link this discussion with (10.4) and (10.5) we must attend to the variable S^3, which is the independent variable in (10.4) and the dependent variable in (10.5). This variable has been defined as one which measures some hitherto unspecified structural element in the foreign-trade sector. We can now define S^3 more specifically as an indicator of the degree of pressure on the balance of payments. With S^3 thus defined, (10.4) and (10.5) clearly provide a concise symbolic representation of the structuralist argument summed up in the previous paragraph.

The next relationship to be introduced is one which explains w^2, the percentage rate of increase of the index of average wage-earnings in the industrial sector. We can write this relationship as:

$$w^2 = h(u, p^*, p^{3*}, S^2),\qquad(10.6)$$

where h denotes 'function of' and the star superscript attached to p and p^3 denotes 'past'. A brief comment will suffice here since (10.6) is a straightforward extension of (2.6), the wage equation of the mark-up model which has been fully discussed in Chapter 2 (see above, p. 30).

Comparison of (10.6) and (2.6) shows that the extension consists of the addition of p^{3*} and S^2 to the two independent variables already present in (2.6) The addition of p^{3*} (past rate of increase in the index of import prices) requires no explanation since the underlying idea is quite straightforward, namely that in the open economy for which the structural model has been devised money wages will respond not only to past changes in the prices of home-produced goods but to past changes in the prices of imported goods as well. However, the addition of S^2 calls for some discussion.

In introducing S^2 the authors of the structural model are attempting to take care of what they believe to be yet another basic structural weakness in the Latin American economies. They argue that economic growth is bound to be accompanied by changes in the composition of demand. This is especially true of developing economies because in these growth is usually accompanied by rapid urbanisation and rapid industrialisation, both of which are likely to have profound effects on the composition of aggregate demand. Given a high degree of labour mobility, these growth-induced changes in the demand mix would involve no special problem. In the Latin American economies, however, this high degree of labour mobility does not exist for various reasons, including lack of education and training and strong social barriers against entry into certain occupations. Consequently, labour shortages develop in the expanding sectors of the economy and labour surpluses in the contracting sectors. The labour shortages cause money wages to rise in the expanding sectors. However, the trade unions are sufficiently strong to prevent money wages falling in the contracting sectors. Thus a *change in the composition of* aggregate demand will lead to an increase in the over-all index of average money wage-earnings, even if there is no increase in the *level* of aggregate demand (no change in u).

The structuralist argument just outlined implies that, at given levels of u, p^* and p^{3*}, w^2 will be an increasing function of the degree of demand instability. This implies, in turn, that the independent variables of the function explaining w^2 should include, in addition to u, p^* and p, an indicator of the degree of demand instability. The variable S^2, defined previously as a variable measuring an unspecified structural element in the industrial sector, can now be defined more specifically as just such an indicator.

The inclusion of S^2 as an independent variable in the wage relationship for the industrial sector takes care, then, of one implication of the structuralist argument. The argument also implies, however, that S^2 is an increasing function of the rate of growth. Hence to do full justice to the argument we need the relationship:

$$S^2 = \theta(y), \tag{10.7}$$

where θ denotes 'increasing function of'.

To round off the model we have the relationship:

$$p = \alpha_1 p^1 + \alpha_2 p^2, \tag{10.8}$$

where α_1 and α_2 are two constants which sum to unity. According to this relationship, the percentage rate of increase in the price index used to measure inflation (the inflation rate) is a weighted arithmetic average of: (i) the percentage rate of increase of the index of prices in the agricultural sector; and (ii) the percentage rate of increase of the index of prices in the industrial sector. This relationship holds provided: (*a*) the *level* of the index used to measure inflation is a weighted arithmetic average of the level of the index of prices in the agricultural sector and the level of the index of prices in the industrial sector; and (b) the indexes are shifting-base indexes with the previous period as base of unity.†

Having presented the relationships of the model, we now categorise the variables into unknowns and data. The variables are: p (current and past), p^1, p^2, p^3 (current and past), S^1, S^2, S^3, w^2, o^2, a, y and u. The variables o^2, a, y and u are treated as data (as imposed on the model) leaving the eight variables, p

† Denote the level of the three indexes involved in (10.7) by P, P^1 and P^2, respectively. In accordance with proviso (a) of the text let P_t be related to P_t^1 and P_t^2 by:

$$P_t = \alpha_1 P_t^1 + \alpha_2 P_t^2 = \sum_{i=1}^{2} \alpha_i P_t^i,$$

where α_1 and α_2 are constants which sum to unity. From this expression it follows that:

$$\frac{P_t}{P_{t-1}} - 1 = \frac{\displaystyle\sum_{i=1}^{2} \alpha_i P_t^i}{\displaystyle\sum_{i=1}^{2} \alpha_i P_{t-1}^i} - 1.$$

Therefore

$$p_t = 100 \left[\frac{\displaystyle\sum_{i=1}^{2} \alpha_i P_t^i}{\displaystyle\sum_{i=1}^{2} \alpha_i P_{t-1}^i} - 1 \right].$$

Now:

$$P_t^i = \left(1 + \frac{p_t^i}{100}\right) P_{t-1}^i.$$

Substituting in the expression for p_t we obtain:

$$p_t = 100 \left[\frac{\displaystyle\sum_{i=1}^{2} \alpha_i \left(\left(1 + \frac{p_t^i}{100}\right) P_{t-1}^i\right)}{\displaystyle\sum_{i=1}^{2} \alpha_i P_{t-1}^i} - 1 \right].$$

Therefore

$$\frac{p_t}{100} = \frac{\displaystyle\sum_{i=1}^{2} \alpha_i P_{t-1}^i}{\displaystyle\sum_{i=1}^{2} \alpha_i P_{t-1}^i} + \frac{\displaystyle\sum_{i=1}^{2} \alpha_i \frac{p_t^i}{100} P_{t-1}^i}{\displaystyle\sum_{i=1}^{2} \alpha_i P_{t-1}^i} - 1$$

(current and past), p^1, p^2, p^3 (current and past), S^1, S^2, S^3 and w^2 to be treated as unknowns (as determined by the model). Since there are eight relationships, the relationships are sufficient in number to determine the unknowns once values have been allotted to the data, that is the model is complete.

Our final task in this section is to present the explanation of inflation in Latin American economies which the structuralists advance on the basis of the above eight-equation model. To facilitate the discussion we first present the model as a whole.

$$p^2 = \beta_1(w^2 - o^2) + \beta_2 p^3 \tag{10.1}$$

$$p^1 = f(S^1) \tag{10.2}$$

$$S^1 = \phi(y, a) \tag{10.3}$$

$$p^3 = g(S^3) \tag{10.4}$$

$$S^3 = \psi(y) \tag{10.5}$$

$$w^2 = h(u, p^*, p^{3*}, S^2) \tag{10.6}$$

$$S^2 = \theta(y) \tag{10.7}$$

$$p = \alpha_1 p^1 + \alpha_2 p^2 \tag{10.8}$$

Unknowns: p (current and past), p^1, p^2, p^3 (current and past), S^1, S^2, S^3, w^2. Data: u, o^2, y, a.

Therefore

$$\frac{p_t}{100} = \frac{\sum\limits_{i=1}^{2} \alpha_i \frac{p_t^i}{100} P_{t-1}^i}{\sum\limits_{i=1}^{2} \alpha_i P_{t-1}^i}.$$

Now put $P_{t-1}^i = 1$ in accordance with proviso (b) of the text. Then, using $\sum\limits_{i=1}^{2} \alpha_i = 1$ we obtain:

$$\frac{p_t}{100} = \sum\limits_{i=1}^{2} \alpha_i \frac{p_t^i}{100}.$$

Therefore

$$p_t = \sum\limits_{i=1}^{2} \alpha_i p_t^i,$$

which is (10.7).

As will be clear from Chapter 2, 'explaining inflation' on the basis of this system of relationships means specifying a particular set of time paths for the four data, and then showing that, with these data time paths, the model will generate continuously positive values for p, that is continuously rising values for the index chosen to measure inflation. A set of data time paths which 'works', and which the structuralists would regard as relevant in the Latin American context, may be formulated as follows. Initially o^2 is constant at zero, a at $\bar{a}$, y at $\bar{y}$ and u at $\bar{u}$. The values of $\bar{a}, \bar{y}$ and $\bar{u}$ are not freely determined but are restricted in such a way that $p = 0$ initially, that is in such a way that there is no inflation in the initial situation.† At a certain point in time, y rises to some higher value and remains at this higher value thereafter, that is there is a 'step' increase in y. The rest of the data remain throughout at their original levels.

The general character of the time path which the model generates for p, in response to this set of time paths for the data , will now be deduced. Initially p is zero, as we have seen already. However, it rises to some positive value in response to the postulated increase in y. This can be seen as follows. The postulated increase in y means an increase in S^1, S^2 and S^3 because (10.3) gives S^1 as an increasing function of y, for fixed a while (10.7) and (10.5) give S^2 and S^3 as increasing functions of y. The increase in S^1 means an increase in p^1 since (10.2) gives p^1 as an increasing function of S^1, that is p^1 now becomes positive.‡ The increase in S^2 with p^* and $p^{3}*$ still fixed at zero and u fixed at $\bar{u}$, means an increase in w^2, and hence, with o^2 fixed at zero, an increase in $w^2 - o^2$, that is $w^2 - o^2$ now becomes positive. Furthermore, the increase in S^3 means an increase in p^3, that is p^3 now becomes positive. But with both $w^2 - o^2$ and p^3 positive, p^2 must be positive (from (10.1)). In short, the immediate effect of the postulated increase in y is to raise both p^1 and p^2 from zero to some positive figure; and this means (from (10.8)) that p must increase from zero to some positive figure.

Once p becomes positive, in response to the step increase in y, it remains positive. To show this, it is necessary (in view of (10.8)) to show that, having once become positive, both p^1 and p^2 remain positive. Take p^1 first. Since y remains fixed at the new, higher level, S^1 remains fixed at the new, higher level. Hence p^1 remains fixed at the new, higher level, that is p^1 remains positive. Turn now to p^2. To show that p^2 remains positive, it is necessary to show that p^3 and $w^2 - o^2$ remain positive. The first is simple; since y and hence S^3 remain fixed at the new,

---

†For p to be zero in the initial situation, both p^1 and p^2 must be zero (from (10.8)). For p^2 to be zero, we require $w^2 = o^2 = 0$ and $p^3 = 0$ (from (10.1)). The latter requires that $\bar{y}$ be such that $g[\psi(\bar{y})] = 0$ (from (10.4) and (10.5)) while the former requires that $\bar{u}$ be such that, with p^* and $p^{3}*$ equal to zero, and S^2 equal to the value given by inserting the required $\bar{y}$ in (10.7), the right-hand side of (10.6) is equal to zero. For p^1 to be zero, the required $\bar{a}$ must be such that when inserted in the right-hand side of (10.3), together with the required $\bar{y}$, a value of S^1 emerges which makes the right-hand side of (10.2) equal to zero.

‡Recall that p^1 was zero initially: see previous footnote.

higher level, p^3 remains fixed, that is p^3 remains positive. To show that $w^2 - o^2$ remains positive, it is enough to show that w^2 remains positive since by assumption o^2 is fixed throughout at zero. This can be done in the following way. We have shown already that in the quarter in which the step increase in y occurs, w^2, p and p^3 will increase from the constant zero figure characterising the initial situation to some positive figure. Since both u and S^2 remain fixed (the former at $\bar{u}$ and the latter at the higher level corresponding to the new, higher level of y) we know from (10.6) that the increase in p and p^3 will lead, after a delay, to a further increase in w^2, that is w^2 continues to be positive.

The general character of the time path which the model generates for p, when set in motion by the postulated set of time paths for the data, is therefore clear; p is zero initially, it then rises to some positive figure, and it remains positive thereafter, that is the price index used to measure inflation moves continuously upward.

To sum up, it has been shown that the structuralist model generates a continuous rise in the price index (inflation) following a jump in the growth rate, with the other data held fixed. The demonstration of this result constitutes a formal structuralist answer to the question, 'How is inflation caused in Latin American economies?' A vague, yet illuminating, translation of this precise formal answer would be that inflation arises in Latin American economies essentially because economic growth meets certain strong resistances. These take the form of an agricultural bottleneck, a chronic weakness in the balance of payments and other such basic structural weaknesses.

10.3 The Structuralist–Monetarist Controversy

We shall now move on from our discussion of the structural model to consider the dispute between the proponents of that model (the 'structuralists') and a rival group who have been dubbed the 'monetarists' — a dispute which has dominated discussion of the Latin American inflation problem since the early 1950s. As we shall show later on, the structuralist–monetarist controversy reflects, at bottom, a deep difference of social and political attitudes. However, it emerges as a dispute about the appropriate way of dealing with inflation in the Latin American context — as a policy dispute. The most natural way to begin the discussion, therefore, is to outline the anti-inflation policy which the structuralists advocate for the Latin American economies and then to contrast this with the policy recommended by their rivals, the monetarists.

The structuralists' view on anti-inflation policy derives directly from their view about the cause of inflation in Latin American economies, that is from the structural model. According to this model, there are two ways of moderating the inflation rate in Latin American economies (cf. Section 7.1). The first is to manipulate the variables u, o^2, y and a — the variables which constitute the data of the model — in an appropriate way. For u, o^2 and a, the appropriate manipulation would be an increase, while for y the appropriate manipulation would be a decrease.† The other possibility is to modify the relationships of the model in such a way as to lessen the upward pressure being exerted on the price index by the data as they stand. The structuralists' proposals for checking inflation represent a combination of both of these approaches. We shall now explain this remark.

It will be recalled that the structuralist analysis of the inflationary process in Latin American economies lays great stress on the intimate connection between inflation and economic growth. Inflation occurs, so the structuralist argues, essentially because the forces of growth encounter certain strong resistances. This being so, the obvious ways of checking inflation are: (i) by reducing the growth rate; and/or (ii) by weakening the resistances to growth. The former they rule out as being politically unacceptable in the Latin American context, and, in any case, undesirable in view of the urgent need to eliminate poverty, illiteracy and other forms of economic and social distress in this part of the developing world. The latter suffers from no such disadvantages and accordingly is the approach which is recommended. The resistances on which the greatest stress is laid are three in number: (*a*) a chronic agricultural bottleneck which, given growth, leads to a persistent upward pressure on agricultural prices; (*b*) a chronic weakness in the balance of payments leading, in the face of growth, to a persistent upward pressure on import prices; (*c*) an exceedingly low degree of labour mobility leading, with growth, to a persistent upward pressure on money wages and hence on industrial prices. Structuralist anti-inflation policy consists, basically, of proposals for weakening these three resistances, for example proposals for land reform as a means of widening the agricultural bottleneck, proposals for export diversification and import substitution as a means of widening the import-capacity bottleneck and proposals for removing illiteracy and improving education as a means of weakening the tendency for low labour mobility to act as a ratchet on money wages. Now weakening resistance (*a*) can be interpreted as increasing one of the data of the structural model, namely a, the rate of growth of agricultural output. Weakening resistance (*b*) can be interpreted as producing a favourable shift in (10.5), so that the degree of strain on the balance of payments associated with any given rate of growth of real G.N.P. is less than before. Finally, weakening resistance (*c*) can be interpreted as producing a favourable shift in (10.6) so that the upward pressure on money wage rates associated with any given degree of change in the demand mix (ultimately, in view of (10.7), with any given rate of growth in real G.N.P.) will be less than before. We see, then, that the structuralist anti-inflation · programme represents a mixture of proposals for manipulating data in a favourable way and proposals for shifting relationships in a

---

†This is clear from the model. Take u as an example. With u higher, w^2 is less than it would have been (from (10.6)), so that p^2 is less than it would have been (from (10.1)) so that p is less than it would have been (from (10.8)).

favourable way, which explains the remark made at the close of the last paragraph.

We turn now to the anti-inflation policy proposals of the rival group, the so-called monetarists. As their label suggests, this group argues that, in the case of the Latin American economies, the most effective way of checking the rate of inflation is to check the rate of growth of the money supply. Further, they argue that, in the Latin American case, the dominant source of growth in the money supply is central-bank borrowing by the central government and that the most effective way of reducing the rate of growth of the money supply is to block off this source of growth. On paper, this can be done either by eliminating the central-government deficits which the borrowing is being used to finance or by substituting private-sector borrowing for central-bank borrowing. In practice, however, given the primitive state of the Latin American capital markets, the former is the only real alternative. Elimination of the chronic budgetary deficits which characterise the Latin American economies thus emerges as the main cure for inflation from the monetarist point of view.

The monetarist anti-inflation policy gets no support from the structural model as it stands. It can be supported, however, by an extended structural model consisting of (10.1)–(10.8) with the addition of five relationships. The additional relationships are:

$$D = D_1 + D_2 \tag{10.9}$$

$$D_1 = s(p) \tag{10.10}$$

$$m = m_1 + m_2 \tag{10.11}$$

$$m_1 = t(D^*) \tag{10.12}$$

$$u = v(m^*, l) \tag{10.13}$$

where s, t and v denote 'function of', D denotes the budget deficit, D_1 the induced, and D_2 the autonomous, parts of the budget deficit, m the rate of increase of the money supply, m_1 the induced, and m_2 the autonomous, parts of m and where l is the rate of increase of the labour force. D_1 and m_1 are to be thought of as increasing functions of p and D^*, respectively, while v is to be thought of as a decreasing function of m^*, given l, and an increasing function of l, given m^*.

Relationships (10.9)–(10.13) introduce seven new variables, namely D (present and past), D_1, D_2, m (present and past), m_1, m_2 and l. Of these, D_2, m_2 and l are treated as data. We have therefore added five new relationships and only four additional unknowns. Thus, taking the model as a whole, we now have twelve unknowns (the eight in the eight equations of the 'basic' model *plus* the four new ones) and thirteen relationships, that is we have one more relationship than we need to determine the unknowns. This allows us to count one of the variables treated as a datum in the basic model as an unknown, and the variable we choose for transfer to the unknown category is u, the unemployment rate.

Relationships (10.9) and (10.11) are definitional — each defines a certain total as the sum of its parts — and hence require no comment. The other three relationships need some explanation, however.

Relationships (10.9) and (10.10) incorporate yet another much-discussed Latin American 'structural weakness'. In developed countries the major part of tax revenue is derived from a progressive income tax. Consequently, in developed countries, tax revenue typically rises more rapidly than the general price level under inflationary conditions. But current government expenditure rises at roughly the same pace as the general price level. In developed countries, therefore, inflation characteristically produces budget surpluses; and the greater the inflation rate the larger will the surpluses tend to be. In the developing countries — in particular in the Latin American countries — the position is the reverse of the one just described. In these countries the bulk of tax revenue comes from regressive indirect taxes rather than from progressive income taxes. Perhaps the main reason for this reliance on indirect taxes is the relative weakness of the public-administrative machine in the Latin American and other developing countries coupled with the relative ease of administering indirect taxes. But whatever the reason, the result is that under inflationary conditions government revenue tends to rise less rapidly than prices. Therefore, given the tendency for current government expenditure to keep pace with prices, inflation tends to produce budget deficits in the Latin American countries; and the faster the inflation, the larger the deficits are likely to be.

This line of reasoning implies that, to some extent at least, chronic government deficits are 'unavoidable' in the Latin American countries, in the sense of being a direct consequence of inflation. Relationships (10.9) and (10.10) attempt to embody this proposition by dividing the total deficit into two parts — an 'unavoidable' or inflation-induced part and an 'avoidable' or autonomous part — and then by making the unavoidable part an increasing function of the inflation rate.

Turning now to relationships (10.11) and (10.12), we note that the rate of increase of the money stock will depend, in part, on the extent to which central-bank credit is used to finance the government deficit. This will depend in turn very largely on the size of the deficit since reliance on this form of deficit finance is necessarily heavy in Latin American countries (see above, p. 247). Relationships (10.11) and (10.12) attempt to capture this point by dividing the total rate of increase into two parts, one of which varies directly with the size of the deficit, subject to a lag, and the other which is treated as a datum.

The starting-point of (10.13), the last of the new relationships, is the observation that the unemployment rate will be a decreasing function of the rate of increase of aggregate demand, given the rate of increase of the labour force, and an increasing function of the rate of increase of the labour force, given the rate of increase of aggregate demand. Arguing along Friedmanite lines,[4] the rate of increase of aggregate demand is then made to depend directly on the past rate of increase of the money stock. In this way we emerge with u as a decreasing function of m^*, *ceteris paribus*, and as an increasing function of l, *ceteris paribus*, which is what (10.13) says.

It was stated earlier that the extended structural model, (10.1)–(10.13), provides theoretical support for the monetarist policy recommendation – a reduction in the rate of increase of the money stock *via* a reduction in the size of the budget deficit. To see that this is indeed the case, let us suppose that there is a reduction in the datum, D_2, that is to say, that the authorities decrease that part of the deficit which is under their control, and let us trace through the effect of this manipulation on the assumption that all other data remain fixed.

We know from our analysis of the basic structural model that p, the inflation rate, is determined once the data of that model are fixed, that is once u, o^2, y and a are fixed. Now the last three are data of the extended model, and hence, by assumption, remain fixed in the face of the postulated decrease in D_2. Also, u remains fixed because, by (10.13), u is determined by m^* and l, and these remain fixed when D_2 is reduced, m^* because it belongs to the past and l because it is a datum and so is fixed by assumption. It follows then, that the postulated reduction in D_2 will have no immediate effect on the inflation rate. Hence it will have no immediate effect on D_1 which is determined by p from (10.10). From this conclusion it follows, in turn, that D will fall in response to the reduction in D_2 (from (10.9)). This fall in D will lead, after a delay, to a fall in m_1 (*via* (10.12)) and hence (*via* (10.11)) to a fall in m. After a further delay, this fall in m will lead to a fall in u *via* (10.13). But, taken together, relationships (10.1)–(10.8) (the basic structural model) imply that, with o^2, y and a fixed, a fall in u will lead to a fall in p (see footnote, p. 246 also). The final conclusion, then, is that a reduction in D_2 will lead to a fall in the inflation rate, p. This, however, is not the end of the story. For the fall in p will mean a fall in D_1 (from (10.10)), and hence, *via* (10.9), a further fall in D, D_2 now being held fixed at its new lower level. Using the same argument as before, we can show that the further fall in D will lead to a further fall in p. This further fall in p will cause D_1, and hence D, to fall still further which, in turn, will cause p to fall still further; and so on.

It is clear, therefore, that given the extended structural model, a reduction in the rate of growth of the money supply *via* a reduction in the budget deficit will lead to a fall in the inflation rate. Thus the model provides theoretical support for the monetarist anti-inflation policy.

It is important to note that the extended structural model provides support for the structuralist policy also. The structuralist manipulations will have no effect on u initially since, according to (10.13), u is determined by m^* and l, neither of which will be affected, the first because it belongs to the past and the second because it is a datum. Also, o^2, y and a are part of the data of the extended model as of the basic model, and so can be regarded as fixed in the face of the structuralist manipulations. Initially, then, u, o^2, y and a can all be regarded as fixed. But we know that, with these four variables fixed, p is determined by the basic structural model (10.1)–(10.8). In other words, the presence of (10.9)–(10.13) notwithstanding, we can still use (10.1)–(10.8) to deduce the initial affect of the structuralist manipulations. We conclude, therefore, that, initially, the structuralist manipulations will produce a fall in p (see also, p. 244). Once again, however, this is not the end of the story. For the reduction in p will mean a reduction in D_1, which, in turn, will mean a (delayed) reduction in m, which, in turn, will mean a (delayed) reduction in u, which, in turn, will mean a further reduction in p via (10.1)–(10.8) (see p. 244 above), and so on. Clearly, therefore, the extended structural model implies that the structuralist manipulations will reduce the inflation rate and so provides a theoretical justification for the structuralists' policy proposals as well as for those of the monetarists.

As pointed out at the beginning of this section, and as emphasised by the whole of the preceding discussion, the structuralist–monetarist dispute emerges as a dispute about the anti-inflation policy that should be followed in the Latin American countries. However, a dispute about policy is invariably the reflection of some more fundamental dispute, even if the parties to the dispute are not fully aware that this is so. What is the more fundamental dispute in the present case? To conclude the section we shall present a possible answer to this question.

A dispute about policy can arise in one of two ways. One possibility is that the two parties to the dispute are working with different models (different explanations) and that the policy advocated by group A is valid in terms of their model but not the policy advocated by group B; and vice versa. The other possibility is that the two parties are working with the same model, that both policies are valid in terms of this model but that group A prefers its policy to that of group B, for example because they believe it to be more feasible politically. Which of these two possibilities apply in the present case?

One cannot give a definite answer to this question since neither the structuralists nor the monetarists have made their theoretical position abundantly clear. However, it seems more than likely that both groups would accept the extended structural model as their theoretical framework. The structuralists would find this model acceptable, one would imagine, because the basic structural relationships, (10.1)–(10.8), are incorporated without modification and because an important feature of the extension is a relationship which reflects structuralist thinking and on which the structuralists themselves lay considerable stress (see above, p. 246). We refer to (10.10), the relationship determining D_1. One cannot be quite so confident about the monetarist attitude because the monetarists are especially inarticulate at the theoretical level. However, they are certainly not disposed to deny the existence of the structural weaknesses which form the focal point of structuralist thinking and would probably regard the basic structural model, (10.1)–(10.8), as correct in so far as it goes. If so, one would expect the extended model to be generally acceptable to the monetarists since it would be surprising if they took issue with the extension contained in (10.9)–(10.13).

Assuming that these judgements are correct, it must be the second of the two possibilities mentioned in the preceding paragraph which applies in the case of the structuralist–monetarist controversy. That is, the situation must be that both groups subscribe to the same model and that both draw support for their anti-inflation policy proposals from this one model, using the arguments presented earlier.

Our conclusion, then, is that the fundamental dispute between the structuralists and the monetarists is not a theoretical dispute, as is often the case when two groups advocate different policies for dealing with some particular economic problem. If the dispute, at bottom, is not about theory, what is it about? Perhaps the best way in which to answer this question is to first answer another: 'Why do the monetarists prefer their policy to that of the structuralists?' A possible answer, of course, is that each group prefers its policy because it believes that, while its policy will work, its opponents' policy will not work. However, we have excluded this answer already by assuming that both groups accept the extended structural model and recognise that both policies are valid in terms of that model by virtue of the arguments presented earlier. Thus, in answering the above question, we shall take it for granted that each group agrees that the policy advocated by the other is technically correct in the sense that it will achieve the desired effect of moderating the rate of inflation.

This being understood, let us now consider the case presented by each group against the proposals of the other, beginning with the monetarists' case against the structuralists' proposals. This seems to be that while the structuralists' policy proposals (measures designed to weaken the various resistances met by growth) will have the intended effect of moderating the rate of inflation, this effect will take a long while to emerge and will be comparatively weak when it does emerge. The latter part of this claim may or may not be correct; the matter is an empirical one and can be settled only by extensive empirical investigation. On the other hand, the monetarists claim that the structuralists' proposals will be slow to work can hardly be denied since they comprise radical changes in the institutional structure, such as the complete reform of the system of land tenure; and the time span for fully implementing these changes would have to be reckoned, not in months, but in years.

Turn now to the structuralists' case against the monetarists' proposals. The structuralists appear ready to admit that the monetarists' proposals (reduction in the rate of increase of the money supply *via* a reduction in the size of the deficit) will have a rapid and substantial effect on the rate of inflation provided that they are carried far enough. They argue, however, that 'far enough' would mean 'to the point where an unacceptably high unemployment rate results'. The essence of the structuralists' objection to the monetarists' proposals, therefore, is that they would impose social costs far in excess of those imposed by the inflation, with which they are intended to deal. This claim, like the monetarists', relates to an empirical matter and can be assessed only in the light of an appropriate empirical investigation. What can be said quite definitely, however, is that, given the extended structural model, *some* increase in the unemployment rate is a necessary consequence of the monetarist remedy. For the only route along which a reduction in the deficit works, according to this model, is *via* a reduction in the money supply, then *via* a reduction in the unemployment rate and finally *via* a reduction in the rate of increase of industrial prices.

Having considered the case mounted by each group against the anti-inflation policy proposals of the other, we can now return to the question, 'What is the exact character of the fundamental dispute between the structuralists and the monetarists?'

From the above discussion it would appear that the two groups have a quite fundamental difference of opinion about the importance of the inflation problem in Latin American countries. To the monetarist, inflation is the key problem. The most urgent task facing the Latin American countries, he believes, is to put an end to the massive inflation rates that have been common in recent years.†[5] Hence this preference for anti-inflation policies that are likely to act quickly, even if painfully. To the structuralist, on the other hand, the inflation problem is secondary. As he sees it, the most urgent task is that of economic, political and social modernisation. Accordingly, he prefers anti-inflation policies that help to accelerate the modernisation process, even if their impact on the inflation rate is likely to be slight, at least in the short run.

This difference of opinion about the importance of the inflation problem probably reflects a more fundamental difference of opinion about the social costs of inflation. In the words of Davis:

> the adverse consequences of inflation are apparent to both Monetarist and Structuralist .... Quantitatively, however, the Monetarist is inclined to assess the real costs as somewhat higher than the Structuralist and to attribute these 'distortions' to inflation *per se* and not, like the majority of Structuralists, solely to the effects of poorly designed and administered controls.[6]

It may even be the case that the difference between the two groups goes much deeper still, as Seers maintains in the following passage:

> This is not just a technical issue in economic theory. At the heart of the controversy between 'monetarists' and 'structuralists' are two different ways of looking at economic development, in fact two completely different attitudes toward the nature of social change, two different sets of value judgements about the purposes of economic activity and the ends of economic policy, and two incompatible views on what is politically possible.[7]

10.4   Tests of the Structural Model

In Section 2.1, we gave a detailed account of the way in which the economist assesses a model. Very briefly, his procedure is to derive the testable predictions

---

†For example, the average annual rate of inflation in the period 1958−67 was 32.6 per cent for Argentina, 47.0 per cent for Uruguay, 24.4 per cent for Chile and 49.7 per cent for Brazil.

of the model and then to test the model by confronting these predictions with the relevant facts. A model is deemed to be useful if, and so long as, it predicts well (tests well), and one model is deemed to be more useful than another if, and so long as, it is a better predictor (has a better test record). Two attempts to assess the structural model from this particular standpoint have been made in recent years, one by Mueller and the other by Argy,[8] and we shall consider these studies in the present section.

We shall begin with Mueller's study. Mueller's test relates to what we have termed the basic structural model, that is (10.1)–(10.8). To explain the nature of her test let us return to that model and begin by noting that the model implies the following expression for the unknown, p: †

$$p = \alpha_1 f(S^1) + \alpha_2 [\beta_1\{ h(u, p^*, p^{3*}, S^2) - o^2\} + \beta_2 g(S^3)] . \qquad (10.14)$$

Suppose now that, on examining the observations on p for some country for a stretch of, say, thirty consecutive years, we find that in, say, the first ten years p was consistently higher than in the subsequent twenty years. Suppose, too, that there was no change in the constants α_1, α_2, β_1 and β_2 between the two periods, no change in unit labour cost in the industrial sector‡ and no shift in either of the functions f and g. Relationship (10.14) implies that, under these circumstances, one or both of S^1 and S^3 will have been consistently higher in the first period.¶ And since this relationship is implied by the model, we can say, instead, that the *model* implies consistently higher levels for at least one of S^1 and S^3 in the first period. In short, the basic structural model predicts that the postulated pattern in the p observations will have been accompanied by consistently higher levels in the first period for either or both of S^1 and S^3.‖

Accordingly, to test the model, Mueller selected a Latin American country with the postulated pattern in the p observations. The country chosen was Mexico, where the inflation rate was consistently higher throughout the 1940s that it was throughout the 1950s. She then examined several different indicators of the unobservable variable S^1, and likewise for S^3, and attempted to determine whether or not these variables were consistently higher in the 1940s than in the 1950s. Her conclusion was that S^1 was consistently higher in the first period but that S^3 was consistently higher ih the second period.[9] Thus the prediction of the

---

† This expression is found by starting with (10.8), substituting for p^1 and p^2 in this expression, then substituting for S^1, w^2 and p^3 in the resulting expression, using (10.2), (10.6) and (10.4) respectively, and so on.

‡ Unit labour cost in the industrial sector is given by:

$$w^2 - o^2 = \{h(u, p^*, p^{3*}, S^2) - o^2\}.$$

¶ This makes use of the restriction that f and g are increasing functions of S^1 and S^3, respectively.

‖ Muller derives a slightly different prediction, namely that *both* S^1 and S^3 will have been higher (p. 153 of her study). This appears to be incorrect in the light of our argument.

model, that at least one of S^1 and S^3 will have been consistently higher in the first period, is not refuted by the data; the model survives this particular test.[†]

We turn now to Argy's test, which can be regarded as a test of the extended structural model. We begin by explaining the basis of the test.

As we have seen already, the basic structural model implies that p is given by relationship (10.14). Now if the functions f, h and g are taken to be linear, (10.14) gives p as a linear function of S^1, S^2, S^3, u, $p*$, $p^3 *$ and o^2 in which the coefficients of S^1, S^2 and S^3 are all positive.[‡] Hence, given the linearity approximation, we can say that the basic structural model implies the existence of a relationship of the form: [¶]

$$p = \tau_0 + \tau_1 S^1 + \tau_2 S^2 + \tau_3 S^3 + \tau_4 u + \tau_5 p* + \tau_6 p^3 * + \tau_7 o^2, \quad (10.15)$$

where the τs are constants and τ_1, τ_2 and τ_3 are positive. This is a testable prediction of the basic model.

By means of a similar argument it can be shown that a testable prediction of the extended structural model is that there exists a relationship of the form:

$$p = \tau_0 + \tau_1 S^1 + \tau_2 S^2 + \tau_3 S^3 + \tau_4 p* + \tau_5 p^3 * + \tau_6 m* + \tau_7 l, \quad (10.16)$$

where the τs are constants and τ_1, τ_2, τ_3 and τ_6 are positive.

Accordingly, to test the extended structural model, Argy estimated a large number of linear relationships with p as dependent variable and various combinations of S^1, S^2, S^3 and m among the independent variables[||] and in each case checked whether the coefficient of the S variables and the m variable are positive and significantly different from zero[††] as predicted by the extended structural model.[†††] In general he found that while the monetary variable

---

[†]Note that the prediction in question follows only if the α and β constants remain fixed, if there is no change in unit labour cost in the industrial sector and no shift in the functions f and g. A limitation of Mueller's work is that she makes no attempt to check that these conditions applied to Mexico in the 1940s and 1950s.

[‡]This uses the restrictions imposed on the signs of α_1, α_2, β_1 and β_2 (all are positive) and those placed on the functions f, g and h (f and g are increasing functions of S^1 and S^3, respectively, while h is an increasing function of S^2, given u, $p*$ and $p^3 *$).

[¶]The procedure is to substitute (10.13) for u in (10.14) and then to linearise the functions f, g, h and v.

[||]Note that m is introduced without a lag in these estimations.

[††]The t test is used for this purpose.

[†††]The data used for the purposes of these estimations were so-called 'cross-section' data. Altogether nineteen estimations are presented. (See Argy's study, p. 76.) For thirteen of these estimations the data used for p was the average inflation rate for the years 1958–65 for each of twenty-two countries (not all Latin American) and similarly for each of the independent variables, that is for these thirteen estimations the data used comprised twenty-two cross-section observations on each of the variables involved in the estimation. For three of the

performed well, in the sense that it generally appeared with a significantly positive coefficient, the structural variables performed badly. Thus the predictions of the model were not strongly supported by the data — on this test the model is found wanting.

10.5 Inflation as a Means to Growth

At the close of our discussion of the structuralist—monetarist controversy we said that the policy clash between these two groups reflected a more fundamental difference of view about the importance of the inflation problem in Latin American countries, the monetarists holding that the problem is one of great urgency, the structuralists that its importance is secondary. It is frequently maintained that one (if not the main) reason why the monetarists lay such stress on the need to curb inflation is that they believe that inflation is damaging to economic growth. Seers, for example, says 'It is only fair to recognize that monetarism is far more than an emphasis on monetary causes of inflation and on the need for restricting the expansion of the quantity of money if inflation is to be ended. A stable price level and a stable exchange rate are considered necessary conditions for growth.'[10] Again, according to Roberto de Oliveira Campos: 'The "monetarists" hold that: (a) Inflation has ceased to promote development and in fact has become incompatible with it; even those countries that managed to have inflation and development are now facing an acceleration of inflation and a deceleration of development.'[11]

In the last twenty years there have been several empirical studies designed to test this view of the relation between inflation and economic growth against the opposite view (also commonly held) that inflation tends to promote growth. Perhaps the most thorough and conclusive of these studies is a recent study by Thirlwall and Barton,[12] and we shall conclude the present chapter by giving a brief account of their method of investigation and conclusions.

The basic data used in the Thirlwall—Barton (TB) study consisted of the average annual inflation rate for the period 1958—67 and the average annual rate of increase of real G.N.P. (average annual growth rate) for the same period for

---

nineteen estimations, the data used comprised eighteen cross-section observations (that is four countries were excluded), while for the remaining three, twenty-one cross-section observations were used.

It should also be noted that Argy experimented with different proxies for the non-observable variables S^1, S^2 and S^3. For example, in some of the estimations in which S^1 was involved the series used for S^1 consisted of cross-section data on the average annual rate of growth of demand for agricultural output *minus* the average annual rate of growth of agricultural production, while for others the series used consisted of cross-section data on the average annual rate of change of food prices *minus* the average annual rate of change of the cost of living.

each of fifty-one countries. It was thus of the cross-section variety rather than the time-series variety.

TB's first step was to divide the fifty-one countries into five groups according to their real *per capita* income, measured in 1963 U.S. dollars. The groups were: (i) less than $200 (ten countries); (ii) $200–99 (ten countries); (iii) $300–799 (fourteen countries); (iv) $800–1650 (ten countries); and (v) over $1650 (seven countries).

Next a scatter diagram, showing the plot of the growth-rate observations against the inflation-rate observations, was drawn for each of these five groups separately. It was apparent from these diagrams that a significant positive relation between the inflation rate and the growth rate existed for the seventeen countries in the top two groups. Accordingly, a linear relationship with the growth rate as dependent variable and the inflation rate as independent variable was estimated for these countries as a group. This estimated relationship suggests that, in the case of developed countries, each one percentage point deviation of the inflation rate from the average inflation rate is associated with a deviation of the growth rate from the average growth rate of a little under two-thirds of one percentage point.

The scatter diagrams for the countries in the bottom three groups showed no significant relation between the inflation rate and the growth rate. However, whereas the countries in the top two groups had much the same inflationary experience in the 1958–67 period (all but three had average annual inflation rates below 4 per cent and none had rates above 6 per cent), the countries in the bottom three groups showed average annual inflation rates ranging from virtually zero to just under 50 per cent. Accordingly, before accepting the scatter diagrams for the bottom three groups as conclusive evidence of the absence of an inflation–growth relationship in the case of the developing countries, TB divided them into two groups: (i) those with an average annual inflation rate in the 1958–67 period in excess of 10 per cent; and (ii) those with an average annual inflation rate of 10 per cent or less. Separate scatter diagrams were then drawn for the seven countries in group (i) and for the twenty-seven countries in group (ii). For the countries in group (ii) no significant relation emerged. On the other hand, for the countries in group (i) there appeared to be a definite *negative* association between the inflation rate and the growth rate.

The findings of the TB study may therefore be summarised as follows: (*a*) in the case of *mildly inflating developed* countries there is a definite *positive* association between the growth rate and the inflation rate; (*b*) in the case of *mildly inflating developing* countries there is *no* clear association between the growth rate and the inflation rate; and (*c*) in the case of *strongly inflating developing* countries there is a definite *negative* association between the growth rate and the inflation rate.

So far as developing countries are concerned, the view that inflation tends to promote growth is clearly inconsistent with these findings. On the other hand, the opposite view is consistent with them – up to a point. More specifically, the claim that the growth rate would rise in a developing country if the inflation rate were reduced from an annual rate of, say, 50 per cent to an annual rate of 20 per cent, is consistent with the TB findings whereas the claim that a reduction in the inflation rate from, say, 10 per cent per annum to 4 per cent per annum would raise the growth rate is inconsistent with them.

Evidently the TB findings have some bearing on the structuralist–monetarist controversy. In general, they support the monetarist position. For they lend weight to the view that the persistently high inflation rates, which several of the Latin American countries have experienced since the war, have been instrumental in lowering their growth rates, and hence, in turn, to the view that it is a matter of urgency to reduce these high inflation rates; and once this latter view is accepted, a preference for the monetarists' anti-inflation policy proposals over those of the structuralists is almost bound to follow.

11

HYPERINFLATION

11.1 The Meaning of Hyperinflation

The dictionary meaning of 'hyper' is 'excessive'. Strictly, therefore, 'hyper-inflation' means 'excessive inflation' or 'abnormally rapid inflation'. To the economist, however, the term 'hyperinflation' means much more than this. Throughout the 1950s and the 1960s the average inflation rate in the advanced industrial countries was, in general, well below 10 per cent per annum. Judged by this standard the inflation rates of around 20 per cent per annum which have begun to appear in these countries since 1970 are certainly 'excessive'; the average inflation rates of around 40–50 per cent per annum, which several of the Latin American countries suffered in the 1950s and 1960s, are 'wildly excessive'. It is not, however, inflation rates of 20 per cent per annum or even 50 per cent per annum that the economist has in mind when he uses the term 'hyperinflation'. What he is thinking of is a situation in which the annual inflation rate runs into hundreds, even thousands, of per cents, a situation in which money loses value so rapidly that spending money as soon as possible after receiving it becomes a major preoccupation of the populace at large. The term 'galloping inflation', which is sometimes used instead of 'hyperinflation', perhaps gives a clearer picture of the situation being described.

For some purposes the general explanation of 'hyperinflation' given in the preceding paragraph is rather too vague, and a precise formal definition is required. One such is the definition devised by Cagan and used by him in his extensive empirical work on hyperinflation. Cagan defines hyperinflation 'as beginning in the month the rise in prices exceeds 50 per cent and as ending in the month before the monthly rise in prices drops below that amount and stays below for at least a year'.[1] On Cagan's definition, therefore, an inflation rate of at least 50 per cent per *month* is required before a state of hyperinflation can be said to exist.

From this definitional discussion it will be clear that hyperinflation, in the economist's sense, is a comparatively rare phenomenon. In fact, for all practical purposes, it can be regarded as something which occurs only during, and immediately after, major wars. This being so, it is reasonable to ask why economists bother to study it. The answer is that, because hyperinflation is a highly dramatic and striking phenomenon, its explanation presents a challenge which they can hardly ignore. In other words, the study of hyperinflation holds great intellectual and scientific interest even though its strictly practical benefits are probably comparatively insignificant.

In Section 10.1 it was argued that a model of the inflationary process (answer to the question, 'What causes inflation?') which works for a developed economy *may* work for a developing economy also, but, in general, is unlikely to do so. The reasoning behind this judgement was that, in view of the marked differences which exist between developed and developing economies, it seems more appropriate to regard them as different things than as different versions of the one thing. But if this view is taken, it must be presumed that the essence of the inflationary process in the two cases will be quite different, and hence that a model which captures the one will, in general, fail to capture the other.

A similar argument can be applied as between normal inflation ('creeping' inflation as it is sometimes called) and hyperinflation. In this case it may be argued that a model of the inflationary process which works for normal inflation may possibly work for hyperinflation but is unlikely to do so. For since the difference between normal inflation and hyperinflation is more a difference in kind than a difference of degree, the essence of a hyperinflationary situation is likely to be quite different from the essence of an inflationary situation of the normal kind. This being so it is not to be expected that a model which captures the former will also succeed in capturing the latter.

This argument has been accepted generally by economists who have worked on hyperinflation, and accordingly a number of special models have been developed to explain the hyperinflationary process. Two of these models will be discussed in Sections 11.2 and 11.3. As we shall see, both are based to a large extent on the New Quantity Theory of Money, which was discussed in detail in Section 2.5.

11.2 The Kalecki Model

In this section we shall present a model developed by Kalecki[2] to explain the upward movement of the price index under hyperinflationary conditions.

All the variables of the Kalecki model relate to instant t but for simplicity they will be introduced without the usual parenthetical t symbol. The notation is as follows:

M – nominal stock of money

P – price index

Y^r – real G.N.P.

Y – nominal G.N.P.

V – income velocity of money (Y/M)

p – inflation rate

p^e – expected inflation rate

$\dot{p}^e$ — increase in p^e per unit of time, that is dp^e/dt

β — positive constant satisying the restriction $0 < \beta < 1$

ϕ — 'increasing function of'

In terms of this notation the relationships of the model are:

$$MV = PY^r \qquad\qquad (11.1)$$

$$V = \phi(p^e) \qquad\qquad (11.2)$$

$$\dot{p}^e = \beta(\dot{p} - p^e) \qquad\qquad (11.3)$$

Since, by definition, V is equal to Y/M and Y^r is equal to Y/P, both sides of (11.1) are equal to nominal G.N.P., Y. Thus (11.1) holds by virtue of the definition of V and Y^r; it is an example of a definitional relationship. Relationship (11.2) is a simplified form of (2.14), the 'income-velocity' version of the N.Q.T. function, in which all of the determining variables apart from p^e are suppressed. Such a simplification seems appropriate in a model of hyperinflation since, under hyperinflationary conditions, p^e is likely to fluctuate much more widely than the income, interest and wealth variables, and hence is likely to be, by far, the dominant influence on income velocity.† Finally, relationship (11.3) is just the expectations-formation equation suitably reformulated to allow for the fact that, in the present analysis, all variables relate to instant t rather than to period t, that is, they are regarded as continuous functions of time.

The data of the model are M, p^e, V and Y', the last being treated not only as given but also as constant over time. Thus the unknowns are p, P and $\dot{p}^e$.

There is one further point relating to the model itself which requires some discussion. As suggested by the argument of Section 2.5, the independent variable p^e takes care of several different influences in the N.Q.T. function, and because of this it is difficult to specify the nature of the dependence of M^d on p^e with complete confidence. However, the general drift of the argument is in the direction of M^d being a decreasing function of p^e, for given levels of the other independent variables. Given this, it follows that Y/M will be an increasing function of p^e, for given levels of the other independent variables, in the income-velocity form of the function given by (2.14). This is the justification for specifying that ϕ is an increasing function of p^e in (11.2).

In diagrammatic terms, the restriction on ϕ is that the curve of V against p^e has a positive slope at all points. Following Kalecki, we shall impose the further restriction that the slope decreases as p^e increases on the ground that 'there exists *some* limit to the velocity of circulation, however high it may be'.[3]

---

†Strictly speaking the dependent variable in (11.2) should be V^d, where $V^d = Y/M^d$ (cf. equation (2.14) above). By making it V instead, we are, in effect, introducing another relationship, namely $M = M^d$ (cf. p. 265 below).

We turn now from the model itself to the explanation which it provides for hyperinflationary movements of the price index.

We begin by putting the model into a more convenient form. First (11.1) is used to obtain an expression for the inflation rate, p, namely:

$$p = m + v, \tag{11.4}$$

where m is the percentage rate of increase in the stock of money at instant t and v is the percentage rate of increase in the income velocity of money.† Then (11.2) is used to obtain the following expression for v: ‡

$$v = \frac{1}{V} \frac{dV}{dp^e} \dot{p}^e. \tag{11.5}$$

† The derivation of (11.4) is as follows. Taking natural logarithms in (11.1) we obtain:

$$\ln M + \ln V = \ln P + \ln Y^r.$$

Therefore

$$\frac{d}{dt} (\ln M) + \frac{d}{dt} (\ln V) = \frac{d}{dt} (\ln P) + \frac{d}{dt} (\ln Y^r).$$

Since Y^r is assumed to be constant over time, the second term on the right-hand side is zero and we have:

$$\frac{d}{dt} (\ln M) + \frac{d}{dt} (\ln V) = \frac{d}{dt} (\ln P).$$

Therefore

$$\frac{1}{M} \frac{dM}{dt} + \frac{1}{V} \frac{dV}{dt} = \frac{1}{P} \frac{dP}{dt}.$$

Therefore

$$p = m + v.$$

‡ The steps are as follows. Noting that V is a function of p^e, where $\dot{p}^e$ is a function of t and using the function-of-a-function rule we obtain from (11.2):

$$\frac{dV}{dt} = \frac{dV}{dp^e} \dot{p}^e.$$

Therefore

$$\frac{1}{V} \frac{dV}{dt} = \frac{1}{V} \frac{dV}{dp^e} \dot{p}^e.$$

Therefore

$$v = \frac{1}{V} \frac{dV}{dp^e} \dot{p}^e.$$

Finally, by substituting (11.3) into (11.5), and then substituting the resulting expression into (11.4), we obtain:

$$p = \frac{m - \dfrac{1}{V}\dfrac{dV}{dp^e}\beta p^e}{1 - \dfrac{1}{V}\dfrac{dV}{dp^e}\beta}. \tag{11.6}$$

Relationships (11.3), (11.4), (11.5) and (11.6) form the basis of the analysis.

We postulate an initial equilibrium in which the actual inflation rate, the expected inflation rate and the rate of increase of the money stock are all constant. This is a 'moving equilibrium' (constant rates of growth) as distinct from a 'stationary equilibrium' (constant absolute levels).† Since p^e is constant, $\dot{p}^e = 0$, whence, from (11.3), $p = p^e$. Thus in the initial equilibrium the actual and inflation rates are not only constant but equal. The common constant value of p and p^e, say p_1, can be deduced from (11.6) by putting both p and p^e equal to p_1 and m equal to some constant, say m_1. Then we get:

$$p_1\left(1 - \frac{1}{V}\frac{dV}{dp^e}\beta\right) = m_1 - \frac{1}{V}\frac{dV}{dp^e}\beta p_1.$$

Therefore

$$p_1 = m_1.$$

That is, in the postulated initial equilibrium the actual inflation rate, the expected inflation rate and the rate of increase of the money stock are all constant and equal.

Now let there be a 'step-increase' in m. That is, let m rise from m_1, the constant level applying in the initial situation, to, say, m_2 and remain at this higher level indefinitely. This step-increase in m will disturb the initial equilibrium, that is p and p^e will no longer remain constant. In fact, assuming that the (positive) magnitude $1/V(dV/dp^e)\beta$ is less than unity, both p and p^e will move towards m_2, which is of course their new equilibrium level.

This can be shown as follows. Suppose that $p^e < m_2$. Then:

$$p^e\left(1 - \frac{1}{V}\frac{dV}{dp^e}\beta\right) < m_2 - \frac{1}{V}\frac{dV}{dp^e}\beta p^e.$$

Since, by assumption, $0 < 1/V(dV/dp^e)\beta < 1$, the bracketed expression on the left-hand side will be positive and hence the direction of the inequality will be

---

†The equilibria postulated from time to time in Chapter 2 were stationary equilibria.

maintained if it is divided through by this expression. Hence, if $p^e < m_2$:

$$p^e < \cfrac{m_2 - \cfrac{1}{V}\cfrac{dV}{d\,p^e}\,\beta p^e}{\left(1 - \cfrac{1}{V}\cfrac{dV}{d\,p^e}\,\beta\right)},$$

that is $p^e < p$. But if $p^e < p$, then, from (11.3), $\dot{p}^e$ must be positive, that is p^e must be increasing. By means of a correponding argument, it can be shown that if $p^e > m_2$, p^e must be *decreasing*. It follows that if p^e is either greater or less than m_2, it will be in motion towards m_2.

Turning now to the actual inflation rate, p, we first note that if p^e is less than m_2 (that is if $\dot{p}^e$ is positive) v must be positive – from (11.5). Hence p must be greater than m_2 – from (11.4). On the other hand, if p^e is greater than m_2, p must be less than m_2. In either case, however, the fact that p^e is in motion towards m_2 implies that p will also be in motion towards m_2 – from the opposite direction.†

---

†With m constant at m_2, (11.4) gives:

$$\dot{p} = \dot{v},$$

where $\dot{p}$ denotes dp/dt and $\dot{v}$ denotes dv/dt. But from (11.5) we have:

$$\dot{v} = \frac{dv}{dt} = \left(\frac{1}{V}\frac{dV}{dp^e}\right)\ddot{p}^e + \dot{p}^e\,\frac{d}{dt}\left(\frac{1}{V}\frac{dV}{dp^e}\right),$$

where $\ddot{p}^e$ denotes $d^2(p^e)/dt^2$.
Now from (11.3) we have:

$$\ddot{p}^e = \beta(\dot{p} - \dot{p}^e).$$

We also have:

$$\frac{d}{dt}\left(\frac{1}{V}\frac{dV}{dp^e}\right) = \frac{1}{V}\frac{d^2V}{d(p^e)^2} - \frac{1}{V^2}\left(\frac{dV}{dp^e}\right)^2.$$

Substituting for $\ddot{p}^e$ and $d/dt(1/V \times dV/dp^e)$ in the above expression for $\dot{v}$, we obtain:

$$\dot{v} = \frac{1}{V}\frac{dV}{dp^e}\,\beta\,\dot{p} - \frac{1}{V}\frac{dV}{dp^e}\,\beta\,\dot{p}^e + \dot{p}^e\left[\frac{1}{V}\frac{d^2V}{d(p^e)^2} - \frac{1}{V^2}\left(\frac{dV}{dp^e}\right)^2\right].$$

Now substituting for $\dot{v}$ in the expression for $\dot{p}$ we obtain:

$$\dot{p} = \frac{1}{V}\frac{dV}{dp^e}\,\beta\,\dot{p} - \frac{1}{V}\frac{dV}{dp^e}\,\beta\,\dot{p}^e + \dot{p}^e\left[\frac{1}{V}\frac{d^2V}{d(p^e)^2} - \frac{1}{V^2}\left(\frac{dV}{dp^e}\right)^2\right].$$

Denote $(1/V)(dV/dp^e)$ by a and

$$\left[\frac{1}{V}\frac{d^2V}{d(p^e)^2} - \frac{1}{V^2}\left(\frac{dV}{dp^e}\right)^2\right].$$

To sum up, if p^e is less than m_2, p will be greater than m_2 and both will be in motion towards m_2. On the other hand, if p^e is greater than m_2, p will be less than m_2 and both will be in motion towards m_2 once again. Thus the actual inflation rate and the expected inflation rate, having been disturbed from the initial constant level, m_1, will eventually settle down at the new, higher level, m_2.

The answer which the Kalecki model gives to the question 'How do hyperinflationary price increases come about?' is now clear. According to the model they come about when the rate of growth of the money stock begins to 'gallop', as it is likely to do, for example, when a government is trying to finance a major war and has to resort increasingly to central-bank borrowing in order to do so. If, in circumstances such as these, the rate of increase of the money stock rises from a steady 4 per cent per month, say, to a steady 10 per cent per month, then the inflation rate will eventually rise also from a steady 4 per cent per month to a steady 10 per cent per month. If, then, the rate of increase of the money stock rises to a steady 30 per cent per month, the inflation rate will eventually climb to a steady 30 per cent per month; and so on. In short, hyperinflation is simply the manifestation of gross monetary mismanagement, according to the Kalecki model.

Our analysis of the workings of the Kalecki model, as well as revealing its explanation of the hyperinflation phenomenon, also reveals its remedy for hyperinflation. By putting the analysis into reverse we see that, just as an increase in the rate of growth of the money supply from a steady 10 per cent per month to a steady 30 per cent per month will lift the inflation rate from a steady monthly figure of 10 per cent to a steady monthly figure of 30 per cent, so a *reduction* in the rate of growth of the money stock from 30 per cent to 10 per cent per month will cause a corresponding *reduction* in the inflation rate. The cure for hyperinflation, then, is a drastic, maintained reduction in the rate of growth of

---

by b. Then:

$$\dot{p} = a\beta\dot{p} - a\beta\dot{p}^e + b\dot{p}^e.$$

Therefore:

$$\dot{p} = \frac{-a\beta}{1 - a\beta}\,\dot{p}^e + \frac{b}{1 - a\beta}\,\dot{p}^e.$$

Therefore:

$$\dot{p} = \left[\frac{-a\beta}{1 - a\beta} + \frac{b}{1 - a\beta}\right]\dot{p}^e.$$

Now by assumption $0 < a\beta < 1$. Hence the first term in the square bracket is negative for all p^e. Further, b is negative for all p^e. (This is because $1/V$ is necessarily positive, $d^2 V/d(p^e)^2$ is negative by assumption (see above, p. 260) and $1/V^2 (dV/dp^e)^2$ is necessarily positive.) Hence the term in square brackets on the right-hand side of the above expression for $\dot{p}$ is negative for all p^e. We conclude that the sign of $\dot{p}$ is always the reverse of the sign of $\dot{p}^e$; if p^e is increasing, p will be decreasing and vice versa.

the money stock, according to the Kalecki model. Of course, this is not a remedy that a government caught in the grip of hyperinflation would be likely to apply, for only a strong government could take drastic policy action of the type envisaged, whereas a government faced with hyperinflation is almost always in the final stages of disintegration. In practice, hyperinflations have usually been brought to a halt, not by any conscious government action, but by the total collapse of the monetary system.

11.3   The Cagan Model

We turn now to another model of hyperinflation which, like the Kalecki model, is firmly linked with the N.Q.T. demand-for-money function. This is the famous model developed by Phillip Cagan to provide a basis for the empirical study of several actual hyperinflationary episodes.[4]

The relationships of the Cagan model are:

$$\frac{M^d}{P} = e^{-(\alpha p^e + \tau)} \tag{11.7}$$

$$\frac{M^d}{P} = \frac{M}{P} \tag{11.8}$$

$$\dot{p}^e = \beta(p - p^e) \tag{11.9}$$

The new symbols are α, τ and e, α and τ being two constants, the first of which is positive, and e the base of the natural logarithms. As in the case of the Kalecki model, all variables relate to instant t, that is, they are to be regarded as continuous functions of time.

Relationships (11.8) and (11.9) require no comment but a brief discussion of (11.7) is in order. This relationship is a simplified form of (2.13), the 'real-balance' form of the N.Q.T. demand-for-money function, all determining variables apart from p^e having been suppressed. As explained in connection with the Kalecki model (see above, p. 260), this is an appropriate simplification in a model of hyperinflation. It should also be noted that (11.7) shows M^d/P as a decreasing function of p^e.† This seems appropriate also in the light of our earlier discussion of the Kalecki model (see above, p. 260).

The variables M, M^d and p^e can be regarded as the data of the model, leaving p, $\dot{p}^e$ and P as the unknowns, as in the case of the Kalecki model.

Having set out the model we turn now to its explanation of hyperinflation. We shall derive this explanation from an analysis of the fundamental properties of the

---

†When $p^e = 0$, $M^d/P = e^{-\tau}$. When p^e is positive, M^d/P is also positive but decreases continuously as p^e increases. Thus the curve of M^d/P against p^e has a positive intercept equal to $e^{-\tau}$ and is asymptotic from above to the horizontal axis.

model similar to the analysis presented in the previous section for the Kalecki model. Here our analysis will be based on the following expression:†

$$p = \frac{m - \alpha\beta p^e}{1 - \alpha\beta}. \tag{11.10}$$

We begin by postulating an initial equilibrium in which m, p and p^e are all constant. Proceeding as before (see above, p. 262) we find that if p and p^e are both constant, they must also be equal and that their common value is m_1, where m_1 is the postulated constant rate of increase of the money stock. Now suppose that there is a step-increase in the rate of growth of the nominal money stock. Specifically, suppose that the rate of growth of the money stock rises from m_1 to m_2, and stays indefinitely at the higher level. Then if we assume that $0 < \alpha\beta < 1$, we can show that both p and p^e will begin moving towards their new equilibrium level, m_2. The argument differs only slightly from the corresponding argument for the Kalecki model and accordingly we shall omit some of the detail.

Suppose that p^e is less than m_2. Then we have:

$$p^e(1 - \alpha\beta) < m_2 - \alpha\beta p^e.$$

Hence, using (11.10) and the assumption that $0 < \alpha\beta < 1$, we can say:

$$p^e < p.$$

From this we can say, using (11.9), that p^e will be rising. Conversely, if p^e is greater than m_2, p^e will be falling. Thus, if p^e is either greater or less than m_2, it will be moving towards m_2.

---

†This expression is derived from the model in the following way. Substituting (11.8) into (11.7) and taking natural logs in the resulting expression we obtain:

$$\ln \frac{M}{P} = -\alpha p^e - \tau.$$

Therefore,

$$\ln M - \ln P = -\alpha p^e - \tau.$$

Now differentiating with respect to time we obtain:

$$m - p = -\alpha \dot{p}^e.$$

Substituting (11.9) into this expression we obtain:

$$m - p = -\alpha\beta p + \alpha\beta p^e.$$

Therefore,

$$p(1 - \alpha\beta) = m - \alpha\beta p^e.$$

Therefore,

$$p = \frac{m - \alpha\beta p^e}{1 - \alpha\beta}.$$

As for p, the actual inflation rate, we first note that if p^e is less than m_2, p must be greater than m_2.† Conversely, if p^e is greater than m_2, p must be less than m_2. In either case, however, the fact that p^e will be moving towards m_2 ensures that p will be moving towards m_2 also, though from the opposite direction.‡

The analytical properties of the Cagan model, therefore, are exactly the same as those of the Kalecki model. Both models imply that if p^e is less than m_2, p will be greater than m_2 and that both p and p^e will be in motion towards m_2; and conversely if p^e is greater than m_2. It follows that the explanation of hyperinflation provided by the Cagan model is exactly the same as that provided by the Kalecki model, as are its policy implications. The discussion of these matters in Section 11.2 is therefore fully applicable to the Cagan model, and, to avoid repetition, we shall ask the reader to look again at this discussion before proceeding.

To round off our treatment of hyperinflation we shall briefly relate the New Quantity Theory models of Kalecki and Cagan to the 'crude' or 'old' Quantity Theory. In the case of the Old Quantity Theory the velocity of circulation is treated as a given constant and the model consists of (11.1) alone, with P as the only unknown. With V constant, (11.1) implies that $p = m$, that is to say, that the actual inflation rate is equal *at all points of time* to the rate of growth of the money stock. In the case of the New Quantity Theory, on the other hand, $p = m$ *only in equilibrium*; out of equilibrium p will be different from m, though it will be moving towards m provided m is constant. Thus, while at first glance the conclusions which emerge from the New Quantity Theory models look very similar to those which emerge from the Old Quantity Theory, the two are really fundamentally different and must not be confused.

† From (11.10) we can say that if p^e is less than m_2:

$$m_2 - \alpha\beta p^e > m_2 - \alpha\beta m_2.$$

Therefore,

$$\frac{m_2 - \alpha\beta p^e}{1 - \alpha\beta} > \frac{m_2 - \alpha\beta m_2}{1 - \alpha\beta}.$$

Therefore,

$$p > m_2.$$

‡ Recalling that α and β are both constants, we can say from (11.10):

$$\dot{p} = -\left(\frac{\alpha\beta}{1 - \alpha\beta}\right)\dot{p}^e,$$

where $\dot{p} = dp/dt$. Now $\alpha\beta$ is positive since both α and β are positive. Also, by virtue of the assumption that $0 < \alpha\beta < 1$, we know that $1 - \alpha\beta$ is positive. Hence the sign of $\dot{p}$ must be the reverse of the sign of $\dot{p}^e$. If $\dot{p}^e$ is positive (p^e increasing), $\dot{p}$ must be negative (p decreasing) and vice versa.

12

CONCLUSION

12.1   Frontiers of Inflation Theory

In the preceding chapters we have expounded the corpus of the theory and policy of inflation as it exists in the mid-1970s. Given the scope and intensity of current research, this corpus is bound to undergo marked changes, even in the next few years. It is not at all easy to predict the direction which these changes will take. Nevertheless in this concluding chapter we shall make the attempt. More precisely, we shall try to identify that part of current work which, because of its excellence and its concentration on fundamental problems, appears destined to become part of the corpus, once it has been more fully developed.

The reader will have gathered from the discussion of earlier chapters that expectations occupy the central position in modern treatments of the inflation problem. He may also have come to suspect that certain fundamental problems which arise in this connection are by no means squarely faced in the literature as it stands. For example, when the 'expected rate of inflation' is entered as an explanatory variable in a money-wage equation, whose expectation of what price index over what time horizon is being referred to? Is the expectation, whatever it might be, held with certainty? Basic questions such as these are effectively passed-by in the current literature, as they are in the exposition of this literature given in the preceding chapters. There should be no surprise, then, when the reader is told that, in the author's judgement, the work which is most likely to make an impact on the corpus in the next few years includes work on certain fundamental problems associated with the measurement of expectations and with their role in the inflationary process. A brief account of this work will be given in the next two sections of the chapter.

It has been emphasised in earlier chapters, notably in Sections 2.1 and 7.1, that to explain inflation and, in doing so, to lay an adequate foundation for the framing of anti-inflation policy, it is necessary to build a model in which the inflation rate appears as a jointly determined, or explained variable. From the professional's standpoint nothing less than a properly articulated model will do. The professional would add that the model should be complete, in the sense of having only genuine data in the data category, but that completeness should be accomplished, if possible, without destroying the comprehensibility of the model. A second area of current work which appears likely to make a permanent mark on the literature in the near future is work directed towards improving existing models from the standpoint of completeness. This work will be briefly discussed in Section 12.4.

It will be recalled that in discussing the demand-management approach to anti-inflation policy in Chapter 7 two forms of demand management were distinguished. Under the first, the policy-maker attempts to shift the economy from one short-run unemployment—inflation rate combination to another, preferred combination. Under the second he attempts to shift the economy from some short-run p, u combination to a desired long-run combination or from one long-run combination to another which is preferred. Now the words 'preferred' and 'desired' in the preceding sentences suggest a need for some form of optimisation in the demand-management context, and the alert reader may have concluded from the absence of any reference to optimisation in Chapter 7 that there is an important gap in the literature at this point. This is so. However, work designed to fill the gap is in progress, and in the author's view this work is also likely to become part of the corpus, once fully developed. A brief account of the work in question will be given in the final section of the chapter.

12.2   Specification of the Expectations-Augmented Wage Relationship

Money-wage relationships of the 'expectations-augmented, Phillips-curve' variety, of which (2.10) is an example, now occupy a prominent position in the inflation literature. When a money-wage relationship of this type is postulated, one usually finds the p^e variable defined somewhat vaguely as 'the expected rate of inflation' without too much attention being given to the twin questions of which group is doing the expecting and which price index they are forming their expectations about. This is obviously unsatisfactory, and workers in the field of inflation have recently faced up to the challenge of devising a tighter specification for wage relationships of the expectations-augmented, Phillips-curve type.

A feature of the most promising research in this area is its attachment to theory; the underlying view is that the only satisfactory way of approaching the specification problem is to devise a model of the labour market and then to use this model to determine which expectation variables should enter the wage equation and also how they should do so.

One such model which has achieved prominence takes, as its starting-point, the definition of labour excess demand as the demand for labour *minus* the supply of labour.[1] The demand for labour is then made to depend on the real wage and likewise the supply of labour. However, it is recognised that the 'real wage' which determines the demand for labour will be different from the real wage which determines the supply of labour. More specifically, the real wage which constitutes the argument of the demand-for-labour function will be the wage *paid by employers* (including payroll and employment taxes) divided by the (expected) price *received by employers* whereas the real wage which enters the supply-of-labour function will be the wage *received by employees* (after direct tax) divided by the (expected) price *paid by employees* (including indirect tax). Proceeding in this way, one finds that the excess demand for labour can be expressed as a function of the money wage actually determined by the market, a group of (expected) price variables and a group of tax variables, and, in turn, that the absolute change in labour excess demand can be expressed as a function of the percentage rates of change of the variables in question. The latter function can then be manipulated to give the percentage rate of increase of money wages as a function of the absolute change in excess demand, and the price variables already mentioned. It is then assumed that money wages are adjusted so as to clear the market, that is so that the change in labour excess demand is equal to the negative of the excess demand actually realised at some earlier point in time. This assumption enables the current change in excess demand to be replaced as an argument in the money-wage function by the prior realised level of excess demand, that is by a variable which can be proxied by the prior unemployment rate.

Thus, by means of the model outlined above, it is shown that a correctly specified money-wage equation of the expectations-augmented, Phillips-curve variety will be much more complex than the equations, such as (2.10), which are commonly encountered. There will be not one expected rate of price increase on the right-hand side of the equation, but several. In addition, the explanatory variables will include a variety of tax variables which are usually overlooked when the equation is formulated without the aid of theory. Also the model implies certain restrictions on the coefficients of the expected price variables and tax variables (these do not emerge from the brief outline given above) which serves to tighten the specification of the relationship still further.

12.3   Direct Measurement of Expectations

Research in the field of inflation has been seriously handicapped in recent years by the absence, even in statistically well-endowed countries, of a time series for the expected inflation rate. This has given rise to difficulties in two main ways. In the first place, it has complicated attempts to test the expectational model. As we have seen in Chapter 3, the most direct way of testing this model is by estimating the coefficient of the expected inflation rate in an expectations-augmented, Phillips-curve wage relationship. But in the absence of time series for the expected inflation rate this can be done only if the expected inflation rate is eliminated from the relationship, in favour of some other variable for which a time series can be obtained. The standard way of achieving this end is to employ some simple hypothesis about the way in which expectations are formed, for example the adaptive expectations hypothesis (cf. Section 3.2 above). But such a procedure immediately weakens the test because it makes it conditional on a particular expectations-formation hypothesis.

The general absence of time series for the expected inflation rate has led to difficulties in a second way also, namely by limiting the opportunity for research into the determinants of the expected inflation rate. The most straightforward way of investigating the determinants of the expected inflation rate would be by estimating a wide variety of expected-inflation-rate equations by some econometric technique and then choosing a preferred equation. However, this approach is not feasible unless a time series can be obtained for each of the variables involved in the equations in question, because without this information estimation cannot proceed. In particular, it is not feasible unless a time series can be obtained for the dependent variable in these equations, that is for the expected inflation rate.

In many countries there is now some regular sample survey in which the members of a sample, chosen either from the population at large or from some segment of the population, are asked to indicate whether they expect prices to rise, fall or stay the same over some specified future time interval. Recently, workers in the field of inflation have taken up the problem of converting such qualitative information about price expectations into a time series for the expected inflation rate. It is the author's view that the work being done in this connection represents a promising way of plugging the gap to which attention has been directed in this section, and that, given further development, it could well be absorbed into the corpus of inflation theory and policy in the near future.[2]

The procedures which have been proposed for converting qualitative sample-survey information on price expectations into quantitative time-series information on the expected inflation rate are fairly complex and no attempt will be made to describe them in detail. The essence of the suggested procedures, however, is a particular set of assumptions about the way in which the member of the sample is behaving when he answers the question, Do you expect prices to rise, fall or stay the same? and a particular definition of the 'expected inflation rate'.

As regards the former, the key assumptions, typically, are: (i) that each individual who gives a definite answer to the above question refers to the prices of the commodities which he, himself, buys; (ii) that each individual has a subjective probability distribution concerning the rate of change of his 'own' price index which varies from period to period; (iii) that each individual who answers 'rise' ('fall') does so because the probability of a positive (negative) value for the rate of change of his own price index, according to his subjective probability distribution of this variable, is greater (less) than 50 per cent; (iv) that the subjective probability distribution referred to in (ii), and hence the median of this distribution, differs from individual to individual; and (v) that the variation in the individual medians is itself covered by a probability distribution – specifically by the normal distribution.

As regards the definition of the expected rate of inflation, this is typically taken to be the mean of the medians of the individual probability distributions. This definition taken together with assumption (v) means that the variable $(m_t - p_t^e)/v_t$ is a standard normal variable, where m denotes the median variable, v its standard deviation and p^e the expected rate of inflation.

Starting with this definition and the above set of behavioural assumptions it is possible to derive a formula for p_t^e. This formula calls only for information from the survey about the proportion of respondents answering 'rise', 'fall', etc. in period t, and certain additional information of a comparatively minor character, and so can be used without difficulty to calculate the required time series for the expected inflation rate.

12.4 Formulation of Complete Models

As the reader will have gathered from the prototype 'mark-up' and 'expectational' models presented in Chapter 2, an important feature of the models of the inflationary process in developed economies, which fall into these two classes, is that the unemployment rate is treated as exogenous, rather than as simultaneously determined, along with the inflation rate, by the model itself. Now this is by no means a satisfactory specification. The unemployment rate, by definition, is $(L - E)/L$ or $1 - E/L$, where L denotes the labour force and E the level of employment. It may be legitimate to treat L as a datum in short-run models, models of the inflationary process included. But the same cannot be said of E. The level of employment is determined by the desired level of real output, which in turn is determined by the level of aggregate demand, which in turn is determined by some more or less complex model of the $IS-LM$, Keynesian type. Thus the unemployment rate is a long way from being exogenous and to treat it as such is to leave the model seriously incomplete.

An obvious way of attacking the problem of the incompleteness of traditional mark-up and expectational models, which is suggested by the discussion of the preceding paragraph, is to retain the unemployment rate as a variable but to explain that variable by tacking on to the existing relationships a production function and a Keynesian model of the determination of real aggregate demand. The difficulty with this approach, however, is that by the time the required relationships have been assembled, the simplicity, which is the attractive feature of mark-up and expectational models as they stand, will almost certainly have been lost.

The alternative is to reformulate the basic relationships of the mark-up, or expectational, model as the case may be, without the unemployment rate as an explicit variable, but with the spirit of the model preserved nevertheless, and then to find some simple way of completing the reformulated model. Some excellent work, which appears destined to find a place in the corpus of inflation theory in the near future, is now being done along these lines and some ingenious models are being produced and tested.[3] The prototype monetarist model presented in Section 2.5 is an adaptation of one of these models and can perhaps be used to explain further the approach which is followed in their construction. To devise this model the price equation of the expectational model, namely (2.7), was reformulated to make $\bar{Y}/\bar{Y}^f$ the independent variable, rather than u. The new relationship is certainly in the spirit of the old and can even be said to be the *same* relationship in another guise (cf. p. 42 above). With the unemployment rate removed, however, it is now possible to complete the model in a comparatively simple way by using the real-balances version of N.Q.T. demand-for-money function. Thus the incompleteness of the expectational model has been removed but without any significant cost in terms of extra complexity.

It should be added, perhaps, that in some cases the authors of these models have not been content to regard them as analytical tools but have devoted considerable effort to estimating them econometrically; and it may well be that, in five or so years' time, an up-to-date account of the econometrics of inflation will be less concerned with single relationships, such as the price equations and wage equations dealt with in Chapters 4 and 5, than with complete models.

12.5 Optimal Demand Management

In Section 9.4 we presented what we believe to be the current consensus on anti-inflation policy, as it relates to advanced industrial economies. In the course of this discussion it was suggested that, at the present time, most economists take the view that the long-run inflation—unemployment curve is a (shifting) downward-sloping curve, not, as some hold, a vertical straight line. Let us suppose that the policy-maker accepts this majority view. It was also suggested that most economists, nowadays, would urge the policy-maker to aim for *some* point on this downward-sloping, long-run curve, that is to aim for a steady inflation rate *via* a steady unemployment rate. Again, let us suppose that the policy-maker accepts this advice. Finally, it was suggested in Section 9.4 that there may well be no point on the long-run curve which is fully acceptable to the community at large – that at the maximum acceptable steady unemployment rate the steady inflation rate is unacceptably high. Suppose, once more, that the policy-maker believes this to be the case. In brief, we have in mind a policy-maker who subscribes to the notion of a downward-sloping long-run inflation—unemployment curve on which there is no fully acceptable point and who believes that the economy should, nevertheless, be at *some* point on this curve. What point should he choose? One possible approach would be to say that the policy-maker should choose the point corresponding to the maximum acceptable steady inflation rate and ask the community to learn to live with the unacceptably high steady unemployment rate which this will involve. A second possible approach would be to say that he should choose the point corresponding to the maximum acceptable unemployment rate and ask the community to learn to live with the unacceptably high steady inflation rate which this will entail. In our discussion of the current policy consensus we suggested that, at the present time, most economists would prefer the second approach to the first. A third possible approach is to say that he should choose the point which is *optimal* in some sense. As yet, this approach is by no means fully developed. However the author's judgement is that economists concerned with anti-inflation policy will find it increasingly attractive and that, in the not too distant future, the corpus of inflation theory and policy will include a substantial literature on optimal demand management.[4]

In this chapter we have tried to pinpoint the current developments in inflation theory and anti-inflation policy that are likely to impose new directions on the subject in the next few years. Our predictions may well prove to be wide of the mark, because of inadequate attention to some current developments and wrong assessment of others. Be that as it may, the chapter will still have served a useful purpose if it has reminded the reader that inflation theory and policy is a highly dynamic field of study whose boundaries are being constantly redrawn as old hypotheses are discarded in the light of fresh evidence, and new hypotheses, still to be tested, are formulated in their place.

REFERENCES

CHAPTER ONE

1. This was the definition advocated by Lerner, for example: see A. P. Lerner, 'The Inflationary Process', *Review of Economics and Statistics* (August 1949) pp. 193–5.

2. See F. W. Paish, *Rise and Fall of Incomes Policy* (London: Institute of Economic Affairs, 1969) p. 20.

3. See Ralph Turvey, 'Theory of Inflation in a Closed Economy', *Economic Journal* (September 1951) pp. 531–5.

4. Ibid. p. 533; italics mine.

5. Ibid. pp. 534–5; italics omitted.

6. These are described in *Australian National Accounts: National Income and Expenditure, 1972–73* (Canberra: Australian Bureau of Statistics, 1974) appendix B.

7. This measure was first used in an international study of inflation made some ten years ago. See *The Problem of Rising Prices* (Paris: Organisation for European Economic Co-operation, 1961) pp. 83–91.

8. See Sir John Hicks, 'Expected Inflation', *Three Banks Review* (September 1970) p. 21.

9. Ibid. pp. 18–19.

10. See Arthur M. Okun, 'The Mirage of Steady Inflation', *Brookings Papers on Economic Activity*, no. 2 (1971) p. 487.

CHAPTER TWO

1. See John Maynard Keynes, *How to Pay for the War* (London: Macmillan, 1940).

2. For the derivation see Ajit K. Dasgupta and A. J. Hagger, *The Objectives of Macro-Economic Policy* (London: Macmillan, 1971) p. 288.

3. For the derivation see ibid. p. 289.

4. See A. W. Phillips, 'The Relationship between Unemployment and the Rate of Change of Money Wage Rates in the United Kingdom, 1861–1957', *Economica* (November 1958).

5. See Phillip Cagan, 'The Monetary Dynamics of Hyperinflation', in *Studies in the Quantity Theory of Money*, ed. Milton Friedman (University of Chicago Press, 1956).

6. See Milton Friedman, 'The New Quantity Theory of Money – A Restatement', in *Studies in the Quantity Theory of Money*.

7.   Support for these statements can be found in *Monthly Bulletin of Statistics* (New York: United Nations).

8.   See Henry Phelps Brown, 'A Non-Monetarist View of the Pay Explosion', *Three Banks Review* (March 1975) p. 17.

9.   Ibid. p. 19.

10.   See W. A. P. Manser, 'Economic Crisis 1974', *National Westminster Bank Quarterly Review* (November 1974) pp. 28–9.

CHAPTER THREE

1.   See Stephen J. Turnovsky, 'The Expectations Hypothesis and the Aggregate Wage Equation: Some Empirical Evidence for Canada', *Economica* (February 1972) pp. 6–8.

2.   See ibid. table 1, p. 12.

3.   See ibid. pp. 9–10.

4.   See Toshihisa Toyoda, 'Price Expectations and The Short-Run and Long-Run Phillips Curves in Japan, 1956–1968', *Review of Economics and Statistics*, vol. 54, no. 3 (August 1972).

5.   See A. W. Donner and F. Lazar, 'Some Comments on the Canadian Phillips Curve', *Economica* (May 1973).

6.   See ibid. p. 201.

7.   See Michael Parkin, 'Incomes Policy: Some Further Results on the Determination of the Rate of Change of Money Wages', *Economica* (November 1970) pp. 389–93.

8.   See Turnovsky, 'The Expectations Hypothesis and the Aggregate Wage Equation'; and Stephen J. Turnovsky and Michael L. Wachter, 'A Test of the "Expectations Hypothesis" Using Directly Observed Wage and Price Expectations', *Review of Economics and Statistics*, vol. 54 (1972).

9.   See Turnovsky, 'The Expectations Hypothesis and the Aggregate Wage Equation', table 1, p. 12.

10.   See Turnovsky and Wachter, 'A Test of the "Expectations Hypothesis" ', table 1, p. 51.

11.   See Robert M. Solow, *Price Expectations and the Behaviour of the Price Level* (Manchester University Press, 1969).

12.   See ibid. table 1, p. 13.

13.   See ibid. table 3, p. 22.

CHAPTER FOUR

1.   See R. R. Neild, *Pricing and Employment in the Trade Cycle* (Cambridge University Press, 1963).

2.   This table has been constructed from Neild's table 2: ibid. p. 13.

3.   See Charles L. Schultze and Joseph L. Tyron, 'Prices and Wages', in *The Brookings Quarterly Econometric Model of the United States*, ed. J. S. Duesenberry, G. Fromm, L. R. Klein and E. Kuh (Amsterdam: North-Holland, 1965) ch. 9.

4. This is the approximate number of equations in tables 9.1–9.4 in ibid. pp. 292–303, after exclusion of repetitions.

5. See ibid. p. 286.

6. See ibid. pp. 292–303.

7. See Otto Eckstein and Gary Fromm, 'The Price Equation', *American Economic Review* (December 1968).

8. These are shown in tables 2, 3 and 4 in ibid. p. 1172 and pp. 1175–6.

9. See ibid. pp. 1172–6.

10. See ibid. p. 1172, table 2, equations 2–(2) and 2–(4). Note that the notation differs slightly from that used by EF: cf. p. 74 above.

11. See R. J. Ball and Martyn Duffy, 'Price Formation in European Countries', in *The Econometrics of Price Determination Conference*, ed. O. Eckstein (Washington: Board of Governors of the Federal Reserve System, 1972).

12. See ibid. pp. 355, 357 and 358.

13. See ibid. pp. 350–3.

CHAPTER FIVE

1. See A. W. Phillips, 'The Relationship Between Unemployment and the Rate of Change of Money Wage Rates in the United Kingdom, 1861–1957', *Economica* (November 1958); and Richard G. Lipsey, 'The Relation Between Unemployment and the Rate of Change of Money Wage Rates in the United Kingdom, 1862–1957: A Further Analysis', *Economica* (February 1960).

2. Phillips, 'The Relationship Between Unemployment and the Rate of Change of Money Wage Rates', p. 284.

3. Ibid. p. 299.

4. Lipsey, 'The Relation Between Unemployment and the Rate of Change of Money Wage Rates', p. 1.

5. See ibid. pp. 11–12.

6. See ibid. p. 4.

7. Typical of these early studies are: Rattan J. Bhatia, 'Unemployment and the Rate of Change of Money Earnings in the United States, 1900–1958', *Economica* (August 1961); and S. F. Kaliksi, 'The Relation Between Unemployment and the Rate of Change of Money Wages in Canada', *International Economic Review* (January 1964).

8. See G. L. Perry, 'The Determinants of Wage Rate Changes and the Inflation–Unemployment Trade-off for the United States', *Review of Economic Studies* (October 1964).

9. See, on this, ibid. p. 293.

10. See Perry's equations (9), (9a), (9b), (9c) and (9d), ibid. pp. 293–4.

11. See ibid. p. 294.

12. See Perry's equations (8), (8a) and (8b), ibid. p. 292.

13. Two, in particular, are worthy of note, namely M. A. Zaidi, 'The Determinants of Money Wage Rate Changes and Unemployment–Inflation "Trade-Offs" in Canada', *International Economic Review* (June 1969); and

Tsunehiko Watanabe, 'Price Changes and the Rate of Change of Money Wage Earnings in Japan, 1955–1962', *Quarterly Journal of Economics* (February 1966).

14.   See John Vanderkamp, 'Wage Adjustment, Productivity and Price Change Expectations', *Review of Economic Studies*, vol. 39, no. 1 (1972).

15.   See ibid. p. 71.

16.   Ibid.

17.   Ibid.

18.   See A. G. Hines, 'Wage Inflation in the United Kingdom, 1948–62: A Disaggregated Study', *Economic Journal* (March 1969).

19.   See ibid. p. 68.

20.   See ibid. pp. 70–4.

21.   See ibid. table III, p. 77 and footnote 1, p. 70.

22.   See G. C. Archibald, 'The Phillips Curve and the Distribution of Unemployment', *American Economic Review* (May 1969). For a more recent and more elaborate study in which Archibald's work is taken as a starting point, see R. L. Thomas and P. J. M. Stoney, 'Unemployment Dispersion as a Determinant of Wage Inflation in the U.K. 1925–66', *Manchester School* (June 1971).

CHAPTER SIX

1.   See A. W. Phillips. 'The Relationship Between Unemployment and the Rate of Change of Money Wage Rates in the United Kingdom, 1861–1957', *Economica* (November 1958) p. 283.

2.   See Bernard Corry and David Laidler, 'The Phillips Relation: A Theoretical Explanation', *Economica* (May 1967).

3.   See William D. Nordhaus, 'Recent Developments in Price Dynamics', in *The Econometrics of Price Determination Conference*, ed. O. Eckstein (Washington: Board of Governors of the Federal Reserve System, 1972) p. 21.

4.   See Edmund S. Phelps, 'The New Microeconomics in Inflation and Employment Theory', *American Economic Review* (May 1969) p. 147.

5.   See ibid. p. 148 (italics not in original).

6.   See Nordhaus, 'Recent Developments in Price Dynamics', p. 21.

7.   See Edmund S. Phelps, 'Money Wage Dynamics and Labour Market Equilibrium', in *Microeconomic Foundations of Employment and Inflation Theory*, ed. Edmund S. Phelps *et al.* (New York: Norton, 1970).

8.   See ibid. p. 134.

9.   See Charles C. Holt, 'Improving the Labor Market Trade-Off Between Inflation and Unemployment', *American Economic Review* (May 1969); and 'Job Search, Phillips' Wage Relation, and Union Influence: Theory and Evidence', in *Microeconomic Foundations of Employment and Inflation Theory*, ed. Edmund S. Phelps *et al.* The following analysis is essentially that contained in the second of these two references.

10.   See Holt, 'Job Search, Phillips' Wage Relation, and Union Influence: Theory and Evidence', p. 62.

CHAPTER SEVEN

1.   See G. L. Perry, 'The Determinants of Wage Rate Changes and the Inflation—Unemployment Trade-Off for the United States', *Review of Economic Studies* (October 1964).

2.   See ibid. pp. 298—300.

3.   See John Vanderkamp, 'Wage and Price Level Determination: An Empirical Model for Canada', *Economica* (May 1966). Two other Canadian studies are: M. A. Zaidi, 'The Determinants of Money Wage Rate Changes and Unemployment—Inflation "Trade-Offs" in Canada', *International Economic Review* (June 1969); and G. L. Reuber, 'The Objectives of Canadian Monetary Policy, 1949—61: Empirical "Trade-Offs" and the Reaction Function of the Authorities', *Journal of Political Economy* (April 1964).

4.   See Ronald G. Bodkin, Elizabeth P. Bond, Grant L. Reuber and T. Russell Robinson, *Price Stability and High Employment: The Options for Canadian Economic Policy*, Economic Council of Canada, Special Study No. 5 (Ottawa: Queen's Printer, 1967).

5.   See ibid. pp. 269 and 271.

6.   The studies in question are reported in O. Eckstein (ed.), *The Econometrics of Price Determination Conference* (Washington: Board of Governors of the Federal Reserve System, 1972).

CHAPTER EIGHT

1.   For a discussion of experience with prices and incomes policy in Western European countries, see Lloyd Ulman and Robert J. Flanagan, *Wage Restraint: A Study of Incomes Policies in Western Europe* (University of California Press, 1971); and Walter Galenson (ed.), *Incomes Policy: What Can We Learn from Europe?* (Ithaca, New York: New York State School of Industrial and Labor Relations, Cornell University, 1973).

2.   The following description of prices and incomes policy in the United Kingdom in the post-war period is based mainly on the official policy statements listed below: *Statement on Personal Incomes, Costs and Prices*, Cmnd. 7321 (February 1948); *Incomes Policy: The Next Step*, Cmnd. 1626 (February 1962); *Prices and Incomes Policy*, Cmnd. 2639 (April 1965); *Prices and Incomes Standstill*, Cmnd. 3073 (July 1966); *Prices and Incomes Standstill: Period of Severe Restraint*, Cmnd. 3150 (November 1966); *Prices and Incomes Policy after 30th June, 1967*, Cmnd. 3235 (March 1967); *Productivity, Prices and Incomes Policy in 1968 and 1969*, Cmnd. 3590 (April 1968); and *Productivity, Prices and Incomes Policy after 1969*, Cmnd. 4237 (December 1969).

3.   The following description of prices and incomes policy in the United States in the post-war period is based on the *Economic Report of the President* for the relevant years.

4.   See P. J. Sheehan and D. S. Ironmonger, 'The Real Income Guarantee: A Fiscal Policy to Control Inflation', *Australian Economic Review* (4th quarter 1973).

5. See Hugh Clegg, *How to Run an Incomes Policy and Why We Made Such a Mess of the Last One* (London: Heinemann, 1971) pp. 57–8.

6. See Henry C. Wallich and Sidney Weintraub, 'A Tax-Based Incomes Policy', *Journal of Economic Issues* (June 1971) and other references given there.

7. See ibid. pp. 13–14.

8. See James E. Meade, *Wages and Prices in a Mixed Economy* (London: Institute of Economic Affairs, 1971).

9. See G. L. Perry, 'Wages and the Guideposts', *American Economic Review* (September 1967) pp. 897–9.

10. See Frank P. R. Brechling, 'Some Empirical Evidence on the Effectiveness of Prices and Incomes Policies', in *Incomes Policy and Inflation*, ed. Michael Parkin and Michael T. Sumner (Manchester University Press, 1972).

11. See National Board for Prices and Incomes, *Third General Report, August 1967 to July 1968*, Cmnd. 3715 (July 1968) pp. 63–7.

12. See D. C. Smith, 'Incomes Policy', in *Britain's Economic Prospects*, ed. R. E. Caves and Associates (London: Allen & Unwin, 1968).

13. See Stanley S. Wallack, 'Wage–Price Guidelines and the Rate of Wage Changes in U.S. Manufacturing, 1951–66', *Southern Economic Journal* (July 1971).

14. See Paul Burrows and Theodore Hitiris, 'Estimating the Impact of Incomes Policy'; and Leslie G. Godfrey, 'Some Comments on the Estimation of the Lipsey–Parkin Inflation Model', both in *Incomes Policy and Inflation*, ed. Parkin and Sumner.

15. See R. G. Lipsey and J. M. Parkin, 'Incomes Policy: A Re-appraisal', *Economica* (May 1970).

16. See A. G. Hines, 'The Determinants of the Rate of Change of Money Wage Rates and The Effectiveness of Incomes Policy', in *The Currrent Inflation*, ed. H. C. Johnson and A. R. Nobay (London: Macmillan, 1971); Jim Taylor, 'Incomes Policy, The Structure of Unemployment and the Phillips Curve: The United Kingdom Experience, 1953–70', in *Incomes Policy and Inflation*, ed. Parkin and Sumner; R. L. Thomas and P. J. M. Stoney, 'Unemployment Dispersion as a Determinant of Wage Inflation in the United Kingdom, 1925–66', *Manchester School* (June 1971).

17. See Brechling, 'Some Empirical Evidence on the Effectiveness of Prices and Incomes Policies', p. 41.

18. See Ajit K. Dasgupta and A. J. Hagger, *The Objectives of Macro-Economic Policy* (London: Macmillan, 1971) p. 349.

19. See ibid. pp. 353–4.

20. See Lipsey and Parkin, 'Incomes Policy: A Re-appraisal', p. 115. It should be noted that some doubt is cast on this conclusion by Kenneth F. Wallis, 'Wages, Prices and Incomes Policies: Some Comments', *Economica* (August 1971) pp. 305–6.

21. See Godfrey, 'Some Comments on the Estimation of the Lipsey–Parkin Inflation Model', p. 146.

22.   Ibid. p. 147.
23.   See Burrows and Hitiris, 'Estimating the Impact of Incomes Policy', p. 154; italics in the original.
24.   See Brechling, 'Some Empirical Evidence on the Effectiveness of Prices and Incomes Policies', p. 45.
25.   See Wallack, 'Wage–Price Guidelines and the Rate of Wage Changes in U.S. Manufacturing, 1951–66', p. 43.

CHAPTER NINE

1.   See in particular Charles C. Holt, C. Duncan MacRae, Stuart O. Schweitzer and Ralph E. Smith, 'Manpower Proposals for Phase III', *Brookings Papers on Economic Activity*, 3 (1971); C. Duncan MacRae, Stuart O. Schweitzer and Charles C. Holt, 'Job Search, Labor Turnover, and the Phillips Curve: An International Comparison', in *1970 Proceedings of the Business and Economic Statistics Section*, American Statistical Association; and Charles C. Holt, C. Duncan MacRae, Stuart O. Schweitzer and Ralph E. Smith, *The Unemployment–Inflation Dilemma: A Manpower Solution* (Washington, D.C.: The Urban Institute, 1971).
2.   See Holt, MacRae, Schweitzer and Smith, *The Unemployment–Inflation Dilemma: A Manpower Solution*, p. 101.
3.   See Charles C. Holt, 'How Can the Phillips Curve be Moved to Reduce Both Inflation and Unemployment?', in *Microeconomic Foundations of Employment and Inflation Theory*, ed. Edmund S. Phelps *et al.* (New York: Norton, 1970).
4.   Ibid. pp. 244–5; italics in original.
5.   See Holt, MacRae, Schweitzer and Smith, 'Manpower Proposals for Phase III', p. 713.
6.   See Holt, 'How Can the Phillips Curve be Moved to Reduce Both Inflation and Unemployment?', p. 248.
7.   Ibid. p. 248.
8.   Ibid. p. 249: italics in the original.
9.   Ibid. p. 249.
10.   See ibid. pp. 247–8.
11.   See, for example, George L. Perry, 'Changing Labor Markets and Inflation', *Brookings Papers on Economic Activity*, 3 (1970); and Charles L. Schultze, 'Has the Phillips Curve Shifted? Some Additional Evidence', *Brookings Papers on Economic Activity*, 2 (1971).
12.   See Amotz Morag, 'For an Inflation-Proof Economy', *American Economic Review* (March 1962) p. 179.
13.   See J. Black, 'A New System for Mortgages', *Lloyds Bank Review* (January 1974).
14.   See ibid. pp. 9–10.
15.   See ibid. pp. 11–13.

CHAPTER TEN

1.   For a contrary view see Roberto de Oliveira Campos, 'Two Views on Inflation in Latin America', in *Latin American Issues: Essays and Comments*, ed. Albert O. Hirschman (New York: Twentieth Century Fund, 1961) pp. 70–1.

2.   See, for example, Joseph Grunwald, 'The "Structuralist" School on Price Stabilization and Economic Development: The Chilean Case', and David Felix, 'An Alternative View of the "Monetarist"–"Structuralist" Controversy', in *Latin American Issues*, ed. Hirschman; Marnie W. Mueller, 'Structural Inflation and the Mexican Experience', *Yale Economic Essays*, vol. 5, no. 1 (Spring 1965); Dudley Seers, 'Inflation and Growth: The Heart of the Controversy', and Joseph Grunwald, 'Invisible Hands in Inflation and Growth', in *Inflation and Growth in Latin America*, ed. Werner Baer and Isaac Kerstenetzky (Homewood, Ill.: Irwin, 1964); Julio H. G. Olivera, 'On Structural Inflation and Latin-American "Structuralism" ', *Oxford Economic Papers* (November 1964); and Osvaldo Sunkel, 'Inflation in Chile: An Unorthodox Approach', *International Economic Papers*, vol. 10 (1960).

3.   See Mueller, 'Structural Inflation and the Mexican Experience', p. 147.

4.   See, for example, A. A. Walters, *Money in Boom and Slump*, Hobart Paper, 44 (London: Institute of Economic Affairs, 1969).

5.   See A. P Thirlwall and C. A. Barton, 'Inflation and Growth: The International Evidence', *Banca Nazionale del Lavoro Quarterly Review* (September 1971) p. 275.

6.   See Tom E. Davis, 'Inflation and Growth in Latin America: Theory, Performance and Policy', *Economic Development and Cultural Change* (July 1966) p. 508.

7.   Seers, 'Inflation and Growth', p. 89.

8.   See Mueller, 'Structural Inflation and the Mexican Experience', and Victor Argy, 'Structural Inflation in Developing Countries', *Oxford Economic Papers* (March 1970).

9.   See Mueller, 'Structural Inflation and the Mexican Experience', p. 192.

10.   See Seers, 'Inflation and Growth', p. 89.

11.   See Oliveira Campos, 'Two Views on Inflation in Latin America', p. 69.

12.   See Thirlwall and Barton, 'Inflation and Growth: The International Evidence'. References to earlier studies and a brief discussion of their main limitations are given on p. 265 of this article.

CHAPTER ELEVEN

1.   See Phillip Cagan, 'The Monetary Dynamics of Hyperinflation', in *Studies in the Quantity Theory of Money*, ed. Milton Friedman (University of Chicago Press, 1956) p. 25.

2.   See M. Kalecki, 'A Model of Hyperinflation', *Manchester School*, vol. 30 (1962).

3.   See ibid. p. 279.

4.   See Cagan, 'The Monetary Dynamics of Hyperinflation'.

CHAPTER TWELVE

1   See J. M. Parkin, M. T. Sumner and R. Ward, 'Wage Behaviour in an Open Economy: Excess Demand, Generalized Expectations, and Incomes Policies in the United Kingdom', in *Conference On Wage–Price Controls*, ed. K. Brunner and A. H. Metzler (Amsterdam: North Holland, 1975).

2.   In particular see, John A. Carlson and Michael Parkin, 'Inflation Expectations', *Economica* (May 1975); and Michael Danes, 'The Measurement and Explanation of Inflationary Expectations in Australia', *Australian Economic Papers* (June 1975).

3.   As an example see David Laidler, 'Simultaneous Fluctuations in Prices and Output – A Business Cycle Approach', *Economica* (February 1973); and David Laidler, 'The Influence of Money on Real Income and Inflation: A Simple Model with some Empirical Tests for the United States, 1953–1972', *Manchester School* (December 1973).

4.   So far the two most important references are R. G. Lipsey, 'Structural and Deficient-Demand Unemployment Reconsidered', in *Employment Policy and the Labor Market*, ed. R. M. Ross (University of California Press, 1965); and E. S. Phelps, 'Phillips Curves, Expectations of Inflation and Optimal Unemployment Over Time', *Economica* (August 1967). For an exposition of these two works, see Ajit K. Dasgupta and A. J. Hagger, *The Objectives of Macro-Economic Policy* (London: Macmillan, 1971) pp. 451–71.

INDEX